GOD'S DESIGN®

Heaven & Earth

| Our Weather & Water | Our Universe | Our Planet Earth |

MASTERBOOKS
CURRICULUM

Debbie & Richard Lawrence

Fourth Edition: January 2016
Master Books Edition fourth printing: July 2022

Master Books, P.O. Box 726, Green Forest, AR 72638

Master Books® is a division of the New Leaf Publishing Group, Inc.

ISBN: 978-1-68344-129-8
ISBN: 978-1-61458-652-4 (digital)

Cover by Diana Bogardus
Book design: Diane King
Editor: Gary Vaterlaus

God's Design® for Heaven & Earth is a complete life science curriculum for grades 3–8. The books in this series are designed for use in the Christian school and homeschool, and provide easy-to-use lessons that will encourage children to see God's hand in everything around them.

The publisher and authors have made every reasonable effort to ensure that the activities recommended in this book are safe when performed as instructed but assume no responsibility for any damage caused or sustained while conducting the experiments and activities. It is the parents', guardians', and/or teachers' responsibility to supervise all recommended activities.

Please consider requesting that a copy of this volume be purchased by your local library system.

Printed in the United States of America

Please visit our website for other great titles:
www.masterbooks.com

For information regarding author interviews,
please contact the publicity department at (870) 438-5288.

Master
Books®
A Division of New Leaf Publishing Group
www.masterbooks.com

Our Weather & Water

Our Universe

Unit 4: Planets   227

Unit 5: Space Program   256

Our Planet Earth

Unit 3: Mountains & Movement · 361

Unit 4: Water & Erosion · 392

Welcome to GOD'S DESIGN®

HEAVEN & EARTH

You are about to start an exciting series of lessons on earth science. *God's Design® for Heaven and Earth* consists of: *Our Universe, Our Planet Earth*, and *Our Weather & Water*. It will give you insight into how God designed and created our world and the universe in which we live.

No matter what grade you are in, third through eighth grade, you can use this book.

3rd–5th grade

Read the lesson.

 Do the activity in the light blue box (worksheets will be provided by your teacher).

 Test your knowledge by answering the What did we learn? questions.

 Assess your understanding by answering the Taking it further questions.

Be sure to read the special features and do the final project.

There are also unit quizzes and a final test to take.

6th–8th grade

Read the lesson.

 Do the activity in the light blue box (worksheets will be provided by your teacher).

 Test your knowledge by answering the What did we learn? questions.

 Assess your understanding by answering the Taking it further questions.

 Do the Challenge section in the light green box. This part of the lesson will challenge you to do more advanced activities and learn additional interesting information.

Be sure to read the special features and do the final project.

There are also unit quizzes and a final test to take.

When you truly understand how God has designed everything in our universe to work together, then you will enjoy the world around you even more. So let's get started!

Our
Weather
& Water

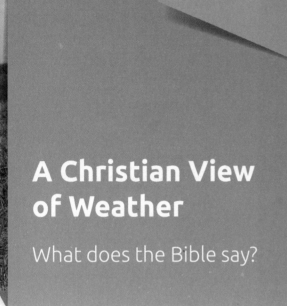

1

A Christian View of Weather

What does the Bible say?

What events in history have affected our weather?

Is there a Christian view of weather? Isn't weather just what happens outside? How can there be a Christian or non-Christian view of precipitation? Many people believe that you can separate your beliefs about God from your understanding of science. However, what you believe about God affects how you approach everything in life, so it even affects your understanding of weather. If you believe what the Bible says, then you know God sends the rain (see Jeremiah 5:24 and Jeremiah 14:22) and withholds the rain (see Amos 4:7). God controls storms (see Matthew 8:23–27). But most importantly, God created the earth and everything in it. He set up the way the weather operates, and He can work within the natural laws He has established as well as outside those laws to accomplish His purposes.

The planet that we live on has been affected by three major events in history. The first was the creation. In the beginning, everything was very good. But man rebelled against God and as a result God cursed the earth. Later, because of man's continual sin, God destroyed all of the people, except those in Noah's family, by sending a worldwide flood. This Flood had a tremendous effect on the planet, including changing the weather. We will look at the weather before and after the Flood in later lessons.

Our belief about God determines whether we recognize the weather patterns as random changes of nature or as a lovely system with an intelligent designer. Do we recognize the water cycle as a gift from God or just a random happening? If we view the planet earth and its weather from a Christian perspective, we will know that it was supernaturally created, it is designed by God, it is relatively young (about 6,000 years), it was created in perfection, and it was created for mankind to show God's love and provision for us. If we recognize these things when we study weather, we will see God's hand and understand Him more clearly. 🌐

What did we learn?

- Is there a Christian view of weather?
- What three events described in the Bible have greatly affected the weather on Earth?
- List three things you can learn about the weather from a newspaper weather report.

Taking it further

- Why is it important to have a Christian view of weather?

- What are some geographical or physical characteristics that affect the weather in a particular area?

 # Weather reports

Look at a weather report from your local newspaper or an Internet site. Most likely you will find information on the temperature and precipitation that your town received yesterday as well as a prediction for the weather conditions for today and several days in the future. What other information does your weather report give? Local weather can be affected by many factors, making it difficult to accurately predict. Do you live near the ocean or a large lake? That will affect the weather. Do you live near the mountains? That will affect your weather too. The amount of humidity and the wind will affect how you feel when you are outside.

Your weather report probably includes information on the weather across your state, as well as across the country. If your newspaper does not have this information, you can find it on the Internet.

Purpose: To compare weather across the country

Materials: weather report from newspaper or Internet, "Weather Across the Country" worksheet

Procedure:

1. Enter your city or town on the first line of the chart and enter the weather conditions for your home town.

2. Enter the predicted weather conditions for each of the cities listed.

Questions:

- How does the weather in your town compare to the weather in other cities across the country?

- Why do you think the weather is so different from one city to another?

Conclusion: You will begin to understand the complexities of weather and how difficult it is to predict the weather as we go through the lessons in this book.

Bible-believing scientists

Today, many people say that if you believe that God created everything you cannot be a good scientist. But is this true? Of course not! Many great scientists in the past believed the Bible. Sir Isaac Newton, considered by many to be one of the greatest scientists of all time, believed in God and was a creationist. Sir Francis Bacon, credited with developing the scientific method, recognized God's hand in the world around him. This is why he believed that you could test your hypotheses to see if you were right, because God had created an orderly universe just waiting for us to discover the wonders that He had placed there.

Today, many scientists believe the Bible and are contributing to scientific research. If you are interested in meteorology and weather, you can be a good scientist, too. If you believe the Bible and recognize that God designed our weather system, you can contribute to a better understanding of our world by being a Bible-believing scientist.

Choose a Christian scientist from the past and research his contributions to science. Write a short report on what you learned and share it with your class or family. You can be encouraged by knowing that many of the greatest scientists have believed that God created this world and not that it evolved by chance. Below is a list of scientists you can choose from.

- Sir Isaac Newton (physics)
- Lord Kelvin (thermodynamics)
- Blaise Pascal (hydrostatics)
- Johannes Kepler (astronomy)
- Carolus Linneaus (biology)
- Robert Boyle (chemistry)
- Charles Babbage (computers)
- Joseph Lister (surgery)
- David Brewster (mineralogy)
- Louis Pasteur (bacteriology)
- James Clerk Maxwell (electronics)
- Dr. Raymond Damadian (inventor of the MRI)

2

Structure of the Atmosphere

Layers above the earth

What is earth's atmosphere like?

Words to know:

atmosphere	ionosphere
troposphere	exosphere
stratosphere	magnetosphere
mesosphere	aurora borealis
thermosphere	aurora australis

Challenge words:

lapse rate

When we think of the earth, we usually think of the solid ground on which we stand. This ball of rock we call earth is a very special place. Unlike the other planets in our solar system, earth has an atmosphere specially suited for life. The atmosphere is the layers of gas that surround the planet. These gases are kept close to the surface of the earth by the earth's gravity. The earth's atmosphere consists of 78% nitrogen, 21% oxygen, and 1% other gases, including hydrogen, helium, argon, and carbon dioxide. This combination of nitrogen and oxygen is the ideal atmosphere for life. Nitrogen is a relatively nonreactive gas. Its purpose in the atmosphere appears to be to dilute the oxygen. Nitrogen also helps protect the earth from gamma rays from the sun. If the oxygen concentration was more than 21%, fires would easily burn out of control. Yet animals and humans need oxygen to breathe, and 21% appears to be the ideal concentration.

The earth's atmosphere not only provides needed oxygen, it also protects life from several harmful effects of space. First, the atmosphere insulates the earth from the extreme temperatures of space. The atmosphere keeps the surface temperature of the earth relatively the same. Temperatures on earth range from −60 to 140 degrees Fahrenheit (−51 to 60 degrees Celsius) at the extremes and are more likely to be between 0°F and 100°F (−17°C to 38°C). However, on the moon, which has no atmosphere, the temperature can be as much as 260°F (127°C) in the sun and −280°F (−173°C) on the side facing away from the sun. The earth's atmosphere protects us from these extremes.

The atmosphere also protects us from the vacuum of space. The air pressure provided by the atmosphere is necessary for our bodies to function correctly. Also, the atmosphere protects us from harmful radiation. The ozone in the atmosphere filters out much of the ultraviolet rays from the sun. These rays can damage our skin and cause skin cancer. Finally, the atmosphere protects the surface of the earth from many impacts. Just compare the surface of the earth with the surface of the moon. The moon's surface is covered with craters caused by impacts. Yet relatively few impacting bodies reach the surface of the earth because most burn up in the atmosphere; when we see this happen, we call them meteors, or shooting stars.

The atmosphere consists of several layers of gases. The layer closest to the surface of the earth is called the **troposphere**. The troposphere is the layer beginning at the surface of the earth. Its thickness varies from 4 to up to about 7 miles (12 km) above the surface. Eighty percent of all air molecules are in the troposphere. All of the weather occurs in the troposphere and there is significant mixing of the air in this layer. In general, the temperature decreases with increasing altitude in the troposphere.

The next layer of the atmosphere is called the **stratosphere**. This layer extends from about 6 to 30 miles (10–50 km) above the earth's surface. The stratosphere contains the ozone layer as well as the jet stream—an area in the atmosphere with very fast-moving air. Most passenger planes fly in the lower stratosphere because of the lack of weather and the jet stream. The temperature in the stratosphere tends to increase with altitude.

Above the stratosphere is the **mesosphere**. The mesosphere is 30 to 50 miles (50–85 km) above the earth. There are variable winds in this layer and the temperature decreases with altitude. The coldest part of the atmosphere is at the top of the mesosphere where the temperatures can be as low as −164°F (−109°C).

The **thermosphere** is the layer that is 50 to 370 miles (85–600 km) above the earth. The molecules in this layer are very far apart and are easily warmed to very high temperatures by the sun. This layer contains the ionosphere. In the **ionosphere**, gas molecules are broken apart into atoms by the radiation of the sun. Some of these atoms lose electrons and become electrically charged ions. These ions reflect short-wave radio waves but allow microwaves to pass through. For

 # Properties of air

Purpose: To demonstrate that air contains oxygen and that air pressure changes with temperature

Materials: candle, modeling clay, glass jar, dish, matches or lighter

Procedure:

1. Attach a candle to the bottom of a dish with a piece of modeling clay.

2. Fill the dish half full with water.

3. Light the candle and quickly place a jar over the candle so that the mouth of the jar is below the level of the water without touching the bottom of the dish and note the water level inside the jar.

4. Watch the candle burn until the flame goes out and now note the water level inside the jar.

Conclusion:

You should have observed two things happening inside the jar. First, the candle only burns for a short period of time. Oxygen is necessary for the candle to burn. The atmosphere consists of about 21% oxygen and 78% nitrogen. Initially there is oxygen in the air inside the jar, but no additional air can enter the jar since the mouth of the jar is underwater. As the candle burns the oxygen is soon used up and the flame goes out.

Second, you should have seen that after the candle goes out the water level inside the jar is higher than the water level outside the jar. The atmosphere is composed of gases. As the flame burns the gas inside the jar heats up and expands. This creates pressure which forces a small amount of water out of the jar. But when the candle goes out the gas inside the jar cools down and contracts. This creates lower air pressure inside the jar than outside the jar so the air outside the jar pushes more water into the jar.

this reason, microwaves are used for communication with astronauts and satellites in space.

The outermost layer of the atmosphere is the **exosphere**, which extends to 60,000 miles (96,000 km) above the earth. Within this layer lies the **magnetosphere**. It consists of protons and electrons from space that have become trapped by the earth's magnetic field. These particles move from pole to pole. Near the poles, some particles move into the lower atmosphere. When they collide with other particles in the atmosphere they give off a beautiful light often called the northern lights, or **aurora borealis**, near the North Pole, and the southern lights, or **aurora australis**, near the South Pole. When the sun experiences solar flares, a higher concentration of particles becomes trapped in the magnetosphere and the northern lights and southern lights are more visible. 🌐

 # What did we learn?

- What are the two main components of air?
- What are the five levels of the atmosphere?
- What are some ways that the atmosphere protects us?

 # Taking it further

- How would the earth be different if there were a higher concentration of oxygen?
- What would happen if the nitrogen in the atmosphere was replaced with a more reactive element, such as carbon?

 # Atmospheric temperature

The temperature in the atmosphere changes as you go up in altitude. If you have ever climbed a mountain, you know that it is often colder at the top of the mountain than at the bottom. The temperature generally goes down as you go up in the troposphere. The temperature drops about 3.5°F per 1,000 feet (6.4°C for each kilometer) that you go up. This rate of decline is called the **lapse rate**. At about 11 kilometers above the earth, the temperature stops declining. It begins to increase at about 12 kilometers.

The temperature tends to increase as you go up through the stratosphere. Temperature again decreases as you go up through the mesosphere and then increases again as you go up through the thermosphere.

Using a chart showing the temperature ranges and altitudes for each layer of the atmosphere, complete the following activity.

Purpose: To create a graph showing how the temperature changes with altitude

Materials: graph paper, pencil or pen, atmosphere temperature chart

Procedure:

1. Begin your graph by labeling the x-axis with temperatures ranging from -100°C to 100°C. Label the y-axis with altitudes from 0 to 110 kilometers.

2. Plot the points from the chart to the right on your graph, and draw lines to show how the temperature increases or decreases as you go up in altitude.

3. Finally, shade and label each layer of atmosphere in your graph. Shade from the bottom to 12 km blue and label it troposphere. Shade from 12–50 km green and label it stratosphere. Shade from 50–80 km yellow and label it mesosphere. And shade from 80 to the top of graph red and label it thermosphere.

Altitude (km)	Temperature (°C)
0	25
12	−50
50	0
80	−80
100	50

3

The Weight of Air

It has weight?

How much does the air weigh?

How much does air weigh? You might think that this is a strange question, because you think that air doesn't weigh anything. You might think that you can't see or feel air, so it must not weigh anything. However, you would be wrong. Although air is very light, it still has mass and weight. As you learned in the previous lesson, the air is made up of mostly nitrogen and oxygen atoms. Each of these atoms weighs a tiny amount, but when you add up the weight of all the molecules in a cubic foot of air it weighs about $\frac{1}{10}$ of a pound, and when you add up the weight of all of the air molecules in the atmosphere, the air surrounding the whole planet weighs about five million billion tons. Now that's a lot of air!

The air has weight because gravity is pulling down on the air molecules. This means that air molecules are pressing against us all the time. In fact, the air presses on our bodies with about 14.7 pounds of pressure per square inch when we are at sea level. So why don't we feel the pressure of the air on our bodies? God designed our bodies to push out with about the same amount of pressure that the air is pushing in, so we don't feel the weight of the air around us. The air pressure is not constant in every part of the world, however. At low elevations, the air pressure is greater, since the molecules of air are compressed from the weight of the air above them. However, at higher elevations, there's less pressure and the molecules are more dispersed, or thinner.

So, what does the weight of air have to do with weather? The weight of air contributes to the air pressure in the atmosphere. Changes in air pressure cause the wind to blow and move weather fronts around the globe. If the air had no weight, the wind would have no force and we would have no changes in the weather. We will be learning more about air pressure in future lessons.

Fun Fact

The Bible speaks about the weight of the air in Job 28:24–27, "For He looks to the ends of the earth, and sees under the whole heavens, to establish a weight for the wind, and apportion the waters by measure. When He made a law for the rain, and a path for the thunderbolt, then He saw wisdom and declared it; He prepared it, indeed, He searched it out." We see that the Bible is true even in small details such as the fact that air has weight.

🧠 What did we learn

- What causes air to have weight?
- How much air pressure do we experience at sea level?
- Why don't we feel the weight of the air molecules?
- Do you expect air pressure to be the same at all locations in the world?

🚀 Taking it further

- Why is it important that air has weight?
- Why must aircraft be pressurized when flying at high altitudes?

⚗️ Demonstrating the weight of air

Purpose: To show that air has weight

Materials: two identical balloons, string, a yard or meter stick, tape

Procedure:

1. Tape an empty balloon one inch (3 cm) from each end of the yardstick.

2. Tie a 2-foot long piece of string to the center of the yardstick.

3. Hold the end of the string on the edge of a table so that the yardstick is hanging down from the table and adjust the string until you are able to get the stick to balance.

4. Have someone hold the string and stick in place while you remove one of the balloons.

5. Fill the balloon with air and tie it shut. Tape it back to the yardstick in the same location that it was in before.

6. Release the stick and watch to see if it is still balanced.

Conclusion: The weight of the air in the balloon should make the stick tip downward on the side with the filled balloon. This shows that even though we cannot see the air, it really does have weight.

🎗 Air pressure

All molecules have weight. You just demonstrated that the nitrogen and oxygen molecules in air have a small weight. Different molecules have different weights. Hydrogen and helium are the two smallest and lightest elements. When a balloon is filled with hydrogen or helium gas it will float because it becomes lighter than the air around it. Gravity does not pull down on the helium-filled balloon as much as it does on the air so the balloon floats. Scientists who study the weather take advantage of this property to fly weather balloons. Weather balloons are filled with either helium or hydrogen and are attached to weather instruments. Then they are allowed to float through the atmosphere and take readings.

Hot air balloons use a similar principle, but instead of using a lighter gas, the air in the balloon is heated. Hot air is lighter than cool air because the molecules are farther apart. This allows the balloon to float.

Purpose: To demonstrate that the weight of air has force

Materials: plastic grocery bag, wide mouth jar, string or rubber band

Procedure:

1. Push a grocery-sized plastic bag into a wide-mouth jar, leaving the edges of the bag hanging over the edge of the jar.

2. Tie a string very tightly below the threads of the jar. You could use a very tight rubber band instead of the string. Think about what is in the jar. If you said a plastic bag you are only partially right. There is also air inside the jar.

3. Carefully pull the bag out of the jar.

Questions:

- What do you observe happening inside the jar?
- Why won't the bag come out?

Conclusion: The bag will not come completely out of the jar unless you force it out. There is air inside the jar. This air is pressing down on the bag. Because the edges of the jar are sealed by the string, no new air can get into the jar to push up on the bag, so the weight of the air holds the bag inside the jar.

Discovery of Air

Air—it's all around us and very important to us. It's mainly important because of what's in it. Three men who all lived during the time of America's Revolutionary War worked to find out what is in the air. Joseph Priestly, Karl Scheele, and Daniel Rutherford each independently discovered what the air is made of.

Joseph Priestly, who studied to be a minister, was not even interested in science. However, while he was in London in 1766, he met a well-known American named Benjamin Franklin. He and Franklin became lifelong friends and through Franklin's influence, Priestly became interested in science. Joseph Priestly's first interest in science was in electricity. Later Benjamin Franklin wrote a letter to Joseph telling him about a gas, or bubbles, that would rise from the bottom of a river and would burn if a flame was held close to the surface of the water.

This letter changed the direction of Joseph's work, and he became interested in the gas that would burn. In his work, he discovered that air was not a single element but was made up of different gases. The first gas that Priestly discovered was carbon dioxide. He also discovered eight other gases in his work. But the most important gas that he discovered was oxygen, which is necessary for combustion, or burning.

Karl Scheele was a scientist who also had an interesting start. At the age of 14 he began working as an apprentice to a pharmacist in Gothenburg, Sweden. He worked for the pharmacist for eight years. There he spent his nights devoted to the study of the standard works of chemistry and to experimental examination. His attention to detail, and a lot of practice, allowed him to make many new discoveries. Around 1773 he discovered that air was made up of two parts—one part would support combustion and the other would prevent it. The gas that supported combustion was oxygen.

Joseph Priestly

The third scientist credited with discovering the components of air is Daniel Rutherford. Rutherford went to the university in Edinburgh, Scotland. There he held the first chair of the Theory and Practice of Medicine. After spending three years learning about continental medical practices in Europe, he set up his own medical practice in Edinburgh. He became a Fellow of the Royal College of Physicians and later went on to become its secretary and president. He conducted many experiments. While working with mice, he found that many of them died. When examining the causes of their death he discovered what he called noxious air. Today we call it nitrogen.

At one time people believed that air was one element, but the work of these three men gave insight into the composition of air and put scientists on the road to understanding our atmosphere and how it works.

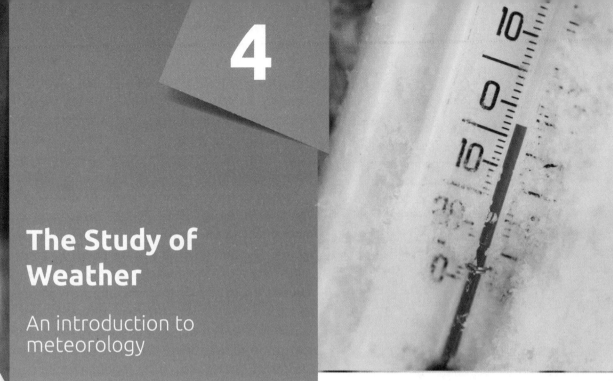

4

The Study of Weather

An introduction to meteorology

What do meteorologists study?

Words to know:

meteorology

temperature

air pressure

atmospheric pressure

humidity

absolute humidity

relative humidity

wind

precipitation

Meteorology <u>is the study of the atmosphere.</u> Most of the studies concentrate on the troposphere and the weather that occurs there. Conditions in the troposphere are most affected by the energy and heat from the sun and their effects on the gas molecules and water molecules in it. Energy from the sun reaches the earth in the forms of visible light, ultraviolet light, and infrared light. Most of the ultraviolet light, which is harmful, is absorbed by the ionosphere. The visible light allows us to see. But the infrared radiation has the most effect on our weather. The infrared light passes through the atmosphere and warms the surface of the earth, which warms the air, causing air currents and leading to most of the weather that we experience.

Meteorologists study five major conditions of the atmosphere. The first condition is <u>temperature.</u> **Temperature** is a measure of the intensity of heat in the air. It measures the movement of the air molecules. The molecules in warm air are moving faster than the molecules in cool air.

The second condition studied by meteorologists is **air pressure**, also called **atmospheric pressure**. The molecules in the air are pulled toward the earth by gravity. The weight of these molecules pushes on everything on the earth. Warmer air expands and is less dense so it has less pressure. Cooler air contracts, so the air molecules are closer together

The air pressure is lower at higher altitudes.

Fun Fact

The energy absorbed from the sun is one of the major factors that drives the weather. Different parts of the earth absorb different amounts of sunlight. Forests are generally dark and absorb over 90% of the rays that reach them. Oceans and lakes absorb between 60% and 96% of the rays that reach them. On the other hand, snow reflects sunlight and absorbs less than 25% of the rays that reach it. This helps explain why tropical rain forests are generally warm and the North and South Poles are colder.

and thus exert more air pressure. Air pressure is also affected by altitude. There are fewer air molecules at higher altitudes than at lower altitudes so there is lower air pressure at higher altitudes. This is why you may become tired more easily when hiking in the high mountains than at sea level. It is also why airplanes pressurize their cabins to maintain a comfortable air pressure during flights.

Meteorologists study areas of high and low air pressure to help determine the weather patterns. Areas with low pressure usually have warm, moist air. This usually results in warm cloudy weather. Areas with high pressure usually have cooler and drier air. This usually results in clear cool weather.

The third condition that meteorologists study is **humidity**. Humidity is a measure of the amount of water vapor in the air. There are two kinds of humidity measurements. **Absolute humidity** measures the actual amount of water in the air. **Relative humidity** measures the ratio of the amount of water in the air compared to the amount of water that the air could hold at that temperature. Warmer air can hold more water than colder air. So, different samples of air could have the same absolute humidity but different relative humidity if they were at different temperatures.

The fourth atmospheric condition which interests meteorologists is **wind**. Meteorologists measure the direction that wind comes from and the speed at which it travels. This helps them determine weather patterns as well.

 # Making air currents

Energy from the sun is the primary source of weather on earth. As the sun heats up the earth and the air, the air molecules move around creating air currents. The same thing happens when water is heated and cooled. You can observe water currents to better understand air currents.

Purpose: To demonstrate how the sun heats our planet and causes air currents

Materials: baking dish (white or light color works best), several Styrofoam™ cups, food coloring, ice, boiling water

Procedure:

1. Place 3 or 4 Styrofoam™ cups (depending on the shape of your baking dish) upside down, and set a baking dish on top of them.

2. Fill the dish half full of room temperature water and allow it to sit until the water is completely still.

3. Place a cup of ice under the dish near one end and a cup of boiling water under the dish at the opposite end.

4. After two minutes, place a drop of food coloring in the water in the baking dish near each end of the dish. Observe how the food coloring moves through the water. Draw several pictures during the next 10 minutes showing how the color moved.

Conclusion: The water in the baking dish was heated by the cup of boiling water so the water molecules in that area began to move more quickly. The water molecules above the ice began to move more slowly. This caused currents in the water. You were able to see these currents as they carried the food coloring around the dish. This same process occurs in the atmosphere. The sun heats areas of the earth and the air molecules in that area move more quickly causing air currents. This uneven heating helps weather systems to move from one part of the earth to another.

Finally, meteorologists study **precipitation**. Precipitation is water that escapes from the atmosphere. Precipitation takes on many forms depending on the atmospheric conditions. These forms can include rain, snow, hail, and sleet. All of these conditions work together to provide the weather on our planet.

 # What did we learn?

- What is meteorology?
- What are the five important conditions in the troposphere that meteorologists study?

 # Taking it further

- Why are meteorologists interested in studying the conditions of the troposphere?
- How does the sun heat areas of the earth that do not receive much direct sunlight?

Weather ingredients

There are basically four main ingredients required to make weather. The first is the earth. Without the planet itself, there would be no sense in talking about the weather. The earth absorbs the energy from the sun and heats up. The sunlight hits different parts of the earth at different times because of the rotation of the earth on its axis and because of the revolution of the earth around the sun. This movement contributes to the various weather patterns that occur around the world.

The second ingredient in weather is the sun. We have already discussed how the sun's rays warm up the earth which in turn warms the air. The sun is the energy source that fuels the weather.

The third ingredient is the air. Without the air molecules to move around, there would be no weather. Planets that do not have an atmosphere do not have weather. The air molecules are heated unevenly and thus move around. You will learn more about how this works in later lessons.

The final ingredient in weather is water. The air contains water all the time. Sometimes that water is in the form of water vapor which is a gas. Sometimes the water is a liquid, such as when it forms clouds or rain, and sometimes it becomes a solid, like snow or hail. The evaporation and condensation of water contribute greatly to the weather that we experience. You will learn more about water's role in weather,

too. These four ingredients work together to create weather everyday.

Now for fun, do the "Weather Ingredients" worksheet to see how much you already know about the things that make up our weather.

UNIT 2

Ancient Weather & Climate

◊ **Distinguish** between weather and climate.

◊ **Identify** the five major climates and their features.

◊ **Identify** possible differences in the climate before the Flood.

◊ **Evaluate** global warming from biblical and scientific perspectives.

5

Weather vs. Climate

What's the difference?

What is the difference between weather and climate?

Words to know:

weather	tropical
climate	monsoon
polar	subtropical
desert	temperate zone

Challenge words:

Coriolis effect

Weather describes the conditions in the atmosphere at a given moment in time. The weather changes from day to day, sometimes from minute to minute. It could be cloudy, sunny, snowing, raining, stormy, calm, or windy. **Climate**, on the other hand, describes the overall pattern of weather conditions in a particular area. It is the average weather conditions in a place over a long period of time. The climate is described in terms of average temperatures and average precipitation amounts. Meteorologists study the weather, and climatologists study the climate.

There are five major climates that occur on the earth. **Polar** areas are cold and are characterized by large, dry, cold air masses. These areas are warmer in the summer but still cooler than in other parts of the world. **Desert** climates are primarily dry. A desert receives less than 10 inches (25 cm) of

Polar

Desert

Tropical

Temperate

Fun Fact

Interesting weather and climate statistics for North America:

- The highest temperature ever recorded was 134°F (56.7°C) in Death Valley, California.
- The lowest temperature ever recorded was −81°F (−62.8°C) at Snag, Canada.
- The heaviest snowfall ever recorded was at Rainier Pardis Ranger Station in Washington State where 1,122 inches (28.5 m) of snow fell in one winter.
- The largest hailstone recorded was 8 inches (20.3 cm) in diameter, had a 18.6-inch (47.2 cm) circumference, and weighed nearly 2 pounds (0.88 kg). It fell in Vivian, South Dakota, in 2010.
- The strongest winds recorded were at Mount Washington, New Hampshire—188 miles per hour (84 meters per second) for five minutes with gusts up to 231 mph (103.3 m/s).
- The fastest winds recorded within a tornado occurred in 1999 in a tornado near Oklahoma City, Oklahoma, measured by Doppler radar at over 301 mph (485 km/hr).
- The most rain falling in one hour was 12.0 inches (305 mm) in 42 minutes at Holt, Missouri, June 22, 1947.

moisture per year. Most deserts are hot, but some areas are classified as deserts because of a lack of moisture even though they are relatively cool.

The third major climate is the **tropical** climate. Tropical areas occur primarily near the equator and are basically wet and warm year round. Tropical areas receive an average of over 80 inches (200 cm) of rain per year. Many tropical areas experience a dry season and a wet season. Areas in Southeast Asia receive very heavy rainfall due to a condition called the monsoon. **Monsoon** is Arabic for "season" and describes the wind that brings the rain from the Bay of Bengal. During the summer, the sun heats the air over the Gobi Desert, pulling moisture from the bay and bringing heavy rainfall to the area. Nearly half of the world's population depends on these rains to provide moisture to grow their crops. In the winter, cooler air from the desert pushes moisture out to sea, bringing dry weather to the area. Shifting monsoon winds often create cyclones, or hurricanes, in the Bay of Bengal. Although the term monsoon originally referred only to the changing winds over the Indian sub-continent, today it is often used to describe changing wind patterns that bring rain in any part of the world.

Subtropic areas receive less average rainfall than tropical areas. These areas are warm most of the year but experience a colder winter than the tropics. The final climate area is the **temperate zone**. Temperate climate areas experience the most seasonal changes. Temperate areas have warm summers and cold winters, usually with a distinct spring and autumn.

Fun Fact

The driest region in the world is Arica, Chile, where the average rainfall was 0.03 inch (0.08 cm) per year over a 60-year period. This included a 14-year period without any rainfall at all.

Fun Fact

For many years it was believed that the highest temperature ever recorded on earth was 136°F (57.8°C) at Al Aziziyah, Liberia. However, in 2012 this record was disqualified as a clerical error so now Death Valley, California, holds the record for the highest temperature at 134°F (55.7°C). The lowest temperature ever recorded was -129°F (-89.4°C) at Vostok, Antarctica.

Because climates are established averages and can be looked up in an atlas or other reference book, we will spend most of our time studying weather to see how it occurs and how meteorologists predict what it will be.

What did we learn?

- What is weather?
- What is climate?
- What are the five major climates found on earth?

 Weather vs. climate

To better understand the difference between weather and climate, complete the "Weather vs. Climate" worksheet.

Taking it further

- How does the Gobi Desert help create the monsoon?
- Which of the following phrases describe weather and which describe climate?
  - Cloudy with a chance of rain
  - Average of 20 inches of rain per year
  - Average summer temperature of 70°F
  - 3 inches of snow in the past 24 hours

Factors affecting climate

As you learned in the last lesson, the interactions between the energy from the sun, the earth, the water, and the atmosphere drive the weather. The tilt of the earth on its axis and the rotation of the earth both play important roles in weather. The tilt of the earth allows the energy from the sun to hit different parts of the earth at different angles and for different periods of time during different parts of the year. This contributes to the seasonal changes in weather.

The energy from the sun heats the earth during the day. The energy absorbed by the earth is radiated back into the atmosphere. Some of that heat is held close to the earth by clouds. Some of the heat escapes back into space. During the summer more heat is gained during the day than is lost at night so temperatures tend to be higher during the summer. During the winter more heat is lost at night than is gained during the day so

temperatures tend to be cooler in the winter. Also, more heat is gained near the equator than is gained near the poles. This is one reason why the equator has a more tropical climate and the poles have a polar climate.

But the situation is more complicated. Although the amount of sunlight is a major factor in weather and climate, the rotation of the earth also plays a role. As the earth spins, the air molecules are dragged with it. So air in the northern hemisphere tends to move to the right and air in the southern hemisphere tends to move to the left. This phenomenon is called the Coriolis effect. The Coriolis effect causes air to spiral around low pressure systems. Thus, in the northern hemisphere low pressure systems spiral counterclockwise and in the southern hemisphere they spiral clockwise.

All of these factors together result in several general circulations of air around the globe. Some air circulates from the equator north to about 30 degrees latitude and back toward the equator. Other air circulates from about 30 degrees to about 60 degrees. A third circulation occurs from about 60 degrees latitude to the poles. Similar circulations occur in the southern hemisphere. These circulations contribute to the climate around the world.

In areas where the circulation of air causes the air to rise, there tends to be lots of rain. Air rises near the equator so the rainy tropical areas are found near the equator. Areas where the circulation generally causes air to fall are drier. Many of the earth's deserts are found near 30 degrees latitude because dry air is falling there, preventing precipitation.

A third important variable in determining climate is the distance from an ocean. Areas near the ocean are wetter than areas farther away.

Finally, mountains also affect climate. The upwind side of mountains is usually wetter than the downwind side of mountains. Overall the climate patterns around the world are very complicated and are not easily changed or predicted.

Using a copy of the world map, color the different climates on your map according to the climate map in a world atlas. Be sure to make a key for your map, labeling all the different climates you colored. Your map may have more than the five basic climates listed in this lesson. Some maps may include more specific climates such as Mediterranean, highlands, or mountainous climates.

6

Pre-Flood Climate

Was it different?

What was the climate before the Flood?

Words to know:

greenhouse effect

What were the weather and climate like before the Genesis Flood? No one knows for sure, but the Bible may give us some clues. We know from Genesis 1–2 that Adam and Eve were comfortable in the Garden of Eden without any clothes. This would indicate that the temperature there was fairly mild.

The second clue we have is from Genesis 7:11–12. These verses state that it rained for 40 days and 40 nights. Where did all this rain come from? It seems most likely that when the "fountains of the great deep" broke up at the beginning of the Flood, steam from inside the earth was catapulted into the atmosphere, where it condensed as torrential rain. While there is not enough water in the atmosphere today for it to rain worldwide for 40 days, there may have been in the past. This higher amount of moisture in the atmosphere before the Flood could have caused the earth to experience a slight greenhouse effect. This means that more of the heat from the sun could have been trapped

inside the atmosphere, creating a warmer and more even climate around the world.

We also know that the weather was different when Adam was created because Genesis 2:5–6 says that God had not yet sent rain but provided streams to water the ground in the Garden of Eden. It is possible that the plants there were watered by underground springs and streams and by dew. It most likely rained elsewhere on earth before the Flood, but it's possible that many of the people of Noah's day may never have experienced heavy rain, making Noah's idea of a global flood completely unbelievable to them.

Another possible explanation for a warmer pre-Flood climate is that God originally created one landmass, which might have looked like this artist's representation of Rodinia.

this supercontinent were centered around the equator, the climate would be much warmer, on average, than today. At the time of the Flood, this landmass broke apart catastrophically and rapidly into plates. This would have caused superheated water from inside the earth (the "fountains of the great deep") to shoot into the atmosphere and then rain back to earth, providing the main water source for the "windows of heaven" mentioned in Genesis 7:11. The various continents moved into their present positions, with some to the extreme south and north, where it is much colder today.

The catastrophic plate tectonic model, though needing further research by creation scientists, provides a plausible explanation for the pre-Flood climate and the sources of the floodwaters.

For more on the climate before the Flood, and where all the floodwaters came from (and went), do a search on the Answers in Genesis website.

What did we learn?

- Using clues from the Bible and science, what was the climate most likely like on earth before the Flood?

Taking it further

- How does the Bible say that plants were watered in the beginning?

- How might the breaking of the earth's crust have contributed to the Flood?

The fossil record also gives us clues to earlier weather and climate conditions. Fossils of large plants, the kind found only in tropical areas today, have been found in nearly every part of the world, including deserts and polar areas. This would indicate that these areas were much warmer before the Flood.

Another possible explanation for the warmer climate is that the original land that God created was one landmass, as suggested by Genesis 1:9. If

Watering without rain

The Bible tells us that at the time of Adam's creation there was not yet any rain. God sent water from under the ground to water the plants in the Garden of Eden. Plants were probably also watered by dew from the air. Warm air can hold more water than cool air. So when warm moist air comes in contact with something that is cool, the air around the object cools and some of the water precipitates out.

Purpose: To demonstrate how plants originally were watered

Materials: mirror, house plant, plate or shallow dish, glass of ice water, dish of hot water

Procedure:

1. Breathe on a mirror. The water from your warm moist breath condensed on the mirror when the air cooled. This is how dew forms on the ground.

2. Hold a glass of ice water over a dish of hot water. Watch as drops of water condense on the outside of the cup. The air above the hot water contains water vapor. As that air gets close to the cup of ice water it cools down. Cool air cannot hold as much water as warm air so the water changes from water vapor to liquid water and clings to the glass. This is another example of how dew could settle on plants and water them.

3. Next, place a house plant on a plate or in a shallow dish.

4. Pour a small amount of water in the dish. Watch as the plant absorbs the water from the dish.

Conclusion: This demonstrates how streams and underground springs could water plants on earth at the beginning.

Climate clues

In order to prove something scientifically, you must be able to observe it and test it. Since we cannot go back in the past and measure the climate, we cannot prove what the climate was like. However, we can look at the evidence and draw some conclusions.

Everyone makes certain assumptions, which affect the conclusions that they draw from the evidence. Some people believe that climate changes very slowly over time and that the processes we see today are the same as the processes that occurred over supposed millions of years. Other people believe that what the Bible says about the past is true and that there was a worldwide flood that changed the climate about 4,350 years ago.

We choose to believe the Bible, God's Word, and use that as our starting point for interpreting the evidence that we find in the rocks and fossils. Complete the "Climate Clues" worksheet to help you interpret the evidence of a pre-Flood climate.

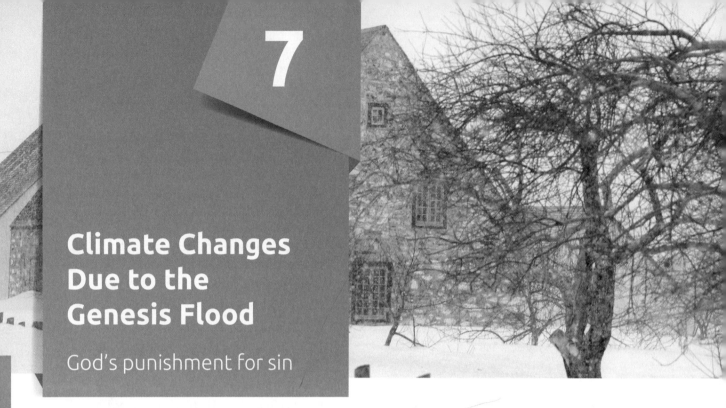

7

Climate Changes Due to the Genesis Flood

God's punishment for sin

How did the Flood affect the climate on Earth?

Challenge words:

permafrost

According to the Bible, how the earth looks today is not the same as how the earth looked at creation. Two major catastrophes have led to changes that have greatly affected the surface of the earth. The first change happened as a result of Adam's rebellion against God in the Garden of Eden. Genesis 3:17–19 says that God cursed the ground, causing it to grow thorns and thistles. The original plan for the earth was for it to produce food without weeds. But all of this changed as a result of man's sin. The apostle Paul tells us in Romans that all of creation has been subjected to futility and is experiencing the effects of this curse (Romans 8:20–22).

The second catastrophe was also a result of man's sin. Genesis 6:3–8 says that man had become so wicked that God was sorry He had created him, and He brought a great flood on the entire earth to destroy the human race. Only those in

the Ark—Noah, his family, and the animals—were saved from the Flood.

The Flood caused major changes in the climate. It is believed that before the Flood, the climate around most of the earth may have been tropical. There is substantial fossil evidence for a much warmer tropical climate worldwide in the past. Some suggest that there may have been more water vapor in the atmosphere surrounding the earth, keeping temperatures warmer and more uniform around the world.

Also, the earth was most likely one continent before the Flood, more centered over the equator. There is evidence that the cause of the Flood was the catastrophic breakup of that supercontintent

Fun Fact

Even during the Ice Age, the middle latitudes had mild weather. People farmed and lived in the warmer parts of the earth. God may have been referring to the Ice Age in Job 38:29–30 when He said, "From whose womb comes the ice? And the frost of heaven, who gives it birth? The waters harden like stone, and the surface of the deep is frozen." Job may have been familiar with the large areas of land covered with ice during the Ice Age.

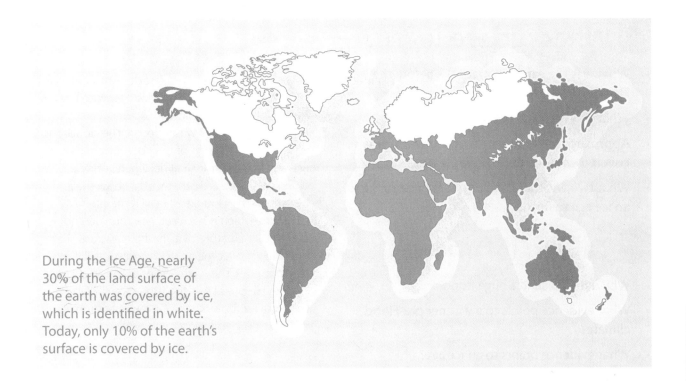

During the Ice Age, nearly 30% of the land surface of the earth was covered by ice, which is identified in white. Today, only 10% of the earth's surface is covered by ice.

and the movement of the earth's plates. The continents we see today got where they are as a result of these rapid plate movements during the Flood.

Directly after the Flood, the climate on the continents was much cooler, partly due to continued volcanic activity throwing ash into the air and blocking some of the sunlight. Because of the catastrophic volcanic activity during the Flood, the oceans after the Flood would have been much warmer than they are today. When the "fountains of the great deep" broke apart, heated water from inside the earth would have caused increased temperatures in the oceans. Warmer water evaporates faster than cooler water. This extensive evaporation would have resulted in huge amounts of precipitation after the Flood. This increase in precipitation, together with much cooler temperatures over the continents, set up conditions that led to the Ice Age.

Many areas of the earth show evidence of a great ice age—a time when much of the earth was covered with snow and glaciers. There is evidence that ice covered about 30% of the earth at one time, including northern Europe, most of Canada, much of the northern United States, and parts of New Zealand. There are areas of land that have been eroded by massive ice movements. And many specimens of animals, and even people, have been found encased in ice.

Scientists believe that the summers during an ice age would have been 20–40°F (10–20°C) cooler than they are today. They also believe that up to 80 feet (24 m) of snow would have fallen each year. At this rate, 40,000 feet (12,000 m) of snow would have fallen in 500 years. This would have compressed into nearly 4,000 feet (1,200 m) of ice, resulting in massive glaciers. The uniformitarian idea of slow climatic changes does not explain what would cause the temperatures to change and does not explain what would cause significantly more snowfall to occur at the same time. On the other hand, the biblical account of the creation of earth followed by the Great Flood explains how a mostly tropical climate was changed quickly into an ice age and eventually into the climate we see today.

Today, a wide variety of climates exist around the world. Areas near the poles are cold all year round. Areas near the equator are generally tropical. Some areas are deserts. Most areas are temperate and experience changing seasons. Despite the effects of the Flood, God has still provided us with a planet that has a climate that allows us to survive and thrive. 🌐

What did we learn?

- What was the earth's climate like before the Flood?
- What was the climate like after the Flood?
- Approximately how much of the world was covered with ice during the Ice Age?
- What two weather conditions are necessary for an ice age to form?

 Taking it further

- Why did God send a huge flood?
- What evidence points to a warmer pre-Flood climate?
- What evidence points to an ice age?
- Do we see new glaciers forming today?

Fun Fact

After Noah and his family left the Ark, God gave them the rainbow as a sign that He would never destroy the world again with a flood. Genesis 9:13–15 says, "I set My rainbow in the cloud, and it shall be for the sign of the covenant between Me and the earth. It shall be, when I bring a cloud over the earth, that the rainbow shall be seen in the cloud; and I will remember My covenant which is between Me and you and every living creature of all flesh; the waters shall never again become a flood to destroy all flesh." When it rains, the water drops in the air act like a prism to spread out the sun's rays, creating a beautiful rainbow. Thank God for His promise the next time you see a rainbow.

Picture of the changing climate

Purpose: To picture how the climate has changed on earth

Materials: paper, drawing materials (colored pencils, markers, etc.)

Procedure:

1. Fold a piece of drawing paper into thirds.

2. In the first third, draw a picture of the pre-Flood earth. It should be very tropical with lots of lush plants.

3. In the middle section, draw a picture of the post-Flood earth. This picture should show the Ice Age.

4. In the last third, draw a picture of what it is like around your home today.

Post-Flood climate

In the last lesson you looked at clues to what the climate might have been like before the Flood. Let's look now at a few clues about what the climate might have been like after the Flood. First, there is extensive evidence that ice sheets and glaciers once covered much of North America, northern Europe, and northern Asia. This evidence includes rounded, U-shaped valleys instead of V-shaped valleys, indicating the movement of ice through the valleys, as well as moraines, which are piles of rock and other debris that were pushed aside and ahead of moving glaciers. Thus, from this evidence we know that there were massive glaciers in the past.

Another clue comes from satellite views of the Sahara Desert, which show large river channels that are now dried up. After the Flood, weather patterns and air flow were different from how they are today. The weather patterns after the Flood likely carried storms to the area that is now the Sahara Desert,

Ancient Weather & Climate

bringing rainfall and allowing many animals and people to live in that area. After the oceans began to cool and ash from volcanoes began to clear, the weather changed to what we see today, and the Sahara Desert no longer receives the rain it once did.

Let's look at another clue. There is abundant evidence that much of the southwest United States was covered with huge lakes. The Great Salt Lake in Utah is the remains of a much larger lake that used to cover six times as much land. Also, Death Valley, California, used to be filled with a lake, as was much of Nevada. Today these areas are very dry and no lakes exist.

So where did that water come from and where did it go? It is very likely that the water came from Noah's Flood. After the Flood, these areas would have been teeming with life. However, eventually the weather patterns changed and water no longer flowed into these areas, allowing the lakes to dry up.

Finally, another interesting clue is found in Siberia and Alaska. Thousands of bones from woolly mammoths have been found encased in ice. Even a few whole mammoths have been discovered. And the further north you go the more bones there are. Think about what a woolly mammoth eats. Like an elephant, it would have eaten hundreds of pounds of grass and other plants each day. But what is Siberia like today? There are grasslands in southern Siberia

but in the area where most of the bones have been found there is very little vegetation, especially during the very long winters. Also, the ground contains permafrost. This means that the top few inches of the ground thaws in the summer, but below that the ground remains frozen, creating a swampy bog that would have been impossible for large animals to walk in.

So what does this tell us about the climate after the Flood in Siberia? Soon after the Flood, the warm waters from the Arctic and North Pacific oceans would have made northern Siberia and Alaska very mild. There would have been warmer temperatures during the winter and plenty of precipitation for lush vegetation, so the mammoths and other animals would have flourished there. However, as the oceans cooled, the weather would have changed and eventually massive dust and snow storms hit the area, trapping thousands of woolly mammoths in the ice. To learn more about woolly mammoths, do a search on the Answers in Genesis website.

We cannot scientifically prove that these were the climate situations after the Flood, but the clues point to changing climates resulting in an Ice Age. The climate changed after the Ice Age, eventually resulting in the climates we have today.

The Sahara Desert used to be much wetter than it is today.

Weather and the Bible

Everybody talks about the weather: "It sure is hot." "We could really use some rain." "Is the sun ever going to shine again?" The weather is something everyone seems to have an opinion about. But what does the Bible say about weather? Let's take a look.

Rain is mentioned in the Bible more than 50 times as both a blessing and a curse. The first place it is mentioned is in Genesis 7:11, "In the six hundredth year of Noah's life, in the second month, the seventeenth day of the month, on that day all the fountains of the great deep were broken up, and the windows of heaven were opened." Here rain was sent as part of the punishment upon man for his wickedness. The last place in the Bible to talk about rain is Revelation 11:6, "These have power to shut heaven, so that no rain falls in the days of their prophecy; and they have power over waters to turn them to blood, and to strike the earth with all plagues, as often as they desire." Here the Lord will stop the rain as punishment upon man for his sins. Most of the other references to

rain in the Bible show how it is used as a blessing or to show the power of God's Word. It shows how God controls everything around us, even the rain.

But God controls more than just the rain. There are references that show God controlling snow, wind, and storms. One of the most well-known examples is in Luke 8:22–25: "Now it happened, on a certain day, that He [Jesus] got into a boat with His disciples. And He said to them, 'Let us cross over to the other side of the lake.' And they launched out. But as they sailed He fell asleep. And a windstorm came down on the lake, and they were filling with water, and were in jeopardy. And they came to Him and awoke Him, saying, 'Master, Master, we are perishing!' Then He arose and rebuked the wind and the raging of the water. And they ceased, and there was a calm. But He said to them, 'Where is your faith?' And they were afraid, and marveled, saying to one another, 'Who can this be? For He commands even the winds and water, and they obey Him!'" Jesus showed that He has power over all of nature.

God can and does control the weather around us. What we look at as a disaster, God may be using for good. In Genesis 42 God allowed a famine to hit the land of Egypt and Israel. God used this famine to bring Joseph and his brothers back together. He also caused the whole family to move to Egypt.

Why is living in Egypt so important? The Egyptians allowed the Israelites to live there but they did not intermingle with them. This may have been because the Egyptians looked down on shepherding, the profession of Joseph's brothers. But whatever the reason, this isolation allowed God's people to grow into a large, strong, identifiable group. Through this experience, the family of Jacob became the nation known as the Israelites.

Later God sent Moses to rescue His people and bring them out of Egypt to the land He had promised to Abraham over 400 years earlier. In the process, God again showed His power over all of nature. One of the plagues sent to persuade Pharaoh was a change in the weather. Exodus 9:23–25 says, "And Moses stretched out his rod toward heaven; and the LORD sent thunder and hail, and fire darted to the ground. And the LORD rained hail on the land of Egypt. So there was hail, and fire mingled with the hail, so very heavy that there was none like it in all the land of Egypt since it became a nation. And the hail struck throughout the whole land of Egypt, all that was in the field, both man and beast; and the hail struck every herb of the field and broke every tree of the field."

God also showed His power over the wind and the sea in the process of rescuing the Israelites from Egypt. First, God turned the water in the Nile River into blood. Then, in Exodus 14:21–28, God used weather to show His power to the world by destroying the most powerful army of the day.

"Then Moses stretched out his hand over the sea; and the LORD caused the sea to go back by a strong east wind all that night, and made the sea into dry land, and the waters were divided. So the children of Israel went into the midst of the sea on the dry ground, and the waters were a wall to them on their right hand and on their left. And the Egyptians pursued and went after them into the midst of the sea, all Pharaoh's horses, his chariots, and his horsemen. . . . Then the LORD said to Moses, 'Stretch out your hand over the sea, that the waters may come back upon the Egyptians, on their chariots, and on their horsemen.' And Moses stretched out his hand over the sea; and when the morning appeared, the sea returned to its full depth, while the Egyptians were fleeing into it. So the LORD overthrew the Egyptians in the midst of the sea. Then the waters returned and covered the chariots, the horsemen, and all the army of Pharaoh that came into the sea after them. Not so much as one of them remained."

As we can see, God is in control of the weather. He can destroy an "invincible" army, while at the same time giving strength and protection to the weak and defenseless. God blesses each with sunshine, rain, snow, and wind (Matthew 5:45). As can be seen by studying His Word, all things in nature are under His control and serve His purposes.

8

Global Warming

Fact or fiction?

Is man causing global climate change?

Words to know:

global warming

You have already learned that climate is the average weather in an area. And you have learned that the climate has changed drastically in the past. So can we expect the climate to change drastically in the future? Some scientists claim that global warming, the increase in the average temperature of the earth due to increased carbon dioxide levels, will drastically change the climate in the future and could lead to drastic consequences for life on this planet. But is this true? Let's look at the facts.

Most scientists will agree that the average temperature on earth has increased about 1.2°F (0.67°C) over the past 130 years. We also know that

carbon dioxide in the atmosphere has increased about 30% since the 1880s. Much of that increase is due to the burning of fossil fuels and to deforestation, which has greatly reduced the number of trees on the planet. It is also true that carbon dioxide is a gas that can increase the greenhouse effect. The greenhouse effect is what causes the heat from the sun to be trapped in the earth's atmosphere rather than escaping back into space.

Many scientists have taken this data and concluded that the increase in carbon dioxide and decrease in trees will cause a serious change in the climate of earth. In fact, many people today no longer talk about global warming; instead they talk about climate change. They point to several indicators that the climate of earth is changing. They claim that ice sheets and glaciers are melting at an unusual rate, and that there are more severe droughts and more severe storms than in the past. They also claim that increased carbon dioxide in the oceans is causing the ocean to become more acidic. Many people predict that if this trend is not stopped, the climate change in the future will be catastrophic and could result in people and animals dying and habitats being destroyed.

Politicians around the world have become very concerned about these predictions and have started passing laws to limit how much carbon dioxide people can put into the air. They are also passing laws

Fun Fact

All of the termites in the world produce more carbon dioxide than all of the cars and factories in the world. People's activities produce only a small fraction of the carbon dioxide in the atmosphere.

to limit how many trees can be cut in the rainforests and requiring new trees to be planted. They believe that these changes are necessary to stop the dire consequences that are looming in the future. Many of these laws will be very harmful to people because it will require companies to change the way they do many things causing products to become much more expensive. This will be especially harmful if energy costs increase and poor people cannot afford to adequately heat their houses in the winter. But are these laws necessary? Is man really responsible for global warming, and will we see the severe global climate changes that some people are predicting?

Computer models

These predictions are based on computer models that take the current data and try to predict what will happen in the future if the trends continue. However, there are many problems with these models.

First, these models assume that carbon dioxide is the cause of the temperature increase that we have seen. However, this is not a proven fact. Carbon dioxide only accounts for about 5% of the total greenhouse effect. The vast majority of the heat that is trapped in the atmosphere is trapped by water vapor and clouds. There are also many natural causes for temperature fluctuations. The amount of energy produced by the sun is not constant. The number of solar flares and sunspot activity affect the amount of energy that reaches the earth. Also, the amount of volcanic activity affects the temperature. When there is a large amount of volcanic activity, more ash is put into the air, which blocks more of the sunlight. When the volcanoes are relatively quiet, there is less ash so more sunlight reaches the surface of the earth.

Fun Fact

The average temperature of Earth has increased since the 1880s, however, this has not been a steady increase. From about 1950–1970 there was a distinct drop in global temperatures, and people were concerned about global cooling until temperatures began to rise again in the 1970s. Since 2000, the global temperatures have been relatively steady and are not rising as fast as computer models have predicted

These events occur in natural cycles that are not well understood and affect the climate in ways that cannot accurately be predicted.

Although many people are predicting droughts and increased hurricane activity, there is very little data to support these ideas. In fact, as the temperature has increased in the past hundred years, the precipitation amounts have increased by about 1% per decade. So it is unlikely that global warming would result in widespread drought. Also, with the exception of the extremely active hurricane season of 2005, the number and severity of hurricanes have remained pretty constant since the 1850s. Again, there is no real data to support the idea that global warming would cause massive hurricanes.

Role of temperature

Another important fact that is often overlooked is the role that temperature plays in evaporation. As temperatures increase, evaporation also increases. This means that more water goes into the air and more clouds are formed. Clouds not only help trap heat in the atmosphere, but also reflect much of the sunlight back into space before it ever reaches the surface of the earth. The atmosphere regulates itself to a large extent so that when it gets too hot, sunlight is reflected. Similarly, when the temperatures drop, fewer clouds are formed allowing more sunlight to reach the surface. So temperatures will not necessarily continue to increase unchecked in the future.

What should we do?

So does this mean that we should not be concerned about global warming? As with any scientific question, we need to look carefully at the facts through a biblical worldview and see what we can learn. At this point, there is simply not enough data to prove that global warming is a problem. This does not mean we can ignore it; it simply means that more investigation is needed before we can draw good conclusions.

The Bible does not tell us what will happen to the climate of the earth in the next 50 years. But the Bible does tell us that God loves us and will take care of us. It also says that as Christians we should be good stewards of the planet. So we need to keep researching the issue and see where God leads. 🌐

What did we learn?

- What is global warming?
- What is the greenhouse effect?
- What is the main cause of the greenhouse effect?
- What amount of greenhouse effect is due to carbon dioxide in the atmosphere?
- How much has the temperature increased over the past 130 years?
- Name at least two possible natural causes for increased temperatures.

 # Taking it further

- Why is it important to know what assumptions are made when looking at computer models?
- Ice core samples from Greenland indicate that rapid climate shifts have occurred in the past. How can your worldview affect the interpretation of this data?

 # Global warming in the news

Look through your local newspapers and magazines, and search online to find articles that mention global warming or global climate change. Read these articles together with your parents. What do these articles have to say? Most of them will probably tell you that global warming is a real problem and we must do something about it right away. Reporters love to talk about the "global warming problem." But if you look at scientific research, you find that most scientists agree that it is too soon to say whether global warming is a real problem or not.

We should not be afraid of what might happen in the future. God designed this world to handle climate changes, and He is in control, despite what reporters say.

 # Benefits of global warming

One of the most important areas that is neglected in the whole global warming debate is the possible benefits of increased temperatures. We often hear of the possible harms such as flooding of coastal areas, more heat-related deaths, and a possible ice age triggered by cool water entering the oceans as the glaciers melt. However, there are many benefits to warmer temperatures.

If there would be more deaths due to heat, then there should be fewer deaths due to cold. Currently, there are about ten times as many people who die each year due to cold than due to heat. Thus, increased temperatures should result in fewer overall temperature-related deaths.

Increased temperatures would also lengthen the growing season in many areas, which would result in more food crops. So even if some areas become too hot for agriculture, other areas that are currently not used could become useful for crops.

As we mentioned earlier, there has been an increase in precipitation in the past hundred years. This is expected with increased temperatures. Increased precipitation should also lead to increased plant growth. This would benefit the entire planet. An increase in plants would also help to reduce the amount of carbon dioxide in the air and would help balance any increase in temperature due to increased carbon dioxide.

Finally, if the glaciers recede there could be increased shipping in the Arctic Ocean. This would be very beneficial to northern countries.

As you can see, the possible benefits must be weighed against the possible harms before any drastic measures are taken. The reality is that at this time scientists cannot accurately predict what would really come to pass, so more study is needed.

UNIT 3

Clouds

◊ **Describe** how water is recycled in the environment.

◊ **Explain** how clouds form.

◊ **Describe** the three basic cloud types.

◊ **Describe** the different types of precipitation.

9

Water Cycle

The ultimate in recycling

How does the water cycle work?

Words to know:

water cycle	transpiration
evaporation	vaporization

Challenge words:

zone of aeration	spring
zone of saturation	impermeable
water table	permeable

Changes in weather are God's way of moving water around the world to be used by plants, animals, and people. This constant moving of water is called the **water cycle** because water is moved and reused over and over again.

Water enters the atmosphere as water vapor—the gas form of water. Water vapor enters the atmosphere one of three ways: evaporation, transpiration, or vaporization. The vast majority of the water enters the atmosphere through evaporation. Nearly three quarters of the earth's surface is covered with water. As the sun heats the surface of the oceans, lakes, and rivers, the water molecules are warmed up. Eventually, these molecules receive enough energy to change state from liquid to gas. This is called evaporation.

Wind increases the rate of evaporation. The wind moves the vapor molecules away from the surface of the ocean or lake. This brings dryer air across the surface, allowing for more water molecules to be absorbed into the air. The dryer the air, the more water it can hold, and the faster the water will evaporate.

The second way that water vapor enters the air is through **transpiration**. Water vapor is released into the air when animals and people breathe. You can see the water vapor in your breath as it condenses in the cold winter air, or when you breathe on a mirror. Water vapor is also released when plants perform photosynthesis.

Vaporization occurs when liquid water is heated to the boiling point. An external heat source is required for this to occur. You can observe vaporization as you are cooking and you see steam rising into the air from the pot of water on your stove. Only a small percentage of the water enters the atmosphere in this manner.

Regardless of how the water enters the atmosphere, warm moist air rises and is moved along by

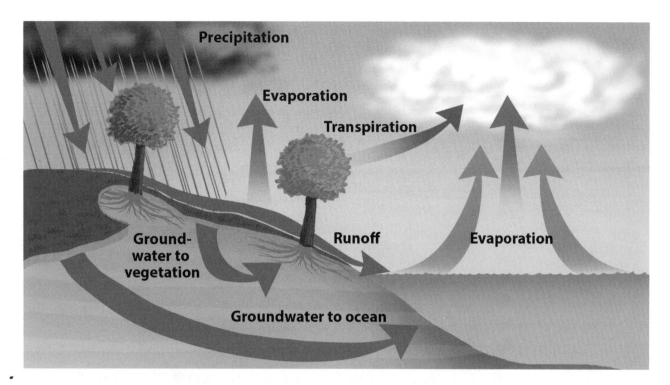

Precipitation

Evaporation

Transpiration

Evaporation

Ground- water to vegetation

Runoff

Groundwater to ocean

winds. Eventually the air cools and can no longer hold all of the water vapor. As this vapor condenses, it forms clouds. As the air cools further, the condensed water leaves the atmosphere in the form of rain, snow, hail, sleet, or dew.

Some of this moisture is used by plants, animals, and people, and is released back into the atmosphere through transpiration. But most of the water finds its way back into the oceans. Some of the water flows into rivers and streams that eventually end up in the ocean. Other water sinks into the ground and finds its way into underground streams that also flow into the ocean. Once the water reaches the surface of the earth, evaporation again puts water vapor into the air, thus completing the water cycle.

 What did we learn?

- How does water vapor enter the atmosphere?
- Which of these processes accounts for most of the water in the air?
- How does water get from the atmosphere back to the earth?

 Taking it further

- What are some factors that affect how fast the water evaporates from the surface of the ocean or lake?
- Why is it better to water your grass early in the morning rather than later in the day during the summer?

Drawing the water cycle

Draw a picture of the water cycle by drawing a landscape that includes the ocean, land, plants, animals, and clouds. Be sure to include evaporation, transpiration, and vaporization, as well as rain or other forms of precipitation. Draw arrows indicating the direction that the water is moving. For example, the picture could show arrows moving up from the ocean's surface and out of an animal's mouth as well as down from the clouds.

Underground water

God designed the water cycle because fresh water is very important for maintaining life on earth. And one important aspect of the water cycle, which many people are not even aware of, is groundwater. Ninety-seven percent of the water on earth is in the oceans. This water is too salty for human use. The remaining 3% is fresh water, but three fourths of that water is permanently frozen in the glaciers and polar ice caps. About 22 percent of fresh water is underground and less than 1 percent of the fresh water is available in lakes, rivers, and other surface water. This makes the groundwater a vital source of fresh water.

Precipitation
Runoff
Recharge area
(permeable rock)
(impermeable rock)
Bedrock (impermeable rock)
Zone of aeration
Water table
Groundwater (Zone of saturation)
Evaporation and transpiration
Discharge area
Lake

It is important to understand how groundwater works. First, water gets into the ground when precipitation seeps into the rock below the surface of the ground. The ground is divided into several zones to help describe this process. The top part of the ground is called the zone of aeration. The rock in this zone has many air holes in it. This is how water flows through it. Below this is the zone of saturation. This level of rock contains many holes that are filled with water. Where the zone of saturation meets the zone of aeration is called the water table. This is the surface of the groundwater.

The water table generally follows the contours of the surface, except it does not go up as high on hills and does not go down as much in valleys, so the water will be farther from the surface on a hilltop and closer to the surface in a valley. Groundwater generally flows downhill and in the same direction as surface water, but it flows at a slower rate. Eventually, most groundwater finds its way to the surface. This happens in one of several ways.

Groundwater can find an opening at a lower level such as in the side of a hill. When it does this it forms a spring. Water often flows continually from a spring. Other times groundwater flows into an underground river which eventually flows into a lake, a surface stream, or into the ocean.

It is important to know the level of the water table, especially if you want to access the water in the ground. Many farmers and some homeowners get the majority of their water from underground wells. Wells are drilled into the ground and the water is then pumped out of the ground. Wells must be drilled below the water table in order for them to fill with water. Since the water table moves up and down with the amount of precipitation and with the seasons, the well must be drilled lower than the lowest level of the water table.

The flow of underground water is greatly dependent on the type of rock in the area. Some rocks do not allow water to flow through them at all. This kind of rock is called impermeable. Most igneous and metamorphic rocks, as well as clay and shale, are impermeable. If there is a layer of impermeable rock near the surface, water will not flow into the ground. Instead, it will flow across the surface until it finds an area where it can sink into the ground or it enters a river or lake.

Rock that allows water to flow into it is called permeable rock. Permeable rock has many air holes that are connected to each other. This allows the water to flow through it. Gravel, sand, and many sedimentary rocks are all permeable surfaces that allow for the flow of water.

Even though you may never see the water that is under the ground, you should remember that it is there. It may be a few feet below the surface or hundreds of feet below you, but it is there nevertheless. And this underground water is what is used to supply much of the water needs for people around the world.

10

Cloud Formation

Pretty white shapes
in the sky

What are clouds, and how do they form?

Words to know:

convection   dew point

condense

Have you ever looked at a cloud and seen the shape of an animal or plant or even a person's face? Looking for shapes in the clouds can be fun. But have you ever wondered what a cloud is made of or how the clouds form to begin with?

Clouds are masses of water droplets or ice crystals suspended in the air. But before a cloud can form, the sun must shine. The sun warms the surface of the earth and the surface of the water causing the water to evaporate. This warm moist air expands and rises; this is called **convection**. It floats up like a hot-air balloon. A bubble of warm

air is called a convection cell. As the air rises, it cools about 5.4°F per 1,000 feet (1°C per 100 m) in altitude. It continues rising as long as the air surrounding the cell is cooler than the air in the cell. As the moist air rises, it cools, causing some of the water vapor in the rising bubble of air to **condense** into droplets of water. This happens when the warm moist air reaches the dew point. The **dew point** is the point where the air holds

Clouds form in much the same way as dew forms on objects.

Fun Fact

A large cloud can weigh up to 700,000 tons—more than the weight of 3,000 jumbo jets.

Fun Fact

Why do clouds look white? Gas molecules such as the nitrogen, oxygen, and water vapor molecules in the air scatter the light like a prism. Blue light has a shorter wavelength and is more easily scattered, whereas yellow light has a longer wavelength and does not scatter much, causing the sky to appear blue and the sun to appear yellow. Water drops in the clouds, on the other hand, reflect the sun's rays evenly and do not scatter the light, so the clouds appear to be white.

as much moisture as it can for the current temperature. This is also called 100% relative humidity. When the air mass cools to the dew point, water droplets begin to condense on dust, pollen, or other particles in the air and a cloud is formed.

Convection is not the only way that warm air reaches the dew point. Sometimes a warm air mass comes in contact with a cold air mass and it is forced to rise over the cold air mass. As it rises, the warm air mass cools and the water begins to condense.

Clouds also form as warm air is forced to rise as it approaches mountain peaks. If an air mass approaching a mountain is lower than the mountain peak, it is forced to rise. As it rises, the air cools, the water vapor condenses, and clouds form.

Once a cloud forms, how does it stay floating in the sky? The upward air pressure holds the clouds up. A cloud can be very heavy, but each individual water droplet is very small and light; the rising air beneath each drop helps to hold it up.

If the air around the cloud is dry, the water will again evaporate and the cloud will vanish. If the surrounding air is moist, the cloud can last for several hours.

What did we learn?

- What is a cloud?
- What is the dew point of air?
- What is another name for dew point?
- How do clouds form?

Taking it further

- Often, one side of a mountain range receives much more rain than the other side. Why do you think this happens?
- Why don't clouds always result in rain?
- What role do pollen and dust play in cloud formation?

Fun Fact

A single raindrop has an average of 1 million droplets of water in it.

🧪 Cloud in a bottle

Purpose: To make your own cloud in a bottle

Materials: jar with a lid, pan of water, ice, plastic zipper bag

Procedure:

1. Pour about one inch of water in a jar and seal the jar with a lid.

2. Place the jar in a pan containing two inches of water, and heat the water over medium heat.

3. Place several pieces of ice in a plastic zipper bag and place the bag on top of the jar.

4. Watch as the water in the jar turns to steam and then condenses at the top of the jar.

Conclusion: The heat of the stove acts as the sun to heat the water in the jar. The warm moist air in the jar rises. The ice keeps the air at the top of the jar cool, causing water to condense at the top of the jar. This is how clouds form in the atmosphere.

🏅 Clouds and snow

Purpose: To make a cloud and snow

Materials: two shoe boxes (one must be at least two inches smaller in each direction than the other), black construction paper, several small pieces of dry ice, newspaper, towel, hammer, flashlight, gloves, lid or cardboard for smaller box

Procedure:

1. Line the inside of the smaller box with black construction paper and place the smaller box inside the larger box.

2. Place small pieces of dry ice in the larger box around the edges of the smaller box and cover the dry ice with newspaper. Always be sure to use gloves when handling dry ice.

3. Cover the small box with its lid or a piece of cardboard so the air inside the box can cool to freezing temperatures. This should take about 10 minutes.

4. Remove the lid and gently breathe into the cooled air. What happened? You should see your warm breath condense in the cool air forming a cloud. Describe the movement of the cloud inside the box.

5. Now, place a small piece of dry ice into a towel.

6. Use a hammer to smash the ice into very small pieces.

7. Turn out the lights and shine a bright flashlight at an angle through your cloud.

8. Using gloves, sprinkle a few tiny fragments of dry ice onto the cloud. You should be able to see moisture crystallize and fall onto the paper as snow.

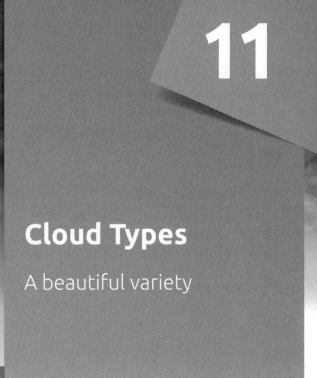

11

Cloud Types

A beautiful variety

How are clouds classified?

Words to know:

stratus	cirrus
cumulus	nimbus

Challenge words:

fog	valley fog
radiation fog	upslope fog
advection fog	condensation nuclei
steam fog	

Clouds form in a variety of shapes and sizes. In 1803 an English pharmacist named Luke Howard developed a system for naming the shapes of clouds. He divided the clouds into three basic shapes. **Stratus** clouds are stretched out clouds that often form an even covering. They form in layers or sheets. An overcast sky is one covered with stratus clouds. The second shape of clouds is **cumulus** clouds. Cumulus is the Latin word for "heap" or "pile." Cumulus clouds are big, fluffy or billowy clouds. **Cirrus** clouds are the final type of clouds. Cirrus clouds are curly or wispy clouds.

The air movement determines a cloud's shape. Horizontal air movement causes clouds to stretch out into layers and become stratus clouds. Vertical air movement causes clouds to clump together to form cumulus clouds.

Stratus clouds

Cumulus clouds

Cirrus clouds

Clouds are also classified by the altitude at which they form. Low clouds, ones that form from 0.5–1 mile (0.8–1.6 km) high, are given the prefix *strato*. Clouds that form from 1–4 miles (1.6–6.4 km) high are called *alto* clouds. And clouds that form from 4–7.5 miles (6.4–12 km) high are called *cirro* clouds. So if you put the prefix for the altitude together with the name for the shape of the cloud you can accurately describe where a cloud is and what it looks like. For example, a billowy cloud at 3 miles (4.8 km) above the earth would be called an altocumulus cloud and a layer of clouds at 3 miles (4.8 km) high would be called altostratus clouds.

If clouds are going to bring rain, they are designated as nimbus clouds. So, low stretched out clouds that are bringing rain are called nimbostratus clouds and billowy thunderstorm type clouds are called cumulonimbus clouds. Cumulonimbus clouds often begin forming close to the earth and can stretch as high as 10 miles (16 km) into the atmosphere, though most are much shorter.

Sometimes thunderstorm clouds have round bumps on the bottom like those shown at the beginning of the lesson. These are caused by updrafts of warm air carrying water droplets into a colder area where they freeze. These ice crystals fall down, pulling cold air with them. The warm air pushes against these cold pouches forming them into round bumps. So, the next time you look at the clouds, don't just look for animals and people, but look for stratus, cumulus, and cirrus clouds.

What did we learn?

- What are the two ways that clouds are classified?
- What are the three main shapes of clouds and how does each look?
- What are rain clouds called?

Taking it further

- What would a fluffy cloud at 0.5 miles (0.8 km) above the earth be called?
- What would a wispy cloud at 5 miles (8 km) above the earth be called?

 ## Cloud picture

Make a picture with different shapes of clouds by pasting cotton balls to a piece of blue construction paper.

The cotton balls can be stretched into layers to form stratus clouds, small pieces can be torn off to form cirrus clouds, and whole cotton balls can be clumped together to form cumulus clouds.

Label each type of cloud.

 ## Fog formation

One special type of cloud that we have not mentioned is fog. Fog is a cloud that comes in contact with the surface of the earth. In general, if condensation in the air reduces visibility near the ground to below 3,280 feet (1,000 meters), it is classified as fog. Just as with other cloud formation, fog occurs when warm moist air is cooled and the water vapor condenses. This can happen in various ways. Each method is given a different name.

The most common type of fog is called radiation fog. **Radiation fog** occurs when the ground radiates heat back into the atmosphere after the sun stops shining on it. This cools the air near the surface of the earth. If the air is moist and there is very little wind, fog can form near the ground. Radiation fog occurs on cool, clear nights. If the sky is cloudy, the heat will be trapped closer to the earth and condensation will not occur. Radiation fog usually dissipates shortly after sunrise.

Another type of fog is **advection fog**. Advection means "moved by the wind," and advection fog occurs when the wind moves a mass of warm moist air over

a cooler surface. Often warm moist air from tropical ocean areas is moved north over cooler waters, and fog forms as the air cools down. Other times the warm air is blown from over the water toward the cooler land. This also cools the air, and fog can form. Advection fog is often called sea fog.

Steam fog is sort of the opposite of advection fog. Steam fog occurs when cool air moves over a warm moist surface. The air just above the surface is cooled by the moving air, causing condensation and fog formation.

Two other types of fog formation are associated with mountains. Frequently, heavy cool air settles into mountain valleys. As warmer air moves over the tops of the mountains, some of it is cooled by the colder air in the valley, causing condensation at lower elevations. This is called **valley fog**.

The second kind of fog associated with mountains is **upslope fog**. Upslope fog forms on windy days. As wind forces warm moist air up a mountain slope, the air cools as it goes up in elevation. Water vapor cools as the air rises forming upslope fog. Upslope fog is very common in the Los Angeles area when the wind blows from the west, and along the eastern slope of the Rocky Mountains when wind blows from the east. I bet you didn't know there are so many ways to make fog.

Purpose: To make your own kind of fog—bottle fog

Materials: clear 2-liter plastic bottle, match, warm water

Procedure:

1. Place ¼ cup of warm water in the bottom of an empty, clear 2-liter soda bottle.

2. Light a match, drop it into the bottle, and tightly cap the bottle. Wait a moment for the smoke to dissipate.

3. Now squeeze the sides of the bottle then quickly release the pressure. Do this several times until fog forms inside your bottle. The fog may last only a few seconds.

Questions:

- Why does fog form inside the bottle?

- Why do you think we have you put a match inside the bottle?

Conclusion: Water vapor does not generally form drops unless it has something to stick to. The smoke particles give the water vapor something to stick to. In the atmosphere, the air is filled with tiny bits of dirt, smoke, pollen, and other particles that water can stick to. These particles are called **condensation nuclei**.

Fun Fact

The foggiest place on earth is the Grand Banks area off the coast of Newfoundland, Canada. The foggiest places on land are Point Reyes, California and Argentia, Newfoundland, Canada; both have with over 200 foggy days each year.

Clouds

12

Precipitation

Rain, rain go away

What different types of precipitation are there?

Words to know:

dew

frost

coalesce

drizzle

sleet

hail

drought

cloud seeding

Challenge words:

acid rain

God controls the weather. He can use it as a blessing or a judgment. The Genesis Flood is the most dramatic use of weather as God's judgment against man's sin. But most of the time, precipitation is a blessing to the people who receive it.

Clouds form when water vapor condenses in the atmosphere. About 10% of all clouds produce precipitation. Precipitation is any form of water falling from the atmosphere. Precipitation can fall in either liquid or solid forms.

Dew and frost occur when the ground becomes cooler than the air around it. When the air near the ground cools, it can no longer hold as much water, and the water vapor condenses on the ground forming **dew**. If the point at which dew forms is below 32°F (0°C), the water freezes instantly, forming **frost**. Crystals of ice that form directly on trees and other structures can make amazing pictures in the winter sunlight.

Most liquid precipitation occurs as rain and drizzle. In a cloud, a water droplet is about 0.0004 inches (0.001 cm) in diameter. As water droplets fall, they begin to **coalesce**. This means that the droplets begin to combine with other droplets. A falling drop creates a vacuum, drawing smaller drops toward it and increasing its size. When a drop of water reaches 0.02 inches (0.05 cm), it is considered **drizzle**—very

Heavy frost

Freezing rain can be extremely dangerous.

Large hailstones

tiny drops of rain. As the drops become bigger, they are classified as rain. Very heavy raindrops can be as big as ¼ inch (0.6 cm) in diameter.

Sometimes rain falls when the temperature near the ground is below freezing. This results in freezing rain, and the rain freezes as it hits the cold ground. Freezing rain, or ice storms, can be extremely dangerous for both drivers and pedestrians.

Precipitation can also occur as a solid in the form of sleet, hail, or snow. When rain falls through a very cold layer of air, the raindrops can become rounded pellets of ice. These small ice pellets are called **sleet**. Hailstones, often just called **hail**, are large pellets of ice that form when ice crystals are forced back up into the clouds by strong updrafts.

These lovely pictures were taken by Wilson Bentley, nicknamed the "Snowflake Man." They were taken in Jericho, Vermont, in the winter of 1902 and were published in an article entitled "Studies among the Snow Crystals" in the annual *Summary of the Monthly Weather Review* for 1902.

The hailstones accumulate water as they fall through the cloud, and then are forced back up by warmer air into the colder part of the cloud where they freeze. Then they begin to fall again. This happens over and over with the hail getting bigger each time until the weight of the hail is greater than the upward force of the warm air. Hail can be very small, but sometimes the hailstones can be as big as golf balls. Medium and large hail can cause severe damage to crops, automobiles, and other structures and can be very dangerous to people and animals.

Probably the most beautiful form of precipitation is snow. Snow occurs when water crystallizes in the clouds and does not melt before it reaches the earth. In 1880 an American named Wilson A. Bentley first examined snowflakes under a microscope. Expecting to see just chunks of ice, he was surprised to find that each flake had a unique delicate shape. He discovered that snowflakes are always hexagonal, or six-sided. He also discovered that every snowflake has a unique design—no two are alike. God created the properties of water in such a way that each snowflake is an example of His creativity.

A prolonged lack of precipitation, called a **drought**,

Drought is a prolonged lack of precipitation.

can have devastating effects on society. Droughts ruin crops and kill livestock. To end drought conditions, people have tried many ways to make it rain. Some have been more successful than others. One popular way to try to make it rain is called cloud seeding. Scientists drop silver iodide crystals from an airplane into cumulonimbus clouds in the hopes that the water droplets will stick to the silver iodide and encourage raindrop formation. Some people believe that this procedure increases rain by up to 15%. However, it is difficult to prove this because the crystals are only dropped into clouds that are likely to produce rain anyway. Another method that has been tried is to drop tiny pieces of dry ice into clouds. Occasionally these clouds have been known to produce snow.

In South America, the country of Chile has taken a different approach to fighting drought. People there have stretched nylon mesh nets that are about 12 yards (11 m) by 4 yards (3.5 m) across the tops of several mountains. As clouds pass through these nets, they lose their moisture. The people have been able to collect up to 2,500 gallons (9,400 liters) of water per day using this method.

Regardless of these different methods, man has been ineffective when it comes to controlling the weather. But we can be thankful that God set up a system that works very well for providing adequate moisture for our needs. 🌐

What did we learn?

- What are the main types of precipitation?
- What is the difference between drizzle and rain?
- What shape do snowflakes have?
- What is coalescence?
- What is the difference between sleet and hail?

Taking it further

- What conditions are necessary for large hailstones to form?
- How effective is cloud seeding?

Fun Fact

The largest snowfall recorded in one day occurred in Capricotta, Italy, March 5, 2015. The storm dumped 100.8 inches (256 cm) of snow in only 18 hours.

Measuring raindrops

Although Wilson Bentley was known for his work with snowflakes, he was actually a farmer by trade and studying the weather was a hobby. From 1898 to 1904 this hobby included the study of raindrops. Bentley devised a way to observe and measure the size of raindrops. He discovered that raindrops falling in a pan of flour produce flour pellets that are very close to the size of the raindrops.

Bentley studied raindrops from over 70 different storms and concluded that about 65% of raindrops are between 0.033 and 0.125 inches (0.8–3.2 mm). Only a very small percent are over 0.2 inches (5 mm) in diameter.

Purpose: To see the size of raindrops

Materials: flour, pie pan or baking dish, oven, rain/water

Procedure:

1. Place a layer of flour one inch thick in the bottom of a pie pan or other baking dish.

2. Place the dish in the rain for 3 or 4 seconds. If you live in an area that does not get much rain, you can make your own rain by dipping your fingers in a cup of water and then sprinkling the water over the surface of the flour. Do this several times so that you get many raindrops to examine.

3. Once you have collected the raindrops, allow the drops to dry. Bentley allowed his drops to dry slowly, but you can place your pan in a 350-degree oven for 20 minutes.

4. Remove the pan from the oven and allow it to cool.

5. When the flour is cool, sift the flour to remove the hard balls. The balls represent the rain drops.

6. Once you have removed all of the pellets, sort them according to size. Like Bentley, you can now see the size and shape of raindrops.

Acid rain

Precipitation is vital for maintaining life on earth. The water is necessary for plant growth and for animals and people. But precipitation contains more than just water.

As you already learned, water vapor will not coalesce unless there is something for the water droplets to stick to. So precipitation already contains particles of dust, smoke, and pollen. But the water in the air chemically reacts with other chemicals in the air as well.

Although air is mostly nitrogen and oxygen, it naturally contains carbon dioxide as well. Some of the carbon dioxide dissolves in the water drops to form carbonic acid. Thus rain water is naturally slightly acidic.

Pure water is neutral, with a pH level of 7.0—neither acidic nor basic. But rain water naturally has a pH level of about 5.6–5.7 because of the carbonic acid in it.

Another natural source of acid in precipitation is the sulfur emitted by volcanoes. The sulfur reacts with the water to form sulfuric acid. God designed the earth to work with precipitation that is slightly acidic. However, in many areas around the world, precipitation has become much more acidic than it naturally would be and is called acid rain.

Acid rain is precipitation—rain, snow, sleet, hail, etc.—that has a lower than normal pH. In some areas the pH of precipitation is as low as 4.5. This higher acid level is due primarily to the addition of sulfur dioxide and nitrogen oxides into the air from the burning of fossil fuels.

There are two main sources of these chemicals. First, energy power plants burn fossil fuels such as coal and oil. Burning these compounds releases sulfur and nitrogen compounds into the air, which react with water to form sulfuric acid and nitric acid.

The second major source of these compounds is automobiles which burn petroleum. This also adds nitrogen oxides to the atmosphere. Areas with high population densities, such as the northeastern part of the United States, often have a higher concentration of acid rain.

Acid rain can be damaging to ecosystems. If the acid level in lakes becomes too high, fish and other wildlife cannot survive. Also, acid in the soil can damage some plants. Red spruce trees are particularly sensitive to additional acid in the soil and have died out in some areas.

Other adverse effects of acid rain include decreased visibility due to the pollutants in the air and the destruction of buildings, statues, and other materials as the acids react with the building materials and wear them away.

Much has been done to reduce the emissions of sulfur and nitrogen compounds from power plants and automobiles. Many power plants have switched to low sulfur coal. Some power plants wash their coal. Others have added scrubbers to their smokestacks to remove sulfur and nitrogen compounds from the smoke that is released. Congress passed the Acid Rain Program in 1990, which requires industries to greatly reduce their emissions of acid rain pollutants.

Other things that can still be done to improve the acid rain situation are to explore alternative fuels such as solar energy, wind energy, and nuclear energy. Also, reducing overall energy usage will help reduce the amount of pollutants in the air. Acid rain is a real problem and we need to continue to work to reduce its effects on our environment.

You can test the acid level of the water where you live if you have pH testing paper. Get several samples of water from various locations near your home. You can test your tap water, water from streams or lakes, or rainwater. Use strips of pH testing paper to determine the level of acid in your water. Remember that pure water has a pH of 7.0, normal rain water has a pH of about 5.6, and acid water would have a pH below about 5.0.

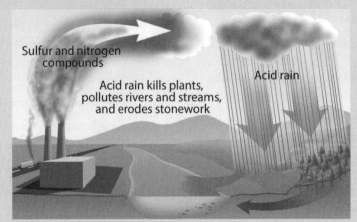

Sulfur and nitrogen compounds

Acid rain kills plants, pollutes rivers and streams, and erodes stonework

Acid rain

The Dust Bowl

The 1930s was a very difficult time for Americans. Following the stock market crash, the country was plunged into the Great Depression. This time was especially difficult for farmers. Many farmers in the Midwest and West lost their farms because of economic difficulties brought on by the depression and by new competition from large-scale agribusiness. On top of all of this, the western United States received little to no rain for several years, bringing on the worst drought in recorded history. The western U.S. became known as the dust bowl.

In 1931 the drought hit Texas, western Oklahoma, eastern Colorado, and New Mexico. The few trees and little native grass that had occupied this land had been removed in order to plant wheat. With the introduction of the tractor, the farmer was able to plant longer unbroken rows of wheat. These longer rows and little to no rain proved to be a disaster to the land. Because very little rain fell for several years, the soil dried out.

Then, in 1932, the winds came and picked up the dry soil, pushing it across the plains creating the "black blizzards." Over the next few years, the drought/dust bowl spread to include most of the Midwest and western states.

A girl named Anne Marie Low, who lived in North Dakota, recorded in her diary what she and her family went through. She talked about how dirt got into every part of their house. After a meal, they would wash the dishes and put them away. Then, they would have to wash the dishes again before they used them for the next meal.

When they went to sweep the rooms, they had so much dirt inside that they almost had to use a shovel. Most of the people left their cars parked and walked or rode an animal because they feared that

all the dust in the air would ruin the cars' engines. When they did go someplace, the roads were covered with so much dirt they had to use the fence posts to find their way. If the wind blew, which it did most of the time, people would have trouble seeing from one post to the next. Sometimes if a person got caught outside when one of these windstorms hit, they did not make it back to safety.

Anne Marie recorded that she would gather dandelions, lamb's quarter, and sheep sorrel to eat as a salad because there was little else to eat. The dust had covered everything, killing most of the plants. She points out that the wheat production in the U.S. went from an average of 170 million bushels per year to 12 million bushels per year during this time. Cattle and horses died from starvation or because of all the dirt they ate with their feed. Thousands of trees died. Anne Marie wrote in her diary that the ground was dry as dust up to fifteen feet (4.5 m) below the surface.

In another eyewitness account, Lawrence Svobida said the dust would completely block out the

During the dust bowl, entire towns were covered by dust.

sun. The visibility would range from 50 feet (15 m) to nothing. Dust would fill the farmers' eyes even when they wore goggles.

When the dust clouds appeared, they looked like dark, low cumulus clouds rolling across the fields (shown above). In front of them, small birds would fly in terror with only the strong able to out fly the storm. Other small animals, like rabbits, would often suffocate from the dust and dirt carried by the winds. The dust not only took the lives of thousands of animals, but many people also lost their lives in these dust storms.

At first, the United States government did not pay much attention to the plight of the farmers hurt by the dust bowl. Then one day, dust was blown into Washington, D.C., from the west. When the dust blotted out the midday sun in Washington, D.C., Congress finally acted and passed the "Soil Conservation Act of 1935," which enacted many changes in the way farmers cultivated their fields. It made changes in everything from the way farmers plowed their fields to the amount of land that could be farmed. The government also helped the farmers with money by purchasing livestock from farmers that were going bankrupt.

Many families in the Midwest and West could not survive the difficulties of the dustbowl years. Thousands of families abandoned their family farms and moved to California where they were eventually able to find jobs and make a living.

The dust bowl changed the farming industry forever. Today, the farming methods are much better. Areas that do not receive a substantial amount of water on a regular basis have built reservoirs to hold water for times of drought. But the attitude of farmers toward the government changed as well. Many farmers now depend on government programs for their livelihood. Most of the government programs and farming practices employed today are a direct result of the hardships encountered during the dust bowl.

UNIT 4

Storms

◊ **Explain** how moving air masses create weather.

◊ **Describe** how wind is generated.

◊ **Explain** the formation of thunderstorms.

◊ **Describe** how lightning is formed.

◊ **Distinguish** between hurricanes and tornadoes.

Air Masses & Weather Fronts

Creating the weather

How do air masses and fronts affect the weather?

Words to know:

air mass	front/weather front
polar air mass	stationary front
tropical air mass	warm front
continental air mass	cold front
maritime air mass	occluded front

Most weather is determined by the location and movement of what are called air masses. An **air mass** is a large amount of air that is a uniform temperature and humidity. An air mass can cover hundreds of square miles and can extend vertically several miles. The weather inside an air mass is stable. Air masses form in locations where there is very little wind, which allows the air to stay in one place for an extended period of time, and thus take on the temperature and humidity of that region.

Cold air masses form in polar regions and are called **polar air masses**. Warm air masses form in tropical regions and are called **tropical air masses**. Air masses can form over land or over water. Air masses that form over land are called **continental air masses**, and those that form over water are called **maritime air masses**. So an air mass that forms over the water near the North Pole would be called a maritime polar air mass. Similarly, an air mass that forms over a Brazilian rain forest would be called a continental tropical air mass.

Eventually, an air mass moves away from the source region. If the air mass is colder than the land over which it is moving, it is classified as a cold air mass. If it is warmer than the land over which it is moving, it is classified as a warm air mass. Air masses are moved around by global winds.

When two air masses meet, they generally do not mix. Instead, the colder air mass usually moves under the warmer air mass like a wedge.

Weather fronts are often heralded by spectacular cloud formations.

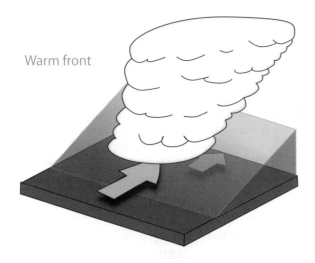

Warm front

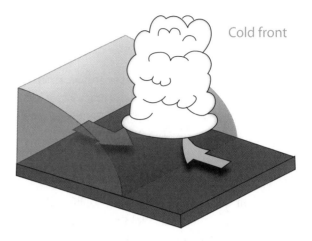

Cold front

The place where two air masses meet is called a **front**. A **stationary front** develops when the two masses of air are not moving. A **warm front** develops when warmer air takes the place of cooler air on the ground. A **cold front** develops when colder air replaces warmer air on the ground. An **occluded front** occurs when a warm air mass becomes trapped between two cold air masses and loses contact with the ground.

Weather becomes very unsettled along a front. Most fronts produce some type of precipitation unless the air along the front is dry. Tracking the movement of air masses and weather fronts is one of the most important things a meteorologist does to help predict the weather. 🌐

What did we learn?

- What is an air mass?
- How do air masses form?
- How does the air pressure compare between warm and cold air masses?

Taking it further

- How would a cold air mass that develops over land be classified?
- Why do most weather changes occur along weather fronts?

Seeing air pressure

Air masses not only differ in temperature and humidity but also in air pressure. Warm air masses tend to have lower air pressure than cold air masses. Since most weather changes occur along fronts, watching the air pressure allows a meteorologist to track where the fronts are moving and help predict the weather.

Purpose: To see the effects of air pressure

Materials: empty 2-liter plastic bottle

Procedure:

1. Look at an empty soda bottle. The air inside the bottle has the same pressure as the air outside the bottle.

2. Now place your mouth over the end of the bottle and suck out as much air as you can. What happened?

Conclusion: When you took air out of the inside of the bottle, you reduced the air pressure on the inside of the bottle. The air pressure on the outside of the bottle was unchanged so the air continued pushing in on the bottle and eventually caused it to cave in. If there was no air pressure, the bottle would be unaffected when the air was removed.

Movement of weather fronts

Predicting where air masses and weather fronts will go and how they will react is the job of meteorologists. Fortunately there are some rules that help meteorologists make these predictions. First, air masses generally move in the direction of high altitude winds. They do not move as quickly as these winds, but they move in the direction of these winds. So meteorologists take high altitude wind measurements several times a day in many different locations.

Second, in the Northern Hemisphere cold fronts and occluded fronts usually move from the northwest toward the southeast and warm fronts generally move from the southwest toward the northeast. Also, warm fronts move toward the poles over time. So warm fronts in the Northern Hemisphere slowly move toward the North Pole. In the Southern Hemisphere the movement of weather fronts is just the opposite. Cold fronts move from southwest to the northeast and warm fronts move from northwest to southeast. And warm fronts tend to gravitate toward the South Pole.

Weather front movement in these general directions is a result of two main causes. First, there are horizontal pressure differences in the atmospheric pressure which cause these different fronts to move. Second, the Coriolis effect, which is caused by the spinning of the earth on its axis, causes the air molecules to move in these ways.

Knowing these guidelines helps scientists to predict where the fronts will go and how fast they will get there. But weather predicting is more complicated than this. The scientists must also take into account geological features that can change the speed and direction of the moving air masses. Large bodies of water such as the Great Lakes, or the ocean, as well as mountain ranges can greatly affect how an air mass moves. All of these factors, and much more, are included in weather predicting software that helps meteorologists decide where the weather fronts are likely to be in the next few days.

Purpose: To show how weather fronts can be affected by high altitude winds and the Coriolis effect.

Materials: Round plate or dish, syrup, food coloring

Procedure:

1. Cover the bottom of a round plate or dish with syrup.

2. Place a drop of food coloring in the center of the syrup. Place another drop on the syrup near the edge of the plate.

3. Hold the plate so the drop of food coloring that is near the edge is close to you. Now blow over the surface of the syrup and watch how the syrup and food coloring move. Did they move in the same direction as your breath? Did they move as quickly as your breath?

4. Set the plate on a flat surface. Spin the plate in a circle. Observe how the syrup and food coloring move. Suddenly stop the spinning. What happened to the syrup?

Conclusion: You should have observed the syrup moving in the same direction as your breath but at a slower rate. The air molecules from your mouth push against the surface of the syrup. Because it is thick, it does not respond as quickly as the air molecules do, but it does move in the same direction. This demonstrates how high altitude winds can cause weather fronts to move in a particular direction. You should also see that the spinning causes the syrup to try to spin as well. Also, it flows outward. This is what happens to air because of the spinning of the earth. This air movement causes weather fronts to move the way they do.

14

Wind

Hold onto your hat!

What causes the wind to blow?

Words to know:

sea breeze   doldrums

land breeze   jet stream

trade winds

One of the most important elements of weather is wind, or moving air. Wind is important because it helps keep the temperatures even around the earth. It also helps to move air masses around so that precipitation will fall all over the earth. Air always moves from an area of high pressure to an area of low pressure. Within an air mass the temperature, humidity, and pressure are fairly uniform so there is little wind within an air mass. However, two separate air masses are likely to have different temperatures, humidity, and air pressure from each other. Therefore, when two air masses meet, the air will move from the mass with the higher pressure toward the one with the lower pressure, creating wind.

Wind speed and direction are also affected by the rotation of the earth. The earth rotates from west to east causing the air to move toward the right in the northern hemisphere. Because winds are moving inward toward a low pressure area, winds tend to circle around areas of low pressure in a counter-clockwise direction in the northern hemisphere and in a clockwise direction in the southern hemisphere.

Winds are often generated along weather fronts. However, winds also occur around the world both locally and globally without being near a weather front. The sun is responsible for most of the winds we experience. Local winds and breezes are generated when one area is heated faster than another area. For example, land warms and cools faster than water does. So during the day, land along a coast will heat up faster than the water. Thus, the air above the land heats up and rises, causing the cooler air over the water to move toward the land. This is called a sea breeze. After the sun sets, the land cools faster than the water so the air above the water is warmer and thus at a lower pressure than the air over the land. Then the air moves from the land toward the water. This is called a land breeze.

Similar breezes occur near mountains. During the day, the sun heats valley air rapidly. As the air heats it becomes less dense and begins to gently rise upslope, causing a valley breeze. At night, the process is reversed. Mountain air cools rapidly at night and "falls" downslope, causing a mountain breeze.

The sun's heat causes winds to move on a global

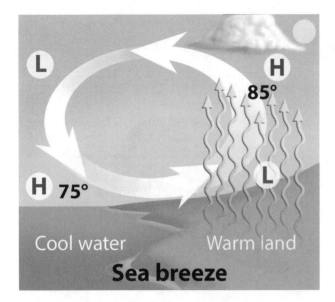

Cool water   Warm land
Sea breeze

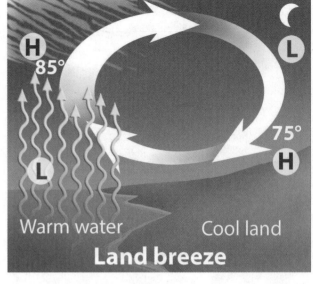

Warm water   Cool land
Land breeze

scale as well as a local scale. The sun's rays are more direct near the equator than they are at the poles, so the sun heats the air more near the equator. This warm air rises, and cooler air moves from the poles to take its place, pushing the warmer air aloft toward the poles. This movement of air from the north or south toward the equator results in **trade winds**, a prevailing pattern of easterly winds found in the tropics. These winds vary from season to season as the sun heats different parts of the earth differently during each season.

Early explorers and traders were aware of many of these winds and used them to their advantage. Near the equator there are some areas with little or no wind. The movement of the air in these areas is straight up

creating a permanent low-pressure area. Sailors call these areas the **doldrums** and avoid them if possible. At 30° latitude, there are areas with permanent high-pressure, with winds blowing straight down. The exact location of these areas shifts with the seasons.

Jet streams are very interesting prevailing winds. Jet streams are very high, fast-moving currents of air. The air in a jet stream can move up to 300 mph (480 km/h). The stream of air can be up to 300 miles (480 km) wide and 7,000 miles (11,300 km) long. Most jet streams flow from west to east. There are many jet streams around the world. They usually occur where air masses of different temperatures meet. Some jet streams appear and disappear suddenly, while others

 ## Making a wind sock

Purpose: To make a simple wind sock to see which direction the wind is blowing

Materials: metal clothes hanger, large trash bag, masking tape

Procedure:

1. Take a metal clothes hanger and bend it so it is shaped like a square by pulling down on the center of the hanger.

2. Tape the opening of a trash bag to the metal hanger frame.

3. Place the wind sock on a pole or take it outside and hold it at arm's length.

4. Spin slowly around until the wind begins to fill the trash bag. The bag or wind sock will point in the direction the wind is moving.

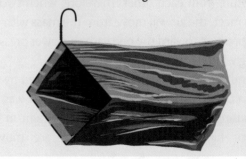

have regular patterns. These currents are called jet streams because they occur at altitudes where jets often fly, and pilots use these currents to help them reach their destinations sooner.

Winds help to circulate the air and bring us needed precipitation. Even though the wind may blow the hat off your head, it is God's provision for our survival. 🌐

What did we learn?

- What is the main cause of wind?
- What is a jet stream?
- What are trade winds?

🚀 Taking it further

- Why was it important for sailors of sailing ships to know about trade winds, doldrums, and other prevailing winds?
- Why does the breeze near the coast blow toward the land in the morning and toward the sea at night?

Storms

Did you know?

Americans first really became aware of the jet stream during World War II when American B-29 bombers suddenly lurched past their targets due to an unknown wind. However, the Japanese knew about the jet stream many years before this. A Japanese meteorologist named Wasaburo Ooishi documented the strong westerly winds above Mt. Fuji in the early 1920s. And the Japanese sent hydrogen filled balloons carrying bombs across the Pacific Ocean during World War II, hoping that the westerly flowing winds would carry them to the United States. About 9,000 bombs were launched and between 300 and 1,000 actually made it to the United States. There is only one recorded incident of a bomb going off and killing people in the United States. A woman and five children with her were killed when she tried to remove the unknown package from a tree.

🏅 Jet streams

You have already learned a little about the jet stream, but this phenomenon is so interesting it is worth taking a closer look at it. We already mentioned that there are many jet streams and that they can come and go somewhat randomly; however, there are primarily four jet streams that occur regularly. Two jet streams form over the polar regions, one in the northern hemisphere and one in the southern hemisphere. Two other jet streams form over the middle latitudes, primarily during the winter (see illustration at right).

The jet streams form because of the temperature difference between the equator and the poles. During the summer the temperature difference is not as great as it is during the winter, so the jet streams are not as strong during the summer as they are in the winter. Although the highest speeds in the jet streams sometimes reach 250–300 mph (400–480 km/h), the average speed of the summer jet streams is only about 35 mph (56 km/h), and the average speed of the winter jet streams is about 90 mph (145 km/h).

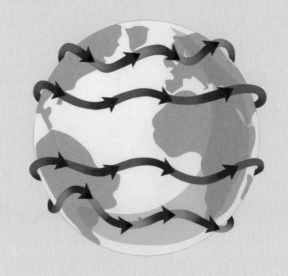

The speed of air within the jet stream is not constant. Some areas may have wind speeds of 75 mph (120 km/h) but another part of the jet stream may be flowing at 200 mph (322 km/h).

The jet streams are constantly changing shape. The wind flows around the globe in somewhat of a zigzag shape. If you viewed the globe from the North Pole, the polar jet stream would form somewhat of a triangular or star-shaped path across North America, Europe, and Asia. The zigs and zags move in and out making the jet stream move up and down in latitude. This brings cooler or warmer air with it as it moves, thus greatly affecting the weather around it. The movement of the jet stream steers storms and plays a large role in tornado formation.

If you placed a balloon in the jet stream as the Japanese did during World War II, it would move north and south as it traveled east through the jet stream. It would speed up and slow down as the speed of the flowing air changed. And it would make it around the world in about 14 days.

Since the development of aircraft and the discovery and understanding of the jet streams, people have put this knowledge to good use. Can you think of any ways people might use the jet stream today? Airlines use the jet stream to cut travel time when flying east. A trip across the United States from west to east takes about 30 minutes less than it does when flying east to west. International flights save even more time when flying east when they are able to fly in the jet stream.

15

Thunderstorms

Lightning and thunder

How are thunderstorms formed, and what causes lightning?

Words to know:

thunderhead   compression wave

ion

Have you ever seen the *Peanuts* cartoons where Snoopy tries to write a story? He always begins with, "It was a dark and stormy night." Storms can make things seem very dramatic. Sometimes storms can be very serious and cause damage to homes and other buildings, but most often, storms, particularly thunderstorms, are what bring needed rain to provide water for crops and people. There are three types of storms: thunderstorms, tornadoes, and hurricanes.

Thunderstorms are rainstorms with huge clouds, strong winds, and usually large amounts of precipitation. In temperate regions, thunderstorms usually form along weather fronts where warm moist air comes in contact with cooler drier air. Thunderstorms often form on hot summer days when there is more heat and thus more energy available for moving the air inside the clouds. In tropical regions, however, thunderstorms can form year-round because of the warm temperatures and abundant moisture. Around the world, there are 40,000–50,000 thunderstorms each day.

Thunderstorm clouds are cumulonimbus clouds and are often referred to as **thunderheads**. Thunderheads can reach as high as 70,000 feet (21,000 m) in the air. That's more than 11 miles high! Inside a storm cloud air moves up and down quickly. As the sun warms the air near the ground, it rises. Then, as it reaches higher altitudes, the air cools and begins to fall. Water condenses very rapidly producing heavy rainfall. In very high clouds hail can also form.

Thunderheads can be more than 11 miles high.

How lightning forms in a thunderstorm

Water droplets and ice crystals inside the cloud rub against each other as the air moves them around. As these particles rub against each other, they form **ions**, which are electrically-charged particles. Positive ions build up at the top of the cloud, while negative ions build up at the bottom of the cloud. Eventually, the built up energy is released as the charged particles move toward each other resulting in lightning flashes. Lightning can occur within a single cloud, between two different clouds, or between a cloud and the ground (see illustration above).

Lightning can reach temperatures up to 50,000°F (27,750°C). This causes the air around the

Fun Fact

A lightning bolt can be up to 90 miles (145 km) long. Lightning strikes the earth an average of 100 times per second.

Fun Fact

Read Psalm 29. This is a beautiful description of the power of God as it is displayed in a thunderstorm. Contemplate God's awesome power as you read this psalm.

lightning bolt to become superheated. As a result, the air violently and rapidly expands. However, the air doesn't stay superheated for long and quickly dissipates its heat. In doing so, it rapidly contracts. It's this rapid expansion and contraction that creates a **compression wave** we know as thunder. Lightning may seem frightening but it serves a very useful purpose. Lightning changes nitrogen in the atmosphere into nitrous oxide, which falls to the ground and enters the soil where it can be used by plants. Lightning is one way God provides for our needs. Thunderstorms help restore nitrogen to the soil and also bring much-needed rain to the land. 🌐

Making lightning

Purpose: To make lightning

Materials: furry stuffed animal, piece of cloth

Procedure:

1. Stand in a dark room holding a fuzzy stuffed animal.

2. Rub the stuffed animal with a piece of cloth, and then slowly remove the cloth and watch the sparks jump between the animal and the cloth.

Conclusion: Rubbing the stuffed animal causes ions, electrically-charged particles, to build up on the animal and the cloth. As the cloth is removed, the ions with opposite charges are attracted to each other. As they connect, the built up energy is released in the form of light, giving you mini-lightning bolts.

What did we learn?

- What is a thunderstorm?
- What causes lightning?
- What causes thunder?

Taking it further

- Why does hail form in thunderstorms that have high clouds?
- Why do thunderstorms usually form on hot summer days?

Fun Fact

Have you noticed that you see lightning before you hear the thunder from a storm? Light travels more quickly than sound does so you see the lightning bolt almost immediately, but there may be a delay before you hear the thunder. Sound travels at about $\frac{1}{5}$ mile per second (344 m/s). So if there is a 15-second lapse between when you see the lightning flash and when you hear the thunder, it means that the storm is about 3 miles (5 km) away. You can only hear thunder up to 10 miles (16 km) away, but you can see lightning much farther. Therefore, sometimes you will see lightning and not hear thunder at all. If you hear the thunder at nearly the same time as you see the lightning, then the storm is very close to you.

Flash floods

Although most thunderstorms are not dangerous and bring needed moisture, some thunderstorms can become dangerous. One of the greatest dangers from a serious thunderstorm is flash flooding.

If a storm lasts for a long time, or if there are a long line of thunderclouds that move in one after another, a large amount of rain can fall in a short period of time. If the ground cannot absorb the rain, it will run off into low areas which can fill very quickly. Flash floods can occur most quickly in canyons where rivers and streams rise very quickly from the water running down the mountain sides.

On July 31, 1976, one of the most deadly thunderstorms occurred in the Big Thompson Canyon in the Rocky Mountains west of Denver, Colorado. Thunderstorms are not an uncommon occurrence in the summertime in Colorado, but weather conditions were unusual this day. As heat from the ground combined with moisture in the air, a thunderstorm formed near Estes Park at the

Flash flood in Utah

western end of the canyon. Usually upper level winds are strong enough to blow thunderstorms east away from the mountains; however this day the upper level winds were weak. This caused the storm to stall and continue dropping rain for nearly three hours.

The thunderstorm dropped nearly 8 inches (20 cm) of rain in one hour, and a total of 12 inches (30.5 cm) in three hours. The canyon has very steep sides and rocky slopes. There was nowhere for the water to go except into the river at the bottom of the canyon. The Big Thompson River is relatively small and usually only 2–3 feet (0.6–0.9 m) deep. But all the rain water that rushed into it turned the river into a 19-foot (5.8 m) wall of water rushing down the canyon.

The water pushed giant boulders ahead of it, tore up the highway that ran through the canyon, and destroyed everything in its path. When it was over, 145 people had been killed. The flood also destroyed 418 houses and 152 businesses. It caused over $40 million in damages.

The highway was rebuilt at a much higher level, about 20 feet (6 m) above the river. Homes and businesses were rebuilt and most importantly the weather service has worked on an early warning system in hopes that people can be warned in time

to get to safety. However, in spite of all these changes, another flood occurred in this same canyon in 2013.

This time the flash flood was not the result of a single thunderstorm but was caused by a very large weather system that became stalled over Colorado from Sept. 9–15, 2013. The cold front was fed with moisture from the Gulf of Mexico and heavy rains fell for nearly a week. Over 9 inches (23 cm) of rain fell on Sept. 12 and another 17 inches (43 cm) of rain fell on Sept. 15. The rain that fell in the mountains poured into the rivers and flooded areas downstream causing damage in a 200 mile (320 km) area from Colorado Springs to Fort Collins. The property damage was estimated to be nearly $1 billion. However, unlike the first flood, because the water built up over several days, people were warned to evacuate ahead of time and only 8 people were confirmed killed in this flood. (To learn more about flash floods, do a search on the Answers in Genesis website.)

So what can you do to be safe in a severe thunderstorm? Make a list of things you think are important to staying safe. Keep in mind that danger can come not only from flash floods, but also from lightning, hail, and strong winds.

16

Tornadoes

Swirling wind

What causes a tornado?

Words to know:

funnel cloud   Doppler radar

waterspout

Challenge words:

Doppler effect   phased array radar

Tornadoes generate flying debris, swirl-ing winds, and a path of destruction. These fearsome storms remind us that only God can control the weather and man is powerless to stop something like a tornado. Tornadoes are also called twisters, dust devils, whirlwinds, waterspouts, and cyclones. Our word *tornado* comes from the Spanish word *tronada*, meaning thunderstorm.

Tornadoes usually form during thunderstorms. They tend to form at the edge of the storm where the warm moist updraft meets a falling downdraft of cool air. The updraft pulls air from the ground creating a low pressure area. The downdraft rushes in to fill the low pressure and then gets sucked up. The falling drier air causes the updraft to begin to spiral and tighten. This increases the speed of the spiraling air, resulting in a tornado. The key to tornado formation is changing wind direction, which causes the spiraling motion. A jet stream above the thunderstorm can enhance thunderstorm growth and contribute to the tornado formation.

If a spiraling cloud does not touch the ground, it is called a **funnel cloud**. The funnel acts like a giant vacuum cleaner, sucking up anything it comes

Fun Fact

The first tornado to be caught on film occurred in 1884.

A waterspout

droplets, dust, and debris that are sucked up by the wind. Sometimes funnel clouds form over water. These storms are called **waterspouts**. They suck water up into the funnel. Waterspouts form mostly along the coast of the Gulf of Mexico.

The average tornado is 400–500 feet (120–150 m) wide, 4,000 feet (1,200 m) from cloud to ground, and has winds from 73 to 112 mph (33–50 m/s). Most tornadoes last only a few minutes and cover a few miles of ground. One of the worst tornados on record had winds up to 300 mph (134 m/s), lasted for more than an hour, and covered 200 miles (320 km) of land, leaving a path of devastation in its wake.

Tornadoes are ranked by the Enhanced Fujita Scale (EF-Scale). The EF-Scale ranks tornadoes by wind speed and potential damage. The chart below shows the EF-Scale, wind speed, and type of damage.

in contact with. If the powerful twisting column of air touches the ground, it is then called a tornado. Tornadoes are visible because of the swirling water

EF-Scale	Wind Speed	Damage
0	65–85 mph	Light damage
1	86–110 mph	Uproots trees and overturns cars
2	111–135 mph	Considerable damage, lifts roofs
3	136–165 mph	Severe damage, flattens forests
4	166–200 mph	Extreme damage
5	Over 200 mph	Levels everything in its path

 # Tornado in a bottle

Purpose: To make a nondestructive tornado in a bottle

Materials: two empty 2-liter plastic bottles, duct tape, plastic tornado tube connector (optional but recommended)

Procedure:

1. Fill an empty 2-liter soda bottle half full with water.

2. Place another empty soda bottle on top of the bottle with water so that the mouths of the bottles are lined up with each other.

3. Use a plastic tornado tube to connect the two bottles together. If you do not have a tornado tube connector,

you can carefully tape the two bottles together tightly with duct tape or other strong tape.

4. Hold the bottles over a sink in case they leak and quickly turn the bottle of water over and swirl the top bottle in a circle for a few seconds.

Conclusion: You should see the water in the bottle begin to swirl, creating a vortex near the mouth of the bottle. This vortex will suck the air from the bottom bottle into the top bottle like a tornado, thus forcing water from the top bottle into the bottom bottle.

In this photo, the engineering committee is examining a 1x5 inch board that was driven through a 2x6 inch plank somewhere along the path of the Tri-State Tornado—the longest-lasting tornado on record.

The awesome power of a tornado is demonstrated as a 33 rpm plastic record was blown into a telephone pole without breaking.

Storms

Tornadoes have occurred in every state and during every season, but most tornadoes occur in the eastern two-thirds of the United States during the spring. So many tornadoes have occurred in Texas, Oklahoma, Kansas, Missouri, Nebraska, and Iowa that a path through those states has been nicknamed "Tornado Alley." About 1,000 tornadoes touch down in the United States each year. There are more tornadoes in America than in any other country.

The National Weather Service (NWS) uses **Doppler radar**, a special radar that can measure velocity as well as distance, to help track storm movement and to watch thunderstorms for signs of tornado development. The NWS tries to give at least 15–20 minutes of warning to people who are in areas where tornadoes are developing. Another technology is being developed, which researchers hope will give even more advanced notice of tornadoes. This technology uses extremely low-frequency sound waves to detect the rotating column of air inside a tornado. This technique is still in development, but it shows promise. Advanced notice has saved many lives and it is believed that more lives will be saved with more notice.

You should pay attention to weather warnings. If a tornado warning is issued for your area, you should go to the basement, or stay under a set of stairs, under a heavy table, or in a bathtub with cushions on top of you. This will help protect you if a tornado does come through your neighborhood. If you are in the open, you should lie down flat in a low area if there is no rain. If it is raining, you should avoid low areas that may flood. Instead, crouch down and make yourself as small as possible. We should all recognize and respect the power of a tornado and not behave unwisely.

What did we learn?

- What causes a tornado to develop?
- What is the difference between a funnel cloud and a tornado?
- What is a waterspout?
- When do most tornadoes occur in the United States?

Taking it further

- How does the jet stream affect tornado formation?
- Why should you take shelter during a tornado?

Fun Fact

In Australia, a dust devil is called a willy-willy.

🏅 Predicting tornadoes

Predicting when and where a tornado will develop can be the difference between life and death in some instances. The National Weather Service (NWS), along with the National Oceanic and Atmospheric Administration, strive to improve their forecasts and increase warning time for severe storms.

There are several different technologies that have been developed in order to study tornadoes and to predict their development and movement. In the mid 1980s the National Severe Storms Laboratory (NSSL), based in Norman, Oklahoma, developed a portable weather center that they hoped to be able to place in the path of tornadoes to take readings during the storm.

TOTO (TOtable Tornado Observatory) was a large cylinder on a wheeled platform that could be rolled off the end of a special truck and left in what was hoped would be the path of a tornado. TOTO contained instruments to measure air pressure, wind speed and direction, and humidity. However, it is very difficult and dangerous to place an instrument in the path of an oncoming tornado. TOTO was placed near a few tornadoes, but only once, in April 1985, was it actually hit by a tornado. After a few years, TOTO was retired and other avenues that were less dangerous were pursued.

TOTO

One of the most important developments in studying tornadoes was the development of Doppler radar. Doppler radar uses the **Doppler effect** to not only figure out where a storm is, but in which direction and how fast it is moving.

The Doppler effect was first discovered in 1842. As an object moves, the frequency of the sound waves, light waves, or radio waves coming from it increases as the object moves toward you and decreases as it moves away. So the radio waves that bounce off of the rain drops in a storm will change frequency indicating whether the storm is moving toward or away from the radar site. Computers can take all of this information and generate a picture or map of the storm so that forecasters can see the storm developing and watch its movements.

In the 1980s and 1990s the NWS installed hundreds of Doppler radar sites across the country. This allows meteorologists around the country to accurately track severe weather and issue severe storm warnings when appropriate. Doppler radar is not only important in forecasting tornadoes, it is also very important in forecasting severe thunderstorms that might cause flash flooding and in forecasting hurricane activity as well.

In addition to Doppler radar, the NSSL has been working to set up a new set of radar transmitters to help them collect weather data more quickly and give even more warning time in the case of severe storms. This new radar is called **phased array radar**.

Traditional radar sends out one beam of energy, waits for the signal to return, raises the angle of the beam a small amount, and sends out another signal until it has scanned the whole atmosphere. Then the radar returns to the bottom and starts over again at a slightly different location. It can take 5–7 minutes to make one complete scan of the atmosphere around the radar site.

A phased array radar sends out multiple beams of energy at a time. This allows multiple bits of information to be gathered at one time. It takes only 20–30 seconds for phased array radar to scan the entire atmosphere around it. This is a great improvement in storm watching and prediction. It will increase warning time for tornadoes, flash floods, hurricanes, and other severe storms.

NSSL is dedicated to developing the best tools for severe storm detection as well as tools for getting help to those who have been harmed by storms. In addition to the tools already mentioned, NSSL and the NWS use airborne radar systems. Airplanes can fly near storms and provide close-up data for weather forecasters on the ground. Finally, one of the newest technologies to be developed by NSSL is called On Demand. On Demand is a web-based application that uses satellite images from Google Earth satellites to confirm where tornados have touched down and to direct rescue workers to damaged areas.

Hurricanes

Typhoons

How does a hurricane form?

Words to know:

tropical cyclone   tropical storm

typhoon   hurricane

cyclone   eye of the storm

tropical disturbance   storm surge

tropical depression

Challenge words:

eyewall   dropsonde

Hurricanes are the largest, fiercest storms in the world. A hurricane can be from 100–600 miles (150–950 km) in diameter, can cover 430,000 square miles (1.1 million km²) and can last for up to three weeks. About 80 hurricanes form each year, with 90% forming in the western Pacific Ocean in areas near Bangladesh, Japan, Indonesia, and the Philippines.

The official meteorological term for these huge storms is a **tropical cyclone**. However, if the storm forms over the North Atlantic Ocean or the South Pacific Ocean, it is called a hurricane. If it forms in the Northwest Pacific Ocean, it is called a **typhoon**. And if it forms in the Indian Ocean, it is called a **cyclone**.

Most hurricanes form within five degrees latitude of the equator. Large areas of water with temperatures greater than 80°F (27°C) are needed for hurricane formation. As warm moist air rises, it eventually cools and the water condenses to form large cumulonimbus clouds. As the water condenses, it releases energy that further heats the air, causing more evaporation and thus more condensation. As this cycle continues, it causes winds to begin to circulate around a center. When several of these storm cells come together, they form what is called a **tropical disturbance**.

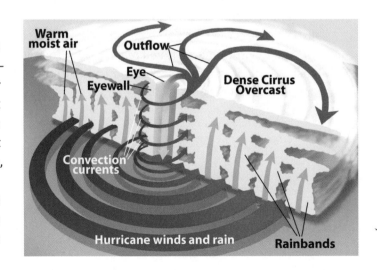

Super Typhoon Maysak tracks west-northwestward toward the Philippines on March 31, 2015. Note the clearly defined eye.

When the spiraling winds reach 25 mph (11 m/s) the storm is labeled a **tropical depression**. If enough energy is available, the winds can increase. A storm with wind speeds from 39–73 mph (17–32 m/s) is called a **tropical storm**. Once the winds reach 74 mph (33 m/s), the storm is classified as a **hurricane**. The storm clouds in a hurricane can reach 50,000 feet (15,000 m) in altitude and the circulating area often reaches 125 miles (200 km) in diameter. The warm air and warm water fuel the storm and encourage it to build.

Global winds slowly move the storm. Eventually the storm will reach an area with cooler water and will begin to die, or it will reach land. When it reaches land, it begins to lose energy and after 2–3 days, the storm dies.

The center of a hurricane is relatively calm and is called the **eye of the storm**. The eye can be from 14–20 miles (22–32 km) across and is an area of low pressure. The edges of a hurricane, just like the edges of a thunderstorm, have erratic winds and can encourage tornado formation. These tornadoes can increase the damage done by the hurricane.

Much of the damage caused by a hurricane is due to the storm surge. **Storm surge** is a sudden rise in sea level due to the water piling up in front of the storm. The ocean level in front of an approaching hurricane can rise as much as 30 feet (9 m), causing huge waves as the storm approaches land. These waves cause massive destruction and flooding.

Meteorologists use Doppler radar and computers to help analyze tropical depressions to

Fun Fact

Winds in a hurricane spin counter-clockwise in the northern hemisphere and clockwise in the southern hemisphere.

Storm word scramble

Complete the "Storm Word Scramble" worksheet.

determine if a hurricane is forming. Unlike tornadoes, which move very quickly, hurricanes move across the ocean relatively slowly. Therefore, meteorologists issue hurricane watches 36–48 hours before a storm is likely to hit land. This gives people time to cover their windows with wood to protect them from flying debris and gives people time to evacuate the area. If a hurricane is predicted for your area, you should leave for a safer place.

Just as with tornadoes, hurricanes are categorized according to their wind speed. The chart below shows the Saffir-Simpson Scale categories for hurricanes as well as the expected storm surge for each level.

Category	Wind Speed	Storm Surge
1	74–95 mph	4–5 feet
2	96–110 mph	6–8 feet
3	111–130 mph	9–12 feet
4	131–155 mph	13–18 feet
5	155+ mph	> 18 feet

Hurricanes can be some of the most deadly and devastating storms that occur around the world.

What did we learn?

- What is a hurricane?
- Where do most hurricanes occur?
- What is the difference between a tropical depression, a tropical storm, and a hurricane?

Taking it further

- Why does a hurricane dissipate once it reaches land?
- How does warm water help create and energize a hurricane?

Storms

🏅 Measuring hurricanes

Detecting and predicting hurricanes is just as important as detecting and predicting tornadoes. Because tornadoes form quickly and move quickly, the amount of warning that the National Weather Service can give is usually only a few minutes. But those few minutes can mean the difference between life and death.

With a hurricane, the warning time is much longer. As we mentioned earlier, the winds inside a hurricane blow very hard, but the storm itself usually moves relatively slowly, so meteorologists can usually warn people 2 to 3 days ahead of an approaching hurricane.

In order to make accurate predictions of the movements of a hurricane, meteorologists must use many different kinds of instruments. You already learned how Doppler radar helps meteorologists measure the location and speed of a storm. This is very helpful for tracking hurricanes when they are close to land where the radars are located. However, hurricanes usually start out in the ocean where most of the radars cannot reach. So other instruments must also be used.

Weather satellites play a very important role in detecting hurricane formation and location. There are many satellites in orbit around the earth that send a constant stream of information to meteorologists. This is one of the best ways for scientists to get a view of the whole storm.

Most hurricanes are so big that the whole storm can only be viewed at once from space. Satellite images show where tropical storms are forming and give other important information. However, satellites give only images of the storms and do not give wind speeds and atmospheric pressure readings that are vital to determining how strong the storm is and how dangerous it might be.

In order to get this information scientists use a somewhat unusual method. They use Hurricane Hunters. The Hurricane Hunters is a group of Air Force pilots who fly planes through hurricanes and drop weather instruments into the storm. This group is designated the 53rd Weather Reconnaissance Squadron, and it is based in Biloxi, Mississippi. There are twenty crews with six crew members each. They work with the National Hurricane Center in Coral Gables, Florida, to obtain needed data on hurricanes.

Hurricane Hunters must be prepared for anything as they fly their WC-130 airplanes through the storm. At the edge of the storm the winds are very erratic. Then, as they fly toward the center, they encounter swirling bands of rain separated by areas that may be completely or nearly completely free of rain. As they get close to the center they must fly through the eyewall. The eyewall is the wall of clouds surrounding the eye of the storm. This is the area of the storm with

Hurricane Hunters in flight

The newest hurricane hunters are drones. Unmanned aircraft can fly through hurricanes, collect weather information and relay it in real time to the storm trackers without endangering human pilots.

Storms

the strongest winds and heaviest rain.

As they pass through the eyewall they enter the eye where there is no rain at all. The air pressure inside the eye of the storm is much lower because of the strong updrafts removing some of the air from the column. Due to the lower air pressure the plane may drop as much as 1,000 feet. The navigator then plots a path back out of the hurricane to the edge of the storm. The plane flies a quarter of the way around the storm then flies another path through the hurricane.

As the plane flies through the storm, crew members release special canisters called dropsondes into the storm. A **dropsonde** is a canister containing many instruments that relay wind speed, wind direction, temperature, humidity, and barometric pressure back to the plane's computers and to the computers at the National Hurricane Center. The dropsondes are connected to parachutes that allow the canisters to slowly fall through the storm so that meteorologists can

obtain readings from various parts of the storm.

The plane will drop at least four dropsondes with each pass, and it is not unusual for several planes to be flying through different parts of the storm at the same time. This allows meteorologists to have a better understanding of the conditions inside the hurricane.

The National Hurricane Center has powerful computers that correlate the data collected from weather satellites, radar, Hurricane Hunters, and even commercial aircraft and ships. All of the data help the scientists to predict where the hurricane will go and how fast it is expected to move.

When scientists think that a hurricane is likely to hit an area within 48 hours, they issue a hurricane watch for that area. If they believe that a hurricane is likely to hit an area within 24 hours, they issue a hurricane warning. This warning system has consistently saved lives. The number of deaths due to hurricanes has greatly decreased as predictions have become more accurate and warning times have increased. Property damage due to hurricanes has increased however, because people are building more buildings along coastal areas that are likely to be hit by hurricanes.

Fun Fact

The first Hurricane Hunter was Major Joe Duckworth who flew through a hurricane on July 27, 1943. He flew a single-engine AT-6 through a tropical storm off the coast of Galveston, Texas.

Although flying through hurricanes sounds like a very dangerous job, the safety record of the Hurricane Hunters is very good. Only four planes have been lost.

Fun Fact

A reality TV series called *Hurricane Hunters* debuted on the Weather Channel in July 2012. This show has featured members of the USAF's 53rd Weather Reconnaissance Squadron as it flew through storms.

UNIT 5

Weather Information

◊ **Describe** the basic measurements used by meteorologists.

◊ **Identify** instruments used to collect weather data.

◊ **Describe** how technology has helped mankind analyze, predict, and report weather.

National Weather Service, Lubbock, TX

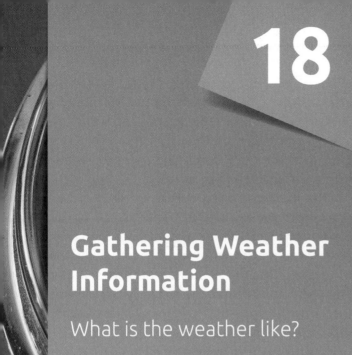

18

Gathering Weather Information

What is the weather like?

What instruments are used to measure the weather?

Words to know:

thermometer   hygrometer

barometer   psychrometer

Challenge words:

heat index   wind chill factor

A meteorologist is someone who studies the weather. The first job of a meteorologist is to gather information about the weather. Understanding what the weather is today helps us to predict what the weather will be like tomorrow. And like any good scientist, a meteorologist needs tools to help do the job. A meteorologist uses several basic weather instruments to gather weather information.

The first thing people usually ask when they want to know what the weather is like is, "What is the temperature outside?" The temperature is determined by the amount of energy the air molecules possess. Warmer air has more energy and the molecules are moving faster than cold air

molecules. The very first instrument used to measure temperature was a thermoscope, invented by Galileo in 1592. The thermoscope was a glass tube suspended over water. As the air in the bulb of the tube heated up it expanded, forcing water down the tube's neck. As the air cooled, it contracted, and water rose up the neck of the tube.

Today, we use thermometers to measure temperature. **Thermometers** are sealed glass tubes containing mercury or alcohol. As the liquid heats up it expands, and as it cools down it contracts inside the tube. The scale on the side of the tube shows the temperature based on how much room the liquid is taking up inside the tube. In order for a meteorologist to use a thermometer to obtain accurate temperature readings, the thermometer must not be in direct sunlight or exposed to a surface that radiates heat.

Most thermometers today are marked with either the Fahrenheit scale or the Celsius scale.

An alcohol thermometer

A modern aneroid barometer

Some thermometers show both scales on their sides. The Fahrenheit scale was defined by the German scientist Daniel Gabriel Fahrenheit in 1714. He chose 100 degrees as the approximate temperature of the human body and 0 degrees as the lowest temperature he could achieve with an ice-salt water solution. On the Fahrenheit scale, water freezes at 32 degrees and boils at 212 degrees. The Celsius scale was defined by the Swedish scientist Anders Celsius with the help of Carl Linnaeus. Celsius chose the freezing point of water to be 0 degrees and the boiling point of water to be 100 degrees on his scale.

The second atmospheric condition that meteorologists measure is air pressure. The instrument they use for this is called a barometer. The first barometer was invented in 1643 by a student of Galileo named Evangelista Torricelli. This early barometer was a sealed glass tube inverted in a dish of mercury. Today's mercury barometers work

Fun Fact

The falling atmospheric pressure and rising humidity that often accompany a warm front can cause human aches and pains. So people really can "feel it in their bones" when a storm is approaching.

in pretty much the same way as Torricelli's barometer. Another type of barometer was invented by Lucien Vidi in 1844. This instrument, called an aneroid barometer, is a round metal can enclosing a vacuum. The can expands and contracts slightly with the changing air pressure.

The average air pressure at sea level is 14.7 pounds per square inch (101.3 kilo Pascals). The air pressure changes with the movement of air masses. Also, the air pressure changes with altitude. As you go up in altitude, the air pressure decreases. The air pressure inside a building is generally the same as the air pressure outside, so barometers are usually kept inside for easier reading.

The third type of reading a meteorologist makes is to measure relative humidity. Relative humidity is the ratio of how much water is in the air compared to how much water the air could hold at a given temperature. The warmer the air, the more moisture it can hold. To measure relative humidity, a meteorologist uses an instrument called a hygrometer (hai-GROM-i-ter). There are several

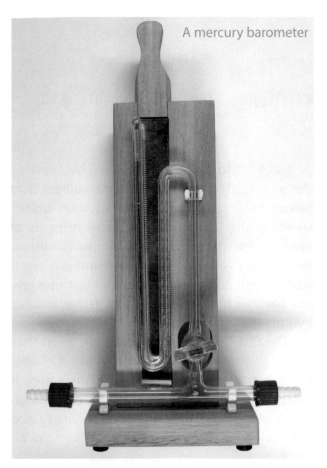

A mercury barometer

types of hygrometers. One of the most common is a psychrometer. A **psychrometer** (sai-KROM-i-ter) uses two thermometers. One thermometer has the bulb wrapped in cloth that is soaked in water. The readings from the two thermometers are referred to as the wet bulb and dry bulb readings. As the water evaporates from the cloth, it lowers the temperature near the bulb. Water evaporates more slowly when the humidity in the air is high and more quickly when the humidity in the air is low. So, the difference in the temperatures will be greater when the humidity is low than when it is high. The difference between the temperatures of the two thermometers is calculated and then a chart is used to determine the relative humidity of the air.

A sling psychronmeter

There are two types of psychrometers. A stationary psychrometer has a reservoir of water with a wick going to the wet bulb thermometer so that the water that evaporates is constantly being replaced. This method requires a longer period of time to determine the relative humidity. The

🧪 Using a psychrometer

Note: You can either use a sling psychrometer, which you can purchase, or make a stationary psychrometer out of two thermometers. If you are using a sling psychrometer please follow the instructions that came with it. If you choose to make you own, please follow the instructions below:

Purpose: To make your own psychrometer

Materials: two nondigital thermometers, cotton cloth, dish of water, rubber band

Procedure:

1. Wrap a small piece of cotton cloth around the bulb of a thermometer and secure it in place with a rubber band.

2. Dip the cloth in a dish of water until it is completely wet then remove it from the dish.

3. Slip one end of a second strip of cloth under the rubber band and place the other end in the dish of water so it will keep the bulb of the thermometer wet.

4. Set the thermometer and dish in a place where they will not be disturbed.

5. Place a second thermometer next to the first. Allow both thermometers to remain undisturbed for at least one hour.

6. At the end of one hour, read the temperature on both thermometers. Subtract the wet bulb reading from the dry bulb reading. Then use the chart below to determine the percent relative humidity in your house.

Relative Humidity in Percent

Air temperature (reading of dry-bulb thermometer) in degrees Celsius

Difference between wet bulb and dry bulb in degrees Celsius

	20°	21°	22°	23°	24°	25°	26°	27°	28°	29°	30°
0.5	96	96	96	96	96	96	96	96	96	96	96
1	91	91	92	92	92	92	92	92	93	93	93
1.5	87	87	87	88	88	88	88	89	89	89	89
2	83	83	83	84	84	84	85	85	85	86	86
2.5	78	79	80	80	80	81	81	82	82	82	83
3	74	75	76	76	77	77	78	78	78	79	79
3.5	70	71	72	72	73	74	74	75	75	76	76
4	66	67	68	69	69	70	71	71	72	72	73
4.5	63	64	64	65	66	67	67	68	69	69	70
5	59	60	61	62	62	63	64	65	65	66	67
5.5	55	56	57	58	59	60	61	62	62	63	64
6	51	53	54	55	56	57	58	58	59	60	61
6.5	48	49	50	52	53	54	54	56	56	57	58
7	44	46	47	48	49	50	51	52	53	54	55
7.5	41	42	44	45	46	47	49	50	51	52	52
8	37	39	40	42	43	44	46	47	48	49	50
8.5	34	36	37	39	40	41	43	44	45	46	47
9	31	32	34	36	37	39	40	41	42	43	44
9.5	28	29	31	33	34	36	37	38	40	41	42
10	24	26	28	30	31	33	34	36	37	38	39

second type is a sling psychrometer. This instrument has a handle attached to the thermometers, allowing them to be swung through the air. Because this method brings air in contact with the wet bulb more quickly, an accurate reading is possible in only a few seconds. Also, no reservoir or wick is needed because the results are very quick.

Other hygrometers do not use thermometers. An older type of hygrometer used a human hair that had the oil removed. The hair was stretched and attached to a needle. As the humidity increased, the hair lengthened and the needle showed the change. More modern hygrometers are electric and use a plate coated with carbon. Electrical resistance of the carbon coating changes as the moisture content of the air changes. These are only a few of the instruments used in meteorology. We will learn about more weather instruments in the next lesson.

- What does a meteorologist measure with a thermometer?
- What is air temperature?
- What are the two temperature scales commonly used?
- What does a meteorologist measure with a barometer?
- What is air pressure?
- What does a meteorologist measure with a psychrometer?
- What is relative humidity?

Taking it further

- Why does a sling psychrometer give faster results than a stationary psychrometer?
- Why do thermometers need to be kept out of direct sunlight?

Heat index

Relative humidity plays a big role not only in the type of weather that you experience, but also in how comfortable or uncomfortable you feel when you are outside.

Your body was designed by God to regulate its temperature in several ways. One of the most important ways that your body regulates temperature is through perspiration. When your body is warmer than it needs to be, you perspire. It takes energy to turn the liquid perspiration into water vapor. Heat from your body causes the perspiration to evaporate, thus cooling your body.

So what does this have to do with relative humidity? When the relative humidity is high, your perspiration cannot evaporate very quickly, so you do not cool down as quickly.

If you live in a part of the world that is often warm and humid, you have probably heard of the term heat index. The heat index is a calculation that takes into account the temperature and relative humidity to determine the apparent temperature. Apparent temperature is what the temperature would have to be in dry air for you to feel the same way.

Heat Index—Apparent Temperatures

		Actual Air Temperature in Degrees Fahrenheit				
		80°F	85°F	90°F	95°F	100°F
Relative Humidity	50%	80.8	86.5	94.6	105.2	118.3
	60%	81.8	89.3	99.7	113.1	129.5
	70%	83.0	92.7	105.9	122.6	
	80%	84.0	96.8	113.3	133.8	
	85%	84.9	99.1	117.5		
	90%	85.6	101.6	121.9		
	95%	86.4	104.2			
	100%	87.2	107.0			

Let's look at an example. If you are outside when the temperature is 90°F and the relative humidity is 50% you would probably feel more comfortable than if you were outside where it was 85°F and 85% relative humidity because your perspiration would evaporate more quickly in the drier air. The heat index would calculate the apparent temperature to be 94.6°F in the first case and 99.1°F in the second case. Even though the second temperature is actually 5°F cooler it would feel like it was nearly 5°F warmer.

On the previous page is a chart showing the heat index apparent temperatures for some sample temperatures and relative humidity readings. Note that there are some numbers missing at the highest temperatures and humidities. This is because as the temperature increases the rate of evaporation also increases. This puts a haze in the air as well as cloud cover, blocking some of the sunshine. Thus, there is a limit to the apparent temperature. This limit is believed to be somewhere between 160°F and 170°F.

Look at the numbers in the chart. What do you notice about the effect of relative humidity at 80°F? It is relatively small. What do you notice about the effect of relative humidity at 95°F? It is much greater. Many weather forecasters use the heat index to warn people about the apparent temperature when the temperature and humidity are high, so they can take care to stay out of dangerously hot weather.

All of these numbers are calculated based on readings taken in the shade. The heat from direct sunlight can make you feel even hotter. The sun may add as much as 15°F to the heat index. So be very cautious when you are outside in hot humid weather not to over exert yourself. Make sure that you drink plenty of fluids and limit the amount of time you spend in those conditions.

Once the temperature drops below 68°F, the relative humidity plays a very small role in how you feel. However, another weather factor begins to come into play. When wind blows across something that has moisture, it increases the rate of evaporation. This is why a sling psychrometer can give a relative humidity reading much faster than a stationary psychrometer. Wind blowing across your body increases the rate at which moisture on your body evaporates as well. Even when you are not hot and perspiring, there is some moisture on the surface of your skin. So when the wind blows you feel cooler. This may be a welcome feeling when the temperature is in the 80s, but when the temperature is in the 40s the wind can make you miserable.

Meteorologists have another calculation that they use in cold windy weather to determine the apparent temperature outside. This calculation is called the wind chill factor. The wind chill factor takes into account the actual temperature and the wind speed to determine the temperature that it would need to be outside for you to feel the same way if the wind was not blowing at all.

Here is an example of how wind chill might affect you. If you were outside when the temperature was 30°F and the wind was blowing at 5 miles per hour, the apparent temperature would be 26.9°F. But if you were outside when the temperature was 40°F and the wind was blowing at 20 mph, the apparent temperature would be 18.2°F. Even though the actual air temperature in the first case was 10 degrees less than the second, it would feel about 9 degrees warmer to you because the wind causes you to lose heat much more quickly in the second case.

Below is a chart showing the apparent temperature for several temperatures and wind speeds.

The effects of wind in cold weather can be dangerous. Be sure to cover up your ears, hands, and other parts that you might not normally worry about if you are going to be outside when the wind is blowing and it is cold.

Wind Chill Factor—Apparent Temperatures

	Actual Air Temperature								
	40°F	35°F	30°F	25°F	20°F	15°F	10°F	5°F	0°F
5 mph	37.4	32.2	26.9	21.7	16.4	11.2	5.9	0.7	-4.6
10 mph	28.2	22.1	15.9	9.8	2.7	-2.5	-8.6	-14.8	-20.9
15 mph	22.4	15.7	8.9	2.3	-4.4	-11.1	-17.9	-24.6	-31.3
20 mph	18.3	11.2	4.1	-3	-10.1	-17.2	-24.3	-31.4	-39.5
25 mph	15.3	8	0.6	-6.8	-14.2	-21.6	-29	-36.4	-43.8
30 mph	13.2	5.6	-2.1	-9.7	-17.3	-24.9	-32.5	-40.1	-47.7

Wind Speed

Weather Myths

Can you really feel the weather in your bones or tell that a storm is coming by the corn on your foot? These, and other weather sayings, have been around for centuries. Some people call them "old wives tales," while other people rely on them. Some have a scientific basis and some do not. Are any weather myths or sayings true? Let's look at a few of them.

1. *Red sky in the morning—sailor takes warning. Red sky at night—sailor's delight.* This saying is very old and is even mentioned in the Bible. Matthew 16:2–3 says, "He answered and said to them, 'When it is evening you say, "It will be fair weather, for the sky is red"; and in the morning, "It will be foul weather today, for the sky is red and threatening." Hypocrites! You know how to discern the face of the sky, but you cannot discern the signs of the times.'" Like many old sayings that have lasted, this saying is based on real science. Red skies occur when air molecules in dry air scatter light, indicating a high pressure system. Because air circles the earth from west to east, the red sky in the morning means a high-pressure system has just passed through and winds from a low pressure system are likely to bring rain. On the other hand, red sky at night indicates a high-pressure system is just moving in and is likely to bring fair weather.

2. *Mare's tails and mackerel scales make tall ships take in their sails.* Mare's tails are a type of cloud that is often found at the leading edge of a warm front and mackerel scales are clouds that are often found at the leading edge of a cold front. Both kinds of fronts can bring changes in the weather, often resulting in storms.

3. *Ring around the moon, rain by noon. Ring around the sun, rain before night is done.* This saying is also true. Small ice particles or crystals in cirrus clouds cause the halo you sometimes see around the sun or moon. This is quite often followed by rain within the next day.

4. *Lightning never strikes twice in the same place.* This saying is false. Lightning strikes the same place repeatedly year after year because electricity flows along the easiest path. This path is often from a storm cloud to the highest object in the area. The Empire State Building was once struck by lightning eight times in 24 minutes.

5. *Opening windows to equalize air pressure will save a roof, or even a home, from destruction by a tornado.* This saying is also false. Buildings are damaged by the high winds, not by pressure changes. Texas Tech's Institute for Disaster Research found that in an F5 tornado, with winds at 260 mph (116 m/s), there was a pressure difference of about only 10% from the inside to the outside of the tornado. Most buildings have enough vents to keep up with pressure changes. If the tornado wants the windows open, it will open them. You need to find a safe place!

6. *Rubber tires on your automobile, or rubber-soled shoes, insulate you from lightning strikes.* This idea is also false. Lightning, like all electricity, will always find the easiest path to ground. Rubber is a better insulator of electricity than air, but only by a small amount, so it will not protect you from lightning. Your protection inside a car comes from being surrounded by metal (as long as your car is made of metal). Any lightning that hits the body of the car will be conducted to the ground through the car's body instead of through yours.

7. *Insects may signal changing weather.* This is true in some cases. Some insects, animals, and plants react to changes in air pressure, humidity, and temperature. If the humidity goes up before a rainstorm, you could see small animals moving to higher ground. Because of the higher humidity, some small insects may fly lower. Some plants' leaves or flowers close because of lower air pressure or higher humidity. God gave these plants and animals these abilities to help them survive. Sometimes just watching the plants and animals around you can tell you a lot about the weather.

Regardless of the signs of the weather, from an aching corn to a ring around the moon, remember that ultimately God controls the weather, and He will take care of you.

19

More Weather Instruments

What else do they use?

What other instruments are used to measure the weather?

Words to know:

anemometer   weather satellite

radiosonde

Challenge words:

geosynchronous orbit   aerosols

polar orbit

In our last lesson we learned that meteorologists have many instruments to help them measure the weather. They use thermometers to measure temperature, barometers to measure air pressure, and psychrometers or hygrometers to measure relative humidity. But these are not the only conditions that meteorologists measure.

Wind is a very important element in weather. Meteorologists measure both wind speed and wind direction. Wind speed is measured with an instrument called an anemometer (an-uh-MOM-i-ter). An anemometer is a pole with three cups at the top. The wind exerts greater pressure on the concave, or

pushed in, side of the cups, thus causing the pole to spin around. The pole is connected to an electrical dial which then shows the wind speed. Wind speed is measured in "knots"—nautical miles per hour. One knot equals 1.15 miles per hour (0.5 m/s).

Wind direction is measured with a wind vane or a wind sock. A wind vane, sometimes called a weather vane, is a pole with a spinning arrow attached to the top. The point of the arrow points into the wind, indicating the direction the wind is coming from. A

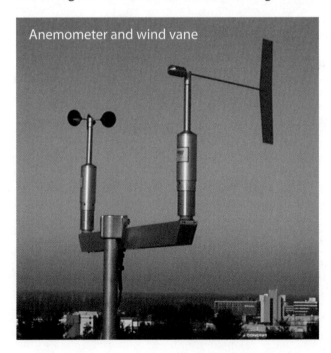

Anemometer and wind vane

Wind sock

Weather balloon being launched

Doppler radar

windsock is a long mesh sock attached to the end of a pole. The mesh catches the wind and stretches out showing the direction the wind is blowing toward.

Another important condition that meteorologists measure is the amount of moisture that falls. A rain gauge is used to measure precipitation, particularly rainfall. This is one of the simplest weather instruments. A rain gauge is simply an open container with straight sides and a scale on the side. Rain gauges are usually placed three to six feet (1–2 m) above ground to catch the rain without interference from objects on the ground. The rain gauge catches the rain that falls and the amount is read from the scale. After a reading is made, the container is emptied and ready to collect more water.

So far we have talked about weather conditions on the ground and how a meteorologist, or even you, could collect information on the weather. However, a meteorologist needs to know what the weather conditions are throughout the atmosphere, even at high altitudes. In order to collect information at higher altitudes, meteorologists use weather balloons with radiosondes. A weather balloon is just a large balloon filled with hydrogen or helium that carries the weather equipment into

the atmosphere. A radiosonde is a box containing a thermometer, barometer, hygrometer, and a radio to relay the readings back to a weather station on the ground. Readings are taken periodically as the balloon rises through the atmosphere. From these readings, meteorologists can get a better idea of the atmospheric conditions above the ground.

Other more sophisticated equipment is also used to collect weather data. Radar antennas send out microwave signals that bounce off water drops and ice crystals. The returned radio signals give the meteorologist a picture of the inside of a cloud or storm. Doppler radar sends signals in such a way that wind speed can be determined, as well as distinguishing between different types of precipitation within a storm.

Weather satellites are also very valuable for collecting weather information. Some weather satellites in orbit around the planet photograph clouds showing movement of storms. Other satellites can detect surface temperatures around the world.

Finally, the most important tool for weather collection and forecasting is the computer. Almost all weather devices used by meteorologists collect data and automatically send the information to computers

Making a rain gauge

Rainfall is a blessing from God. Rain provides us with the water we need for nearly everything we do. Measuring the amount of rainfall that you receive around your house is easy—you just need a rain gauge.

Purpose: To make a rain gauge

Materials: jar with flat bottom, masking tape, waterproof marker, ruler

Procedure:

1. Place a 6-inch strip of tape vertically on the side of the jar with the edge of the tape even with the bottom of the jar.

2. Using a waterproof marker, carefully mark the tape with lines that are ½ inch apart and label each inch.

3. Place the rain gauge in an open area where the rain will fall into it. Choose an area without a lot of bushes or trees that might block the rain.

Conclusion: When it rains, your rain gauge will collect the water and you can read the amount after the rain stops. Be sure to empty the jar after you read the amount of rain so you can measure the next rainfall amount.

to be analyzed. By taking all of the data that is collected and analyzing it with a computer, meteorologists can develop a picture of the weather patterns and conditions that exist around the world.

 # What did we learn?

•   How do meteorologists measure wind?

•   How do meteorologists measure weather at higher altitudes?

•   What sophisticated instruments do meteorologists use?

 # Taking it further

•   Why is it important for a meteorologist to take weather readings at higher altitudes?

•   Why might a weather satellite be useful for tracking a hurricane?

•   Why are computers necessary for weather tracking and forecasting?

 # Weather satellites

You learned earlier in the lesson that weather satellites play an important role in weather forecasting. Before weather satellites, meteorologists could not see much of the weather beyond the land. Some weather measurements were made by ships and later by airplanes, but there was no consistent way to see what was happening over the oceans. This is a real disadvantage when it comes to weather forecasting since the oceans play a very large role in the formation of our weather systems.

With the invention of rockets and other technological advancements, the first weather satellite was launched on April 1, 1960. This satellite was named TIROS 1, for Thermal InfraRed Observation Satellite. It sent about 4,000 pictures a week to earth and allowed scientists to see weather from space for the first time.

Early satellites helped scientists realize that they did not really understand the global nature of storm systems. The images showed that global phenomena such as jet streams helped to push weather systems around. This information encouraged scientists to send up more satellites.

As technology improved, satellites were launched that were able to measure energy absorbed by different layers of the atmosphere, thus giving

TIROS 1

scientists a picture of the temperatures in the atmosphere. Other satellites were launched that could measure the reflection of infrared energy. This allowed the satellites to take pictures at night as well as during the daytime. This information greatly improved meteorologists' ability to forecast the weather.

Today, there are several different kinds of weather satellites that collect data and transmit them back to earth. There are some satellites that are in geosynchronous orbit. This means that they orbit at the same speed and in the same direction that the earth is moving, so they stay in the same location above the equator.

There are primarily two satellites in this kind of orbit, one over the Indian Ocean that sees the eastern hemisphere and one over the Pacific Ocean that sees the western hemisphere. These satellites provide pictures of cloud cover, surface temperatures, cloud temperatures, moisture content, and ozone distribution. These satellites also have instruments that measure emissions from the sun including x-rays, protons, and electrons. This helps scientists better understand the role that the sun plays in the earth's weather.

In addition to these satellites, there are several satellites that orbit the earth from the north pole to the south pole and back. This is called a polar orbit. These satellites give more detailed information about temperatures on the surface and in the atmosphere. Information from these satellites is never more than six hours old.

Information from all the weather satellites, as well as information from ground-based instruments and radiosondes, is fed into massive computers that model the weather and predict what will happen in the future. The weather satellites provide a vital element in these calculations.

A very important set of weather satellites has been dubbed the A-Train. The A-Train is a set of satellites that follow one another around the earth, collecting data and sending it back continuously. The train of satellites crosses the equator at 1:30 PM solar

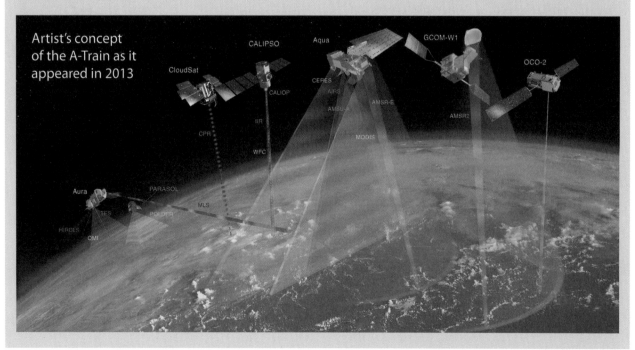
Artist's concept of the A-Train as it appeared in 2013

time each day, which is why it is called the Afternoon Train or A-Train for short.

The satellites in the A-Train collect various types of data. Aura measures greenhouse gases and Aqua measures the water in the atmosphere. CloudSat uses very sensitive radar to scan clouds and sends back slice-by-slice pictures of the insides of storms. This helps scientists better understand how precipitation forms inside of storm clouds. CALIPSO measures aerosols, which are any tiny particles that are suspended in the air. GCOM-W1 is a satellite that measures the water cycle on earth. It will be joined by GCOM-C1 which will measure climate conditions on earth as well as carbon in the atmosphere to help determine global climate change. These two satellites were launched by Japan. The most recent member of the A-Train is OCO2, which measures carbon dioxide concentrations in the atmosphere. The A-Train satellites were launched between 2002 and 2014.

In addition to the A-Train, there are many other weather satellites as well. One of the most recent weather satellites to be launched is the DSCVR satellite which is owned and operated by NOAA and was launched by SpaceX in February 2015. DSCVR, which stands for Deep Space Climate Observatory, orbits at a distance of 930,000 miles (1.5 million km) from earth, about a tenth of the way to the sun. It is in a position where it can always see the sun as well as the lighted side of the earth. Its main purpose is to monitor solar activity. Major solar events can affect earth's climate and can send massive amounts of charged particles to earth, which can disrupt electrical devices. Early warning can help people take measures to protect these devices. This can be very helpful in many situations. For example, with enough warning a space launch could be delayed, which could prevent the launch from failing due to electrical interference. DSCVR also monitors changes in ozone, aerosols, dust and volcanic ash, cloud height, vegetation cover, and climate on earth. Images of these phenomena are sent to earth every two hours.

As new satellites are developed and launched, scientists will continue to gain a better understanding of the infinitely complex system that God has designed to produce our weather.

The SpaceX Falcon 9 rocket carrying NOAA's DSCOVR, lifts off at Cape Canaveral Air Force Station in Florida on February 11, 2015.

20

Reporting & Analyzing Weather Information

Making it all make sense

How do we read a weather map?

Words to know:

weather station model

Meteorologists across the United States and around the world collect large amounts of weather data each day. There are about 15,000 individual ground-based weather stations that report information to the National Weather Service. This information is sent to the Weather Service computer located at the National Meteorological Center in College Park, Maryland. This computer also receives over 25,000 radiosonde reports, 1,500 reports from ships at sea, 2,500 aircraft reports, 500 radar reports, and multiple satellite reports every day. The computer sifts through all of this information to generate reports and summaries of weather conditions, and makes general weather forecasts.

In order to simplify the transmission of so much data, a standard format for data, called the **weather station model**, has been developed to give the most information in the shortest amount of time. The weather station model is a picture (see right) that quickly shows wind speed and direction, cloud cover, precipitation, temperature, dew point, and air pressure.

The circle in the center indicates the percent of the sky covered by clouds. The long line shows the direction the wind is coming from with straight up representing winds from the north. The shorter lines, called flags, indicate the wind speed. Full flags represent 10-knot winds and half flags represent 5-knot winds. The number to the upper left of the circle indicates the current temperature. The number to the lower left indicates the dew point. If precipitation is falling, a symbol showing the type of precipitation is placed between

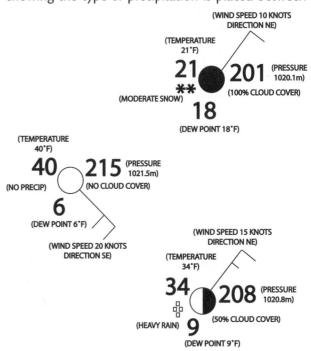

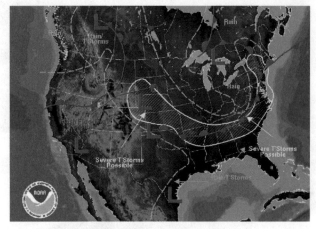

A sample weather forecast map

these two numbers. Rectangles represent rain, stars represent snow, and an apostrophe represents drizzle.

The number to the right of the circle indicates the current air pressure. To convert this number to air pressure in millibars (the average pressure at sea level is 14.7 pounds per square inch, or 1,013.25 millibars), one must add 10,000 to the number and then move the decimal point one place to the left. For example, if the model shows 205 you add 10,000 to 205 and you get 10,205. Then you move the decimal point to the left to make it 1,020.5 millibars. If the number on the model is greater than 500, you add 9,000 instead of 10,000.

The model shown here gives the weather conditions in three different locations. The information in parentheses would not actually be included on the model; it is added to help you understand the symbols.

Once the central computer has analyzed all of the data, the information is sent to local offices called Weather Forecast Offices (WFOs) where local meteorologists use the information to make local weather predictions as well as to generate warnings of severe weather such as severe thunderstorms, flash floods, or severe winter storms. There are over 120 WFOs across the United States.

The weather information collected by the NWS is also posted on the website www.weather.gov. This information is available to anyone who wants to use it. It includes maps that show forecasts for precipitation, cloud cover, high and low temperatures, wind speed, and storms. You can go to the website and click on any part of the map to find out the forecast for that location. You can also see satellite images, air quality information, locations of weather radar sites, and much more.

If you want to know what the weather is likely to be like tomorrow, there are many ways to get the weather forecast. You can watch a TV report, listen to the radio, check in a local newspaper, visit a weather website, or use a weather app that gives weather forecasts, but all of the information used to generate these forecasts originates with the information provided by the National Weather Service. 🌐

🧠 What did we learn?

- What happens to the weather data collected at weather stations?

- Other than from land-based weather stations, where does the National Weather Service get weather information?

- What group of the National Weather Service generates local severe thunderstorm and flash flood warnings?

🚀 Taking it further

- Why is it necessary for one location to collect and analyze all of the weather data across the United States?

- Why is a standard picture or model needed for reporting weather information?

- Why must the information in the model be converted to electrical signals before it is transmitted to the National Weather Service's computer?

🧪 Analyzing weather information

Complete the "Weather Station Model" worksheet.

ⓘ History of the NWS

Weather information is collected from thousands of sources around the world—from land-based weather stations, radiosondes, satellites, and many other sources as well. Yet this information would be useless without the National Weather Service to correlate all the data and send the information back out to meteorologists across the world. The National Weather Service has been helping people make weather forecasts since 1870.

People have been interested in the weather since the beginning of time. And many people have taken weather readings and tried to make their own predictions of the weather, but an official government supported weather organization was not formed until after the Civil War. The Smithsonian Institute started an organized weather system in 1849 by giving out weather stations and having the operators telegraph the readings to the Smithsonian each day. They continued to expand their network until they had 500 stations in operation in 1860. However, their efforts were interrupted by the United States Civil War.

After the war ended, many people pressed Congress to form a weather bureau. One of the main reasons for this was that many ships were lost each year due to unforeseen storms on the Great Lakes and along the Atlantic coast. So in 1870 President Ulysses Grant signed the bill that established the Division of Telegrams and Reports for the Benefit of Commerce. This group was under the oversight of the War Department and was part of the Signal Service Corps.

Meteorologists were trained and were required to telegraph temperature, barometric pressure, relative humidity, wind speed, cloud cover, and general weather information to Washington, D.C., three times each day. This allowed the meteorologists in Washington to have a glimpse of the weather all over the country three times a day. They took this information and made predictions of the weather in each part of the country. These predictions were telegraphed around the country and people began to have their first glimpse of weather forecasting.

The benefits of accurate weather forecasts were quickly seen and the Weather Service was expanded. In 1891 they were given the responsibility of issuing flood warnings, and in 1898 they established a hurricane warning network in the West Indies. By 1909 the Weather Bureau was using balloons for weather observation. With increased use of airplanes in the early 1900s, it became necessary for the Weather Bureau to look at severe weather that could affect airplanes. In 1918, the Weather Bureau began issuing forecasts for air mail routes.

From 1891 to 1940 the Weather Bureau was part of the Department of Agriculture. In 1940 the Weather Bureau was transferred to the Department of Commerce. In 1967 the Weather Bureau was renamed the National Weather Service and was placed under the Environmental Science Services Administration (ESSA). In 1970 the ESSA was renamed the National Oceanic and Atmospheric Administration (NOAA). The National Weather Service continues to operate as part of NOAA today.

Technology has been the driving force in better weather prediction. The first important technological development was the telegraph. Before the telegraph people could make weather readings but it was very difficult to get information from multiple locations at the same time, which is necessary for accurate predictions. The telegraph allowed for nearly instantaneous reporting of weather readings.

The invention of the radio was the next important advancement. Radio and television have been instrumental in getting the weather forecasts out to the general public. The first radio broadcast of a weather forecast was in 1921.

Other important inventions include weather satellites and radar. But the most important invention is the computer. Scientists began the development of mathematical models in the 1950s, when computers first became powerful enough to process them. Today, powerful computers can process huge amounts of information in a short period of time. As more information is gathered, the models are improved and today the weather forecasts are much more accurate than they have ever been.

Even with all of the computing power and technological advancements, however, meteorologists will be the first to admit that they really understand very little about the way that weather works. God designed a very complex and beautiful system for the weather on our planet.

Weather Information

21

Forecasting the Weather

Keeping people safe

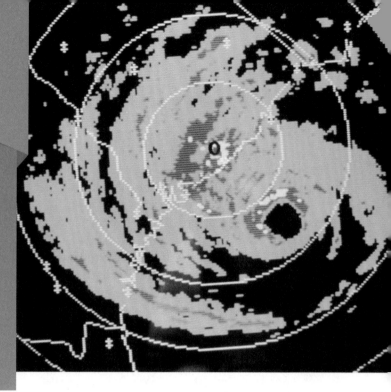

How can weather forecasts keep people safe?

Challenge words:

weather outlook

weather advisory

weather watch

weather warning

Do you want to plan a picnic or a trip to the swimming pool? How do you decide what clothes to pack for a trip? It helps if you know what the weather is going to be like, so you might watch the TV weather report or look at the weather forecast in the newspaper or on the Internet before you make your plans. Meteorologists collect and analyze weather data in order to make weather forecasts.

You are probably very familiar with local weather forecasts. Although these are important, the National Weather Service does much more than just generate local weather forecasts. The NWS is dedicated to providing information about the weather that can help keep people safe so they send out weather information to many different groups in addition to local weather forecasters. For example, fire weather reports are sent out to help forest rangers and other groups predict the likelihood of forest

fires. When conditions are hot, dry, and windy, forest fires can easily be started by lightning or campers who are careless with their campfires. Rangers are very diligent to watch for fires when conditions are bad. Once a fire starts, the fire weather reports help people decide how best to fight the fires to keep them from spreading and to put them out quickly.

Another special type of weather forecast is the Terminal Aerodrome Forecast (TAF). This forecast is sent every few hours to major airports. It includes information on wind, visibility, cloud cover, and wind shear specific to that airport. These are weather conditions that specifically affect airplane take offs and landings. These reports help the people at the airport make good decisions to keep the pilots and passengers safe.

The NWS's Ocean Prediction Center generates several forecasts that are specific to ocean going

Fun Fact

Benjamin Franklin began publishing *Poor Richard's Almanac* in 1732, and printed a new volume every year for 25 years. The *Almanac* contained calendars, astronomical data, weather forecasts, and generous doses of humorous sayings from the fictional character Richard Saunders.

vessels. These include the Coastal Waters Forecast and the Offshore Waters Forecast. In addition to regular weather information, these forecasts include predictions of wave heights and other conditions that might affect ships in the area.

The National Hurricane Center in Florida and the Central Pacific Hurricane Center in Hawaii monitor tropical depressions and tropical storms. They send out forecasts of hurricanes whenever conditions seem likely for a hurricane to develop. They are also responsible for tracking hurricanes and forecasting when and where they are likely to make landfall. This advanced notice can help people to evacuate areas that are likely to be in the path of the storm.

Finally, the NWS has a Climate Prediction Center that issues more long-term weather forecasts that are related to climate changes. These forecasts can be a week, a month, or several months in the future. These forecasts cover land, water, and atmospheric conditions.

All of these different forecasts are designed to help keep people safe by giving them as much warning about dangerous weather conditions as possible.

With the use of sophisticated computer technology, weather forecasting has greatly improved. The weather forecasts are much more accurate now than they were in the past. However, predicting the weather is still tricky and complicated and often defies complete understanding. God still controls the weather. He can withhold the rain or send a flood at His will, though the weather normally follows the physical laws that He has set in place. We must never forget that He is in charge. But, we must also remember that God loves us and has a purpose for everything He does. Psalm 95:6–7 says, "Oh come, let us worship and bow down; Let us kneel before the LORD our Maker. For He is our God, And we are the people of His pasture, And the sheep of His hand." So we can rejoice in the weather, even when it spoils our picnic.

What did we learn?

- How do meteorologists predict what the weather will be like?

- What is an important function of local National Weather Service offices?

- Other than local weather forecasts, what types of weather forecasts are generated by the NWS?

Taking it further

- Why are weather forecasts more accurate today than they were 20 years ago?

- Are weather forecasts always reliable?

Forecasting the weather

Follow the directions on the "Weather Forecasting" worksheet to try your hand at predicting the weather. At the end of a week, compare how well you predicted the weather to how well the meteorologist predicted the weather.

🏅 Severe weather terminology

In order to quickly convey how dangerous the weather is at the moment the National Weather Service has defined a set of terms the helps people understand how urgent the danger is. A hazardous **weather outlook** is a daily forecast of potentially hazardous storms that might develop. This alerts local weather people to watch for a possible storm. A **weather watch** is a little more serious. A watch occurs when conditions worsen and a serious storm or other hazardous weather is possible, but it is still uncertain when and where it will occur. Weather watches are intended to give people enough time to change important plans if weather is a consideration. A **weather advisory** is issued when hazardous conditions are likely or imminent. This warns people to pay attention to bad weather that is likely to start soon and take precautions. A **weather warning** is issued when severe weather is occurring or is very likely and the conditions are likely to cause great harm. People in an area where a severe weather warning has been given should take immediate action to be sure they are safe. If the warning is for a severe winter storm it would be wise to stay home and not drive anywhere. If it is a flash flood warning, people should immediately climb to higher ground to be out of the path of the flood. If you understand these terms, you will better understand the information given by the NWS and you will be much safer.

Graphing Data

One of the easiest ways to interpret data is to graph the data points. This gives a visual picture of the data. You are going to make two graphs of the data that you collect.

Purpose: To practice graphing data for easy interpretation

Materials: Graph paper, colored pencils, data from the "Weather Forecasting" worksheet

Procedure:

1. Using the data you collect on the "Weather Forecasting" worksheet, make one graph of the high temperatures and one graph of the low temperatures. On each graph put the dates along the x-axis and put the temperatures along the y-axis. Use a different color for each set of data, one color for your predicted temperatures, one color for the meteorologist's predicted temperatures, and one color for the actual temperatures. Be sure to label what each color represents.

2. Look at how close your predicted data points are to the actual points. Compare this with how close the meteorologist's points are to the actual points.

Question: Who made the best weather forecasts, you or your local meteorologist?

Weather Station: Final Project

Collecting your own data

How can you make your own weather station?

Collecting your own weather data can be fun and educational. All you need are a few instruments for your own weather station. You have already built a wind sock for measuring wind direction, a psychrometer for measuring relative humidity (which includes a thermometer for measuring the temperature), and a rain gauge for measuring precipitation. The only instruments you are missing are a barometer to measure changes in air pressure, and an anemometer for measuring wind speed.

Once you have all of your instruments made and in place, you can measure the weather conditions at your house every day, and you can compare your results with those printed in the newspaper or given on TV. You will most likely get different results from the meteorologist because your instruments are in a different location from the instruments used to make official reports, and your instruments are probably less accurate. 🌐

🧠 What did we learn?

- What does each instrument in your weather station measure?

🚀 Taking it further

- Why might you want to have your own weather station?

- Why might your weather readings be different from what is reported in the newspaper or on TV?

- Did you see any relationship between air pressure and wind and rain?

- What changes did you see in your temperature readings from day to day?

⚗️ Making a weather station

Activity 1

Purpose: To make a barometer

Materials: clear plastic tubing, duct tape, food coloring, string, waterproof marker

Procedure:

1. Bend an 8–10 inch piece of clear plastic tubing in a U shape, and seal one end tightly with duct tape.

2. Pour colored water into the open end until it goes up one inch on each side of the U.

3. Tie your barometer to a post, tree, or other pole.

4. Use a waterproof marker to mark the level of the water on the plugged side of the tube.

Conclusion: As the air pressure increases, the water will go up on the plugged side of the U. As the air pressure decreases, the water level will go down on the plugged side.

Activity 2

You may wish to use a purchased weather station that includes an anemometer. If not, you can make your own.

In lesson 19 we learned about an anemometer made with three cups on a pole. We will make a different kind of anemometer from the one mentioned in lesson 19; we will make one that moves a ruler as the wind pushes against it.

Purpose: To make an anemometer

Materials: empty 2-liter bottle, cardboard or tagboard, marker, tape, ruler, modeling clay, soda straw, thin stick or skewer

Procedure:

1. Fill an empty 2-liter bottle with water and put on the cap.

2. In an 8-inch square piece of cardboard or tagboard, cut a smooth curve from one corner to the opposite corner.

3. Draw lines on the cardboard from the corner to the edges of the curve so the lines are 1 inch apart on the curve. This will be the scale.

4. Tape the cardboard to the front of the bottle so that the edge of the cardboard is in the center of the bottle.

5. Tape the ruler to the end of a thin stick at a 90° angle.

6. Tape a soda straw to the top of the bottle so the end of the straw just reaches the front of the bottle.

7. Put the stick through the straw so the ruler hangs down in front of the scale.

8. Place a piece of modeling clay or tape on the end of the stick where it sticks out of the straw to prevent the stick from coming back out. The ruler should move freely in front of the scale when the wind blows on it. The harder the wind blows, the further up it will push the ruler.

Activity 3

Now, select a place for your weather station and place these instruments, as well as the ones you made in previous lessons, outside so you can measure the weather. Be sure to place them where they will not be blocked by buildings or plants.

To get accurate temperature measurements, the thermometer needs to be shaded so the sun does not directly shine on it.

Review what you learned in previous lessons to understand how to properly use each instrument. Now you are ready to be a junior meteorologist. Use a copy of the "Weather Data Sheet" to record your readings.

UNIT 6

Ocean Movement

◊ **Identify** and **locate** on a map the five major oceans.

◊ **Describe** the cause of ocean currents.

◊ **Describe** the cause and features of ocean waves.

◊ **Describe** the cause of the ocean tides.

◊ **Explain** how moving seawater affects mankind.

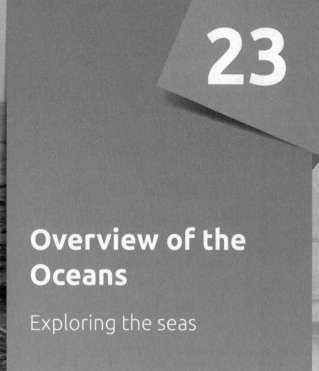

23

Overview of the Oceans

Exploring the seas

What are the major oceans around the world?

Words to know:

sea   gulf

Challenge words:

fauna

As you have seen from studying the weather, the oceans play a major role in the earth's weather patterns. Many storm systems develop over the oceans and then move toward land. Evaporation of seawater provides most of the moisture for the storms across the globe. And because water changes temperature more slowly than land does, the sun's heating of the oceans causes much of the wind around the world. Also, coastal areas have milder winters and cooler summers than inland areas because of the heat stored in the oceans.

Technically, there is only one ocean. All of the water in the oceans is connected around the globe. However, we generally divide the ocean into five main areas: the Pacific, Atlantic, Indian, Arctic, and Antarctic Oceans. The oceans cover about 71% of

the surface of the earth and account for 97% of the water supply. This ready supply of water is what makes earth unique and able to support life.

The Pacific Ocean, located west of North and South America and east of Asia and Australia, is the largest ocean. It covers more of the earth than all of the landmasses put together—nearly one-third of the entire planet. It is more than twice as big as the Atlantic Ocean, which is the second largest ocean. The Pacific Ocean contains the lowest point on earth. The bottom of the Mariana Trench is 36,200 feet (11,034 m) below sea level. And more volcanoes and islands are found in the Pacific than anywhere else on the planet.

The second largest ocean is the Atlantic Ocean. It is located east of North and South America and west of Europe and Africa. The Atlantic Ocean contains the longest mountain range in the world. The Mid-Atlantic Ridge runs from north to south under the water nearly from pole to pole. The majority of fish eaten by people are caught in the Atlantic Ocean.

The Indian Ocean is the third largest ocean. It is located east of Africa, south of Asia, and west of Australia. There have been established trade routes on the Indian Ocean longer than on any other ocean. This is mainly because the monsoon winds supply a reliable source of locomotion that change direction twice a year.

The fourth largest ocean is the Antarctic Ocean, also called the Southern Ocean. It is located around the continent of Antarctica near the South Pole. The Antarctic Ocean is defined as all of the water south of 55° south latitude. More than half of the Antarctic Ocean is covered with ice and icebergs in the winter.

The smallest ocean is the Arctic Ocean. This ocean consists of all water north of 55° north latitude. The Arctic Ocean is almost completely surrounded by land. It is mostly frozen year round.

Often we use the term *sea* or *the seas* to mean the oceans, but technically there is a difference. A **sea** is a part of an ocean that is partially enclosed by land. For example, the Mediterranean Sea is connected to the Atlantic Ocean but is mostly surrounded by parts of Europe, Africa, and the Middle East.

Another term often associated with the ocean is a gulf. A **gulf** is a part of the ocean that dents into the land. A well-known example is the Gulf of Mexico, which dents into the southern United States.

Oceans are vitally important to keeping the water cycle going and bringing needed moisture to all parts of the world.

What did we learn?

- What are the names of the five oceans?
- Which ocean is the largest?
- How much of the earth is covered by the oceans?

Taking it further

- How do the oceans affect the weather?
- Why do some people say there is only one ocean?
- Why was the Indian Ocean the first ocean to have established trade routes?

A topographical map of the earth

Labeling the oceans

Using a copy of the world map, label the oceans and continents. Older children can label seas and gulfs, as well. Use an atlas or labeled world map as a reference. Then color the map with colored pencils or markers.

 # Challenger expedition

The study of the ocean is vital to the study of the atmosphere, but the study of the ocean is broader than just its effects on weather.

Oceanography is the study of the ocean and is broken down into four main areas of study. Biological oceanography is the study of the plants and animals in the ocean. This is often called marine biology. Chemical oceanography is the study of the chemical make-up of the oceans. Geological oceanography is the study of the ocean floor and includes the study of plate tectonics and the movements and formation of the ocean floor. Finally, physical oceanography is the study of the temperature, salinity, tides, and currents of the ocean. This is the area of oceanography most closely associated with meteorology.

Oceanography officially began with the Challenger Expedition in 1872, although people had been studying the ocean long before this. The Challenger Expedition was a 3½-year mission to study the oceans of the world.

The HMS *Challenger* was a three-masted wooden ship with a steam engine. The sails were used the majority of the time, but the engine was used for deploying equipment and taking scientific readings. There were 20 naval officers on board the ship along with 200 crew members.

The expedition was headed by Charles Wyville Thompson and Sir John Murray. The ship left England on Dec. 7, 1872 and spent the next 40 months sailing around the world. They returned on May 24, 1876 after traveling 68,890 nautical miles. During their journey they covered the extremes of the Atlantic and Pacific Oceans and traveled as near as they could to Antarctica.

The *Challenger* stopped at 362 different locations around the world. At each location the crew measured the depth of the water, temperature of the water at various depths, and the direction and rate of flow of surface currents. They also collected fauna,

samples of the animal life, from different levels of the ocean including many samples dredged from the bottom at each location. They collected water samples from various depths and soil samples from the bottom. They also recorded the atmospheric conditions and meteorological data at each location.

This expedition was the first organized effort to thoroughly and systematically study the entire ocean. After returning, over 100 scientists analyzed the data collected and published their findings in over 50 volumes. These volumes gave full details of the currents, temperatures, depths, topography, geology, and biology of most of the world's oceans.

Although in reality the data collected on this expedition only scratched the surface, it greatly added to people's understanding of the oceans and encouraged more expeditions to gather more data. Today, because of the vastness of the ocean, there are still many areas of the ocean that remain unexplored; however, what we have learned continues to reveal the glory of God through the ocean's magnificence and complexity.

Fun Fact

The U.S. Space Shuttle *Challenger* was named for this ship.

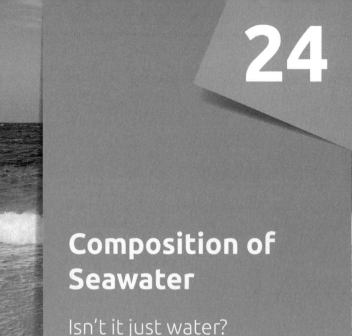

24

Composition of Seawater

Isn't it just water?

What is seawater made of?

Challenge words:

desalination   reverse osmosis

distillation   brackish

Oceans play a vital role in the ecology of the earth. The oceans cover 71% of the earth's surface and 97% of all of the earth's water is in the oceans. Unfortunately for humans, the water in the oceans is too salty to drink or to use for irrigation of crops.

How did the oceans become so salty? The Bible does not tell us if God created the oceans with salt to begin with or not. It is likely that there was some salt for the fish and other sea creatures. Also, we know that the worldwide Flood would have washed salt from the land into the oceans. So, after the Flood there was salt in the oceans. But the oceans are continuing to get saltier all the time.

The process that causes salt to accumulate in the oceans today is evaporation. As water falls on the earth and flows over the ground and through rocks, it dissolves salt and other minerals in small amounts. This small amount of salt is not noticeable in the streams, rivers, and lakes. However, after

this water flows into the ocean, the only way for the water to leave is through evaporation. When the water evaporates, it leaves behind any minerals that had been dissolved. Over time, these small amounts of salt and other minerals build up, causing the ocean to become saltier and saltier.

The saltiness of the ocean is actually a testimony to a young earth. If salt had been accumulating at the current rate for billions of years, as many evolutionary scientists believe, the oceans would be much too salty to support any life at all. Instead, if we assume that the oceans had no salt at all to begin with, the current saltiness of the oceans indicates that they cannot be any older than 62 million years, much younger than most secular scientists claim the earth to be. This may sound like the salt in the oceans does not support a young earth, but as we mentioned above, the oceans likely had some salt to begin with, and the Flood washed large amounts of salt into the ocean, so the current saltiness actually can support a 6,000-year-old earth but cannot support a billions-year-old earth.

The most common mineral found in seawater is salt. But many other minerals are found there as well. Magnesium and bromide, along with table salt (sodium chloride), are available in high enough concentrations to be removed and sold commercially. All together, there are 55 different elements

Rivers like this one carry minerals to the ocean.

that have been identified in seawater. In 1,000 grams (35 ounces) of seawater, there are about 35 grams (1.2 ounces) of minerals. Of the minerals in the seawater, about 75% is salt, although the salt concentration varies from place to place.

In addition to minerals, gases such as oxygen, nitrogen, and carbon dioxide are also dissolved in the water. The concentration of oxygen is highest near the surface of the ocean. Some oxygen dissolves from the air into the water, but most of it is produced by tiny ocean plants, called phytoplankton, that grow near the surface of the water.

The ocean is a wonderful mixture of water, minerals, and gases that God has provided to support all life on earth.

What did we learn?

- What are the main elements found in the ocean besides water?
- How does salt get into the ocean?
- What is one gas that is dissolved in the ocean water?

Taking it further

- Why is there more oxygen near the surface of the ocean than in deeper parts?
- How does the saltiness of the ocean support the idea of a young earth?

Salting the ocean

The oceans are much saltier than the rivers and lakes. This is because water flowing into them contains small amounts of salt that are left behind when the water evaporates.

Purpose: To help you visualize how the ocean becomes salty

Materials: stove, pan, salt, dark construction paper, paintbrush, water

Procedure:

1. Heat a cup of water until very warm.
2. Stir in as much salt as can be dissolved.
3. Use the salt water to paint a picture on a piece of dark colored construction paper and allow the paper to dry overnight.

Conclusion: After the water is gone, a salty picture will remain behind. The water evaporates but the salt does not, just like in the oceans.

Desalination

Ocean water is not useful for human consumption or for growing plants because of its high salt content. Yet the vast majority of the water on earth is in the oceans, so people have developed many methods for removing the salt from the ocean's water.

The removal of salt from sea water is called desalination. Desalination plants remove salt from ocean water to produce fresh water. There are several methods of desalination but the two most common are distillation and reverse osmosis.

Distillation is a process that heats the water until it evaporates, leaving the salt and other minerals behind. The steam is then allowed to condense in another container.

Reverse osmosis is a process that passes the sea water through a special permeable membrane, which is like a special filter that allows the water molecules to pass through without letting the salt and other minerals pass through.

Before seawater can be desalinated, it usually has to be treated to get rid of the bacteria, algae, and other marine life in the water. This is done by adding a small amount of chlorine or ozone to the water, or by shining ultra-violet light on the water to kill the microorganisms. The water is then filtered to remove any sand or other solids from the water. These filters and membranes must be cleaned periodically. Also, the pipes carrying the seawater must be cleaned periodically because of the chemicals that build up inside the pipes.

Currently, most of the desalination plants in the world are located in the Middle East. Desalination is an expensive process compared to obtaining fresh water from the ground or many other sources. Therefore, desalination plants are mostly built in areas where there is little available water.

In the United States, many desalination plants treat brackish water. Brackish water is water that is too salty to drink but is much less salty than

A view across a reverse osmosis desalination plant.

seawater. Water can become brackish if it is near the ocean but not part of the ocean.

Saudi Arabia and other countries in the Middle East have led the way in developing desalination plants. Some of the largest desalination plants include the Ashkelon seawater reverse osmosis plant in Israel, which opened in 2005, and the Ras Al Khair desalination plant in Saudi Arabia, which came online in 2014. Over 40% of the domestic water used in Israel is produced by desalination. There are over 16,000 desalination plants worldwide, which produce enough water for more than 300 million people and that number is increasing every year.

Although desalination is expensive, new technologies are reducing the costs. With the demand for fresh water continually increasing around the world, more work will be done and the costs of desalination are expected to decrease.

Ocean Currents

Moving around the world

What causes the currents in the ocean?

Words to know:

surface current

subsurface current

density current

Challenge words:

upwelling

gyre

Imagine if the ocean water did not move. The water would become stagnant and eventually all life in the oceans could end. This would be a disaster. However, God designed the oceans to be very active. The water in the oceans is affected by three main forces. First, the sun heats the water and the air, causing currents that move the water around the globe. Second, gravitational pull from the moon causes tides. And third, winds cause waves to be generated. Currents, tides, and waves all keep the ocean moving. We will examine tides and waves in the following lessons. First, we will study the ocean currents.

Just as the heat from the sun warms the air near the equator, causing global winds, so also the sun heats the water near the equator. This warmer water is moved by the wind on the surface of the ocean from the equator toward the poles. Cooler water moves from the poles toward the equator to take its place. These surface currents are also affected by the rotation of the earth. So, currents in the northern hemisphere primarily flow clockwise and in the southern hemisphere they primarily flow counter-clockwise.

Surface currents move at about 2–3 mph (0.9–1.3 m/s). This constant movement of water helps to distribute the heat from the equator to cooler regions. This is God's design for keeping the tropics from getting too hot and the polar regions from getting too cold.

Fun Fact

American naval officer and oceanographer Matthew Maury (1806–1873) was a Christian who loved reading his Bible. He also had no doubts about its accuracy. In his Bible studies, the words of Psalm 8:8 stuck in his mind: "whatsoever passeth through the paths of the seas." Maury determined that if God's Word said there were "paths" in the seas, then there must be paths. So he set out to find them. And using his ingenuity and creativity, Maury found them. In 1855 he wrote the first textbook on modern oceanography.

Ocean Movement

Ocean currents

The Gulf Stream is one of the best known warm ocean currents. It flows from the Gulf of Mexico, along the east coast of the United States, then out toward England. This flow of warm water allows England to experience milder winters and warmer weather than many areas in more southern latitudes.

Similarly, cold currents bring drier weather to neighboring land because the colder water cools the air, and cold air cannot hold as much moisture as the warmer air. A cool current flows south along the western coast of the United States causing the Baja area of Mexico to be very dry.

In addition to surface currents that are primarily driven by the wind, the ocean also experiences **subsurface currents**. One type of subsurface current is a **density current**. Colder, saltier water is more dense than warmer, less salty water. For example, the Mediterranean Sea is saltier than the Atlantic Ocean. Where their waters meet, the water from the Mediterranean Sea tends to sink into the Atlantic Ocean and the less salty ocean water flows into the sea above the saltier water. Similarly, the colder more dense water near the poles flows toward the equator along the bottom of the oceans as warmer water flows toward the poles above the colder water.

God designed the oceans so that currents would help move the water around the earth, helping to equalize the temperatures of the water and keeping the oceans viable.

What did we learn?

- What is a surface ocean current?
- What are the main causes of surface currents?
- How fast do surface currents usually move?
- What is a subsurface ocean current?
- What are the main causes of subsurface currents?

Taking it further

- What climate changes do warm surface currents cause?
- What climate changes do cool surface currents cause?
- Why do warm surface currents move away from the equator while cooler currents move toward the equator?

⚗️ Observing currents

Purpose: To observe water currents on a small scale

Materials: large glass bowl, small bottle or jar, red and blue food coloring

Procedure:

1. Fill a large glass bowl with cold water; fill a very small bottle or jar with very warm water.

2. Add a couple drops of red food coloring to the warm water.

3. Place your finger over the opening of the bottle and place the bottle on its side on the bottom of the glass bowl.

4. Carefully remove your finger from the opening of the bottle and take your hand out of the water. Watch as the warm water slowly swirls to the top of the bowl. This is how warm water currents move across the top of colder water.

5. Empty the bowl and the bottle.

6. Now fill the bowl with very warm water and the bottle with cold water.

7. Add a couple of drops of blue food coloring to the water in the bottle.

8. Place your finger over the opening of the bottle and hold the bottle sideways just under the surface of the water in the glass bowl.

9. Carefully remove your finger from the opening of the bottle. While holding the bottle in place, watch as the cool water slowly swirls to the bottom of the bowl. This is how cool water currents move under warmer water.

Repeat this experiment with salty and non-salty water of the same temperature.

1. Fill the bowl with plain water and fill the bottle with salt water.

2. Add a couple of drops of food coloring to the salt water.

3. Hold the bottle just below the surface of the water. The salt water will drift to the bottom.

4. Add several tablespoons of salt to the bowl of water.

5. Replace the water in the bottle with plain water and add a couple of drops of food coloring.

6. Place the bottle on its side on the bottom of the bowl of salt water.

Conclusion: The fresh water will drift up to the surface of the water. This shows the differences in the density of plain and salty water and how density currents occur because of higher and lower salt concentrations in ocean water around the world.

Ocean Movement

Surface currents

One of the effects of surface currents is that the trade winds push the surface water away from western coasts. This allows cooler, nutrient-rich water from lower in the ocean to rise up and fill the area where the warmer water was. This process is called upwelling. Upwelling is God's way of stirring up the nutrients that have settled to the bottom of the ocean. These nutrients are vital to life along the coastal areas.

There are seven main surface currents in the oceans and many smaller ones as well. These currents converge to form five huge swirling masses of water called gyres. A gyre is any swirling vortex of air or water, but with respect to ocean currents the gyres are the prevailing currents around each major part of the ocean. Two of the gyres are located in the Pacific Ocean, two in the Atlantic Ocean, and one in the Indian Ocean. These gyres are a result of the Coriolis effect that you learned about in lesson 5.

As you learned earlier in the lesson, some of the surface currents are warm currents and others are cold, and these currents have a large impact on the weather along the coasts where they flow. As we already mentioned, the Gulf Stream current is a very warm fast-moving current flowing northward along the east coast of the United States. The California current is a cool, slow-moving current that flows south along the western coast of the United States. This current brings much cooler weather to the coast of California.

The Somali current is found off the east coast of Africa. It is an unusual current because it flows northward from May to September and southward from November to March. Upwelling occurs while the current is flowing north but dies out when the current is flowing south, so the marine life is much more abundant in the summer months.

On the Internet or in a book, find a map showing the predominant surface currents. Draw these currents on your copy of the world map from lesson 23. Mark warm currents with red lines and arrows and cold currents with blue lines and arrows. Also label the five gyres on your map if you can locate them.

El Niño

If you have watched a weather report on TV or read about the weather in the newspaper, it is likely that you have heard of El Niño (el NEEN-yoh). But what is El Niño and why is it named so? El Niño is a body of warm water in the west Pacific Ocean. It got its name, which means "The Child" in honor of the Christ child, because the effects of the warmer water are felt along the coast of Peru around Christmas time. However, the weather effects of El Niño are felt around the world at various times of the year.

El Niño is like a warm lake in the middle of the ocean. Many scientists believe El Niño to be caused by the trade winds that blow from east to west across the tropical Pacific. The warmer surface water piles up in the west Pacific around Indonesia because of the prevailing winds. When the trade winds weaken or reverse direction, the warm body of water moves eastward along the equator until it reaches the coast of South America. This extra warm water causes changes in the weather and in fishing patterns along the South American coast. This phenomenon is called El Niño and it happens every 3 to 7 years.

The water in El Niño can be as much as 14.4°F (8°C) warmer than the surrounding water and can extend 50 to 150 yards (45–135 m) below the surface. At times, El Niño can cover an area one and a half times the size of the continental U.S.

The water in El Niño also has less salt in it than what is found in the surrounding cooler waters. This is a result of the heavy rainfall that occurs over this warm body of water. Because of the lower salt content and higher temperatures, this water is lighter than the cooler, saltier water around it. It floats above the cooler, heavier water and does not mix with it very well.

Sometimes cooler than normal currents form off of the coast of Peru. This effect is called La Niña

Buoys like this have instruments that measure ocean temperature at varying depths and forewarn of El Niño or La Niña events.

(la NEEN-yah) and it occurs in the eastern part of the Pacific Ocean. This cooler water pushes out along the equator toward the west in a somewhat thin line. This is sometimes called a "cold tongue" because of its shape. The result of El Niño and La Niña going back and forth every 3 to 7 years is sometimes called the El Niño Southern Oscillation, or ENSO, by the scientific community.

ENSO affects the weather around the world. While El Niño brings warmer than normal winter temperatures to the north central United States, and cooler than normal temperatures to the southeastern and the southwestern United States, La Niña brings winter temperatures that are warmer than normal for the Southeast and cooler than normal in the Northwest.

Some areas of the world experience better weather during El Niño years while others experience very severe weather. In 1997–98, there was a very large El Niño containing as much energy as one million atomic bombs the size of the bomb that was dropped on Hiroshima. This is more energy than has been produced in the U.S. in the last 100 years. The weather patterns created by this El Niño caused damage around the world. There was an increase in hurricanes in 1998. It is estimated that 2,100 people died because of this El Niño, and in the U.S. alone, there was over 33 billion dollars in property damage from severe storms.

The entire world does not get more rain and severe storms because of El Niño, however. In eastern Australia, El Niño brings drought. However, La Niña, which is the opposite of El Niño, brings flooding to eastern Australia and drought to other parts of the world including parts of the United States.

Some people have asked if there is any way to stop El Niño from happening. Is there a way to cool the water off so we will not have such severe weather? To cool the water in El Niño down to the normal water temperature for that area would take an iceberg 33 feet (10 meters) thick covering an area the size of the continental U.S. This is an enormous amount of ice. So it is not feasible to try to change the temperature of El Niño.

We can try to predict when this weather phenomenon might occur and its possible effects, but only God is ultimately in control of the weather.

26

Waves

Gently lapping the shore

What causes waves, and how do they move?

Words to know:

wave height	breaker
crest	rip current
trough	rip tide
wavelength	tsunami

Have you ever had the chance to lie on the beach and listen to the waves crashing against the shore? It is a very soothing sound. Waves can be lots of fun to play in, too. People enjoy surfing and swimming in the waves. But what causes the waves?

The wind on the surface of the ocean causes currents that move water around the world. But wind has another effect on the surface of the ocean—it produces waves. The friction of the wind with the water molecules moves the water a short distance. When the water falls down, it forces some water molecules to move back, thus creating a wave.

The energy from one wave is transferred to the next, so the actual water molecules do not move across the ocean, but the wave's energy does. Waves can travel hundreds or even thousands of

miles across the ocean, but particular water molecules are lifted, moved forward, dropped down, and pushed back. Individual water molecules travel in a circular motion and stay in relatively the same location, while the energy from the wind moves across the surface of the ocean (see illustration).

There are two main ways that waves are measured. First, the difference between its highest and lowest points is called the **wave height**. The highest point is the **crest** and the lowest point is the **trough**.

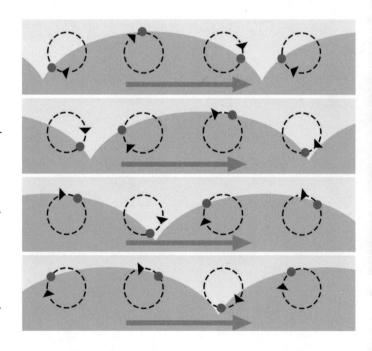

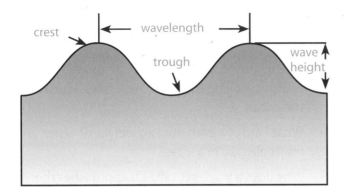
crest — wavelength — trough — wave height

The second measurement is the **wavelength**, which is the distance from one crest to the next.

On the open ocean, a typical wave may have a wave height of three feet. But the shape of the wave changes as it approaches the shore. As the wave reaches shallow water, the base begins to drag on the shallow ocean floor, causing it to slow down more quickly than the top of the wave. This causes the water to build up on top until it becomes unstable and falls over. This is called a **breaker**.

As the waves break on the shore, the water flows down the beach and back into the ocean. Occasionally, the backflow from the beach moves rapidly through a narrow gap in the breakers. This is called a **rip current** or a **rip tide**. A rip current can be dangerous to swimmers as it pulls the swimmer quickly out to sea. Most rip currents are narrow, however, and a person swimming parallel to the shore can usually escape the current and then swim back to shore.

Although most waves are caused by wind, earthquakes or volcanoes generate some very dangerous waves called **tsunamis**. These waves often move at great speeds, up to 600 mph (268 m/s). In the open ocean these waves may be only 20 inches (50 cm) in height, but due to their huge speed and energy, they rapidly build up as they approach the shore. A tsunami can reach heights of over 100 feet (30 m). When these giant waves crash onto the shore, they can cause massive death and destruction due to the rapid flooding that occurs. An earthquake in the Indian Ocean in December of 2004 caused a series of tsunamis that killed over 230,000 people in Indonesia, Sri Lanka, South India, and Thailand.

Tsunamis are very dangerous, but they are also rare. Most waves are harmless. In fact, waves serve a very important function. The moving water keeps the ocean clean by circulating oxygen, and moving debris out to sea where it can be eaten or decomposed by the many sea creatures that live there. Waves are another reminder of God's wonderful design for the earth. ⊕

A U.S. Navy hovercraft delivers supplies to the city of Meulaboh, on the island of Sumatra, Indonesia, following the 2004 tsunami.

A fishing boat and debris block a road following a 2011 tsunami triggered by a 9.0 magnitude earthquake that struck 230 miles off the coast of Japan.

🧠 What did we learn?

- How are waves generated?
- How far does a particular water molecule move when a wave is generated?
- What is the crest of a wave?
- What is the trough of a wave?
- What are two ways to measure a wave?

🚀 Taking it further

- Explain how a wave can move across the ocean without moving the water molecules across the ocean.
- What kind of a path does an individual water molecule take in a wave?
- Why does a wave get tall as it approaches the shore?
- Why are tsunamis such dangerous waves?

🧪 Making waves

Purpose: To see the movement of a wave

Materials: string, slinky

Activity 1—Procedure:

1. Tie a piece of string to a coil in the center of a slinky.

2. Have two people hold the ends of the slinky and stretch the slinky out on the floor. The surface must be smooth so do not try this on the carpet.

3. While one person holds their end still, the other person should move the slinky back and forth to make a wave travel to the other end of the slinky. Pay attention to what happens to the string.

Conclusion: The string moves back and forth but does not move to the end of the slinky. This is similar to the movement of the individual water molecules in the ocean. They move up, forward a little, down and back, but do not move toward the shore. Just as the wave energy moved down the slinky, so the wave energy moves across the ocean.

Materials: small bottle, large bottle, tub or sink

Activity 2—Procedure:

1. Fill a sink or tub with a few inches of water.

2. Place a small cup or bottle on its side against the edge of the sink nearest you and plunge it into the water.

3. Repeat this several times and watch the small waves travel across the sink and break against the other side.

4. Repeat this process using a larger bottle. This produces much larger waves. The larger bottle allows you to add more energy to the water, just as a storm adds more energy to the water and creates bigger waves.

🏅 Wind scale

Wind and waves go together. Sailors need to know the wind and sea conditions before they head out to sea, so a standardized method was developed to help seamen know what they could expect in the open ocean. This method is called the Beaufort Wind Scale.

The Beaufort Wind Scale was developed by Sir Francis Beaufort in 1804. At that time the scale made reference to how the wind would affect a man-of-war, the common ship of the British navy. In 1823 the scale was standardized to wind speed, and in the 1850s the scale was changed to reference how fast an anemometer was spinning in the wind.

The Beaufort Wind Scale uses numbers from 0–12 to indicate the wind speed and also references wave heights on the open ocean. If there is no wind and the sea is glassy, it is given a reading of 0. If the conditions are given a 2, it means the wind is blowing 4–7 miles per hour (7–11 km/h). The wind is described as a light breeze and waves of up to 0.66 feet (0.2 m) can be expected.

Below is a complete chart showing the conditions associated with each level of the Beaufort Wind Scale. These numbers help fishermen and other seamen know what to expect in a certain part of the ocean.

Although the scale goes up to 12, there are 5 different levels of hurricanes, so some countries have extended the scale to describe the actual level of the hurricane.

The Beaufort Wind Scale can be used to describe wind on land as well, but its original usage was for the ocean.

Beaufort Number	Wind Speed Miles per hour (km/hr)	Description	Wave Height Feet (Meters)	Sea Description
0	0 (0)	Calm	0 (0)	Flat
1	1–3 (1–6)	Light air	0.33 (0.1)	Ripples without crests
2	4–7 (7–11)	Light breeze	0.66 (0.2)	Small wavelets; crests of glassy appearance, not breaking
3	8–12 (12–19)	Gentle breeze	2 (0.6)	Large wavelets; crests begin to break; scattered whitecaps
4	13–18 (20–29)	Moderate breeze	3.3 (1)	Small waves
5	19–24 (30–39)	Fresh breeze	6.6 (2)	Moderate waves; some foam and spray
6	25–31 (40–50)	Strong breeze	9.9 (3)	Large waves with foam crests and some spray
7	32–38 (51–62)	Near gale	13.1 (4)	Sea heaps up and foam begins to streak
8	39–46 (63–75)	Gale	18 (5.5)	Moderately high waves with breaking crests; streaks of foam
9	47–54 (76–87)	Strong gale	23 (7)	High waves with dense foam; wave crests start to roll over; considerable spray
10	55–63 (88–102)	Storm	29.5 (9)	Very high waves; the sea surface is white and there is considerable tumbling; visibility is reduced
11	64–72 (103–117)	Violent storm	37.7 (11.5)	Exceptionally high waves
12	>72 (>117)	Hurricane	46+ (14+)	Huge waves; air filled with foam and spray; sea completely white with driving spray; visibility very greatly reduced

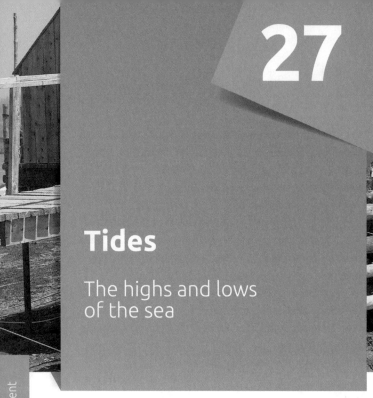

27

Tides

The highs and lows of the sea

What causes the tides on earth?

Words to know:

high tide   spring tide

low tide   neap tide

Challenge words:

tidal range   maelstrom

Currents and waves are two ways that the ocean moves. The third major type of motion is tides. If you stay on the beach for several hours, you will notice that the distance the waves reach up onto the shore changes over time. If you build a sandcastle on the shore where the sand is moist but the waves do not reach, you may be disappointed to find that a few hours later the waves are covering your master-piece and washing it away. This change in water level along the shore is called the tide. At **high tide**, the water level is high and the waves reach farther up on the beach. At **low tide**, the water level is low and the waves do not come up as far on the beach.

Tides are caused by the gravitational attraction between the moon and the oceans. As the moon revolves around the earth, its gravitational pull causes the oceans to bulge toward the moon. This causes the water level along the shores nearest the moon to rise. This is called high tide. The rotation of the earth and moon as a system also causes a bulge to occur on the opposite side of the earth at the same time because of inertia of the ocean water and because the earth is being pulled toward the moon by its gravitational field, yet the ocean water remains left behind. As the moon moves relative to the earth, the bulges of water move as well. When the water is pulled away from the shore, it is called low tide.

The tidal bulge that occurs during high tide in the world ocean follows the revolution of the moon, and the earth rotates eastward through the bulge once every 24 hours and 50 minutes (called the tidal day). Thus, because there are two bulges in the ocean, the moon's movement causes two high tides and two low tides each day. The high and low tides are approximately six hours apart. Coastal areas often publish tide charts to notify people when that area will experience high and low tide. This is particularly helpful for shipping, so ships' captains know what the water level will be at a particular time.

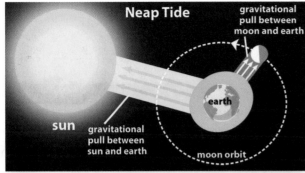

Neap Tide

gravitational pull between moon and earth

earth

sun

gravitational pull between sun and earth

moon orbit

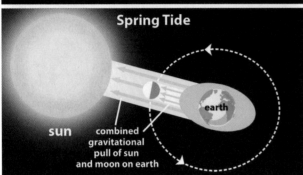

Spring Tide

earth

sun

combined gravitational pull of sun and moon on earth

To a much lesser degree, the sun also pulls on the earth's oceans. When the sun lines up directly with the earth and the moon it causes especially strong tides called spring tides. This occurs twice each month—at full moon and at new moon. Similarly, twice each month the sun is at right angles to the line of the earth and the moon. This results in especially weak tides called neap tides. Neap tides happen halfway between the full and new moons.

All of the motions of the ocean were designed by God to keep the earth a healthy place to live.

This movement helps to more evenly distribute the heat of the sun. It also helps to clean the oceans and keep the plants and animals alive.

What did we learn?

- What is a high tide?
- What causes the water level to change along the shore?
- How often does a high or low tide occur each day?

Taking it further

- Why does a spring tide only occur when there is a full moon or when there is a new moon?
- Since the sun is so much larger than the moon, why doesn't it have a greater effect on the tides than the moon?
- Where should you build your sandcastle if you don't want the water to knock it down?

Ocean movements

Complete the "Ocean Movements Word Search."

🎖 Tidal motions

When we think of the effects of tides we often consider the changes along a relatively flat beach. This is where many people often spend their time near the ocean. While having your sandcastle washed away by high tide may be disappointing, there are serious challenges associated with rising and lowering tides.

The difference between the level of the water at high tide and the level of the water at low tide is called the tidal range. The greatest tidal ranges occur in bays and estuaries where the water is somewhat surrounded by land. Here people must plan for large differences in water levels. The Bay of Fundy in Canada has the highest tidal range with a difference of 49 feet (15 m) between high tide and low tide. This difference can create many challenges for boats and other activities in the areas with large tidal differences. Docks and buildings must accommodate these large differences.

Another challenge created by changing tides is a maelstrom. A maelstrom is a whirlpool or vortex of spinning water (see upper right). You have probably seen a vortex of water when you have watched the water spinning down the drain of a sink or bathtub. However, the vortex formed in a maelstrom is not caused by gravity but by the changing directions of the water during the changing of the tides.

Maelstroms form in narrow shallow straits where the water moves quickly in and out as the tide changes. Opposing currents meet in these shallow areas and cause the water to spin

A maelstrom

downward. These whirlpools form twice a day as the tides change direction.

Although many stories have been written about giant whirlpools in the ocean that can suck a ship into them, actual whirlpools are not very strong. The strongest maelstrom is the *Moskstraumen*, which forms off the coast of Norway. The water can reach speeds of up to 25 mph (40 km/h) and the sound from the crashing waters can be heard miles away. Although unsuspecting people with very small boats could have a problem in a maelstrom, most maelstroms are well documented, and seamen know to avoid them.

28

Wave Erosion

Wearing down the shore

How does wave action affect the shoreline?

Words to know:

erosion

Challenge words:

spit   hook

bay barrier   barrier island

The movement of the oceans is very ben-eficial to the earth. It helps keep the temperatures more even around the world. It helps to keep the water clean and prevents it from becoming stagnant. However, not all ocean movement is beneficial.

As we learned when we studied waves, tsunamis are giant waves that can be generated by earthquakes, volcanic eruptions, or other unusual occurrences. These waves can be very devastating by causing massive flooding and by destroying buildings and damaging shorelines. But tsunamis are not the only kind of waves that cause damage to the shore. Everyday movement of water has an eroding effect on the shoreline. **Erosion** is the gradual wearing away of the land.

When waves reach the shore, the water flows back into the sea. As it does, it drags bits of sand and loose debris with it. Over time, shorelines can be worn away by this constant pounding of waves. People must take this shoreline erosion into consideration when they build near the shore. Buildings built too close to shore may lose their support as the waves wear away the sand and stone around the foundation. Storms that cause high waves, such as hurricanes, can do extensive damage to shores and to the buildings that are built too near the ocean.

Waves wear away the shore as the moving water picks up sand and debris and carries them

The effects of water erosion

out to sea. When the water slows down it drops the sand and debris. The water usually slows down when it hits an obstacle. This causes sand to build up in a particular area. Sometimes the sand can build up near the entrance of a bay and can eventually close the mouth to the bay. This can have devastating effects on the wildlife in the bay as well as on the shipping in and out of the bay.

Finally, water can erode rocks and cliffs near the shore. Sea caves, arches, and pillars have all been built as the waves wear away the rock. Moving water is a very strong force. Whether it comes as a giant tsunami or as a small breaker, moving water can wear away the shore and damage buildings built near the ocean.

What did we learn?

- What causes erosion along a beach?

- What are some problems that can arise from wave erosion?

- What features have been formed along the shore by the erosion from waves?

Taking it further

- Why don't shores completely erode if water is constantly pulling sand away from them?

- How can you protect your building from the damaging effects of tsunamis and other storm-generated waves?

Observing erosion

Purpose: To observe erosion

Materials: sand, paint roller pan, empty plastic bottle

Procedure:

1. Place an inch of sand in the bottom of a paint roller pan. Press the sand firmly up the ramp as well.

2. Carefully pour water into the tray until it begins to go up the ramp.

3. Place an empty plastic bottle in the deepest part of the water and gently move the bottle up and down in the water to create small waves.

4. Observe the effects the waves have on the sand on the ramp of the tray.

Conclusion: The water will eventually wash all of the sand into the deep part of the tray. This is similar to the erosion that occurs along the shores of the ocean.

Erosional landforms

As waves erode the shoreline, they move sand and debris. Sometimes they move the debris back out to sea and other times they move it a short distance before they redeposit it nearby. When the debris is deposited, new landforms develop.

As we mentioned earlier in the lesson, many times the sand is deposited across the mouth of a bay. A land formation called a spit is formed when sand builds up and juts out from the shore into the entrance to the bay. Often a spit forms on both sides of the bay's entrance, but a spit can be on only one side depending on how the waves and currents move. If the spit eventually closes off the mouth of the bay it becomes a bay barrier.

Sometimes the sand is deposited in a curved shape instead of a straight line. This formation is called a hook.

Often the sand is deposited in the bay but it is not connected to the land. This formation is called a barrier island. There are many barrier islands off the southeast coast of the United States.

Demonstrate your understanding of the landforms that are made by wave erosion by completing the "Erosional Land Formations" worksheet.

Breton Island is a barrier island off the coast of Louisiana.

Energy from the Ocean

Making it work for us

How can we use the ocean to produce energy?

Words to know:

tidal barrage

We have learned that the movement of the ocean can be very beneficial and can be very destructive as well. The movement of the ocean is a result of energy being applied to the water. Scientists and engineers would like to be able to harness this energy and convert it to electricity for people to use. Several different ideas have been tried to collect and use the ocean's kinetic energy.

One way to use the movement of the ocean to generate electricity is by building a tidal barrage. A tidal barrage is a wall or dam that is built across a tidal channel where a large river flows into the ocean. The water flows through the barrage as the tide rises and lowers. The movement of the water through this wall causes a turbine to rotate and thus generate electricity. A tidal barrage power station has been built and is in use in La Rance in northwest France. However, tidal barrages can only be built in a few areas around the world where there is a continuous flow of water in and out of the river and where there is a large difference between low tide and high tide. Also, tidal barrages can drastically change habitats for birds, fish, and other wildlife near the river and in the ocean so they are not widely used.

Another way to get energy from the ocean is to use the power of the waves. Many different ideas are being tested to convert wave energy into electricity. Some wave energy converters float in the water like a buoy. These buoys move up and down with the waves. This movement is then converted into electricity which is transmitted to shore through underground cables. Other

Scientists want to generate electricity from the motion of the tides and waves.

wave energy converters are installed below the surface of the ocean and use the movement and pressure differences below the surface to generate electricity. A third method that is being tested to generate power from the ocean does not use the motion of the water but uses the difference in temperature between the surface of tropical waters and the temperature of the water at lower depths. A heat exchanger uses the heat from warm water near the surface to evaporate ammonia. Then, cool water pumped from 1,600 feet (488 m) below the surface is used to cool the ammonia. When the ammonia condenses, it produces heat that is then used to turn water into steam, which in turn moves turbines to generate electricity. This is not a very efficient way to generate electricity, but scientists will continue to develop better methods of using this energy.

Although there are no solid answers as to how best to use the power of the ocean, as scientists learn more about the ocean they will continue to search for ways to harness its awesome power to help provide the energy needs of the world.

What did we learn?

- What are three ways that people are using the ocean to generate electricity?

Taking it further

- Why are tidal barrages used infrequently?

- Why do heat exchangers have to be built near the equator?

- Scientists hope to use the warm tropical waters to generate electricity. What natural weather phenomenon is fueled by these warm tropical waters?

 ## Read about the ocean

Read *The Magic School Bus on the Ocean Floor* by Joanna Cole. This is a fun way to review all you have learned about the ocean and to prepare you for the remaining lessons.

 ## Ocean energy research

Scientists are constantly looking for new ways to harness the energy of the oceans. Do your own research and see what other methods you can discover. Present what you have learned to your class or family so they can know what is happening, too.

UNIT 7

Sea Floor

◊ **Explain** how technology has improved our understanding of the oceans.

◊ **Describe** the basic features of the ocean floor.

◊ **Identify** the ocean zones and the living things found in each.

Sea Exploration

Exploring the depths

What tools do we have to explore the oceans?

Words to know:

submersible

oceanographer

remotely operated vehicle (ROV)

Challenge words:

aquanaut

Exploring the unknown has been a driving passion for many people throughout history. People have explored the land around them. They have crossed oceans and discovered new lands. People have developed technology to explore space. And people have explored the ocean.

At first, people explored what was beneath the surface of the ocean by diving down as far as they could go while holding their breath. This allowed divers to discover many interesting things in shallow areas. Today, snorkeling in shallow water is still very fun and interesting. In some parts of the world, particular groups of people have become so good at diving that they can hold their breath for a minute or more and gather pearl oysters for a living.

But diving in shallow water does not reveal all there is to know about the ocean, so man has developed ways to go deeper and stay under the surface longer. The first diving suit was developed in 1830. It had a helmet with an air tube that went up to an air pump on the deck of the diver's boat. This allowed the diver to stay down for a longer period of time and explore a larger area of the ocean floor.

Then, in 1942, two scientists, Jaques-Yves Cousteau and Emily Gagnan, developed the Aqua-Lung. This was a portable air tank that divers could strap on their backs. This allowed divers to stay down much longer and to have much more freedom to explore the ocean. Improved versions of the diving

Scuba divers

Fun Fact

Many people are familiar with the term *scuba diving*, but few people realize that the term **scuba** means Self-Contained Underwater Breathing Apparatus.

The submersible Alvin descends after launch.

suit and air tanks are used by scuba divers today. Divers can now explore the ocean for several hours at a time.

Unfortunately, even the best diving suit cannot be used in very deep water. The deeper the water, the greater the water pressure, and the human body cannot withstand the pressure in the deeper parts of the ocean. So scientists have developed **submersible** vehicles, mini-submarines that can withstand the great pressure in the deepest parts of the ocean. The first submersibles were developed in the 1960s.

Today, **oceanographers**, scientists who study the ocean, use submersible vehicles to explore many parts of the ocean. These vehicles can carry one or more people, have video cameras to record what they see, and have manipulator arms and storage containers for collecting samples. Submersibles have allowed people to explore and understand many

areas of the ocean that were previously unexplored. Since the development of submersibles, scientists have gained a greater understanding of the ocean's complex ecosystem and have even discovered an unusual ecosystem that survives near the deep-sea vents on the ocean floor.

Submersibles can go as deep as 22,000 feet (6,700 m). To explore below this depth, scientists use **remotely operated vehicles (ROVs)**. ROVs can be

Fun Fact

Ninety-eight percent of the ocean floor is still unexplored. We know more about the surface of the moon than we do about many areas of the ocean.

🧪 Practice diving

How long can you hold your breath? Before the invention of the Aqua-Lung air tank, divers could only explore underwater as long as they could hold their breath. This limited how much of the ocean they could explore.

Purpose: To use a game to explore the importance of air tanks

Materials: deck of playing cards

Procedure:

1. Shuffle a deck of cards and place all of the cards face down in rows on a table.

2. Hold your breath and turn over two cards. If they match, you get to keep them. If they do not match, turn them back over and turn over two more cards.

3. Continue doing this until you can't hold your breath any longer.

4. Try this two or three times to see how many matches you can make in one breath. How many matches did you make in the length of time you could hold your breath?

5. Now repeat, but this time you can breathe normally. How many matches were you able to make in five minutes?

Conclusion: It is much easier for a diver to explore the ocean when he/she can breathe normally.

The ROV Hercules on a deep sea mission

controlled by the mother ship or by a submersible. These ROVs are too small to carry a person, but they still have manipulator arms and cameras, and can

explore nearly anywhere in the ocean. In 1989, the submersible called Alvin sent an ROV named Jason Jr. into the wreckage of the famous Titanic. Jason Jr., or JJ, was able to explore much of the ship and videotape the wreckage for all to see.

Exploration of the ocean's depths has revealed that God designed the ocean with as much diversity and beauty as he designed the land.

🧠 What did we learn?

- What invention in the 1940s allowed divers to more freely explore the ocean?

- How do oceanographers study the ocean today?

- What special equipment do submersibles have?

🚀 Taking it further

- Why does a submersible or ROV need headlights?

- Why can't scuba divers go very deep in the ocean?

- How are submersibles similar to spacecraft?

Fun Fact

The deepest manned ocean descent occurred on January 23, 1960, when Dr. Jacques Piccard (Switzerland) and Lt. Donald Walsh, USN, piloted the U.S. Navy bathyscaphe (submersible) *Trieste* to a depth of 35,797 feet (10,911 m) to the bottom of the Mariana Trench.

🏅 Aquarius laboratory

Most people have heard about the International Space Station, an orbiting laboratory in space where astronauts can conduct experiments in microgravity; however, very few people have heard of *Aquarius*, which is the equivalent of the space station for underwater experimentation. *Aquarius* is an underwater laboratory that can operate up to 120 feet (37 m) below the surface of the water.

Aquarius is a metal cylinder that is approximately 9 feet (2.7 m) in diameter and 43 feet (13 m) long. It is designed to hold up to six explorers, referred to as aquanauts, at a time. It contains many of the luxuries of home including six bunks, a shower with hot water, a microwave oven and refrigerator, computers, and a myriad of scientific equipment.

Missions at *Aquarius* usually last 10 days, but some missions are shorter and some future missions

may be longer. The missions that are conducted at *Aquarius* have several purposes. The U.S. Navy trains divers there and NASA trains astronauts. Also, many oceanographers conduct research on ocean life from *Aquarius*.

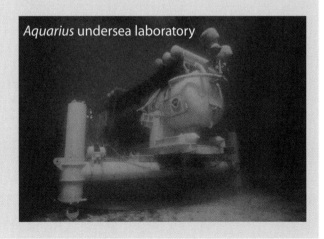
Aquarius undersea laboratory

Although divers can start at the surface and dive down to the level of the *Aquarius*, they cannot stay more than about an hour at a time. Researchers who live in the *Aquarius*, however, can work in the depths of the ocean for long periods of time. The main reason they can work for longer periods is because the pressure inside the *Aquarius* is the same as the pressure outside. When the person's body has become adjusted to the pressure, he/she can stay down in the *Aquarius* for an unlimited length of time and work out of the laboratory. When the mission is completed, the aquanauts go through a 17-hour decompression inside the *Aquarius* before swimming to the surface.

The first underwater laboratory was *Hydrolab*, which was operated by NOAA from 1966–1985. *Aquarius* was first deployed in 1988. After refurbishing, it was redeployed in 1992 in its present location in the Florida Keys National Marine Sanctuary. These permanent underwater laboratories have been instrumental in helping scientists better understand the oceans and the wildlife that is found there.

31

Geography of the Ocean Floor

Mountains and valleys

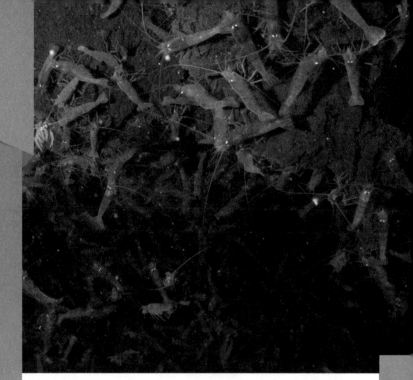

What features are on the ocean floor?

Words to know:

echo sounding	abyssal plain
SONAR	seamount
continental shelf	guyot
continental slope	trench

Looking out at the ocean, one might imagine that it is a giant bowl filled with water. The surface appears relatively flat and smooth. But don't let the surface fool you. Just as the land around us varies greatly, so also the floor of the ocean changes from one location to another. On land we see mountains, valleys, plains, and hills. The ocean floor has many of these same features.

The first record of a group studying the ocean floor was the crew of a British ship called the *Challenger* in 1872. Using a weighted rope, they measured the depth of the water in many locations. They discovered that the ocean floor has mountains, plains, and valleys just as varied as those on land.

Today, we have many different technologies to help us study the sea floor. One method for mapping the floor is **echo sounding** or **SONAR**. A ship sends out a sound wave and measures the time it takes for the sound to bounce back. The deeper the water, the longer it takes for the sound to return. Much of the ocean floor has been mapped in this way.

In addition, divers can explore shallower areas of the ocean firsthand. However, to really see and

The *Challenger*

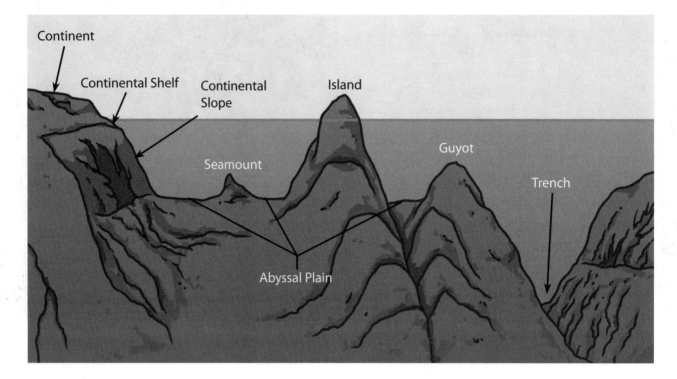

understand the sea floor, scientists use submersible vehicles that are designed to withstand the tremendous pressures of the water at great depths. Some of these vehicles are manned mini-subs and some are remotely controlled vehicles equipped with cameras to send back pictures of remote areas.

The research done in the past 150 years has revealed that the ocean floor has three general areas. First, stretching out from most of the continents is an area called the **continental shelf**. This is a relatively shallow area that slopes gently down from the shore. The width of this shelf varies greatly from one area to another. It can be from 40 to 1,200 feet (10–365 m) wide and has a depth of 0 to 700 feet (0–210 m).

Past the continental shelf, the sea floor drops sharply at what is called the **continental slope**. Past this slope is the third area of the sea floor—the relatively flat area called the **abyssal plain**.

The abyssal plain is not really flat. It is covered with rises, trenches, hills, mountains, and other features.

Fun Fact

The deepest known trench is the Mariana Trench in the Pacific Ocean. Its bottom is more than 35,000 feet (11,000 m) below sea level.

🧪 Seeing the ocean floor

Purpose: To make a model of the ocean floor

Materials: empty aquarium or other glass case, modeling clay

Procedure:

1. In the bottom of an empty aquarium or other clear container, use modeling clay to mold the ocean floor. Start with a thick area near one edge that gently slopes down toward the center. This will be the continental shelf. This should then quickly taper down to the bottom. This sharp drop is the continental slope. The bottom is the abyssal plain.

2. Also include mountains and trenches in the abyssal plain.

3. After you finish the model, fill the tank with water nearly to the top of the continental shelf, leaving a little room for a beach.

4. Review each feature of the ocean floor.

Fun Fact

The pressure at the deepest part of the Mariana Trench is over 8 tons per square inch (11,250 tons/m²).

Underwater mountains are called **seamounts**. If the top of the seamount is flat, it is called a **guyot** (JEE-oh). If the top of the seamount extends above the surface of the ocean, it is called an island.

Deep valleys in the ocean floor are called **trenches**. Many trenches occur near strings of islands. They usually have a very sharp drop on the side near the islands and then slope more gently up on the other side of the trench. So, the next time you look at the ocean, remember that there is much more to see below the surface.

What did we learn?

- What are the three areas of the ocean floor?
- What are some features of the abyssal plain?
- What is a guyot?

Taking it further

- What part of the ocean floor is most difficult to observe?
- What do you think is the most likely cause of seamounts?

Trenches & ridges

Trenches and ridges are two remarkable features of the ocean floor. Trenches are very deep valleys in the ocean floor, and ocean ridges are long mountain chains on the ocean floor. Both of these features are believed to be the result of plate tectonics.

Scientists believe that the earth's crust is composed of several large pieces called tectonic plates. Today, these plates slowly move as they float on the earth's mantle, though they may have moved rapidly during the time of Noah's Flood.

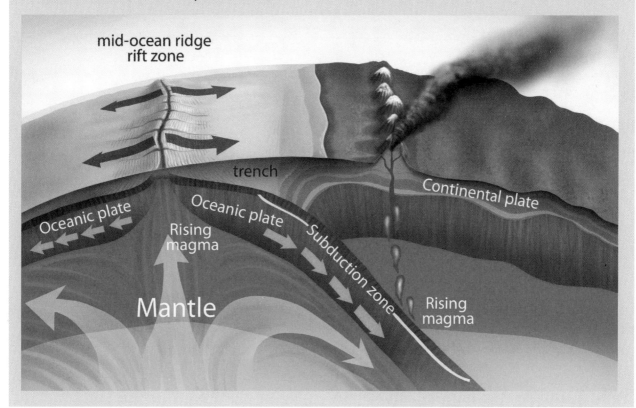

In some parts of the ocean the tectonic plates are slowly moving away from each other. This allows magma (melted rock) to move up onto the ocean floor, creating new land. This is how the ocean ridges are formed.

In other areas, the plates are moving toward each other. When they meet, one plate is pushed down into the mantle under the other plate. This is called subduction. This can cause a deep trench. Most of the trenches in the ocean are believed to be the result of subduction.

Below is a list of some of the most famous ocean trenches and ocean ridges. See if you can find where each is located and draw them on a copy of the world map. Be sure to label each feature on your map.

Famous Trenches

Aleutian Trench	West of Alaska
Cayman Trench	Western Caribbean Sea
The Gully	East of Nova Scotia
Hikurangi Trench	East of New Zealand
Japan Trench	Northeast of Japan
Mariana Trench	Western Pacific ocean; east of Mariana Islands
Puerto Rico Trench	Boundary of Caribbean Sea and Atlantic Ocean
Peru-Chile Trench	Eastern Pacific ocean; off coast of Peru & Chile
Philippine Trench	East of Philippine Islands

Famous Ocean Ridges

Mid-Atlantic Ridge	Middle of Atlantic Ocean
East Pacific Rise	Eastern Pacific Ocean
Emperor Seamounts	Pacific Ocean includes Hawaiian islands
Juan de Fuca Ridge	Off the west coast of Canada and USA
Pacific-Antarctic Ridge	Where Pacific and Antarctic plates meet
Southwest Indian Ridge	Southwest Indian Ocean
Southeast Indian Rise	Southeast Indian Ocean

Sea Floor

32

Ocean Zones

Visiting the different levels

How are the zones of the ocean classified?

Words to know:

sunlit (euphotic) zone	midnight (aphotic) zone
twilight (disphotic) zone	abyss
bioluminescent	

Most sea life can be found in the area above the continental shelf. Here sunlight penetrates the water, allowing abundant algae and plant growth to occur, thus feeding most of the animals in the ocean. However, many interesting creatures live in deeper parts of the ocean as well. But, in deeper parts of the ocean, animals are not found in the quantities that they are found in the shallower waters.

Scientists divide the ocean depth into five zones based on the amount of sunlight that penetrates the water. The first zone is the **sunlit** or **euphotic zone**. This is the water from 0 to 660 feet (0–200 m) below the surface. All plants and algae grow in this zone and most varieties of animals live here as well. Sharks, coral, jellyfish, whales, and most commercial fish and seafood are found in the sunlit zone.

The **twilight** or **disphotic zone** extends from 660 to 3,300 feet (200–1,000 m) below sea level. There are no plants in this zone, but you are likely to see some very interesting animals. The sperm whale, a few coral, the octopus, sponges, and hatchetfish are often seen in the twilight zone. Some of the most interesting animals found in the twilight zone are the **bioluminescent** creatures. These creatures have bacteria living inside them that perform a chemical reaction that produces light. The

Fun Fact

The greatest depth at which a fish has been found is 26,722 feet (8,145 m) below sea level. Sea anemones and sea cucumbers have been found at 35,194 feet (10,727 m) below sea level. A sponge and a sea star were found at 32,767 feet (9,987 m) below sea level.

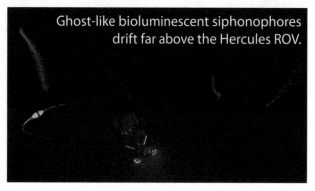

Ghost-like bioluminescent siphonophores drift far above the Hercules ROV.

flashlight fish has light-generating organs under its eyes as well as special eyelids that can be used to cover these organs. The lanternfish has light organs along its sides and bottom. The exact reason for light production in many of these animals is uncertain. Some scientists believe that the light blinds predators. Others believe that these animals use the light to attract mates. But the purpose of the light-generating organ is well known in one bioluminescent fish. The viperfish has an organ that hangs down in front of its face and lights up to attract smaller fish to within striking distance. This feature allows it to capture its dinner. Whatever the reasons for these lights, God created these creatures with a unique and interesting ability.

Below the twilight zone is the **midnight** or **aphotic zone**. No sunlight penetrates to these deep waters. The midnight zone is defined as water that is 3,300 to 13,200 feet (1,000–4,000 m) below sea level.

The water pressure is very high in the midnight zone and only a few creatures can survive here. Some animals that make their home in this zone include eels, anglerfish, sea spiders, and rattail fish. Like the viperfish, anglerfish have the ability to light up to attract prey. An anglerfish can also expand its stomach to allow it to eat something that is twice its own size.

Some animals in the midnight zone serve a very useful purpose by eating bits of dead algae and animals that sink to the ocean floor. The gulper eel can unhinge its jaws. It opens its mouth very wide and scoops up anything that comes in its path, usually dead plants and animals. The sea cucumber also eats the remains of dead plants and animals from the ocean floor. These and other animals help to keep the ocean clean.

The fourth zone in the ocean is called the **abyss**. The abyss is any water that is more than 13,200 feet (4,000 m) below sea level. The water in the abyss

giant trevally

Sunlit zone
(0 to 660 feet)

gray reef shark

octopus

hagfish in sponge

Twilight zone
(660 to 3,300 feet)

anglerfish

rattail fish

Midnight zone
(3,300 to 13,200 feet)

sea cucumber

sea lily

Abyss (deeper than
13,200 feet)

Trench
(very deep canyons)

A field of brachiopods and ophiuroids on the seafloor with several fish, corals, and a sea star in view. Image captured by the Little Hercules ROV at 1,970 feet (600 m) depth on the Paramount seamounts. Notice the large anglerfish in the bottom center of the image.

area is always 32°F (0°C) and the water pressure is extreme. Blood-red prawns have been found in waters up to 16,000 feet (4,875 m) below sea level. Other animals in the abyss include sea cucumbers, starfish, and the tripod fish. Sea lilies, animals that look like feather dusters, have also been seen at these extreme depths. Sea lilies use their feathery arms to push tiny bits of food into their mouths.

The final zone in the ocean is the trench. Trenches are very deep canyons in the ocean floor. Water pressure in the trenches can be more than 14,000 pounds per square inch (1 ton per cm²). This is 1,000 times greater than the air pressure at sea level. Very little life exists in the trenches, although a few sea creatures have been found in these depths.

All of the animals listed in this lesson are ones that are likely to be found in each zone, but you should keep in mind that these zones have been defined by people and the animals don't recognize any barriers in the ocean. So many of these animals can be found in zones other than the ones mentioned.

 ## What did we learn?

- What are the five ocean zones?
- What zone has the most life?
- Where is the sunlit zone located?

Taking it further

- Why is all algae and plant life found in the sunlit zone?
- Why are so few animals found in the very deepest parts of the ocean?

Fun Fact

The giant sea spider that lives in the midnight zone can have a two-foot leg span. It injects its proboscis into soft-bodied animals such as worms to suck out its dinner.

 ## Ocean zones worksheet

Label each zone on the "Ocean Zones" worksheet and draw pictures of plants and animals that have been found in each zone.

 ## Sea creature report

God has created an unimaginable variety of life in the oceans. We have listed only a very few of the interesting sea creatures. Choose a sea creature that you know very little about. Do some research and see what you can learn about it. Be sure to find out which zone it lives in, what it eats, and what its predators are. Find out what makes that animal different from other animals and see what unique characteristics God gave it. Get a picture of your animal to include in your report.

Intertidal Zones

Have you ever been to the beach and seen the tide come in and go out and seen waves crash on the rocky shore? Did you ever wonder what kind of life could live in an area that is under water for hours at a time then dry for several more hours? This area is called the intertidal zone and God designed many algae, plants, and animals that flourish in this area.

The intertidal zone is divided into four subzones. The highest area is called the spray zone and by its name you can tell that it is above the water level most of the time. The water sprays it at high tide. It may get covered with water during very high tides that can be caused by storms, but it is usually not underwater. The plants and animals that live here must be able to go several hours each day with no water. The organisms that live here include barnacles, limpets, lichens, lice, isopods, periwinkles, and whelks.

The next area as we head down the beach is called the high tide zone. This area is flooded during high tide so it is under water two times a day. Since this area is wet or under water more often than the spray zone, it has a wider variety of organisms living in it. These organisms include anemones, barnacles, brittle stars, crabs, green algae, sea stars, isopods, snails, limpets, mussels, whelks, and some marine vegetation. In order to survive during the low tides, anemones, mussels, and other animals close up to keep in the necessary moisture. Also, there are often small fish that make their home in the small permanent tide pools that are formed when seawater is trapped in the rocks after the tide goes out.

The third area is called the middle tide zone. This area is uncovered twice a day as the water goes out during normal low tides. Since this area is under water most of the time the organisms that

A tidal pool on a Welsh beach

live here only have to live a few hours out of the water. Because of this, many types of seaweed grow here. Many of the same animals found in the high tide zone are also found here. In addition, you will often find sea lettuce, sea palms, and sponges.

The last or lowest area is not uncovered on a regular basis. The low tide zone is only uncovered in unusually low tides. The organisms that live in this area can't handle much sun or air. They will dry out quickly. They also can't handle big changes in the temperature. Some of the organisms that live here that are not found in the other areas include abalone, brown seaweed, hydroids, sea cucumbers, shrimp, surf grass, tube worms, and sea urchins.

Looking at the conditions along the shore, it might be hard to believe that anything could live there. But remember that God has a plan and a reason for all things. The pounding waves that make it hard for many animals to live in this area also serve to protect the animals that do live there. We see that God has a plan for every part of the earth.

33

Vents & Smokers

Underwater volcanoes?

What kinds of animals live in the deep ocean?

All plants and algae in the ocean can be found in the sunlit zone, in waters less than 660 feet (200 m) deep. This is because they depend on sunlight. For years, scientists believed that all life in the ocean could be traced back to these producers through the food chain. However, in 1977 divers in deep-sea submersibles discovered an ecosystem that does not depend on plants and sunlight. This eco-system was discovered near what are called deep-sea vents.

Deep-sea vents are found in the midnight zone of the ocean in areas where there is a rift in the sea floor where two tectonic plates are moving apart. The rift fills with hot magma and water flows down into the rift. The water is super-heated by the magma and eventually shoots its way back up to the ocean floor. This water is very hot, sometimes up to 700°F (370°C). This water can be hotter than

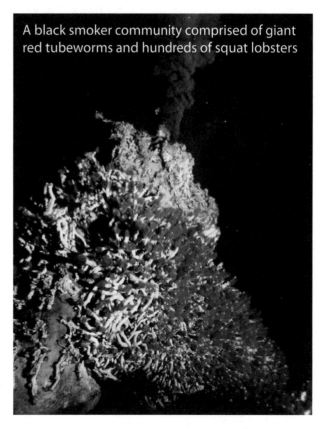

A black smoker community comprised of giant red tubeworms and hundreds of squat lobsters

Fun Fact

In addition to hydrothermal vents, there are thousands of volcanoes on the ocean floor. Usually these volcanoes occur where two tectonic plates are moving apart or where one is sliding under another one. Most of these volcanoes remain unnoticed until their height reaches sea level and an island is formed. Although unnoticed, these volcanoes often produce new land underwater.

A dense bed of hydrothermal mussels covers the slope of Northwest Eifuku volcano near a seafloor hot spring called Champagne vent. Other vent animals living among the mussels include shrimp, limpets, and Galatheid crabs.

the normal boiling point because of the extreme water pressure in the depths of the ocean.

The water flowing from these vents contains high concentrations of sulfur. As the hot water mixes with the cold seawater, the sulfur precipitates out and forms columns of sulfur resembling chimneys. These formations are called black smokers because the water flowing from them is often black with the minerals they contain. Some black smokers have been discovered to be over 30 feet (9 m) tall.

But the most amazing aspect of these vents is the animal life that has been discovered living near them. The key to life near the vents is a very special kind of bacteria. These bacteria thrive on the sulfur in the hot water and provide food for all the other animals that live in this ecosystem. Among these animals are giant tube worms. Some tube worms have been measured to be 10 feet (3 m) long. These worms live in huge colonies around the vents. There are also giant clams, white crabs, and lobsters living near these vents that eat bits of food stirred up by the flow of the water.

This amazing ecosystem shows God's wonderful imagination and creativity in creating systems we did not even expect.

What did we learn?

- What is a deep-sea vent?
- What provides the food source for the animals living near these vents?

Taking it further

- Why were scientists so surprised to find an ecosystem thriving near the deep-sea vents?
- Why can the water stay so hot near the vents without turning to steam?

Discovering new life forms

Imagine what it would be like to be a deep-sea diver who discovers a new habitat. Draw a picture of your new habitat. What types of animals live there? What makes it different from other habitats? Where do the animals get their food?

Studying vents

Ocean vents are located in areas under the ocean where the magma is close to the surface of the sea floor. Thus, most of the vent systems are located in ocean ridges and trenches near the edges of tectonic plates. This is where most of the volcanic activity takes place, and many of the vent systems are actually in calderas or craters of underwater volcanoes. Since the discovery of vent systems on the ocean floor, scientists have wanted to learn more about these interesting ecosystems and to understand the effect these heat vents have on the overall temperature of the ocean.

For over 20 years NOAA has been operating the PMEL (Pacific Marine Environmental Laboratory) Vents program to study the vent systems around the world. Over 70% of all volcanic activity takes place below the surface of the ocean, so it is important to understand the effect that this activity has on the world's oceans.

NOAA uses remote sensors in vent areas to detect temperature changes from the vents as well as to detect earthquake and volcanic activity. The PMEL program also collects water and soil samples so scientists can better understand the effects of mixing the super-heated water from the vents with the colder water in the rest of the ocean.

One of the newest parts of the PMEL program is the deployment of NeMO, the New Millennium Observatory. NeMO is a series of instruments deployed at Axial Volcano on the Juan de Fuca Ridge just west of Oregon. NeMO regularly collects samples of the microbial life around the vents to see the effects that volcanic activity has on these colonies.

NeMO also includes temperature sensors in the hot springs and physical sensors that continuously monitor the movement of the ocean floor. The information from these sensors is relayed to a two-way communication network called NeMO-Net, giving scientists continuous readings from the ocean floor.

With the information that scientists have gained from the PMEL Vents program, they have discovered that volcanic activity under the ocean has a global effect. Therefore, the Vents program has now been divided into two separate groups. The earth-Oceans Interaction Group continues to study the ecosystems around the hydrothermal vents, and the Acoustics group develops tools and technologies to better understand the volcanic activity and other acoustical events in the ocean. They hope to be able not only to detect volcanic and earthquake activity, but also to predict the effects on people and the environment.

Sea Floor

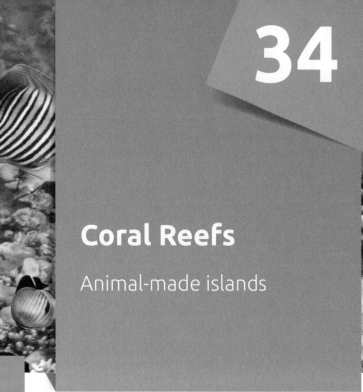

34

Coral Reefs

Animal-made islands

How are coral reefs formed, and what kinds of animals live there?

Words to know:

coral reef   fringing reef

barrier reef   atoll

Challenge words:

uniformitarianism

How can an animal build an island in the ocean? "Impossible" you might say, yet it's true. And most amazing of all, the islands are built by very tiny animals about the size of a pinhead. These tiny animals are called corals. Each coral polyp is shaped a little like an upside-down jellyfish with stinging tentacles. The coral polyp builds a hard cup around itself. As old polyps die, new polyps grow on top of the now empty cups. Eventually, enough coral polyps grow together to form a colony. Many colonies grow together to form a **coral reef**, which is an animal-made island.

Coral reefs can be found in warm clear waters near the equator. Corals obtain food in two ways. First, they can sting tiny animals that float nearby and then pull them into their mouths. But the main way that corals get food is from the algae that live inside their bodies. These tiny algae can convert sunlight into food for themselves and the coral. Because of this need for sunlight, reefs only grow in water less than 250 feet (75 m) deep.

Coral reefs grow in three different formations. A reef that grows from the shore out into the ocean

Fun Fact

An estimated 4,000 species of fish (18% of all living fishes) live on coral reefs and associated habitats of the Indo-Pacific and Atlantic oceans.

Aerial view of a prominent fringing reef in Western Samoa

Aerial view of the Great Barrier Reef

Aerial view of atoll reef formations

Fun Fact

The Great Barrier Reef off the coast of Australia is more than 1,250 miles (2,000 km) long. It is the largest structure on earth built by living creatures. It is larger in area than anything built by man including the Great Wall of China, and it is visible from the moon.

is called a fringing reef. Fringing reefs are found in many areas along the coasts of Mexico and Central America. Other coral reefs grow several miles out from the shore, creating a barrier between the shore and the open sea. These reefs are called barrier reefs. The largest barrier reef in the world is off the coast of Australia and is called the Great Barrier Reef. Finally, some reefs grow in a circle formation. These reefs are called atolls. Atolls begin as fringe reefs surrounding a volcanic island; then, as the volcano sinks (or the ocean level rises), the reef continues to grow and eventually only the reef remains. Atolls can be very small, but some atolls near India are so big that people have built cities on them.

A coral reef is an amazing place. There are more different kinds of animals living in or near a coral reef than in any other ecosystem except the rainforest. First, there are many different kinds of corals. Each type of coral builds a differently shaped colony. Brain coral grows in curving lines that resemble a brain. Staghorn coral looks like the antlers of a deer. Other corals look like fans, whips, or feathers.

Corals alone make the reef an amazing place to visit, but many other amazing animals live in a coral reef as well. There are starfish, sea urchins, sponges, and sea anemones. You will also find eels, crabs, colorful snails, and many different kinds of fish. All of these animals have a unique place in the reef ecosystem. The coral reef is another testimony to God's creativity. ☺

What did we learn?

- What is a coral?
- What is a coral reef?
- What are the three types of coral reefs?

 # Taking it further

- Why are coral reefs only found in relatively shallow ocean water?
- Why might a coral reef be a hazard to ships?
- What could happen to a coral reef if the water became cloudy or too warm for the algae to survive?

 # Coral models

Make a model of a coral colony using modeling clay. Remember that a colony is a collection of thousands of tiny polyps that grow in a unique shape. Colonies of coral can be shaped like ropes, flowers, tubes, or the other shapes mentioned in the lesson. Be creative.

 # How old are coral reefs?

The Great Barrier Reef near Australia is an amazing ecosystem. The reef itself is 260 to 460 feet (80–140 m) thick. The reef has many layers of growth. Evolutionary scientists claim that this thickness represents 600,000 years of coral growth. Yet the Bible indicates that the earth is only a few thousand years old. How can we reconcile these two ideas?

The scientists who claim that the reef is hundreds of thousands of years old are basing that number on the rate of growth that they see currently taking place on the reef. The idea that what we see today has remained constant for very long periods of time is called uniformitarianism. This idea is usually used in looking at geological formations, but is also applied to reef formation. Some scientists say that if the rate of reef growth has remained constant, then the bottom of the reef had to have been formed about 600,000 years ago.

But is this a valid assumption? Does the rate of coral growth remain constant? The rate of growth is dependent on many things, including food availability, water temperature, mineral content of the water, and other conditions in the ocean. Also, scientists have observed growth rates that were much higher than the current rate. In 1997 the growth rate of coral in the Great Barrier Reef was measured to be 5 inches (13 cm) per year at the tips. At this rate the reef could grow to be 1,400 feet thick in only 3,500 years, so it could easily reach a thickness of 460 feet in about 4,500 years. If the growth rate was equal to or greater than the 1997 rate for an extended period after the Great Flood, the reef could have easily reached its current height in the time given in the Bible.

We don't know exactly what the conditions were like in the area near Australia shortly after the Flood, but the conditions could have been good for rapid coral growth. Although we don't have all the answers, we do not have to accept the long-age ideas proposed by evolutionary scientists. God knows the answers and He has given us the truth in the Bible.

The Great Barrier Reef is an extraordinary ecosystem. Research this reef and see what you can find out about it. It will open your eyes to another part of the amazing world that brings glory to God.

35

Conclusion

Appreciating our weather and water

Reflecting on God's creation

We live on a planet that was created "very good." But the Fall changed that, and the Flood reshaped the surface of the earth, and changed its weather patterns.

The earth is mostly covered with water. This water makes life possible on earth. God designed the earth to be the home of man and set the weather patterns in place that bring needed rain and sunshine.

Take a few minutes to read some Scripture verses that describe God's creation of our weather and water, and reflect on what God has made and appreciate the beauty of our world. Read Genesis 1, Psalm 19:1, Psalm 24:1, and Psalm 104.

What is the best thing you learned about our weather and water? Now take a few moments and thank God for what He has done.

Our Weather & Water — Glossary

Absolute humidity   Actual amount of water in air

Abyssal plain   Relatively flat area of the sea floor

Abyss   Water more than 13,200 feet (4,000 m) below surface

Air pressure/Atmospheric pressure   Pressure produced by the weight of air molecules

Air mass   Large amount of air with uniform temperature and humidity

Anemometer   Instrument used to measure wind speed

Atmosphere   Layers of gas that surround the planet

Atoll   Reef growing in a circle formation, usually around a volcanic island

Aurora australis   Southern lights

Aurora borealis   Northern lights

Barometer   Instrument used to measure air pressure

Barrier reef   Reef forming a barrier between the ocean and the land

Bioluminescent   Living animals able to glow in the dark

Breaker   Top of a wave falling over

Cirrus   Clouds that are wispy and curly

Climate   Average weather conditions over a long period of time

Cloud seeding   Dropping silver iodide or other chemicals into clouds to encourage raindrop formation

Coalesce   Water droplets stick together to form larger drops

Cold front   Where colder air replaces warmer air on the ground

Compression wave   Energy wave created by rapid expansion and contraction of air inside a cloud resulting in thunder

Condense   When water vapor cools and turns into liquid water

Continental shelf   Shallow area of land sloping away from the continents

Continental slope   Steep drop off from continental shelf to sea floor

Continental air mass   Air mass that forms over land

Convection   Rising of warm air

Coral reef   Island formed by the collective growth of coral polyps

Crest   Highest point of a wave

Cumulus   Clouds that are fluffy and billowy

Density current   Movement due to differences in density

Desert   Climate with less than 10 inches (25 cm) of precipitation per year

Dew point   100% relative humidity

Dew   Water condensed on the ground

Doldrums   Area with consistently little or no wind, air moving vertically

Doppler radar   Special radar that measures velocity as well as distance

Drizzle   Very tiny rain drops

Drought   A long period of time without significant precipitation

Echo sounding/SONAR   Use of sound waves to measure distances in water

Erosion   Gradual wearing away of rocks and land by moving water

Evaporation   Changing of water from liquid to a gas without boiling

Exosphere   Outermost layer of the atmosphere

Eye of the storm   Center about which a hurricane rotates

Fringing reef   Reef that grows from the land into the ocean

Frost   Water vapor that condenses and freezes on the ground, plants, or other objects

Funnel cloud   A spiraling cloud that does not touch the ground

Global warming   Increase in earth's temperature due to increased carbon dioxide

Greenhouse effect   Trapping of heat in the earth's atmosphere

Gulf   Part of ocean that dents into land

Guyot   Flat topped underwater mountain

Hail   Larger pellets of ice

High tide   When the level of the ocean is high up on the shore

Humidity   Amount of water vapor in the air

Hurricane   Storm forming over the ocean with winds greater than 74 mph (120 km/h)

Hygrometer   Instrument used to measure humidity in the air

Ionosphere Area in the thermosphere where gas molecules are broken into ions by the sun's radiation

Ions Electrically charged particles

Jet stream Very high, fast-moving air currents

Land breeze Cooler air over land moving toward the water

Low tide When the level of the ocean along the shore is low

Magnetosphere Area in the exosphere where protons and electrons become trapped by the earth's magnetic field

Maritime air mass Air mass that forms over water

Mesosphere Layer of atmosphere 30–50 miles (50–85 km) above the surface of the earth

Meteorology Study of the atmosphere

Midnight zone/Aphotic zone Water from 3,300 to 13,200 feet (1,000–4,000 m) below surface

Monsoon Wind that brings moisture from the Bay of Bengal

Neap tide Lower than normal low tide

Nimbus Clouds that are likely to bring rain

Occluded front Where a warm air mass is trapped between two cold air masses

Oceanographer Scientist who studies the ocean

Polar air mass Cold air mass that forms over polar regions

Polar climate Climate characterized by cold temperatures and dry air masses

Precipitation Water that escapes from the atmosphere

Psychrometer Instrument used to measure relative humidity using wet and dry bulb thermometers

Radiosonde Portable weather station taken into the atmosphere by weather balloons

Relative humidity Ratio of the amount of water in the air to the amount of water the air could hold at a particular temperature

Remotely operated vehicle (ROV) Vehicle too small for people, used for exploring deeper than a submersible

Rip current/Rip tide Backflow of waves through a narrow gap in the breakers

Sea breeze Cooler air over the water moving toward land

Seamount Underwater mountain

Sea Part of ocean partially enclosed by land

Sleet Small round pellets of ice

Spring tide Higher than normal high tide

Stationary front Where air masses are not moving

Storm surge Sudden rise in sea level due to movement of a hurricane

Stratosphere Layer of atmosphere 6–30 miles (10–50 km) above the surface of the earth

Stratus Clouds that are stretched out in layers or sheets

Subtropical climate Climate that is mostly warm and moist but with cooler winters

Submersible Mini-submarine for exploring deep in the ocean

Subsurface current Movement below the surface

Sunlit zone/Euphotic zone Water 0 to 660 feet (0–200 m) below surface

Surface current Movement of surface water primarily due to wind and solar heating

Temperate zone Climate that experiences four distinct seasons

Temperature Measure of the intensity of heat in the air

Thermometer Instrument used to measure temperature

Thermosphere Layer of atmosphere 50–370 miles (85–600 km) above the earth

Thunderhead Cumulonimbus clouds forming a thunderstorm

Tidal barrage Wall across the tidal channel of a river to harness energy

Trade winds Winds that blow consistently in one direction

Transpiration Releasing of water vapor into air by breathing or photosynthesis

Trench Deep valley in the sea floor

Tropical air mass Warm air mass that forms over tropical regions

Tropical climate Warm temperatures and more than 80 inches of rain per year

Tropical cyclone/Typhoon/Cyclone Various names given to hurricanes

Tropical depression Spiraling storm forming over the ocean with winds from 25–38 mph (40–60 km/h)

Tropical disturbance   Formed when several tropical storm cells combine over the ocean

Tropical storm   Storm forming over the ocean with winds from 39–73 mph (60–118 km/h)

Troposphere   Layer of atmosphere closest to the earth

Trough   Lowest point of a wave

Tsunami   Giant wave generated by an earthquake or volcanic eruption

Twilight zone/Disphotic zone   Water from 660 to 3,300 feet (200–1,000 m) below surface

Vaporization   Changing of water from liquid to gas by boiling

Warm front   Where warmer air replaces colder air on the ground

Water cycle   Circulation of water primarily by evaporation and precipitation

Water spout   Funnel cloud that forms over water

Wave height   Distance between the highest and lowest part of a wave

Wavelength   Distance between two crests

Weather station model   Standardized method for transmitting weather information

Weather front   Location where two air masses meet

Weather satellite   Satellites which orbit in space and collect weather information

Weather   Conditions in the atmosphere at a given time

Wind   Moving air

Our Weather & Water — Challenge Glossary

Acid rain   Rain with a lower than normal pH level

Advection fog/Sea fog   Forms as wind moves warm moist air over cooler surface

Aerosols   Tiny particles suspended in the atmosphere

Aquanaut   Undersea explorer

Barrier island   Deposited material that forms an island

Bay barrier   Deposited material that closes the mouth of a bay

Brackish   Water that is somewhat salty but less salty than sea water

Caldera   Crater of a volcano

Condensation nuclei   Particles to which water droplets stick when coalescing

Coriolis effect   Circular motion of air due to rotation of the earth

Desalination   Removal of salt from seawater

Distillation   Removal of salt by evaporation

Doppler effect   Frequency of sound or light changes as an object approaches or moves away from the observer

Dropsonde   Canister containing weather instruments dropped from airplanes

Eyewall   The wall of clouds surrounding the eye of a hurricane

Fauna   Animal life

Fog   A cloud that touches the earth

Geosynchronous orbit   Orbiting the earth in the same direction and same speed that the earth moves

Gyre   Large vortex of water formed by converging surface currents

Heat index   Apparent temperature based on actual temperature and relative humidity

Hook   Deposited material that forms a curved shape

Impermeable   Rock that does not allow water to flow through it

Lapse rate   Rate at which temperature decreases as you go up in altitude

Maelstrom   A whirlpool or vortex of spinning water due to changing tides

Permafrost   Soil that never thaws below the surface even in summer

Permeable   Rock with holes that allows water to flow through it

Phased array radar   Radar that sends out multiple signals at one time

Polar orbit   Orbiting the earth from Pole to Pole

Radiation fog   Forms as the earth cools at night

Reverse osmosis   Removal of salt by a special kind of filter or membrane

Spit   Deposited material that forms a straight line from the land into a bay

Spring   A place where ground water comes to the surface

Steam fog   Forms as cool air moves over a warm moist surface

Tidal range   The difference in the level of high tide and low tide

Uniformitarianism   Idea that the rate at which things happen today has been constant throughout history

Upslope fog   Forms as warm air cools as it is forced up the slope of a mountain

Upwelling   Rising of cool, nutrient rich water

Valley fog   Forms as warm air passes over cool air in a mountain valley

Water table   Where the zone of aeration and zone of saturation meet

Weather advisory   Hazardous weather is imminent

Weather outlook   Daily forecast of possible hazardous weather locations

Weather warning   Extremely dangerous weather is occurring or imminent

Weather watch   Hazardous weather is likely but not certain

Wind chill factor   Apparent temperature based on actual temperature and wind speed

Zone of aeration   Top layer of rock through which water flows but does not stay

Zone of saturation   Lower layer of rock filled with water

Our
Universe

UNIT 1

Space Models

◊ **Identify** models used to understand the universe.

◊ **Describe** how models are used in science.

◊ **Describe** how lenses and mirrors are used to explore space.

Introduction to Astronomy

Study of space

What is astronomy, and why should we study it?

Words to know:

astronomy   big bang theory

Psalm 19:1 says, "The heavens declare the glory of God." Since the Bible is always true, we should want to study and understand the heavens so that we can better understand God's glory. The study of the heavens is called astronomy. Astronomy is the study of the planets, moons, stars, and other things found outside of the earth. In this book you will learn about these things and many other things in the universe as well.

Have you ever looked at the stars and wondered what they were or how they got where they are? Have you ever observed the movement of the sun through the sky and wondered how it moves like it does? Then you are asking some of the same questions that astronomers have asked for hundreds of years. Scientists cannot prove where the universe came from. A popular theory among some scientists is the big bang theory—the idea that the universe suddenly came into existence nearly 14 billion years ago and has been expanding ever since. However, in Genesis 1:14–19, the Bible says that God created the sun, moon, and stars on the fourth day of creation, so we know how the sun, moon, and stars got where they are—God created them. Many of the other questions have been answered by scientists as they have observed the universe and studied how things move and work together. In this book, you will learn many of the things that astronomers and other scientists have discovered as well as many things that the Bible has to say about the universe that we live in.

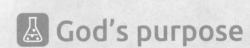

God's purpose

Complete the "God's Purpose for the Universe" worksheet.

🧠 What did we learn?

- What is astronomy?
- Why should we want to study astronomy?

🚀 Taking it further

- What is one thing you really want to learn during this study?
- Write your question or questions on a piece of paper and save it to make sure you find the answers by the end of the book.

🎖️ Knowledge of the Stars

The word *astronomy* comes from two Greek words, which mean "star arranging." It means to arrange or systematize our knowledge of the stars. What knowledge do you have of the stars? Test your knowledge of the stars by completing the "Knowledge of the Stars" worksheet. Try to find the answers to the questions you are not sure of in any books you may have on astronomy or on the Internet.

Space Models

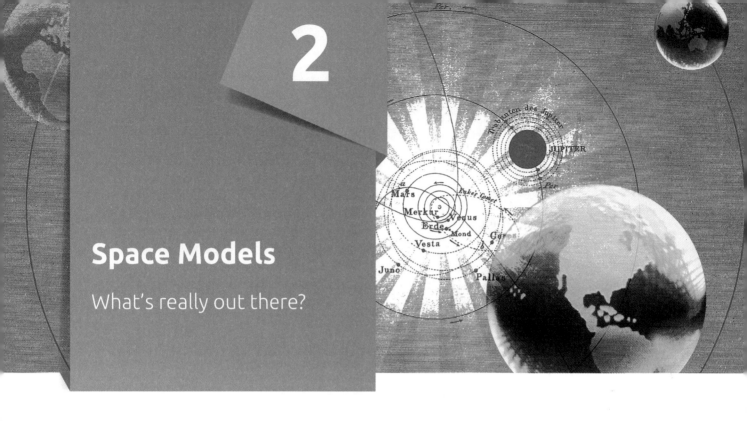

2

Space Models

What's really out there?

How do we know what our solar system looks like?

Words to know:

geocentric model

heliocentric model

law of gravitation

gravity

Have you ever played with a model car or a model airplane? Have you ever built a model train or seen a model space ship? A model is a smaller version of the real thing. It allows you to see and touch something that is too big to actually hold or play with. Space is much too big to hold or even to see completely. So man has invented models to help us understand what the universe looks like and how it works. A model of space can be very useful. These models are often drawings and not three-dimensional toys, although we sometimes see three-dimensional models of our solar system. But how did people figure out what the universe and our solar system looked like and how they work?

Geocentric model

One ancient model of the solar system was based on what is called the **geocentric model,** which means that the earth was believed to be the center of the universe. This model was developed based on several observations. First, the earth appears to be stationary while the sun, moon, and stars seem to move around it. The sun rises in the east and sets in the west. The moon also rises in the east and sets in the west. And the stars move across the sky. Therefore, it made sense to early observers that the earth was in the center and everything else moved around it.

Careful observation also revealed that the sun, moon and the five visible planets appeared to move among the stars. So the early model showed the earth in the center with the sun, moon, and planets

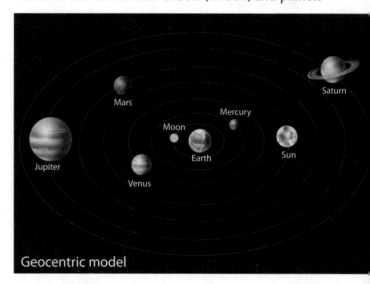

Geocentric model

each in its own sphere spinning around the earth. The stars were believed to be in the outermost sphere. The spheres were thought to be crystal or some other transparent material that allowed the people on earth to view the objects in them.

This model was developed over several hundred years. A Greek scientist named Ptolemy did much of the work, and the geocentric model is sometimes referred to as the Ptolemaic model. However, Ptolemy and others made observations that did not fit well within the theory. Sometimes planets seemed brighter and nearer, and at other times they seemed dimmer and farther away. Also, the planets sometimes appeared to slow down and even move backward with respect to the stars. To accommodate these observations, Ptolemy shifted the earth so it was not in the exact center of the model. He then said that the planets moved in small circles within their spheres to account for the apparent backward motion. This model did not fully explain all of the inconsistencies that were observed, but it was the best model available and, for centuries, was accepted as the way the universe was.

Heliocentric model

Then, during the Renaissance, there was a renewed interest in art, science, and learning. Many scientists began to make careful observations of the heavenly bodies, and new ideas began to emerge. A Polish astronomer named Nicolaus Copernicus developed the idea that the sun, not the earth, was the center of the solar system. This has been called the Copernican or heliocentric model. His model was able to explain many of the problems that had been observed in the geocentric model. Earth moving around the sun just like the other planets would explain why sometimes the planets appeared to move backward. The earth would catch up with slower moving planets, causing them to seem to slow down. Then after passing them, the planets' forward motion could be seen again.

Other scientists that followed Copernicus built on his foundation and were able to explain even more of what was observed. Johannes Kepler was a mathematician who very carefully plotted the movements of the planets and proved that the planets move in elliptical (or stretched) orbits instead of circular orbits, which helped explain why planets sometimes appeared closer than at other times.

The same year that Kepler published his work, another scientist, Galileo Galilei, designed and built his first telescope. He was the first one to study the heavens with a telescope. This invention allowed for much more precise measurements of the heavenly bodies and even better understanding of the workings of the planets and stars.

Finally, in the late 1600s Sir Isaac Newton used his knowledge to explain how all of these heavenly bodies were able to move the way they do. He devised his law of gravitation, which explained how gravity helps to hold all of the planets in their orbits around the sun. Throughout the years many improvements have been made to these theories, but the basic ideas of the Copernican model have

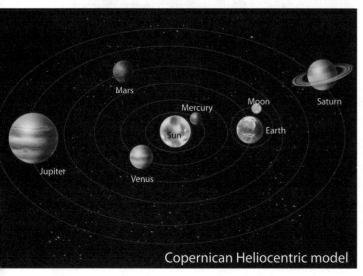

Copernican Heliocentric model

The motion of stars across the sky can be seen with a long exposure photograph.

remained the same. Today we know that the universe is much, much larger than was believed in the 17th century, but the heliocentric model explains what we observe in our solar system.

Law of gravitation

Newton's **law of gravitation** states that everything exerts a pull on everything else. The more massive something is, the stronger its gravitational pull, and the closer something is to an object, the stronger its gravitational pull. Because the moon is very large and very close to us, it has a strong gravitational pull on everything on the surface of the earth.

The earth and moon exert a gravitational pull on each other. Because the earth's mass is much larger than the moon, the moon orbits the earth. Similarly, the sun and the earth exert a gravitational pull on

 # Gravitational pull

Purpose: To demonstrate that the speed at which an object falls due to the pull of gravity does not depend on the weight of the object.

Materials: ping-pong ball, golf ball, piece of paper, book

Procedure:

1. Hold a ping-pong ball and a golf ball. Which one is lighter?

2. Hold them both at the same height and release them at the same time. Which one hit the ground first?

3. Hold a book and a small, flat sheet of paper out at the same height and release them at the same time. Which one hit the floor first? Why?

4. Place the paper on top of the book and drop them at the same time. Did the paper float down slowly this time?

5. Finally, crumple the piece of paper into a small ball. Now, hold the book and the paper ball at the same height and drop them at the same time. Did they land at the same time?

Questions:

- Why did the book hit the ground before the sheet of paper?

- Why did the sheet of paper on top of the book stay with the book?

- Why did the crumpled piece of paper hit the ground at the same time as the book?

Conclusion:

People used to think that heavier items fell faster than lighter items—that seems logical, right? Our activity showed this to be false. The ping-pong ball and golf ball

Leaning Tower of Pisa

should have hit the ground at about the same time even though the golf ball is much heavier. You may think that the book hit the ground before the paper because it is heavier. But you have now shown that is not the reason the paper floated slowly down. The sheet of paper floated down because of air resistance, not the pull of gravity. The paper ball did not have as much resistance to the air as the flat sheet of paper did, so it fell at about the same rate as the book. Understanding gravity is important because the force of gravity pulls objects down, holds our atmosphere in place, and keeps planets in orbit around the sun.

Johannes Kepler

Galileo Galilei

each other. But because the sun is much more massive than the earth, the earth revolves around the sun.

Although Newton is credited with proving the law of **gravity**, he was not the first to recognize that the earth pulls down on objects, nor was he the first to do experiments to test the pull of the earth. According to popular legend, Galileo did many experiments by climbing to the top of the Tower of Pisa and dropping various objects over the side, but this legend is probably not true. Nonetheless, Galileo did perform some ingenious experiments while at Pisa. He experimented with falling objects, projectiles, inclined planes, and pendulums. Galileo discovered that the speed at which an object falls is the same regardless of the weight of the object.

What did we learn?

- What are the two major models that have been used to describe the arrangement of the solar system?
- What was the main idea of the geocentric model?
- What is the main idea of the heliocentric model?
- What force holds all of the planets in orbit around the sun?

Taking it further

- Which exerts the most gravitational pull, the earth or the sun?
- If the sun has a stronger gravitational pull, then why aren't objects pulled off of the earth toward the sun?

Research the scientists

Choose one of the following scientists to research.

- Hipparchus
- Ptolemy
- Tycho Brahe
- Johannes Kepler
- Galileo
- Sir Isaac Newton
- Nicolaus Copernicus

Try to find the answers to the following questions:

1. When did he live?
2. What was the accepted space model at that time?
3. What problems were observed with the accepted model?
4. What contributions did he make to the space model that he believed in?
5. What arguments did he have to answer and how did he answer them in support of the model he believed in?

Write up your answers and present them to others so they can have a better understanding of how we developed the model of space we have today.

Space Models

Nicolaus Copernicus

1473–1543

Nicolaus Copernicus is known as the person who changed the way the world views the universe. However he was not always known as "Nicolaus Copernicus," which was the Latin form of his name. His birth name was Mikolaj Kopernik or Nicolaus Koppernigk.

Nicolaus was born in 1473, in Poland. His father traded in copper and was a magistrate. When Nicolaus was about 10 years old, his father died and his uncle Lucas Waczenrode took him and his family in. His uncle was a canon, or clergyman, at the time.

When Nicolaus was about 15, his uncle sent him to a Cathedral school for three years. After that, he and his brother went on to the University of Krakow. Nicolaus studied Latin, mathematics, astronomy, geography, and philosophy. He later said that the university was a big factor in everything he went on to do. It was there that he started using his Latin name.

After four years of study, he returned home without a degree, a common practice at the time. His uncle wanted him to have a career in the church. To give him the needed background, he sent Nicolaus to the University of Bologna (Italy) to get a degree in canon law. While there, through the influence of his uncle, he was appointed canon at Frauenburg, which provided him with a nice income.

Shortly after this, he asked his uncle if he could return to school to complete his law degree and to study medicine. His uncle probably would not have let him go if he were not going to study medicine. The leader of the Cathedral Chapter thought it worthwhile and gave him the necessary funds. The study of medicine may have been an excuse to study his real passion, astronomy. At this time astronomy was little more than astrology and, therefore, used in medicine. It is not known if Nicolaus ever completed his medical training, but upon

returning home, he worked for about five years as his uncle's doctor.

Although he worked as a doctor, Copernicus continued to study astronomy. At the time, most people believed that earth was the center of the universe and all heavenly bodies orbited around it. However, Copernicus came to a different conclusion based on his studies of the heavens. And in 1514 he distributed a handwritten book on astronomy, without an author's name in it. The book made the following points:

The earth's center is not the center of the universe; the center of the universe is near the sun.

The distance from the earth to the sun is imperceptible compared with the distance from the earth to the stars.

The rotation of the earth accounts for the apparent daily rotation of the stars.

The apparent annual cycle of movements of the sun is caused by the earth revolving around it.

The apparent retrograde motion of the planets is caused by the motion of the earth from which one observes the planets.

These ideas were revolutionary and not commonly accepted, which is why Copernicus published his book without his name in it. This little book was a precursor to his major work, which was completed at the end of his life. Copernicus did not spend his whole life studying and writing, however. In 1516, Copernicus was given the administrative duties of the districts of Allenstein for four years. In 1519, when war broke out between Poland and the Teutonic Knights, he was in charge of defending his area. In 1521 he was able to successfully lead the defense of Allenstein Castle, and an uneasy peace was restored. He was next appointed Commissar of Ermland and given the job of rebuilding the area after the war. Around 1522, he returned to Frauenburg and finally got the peaceful life he was looking for.

Even during the war, Copernicus continued his observations of the heavens. And after returning to Frauenburg, he began to work continuously on his book. Copernicus's theory of the solar system may have remained unknown, however, if not for a young Protestant named Rheticus who came to visit Copernicus in 1539. It was an unusual thing for a Protestant to visit a Catholic stronghold at this time, but Rheticus lived with Copernicus for about two years and helped him get his book published.

Rheticus took the manuscript to a printer named Johann Petreius in Nürnberg. He was unable to stay around and watch over the printing of the book, so he asked a friend named Andreas Osiander, a Lutheran theologian, to oversee it. Andreas Osiander removed the introduction letter originally written by Copernicus, and inserted his own. This substitute letter said that the book was to be used as a simpler way to calculate the positions of the heavenly bodies and not to be taken as truth. Copernicus received his first copy of the book on the day he died, so the switch was not discovered for 50 years.

When Osiander's switch was discovered, some people were appalled; others felt it was the only reason the work was not immediately condemned by the Catholic Church. Regardless of the reasons for the switch, the publication of the book changed the way man looks at the universe. Copernicus's work went on to inspire Galileo and Newton and generations of scientists to follow.

The Earth's Movement

Rotating and revolving

3

How does the earth move, and how does that affect us?

Words to know:

rotation

revolution

solstice

equinox

Challenge words:

Foucault pendulum

Various models of the universe were based upon observations about how the earth and other heavenly bodies move. When the geocentric model was the accepted model, scientists observed that the sun rose in the east and set in the west and that a day was 24 hours long. They also observed that the stars appeared to move through the sky. This led them to believe that these objects moved around the earth. However, these observations can be accounted for in the heliocentric model as well by showing how the earth moves with respect to the sun and the stars.

The earth's movements

Once the heliocentric model was accepted, scientists began to make very careful measurements of how the earth moves. The earth moves in two different ways. First, it rotates on its axis, an imaginary line going from the North Pole to the South Pole through the center of the earth. Second, the earth revolves around the sun.

Rotation

The **rotation** of the earth on its axis explains how we experience the rising and setting of the sun and the relative movement of the stars. It also explains other observations that could not be easily explained by a stationary earth.

The earth bulges slightly around the equator. The diameter of the earth measured at the poles is approximately 7,900 miles (12,700 km), but the diameter at the equator is about 7,927 miles (12,756 km). This difference is caused by rotation. Accurate measurements of Jupiter and Saturn show that they bulge even more around the center because they are more massive and spin faster than the earth. On the other hand, Mercury and Venus bulge less around the center because they spin at a slower rate than the earth.

Another indication of a spinning planet is the movement of air and water masses on earth. The rotation of the earth causes something called the Coriolis effect. Hot air near the equator rises and colder air from the poles moves in to take its place. Without the rotation of the earth, this air would

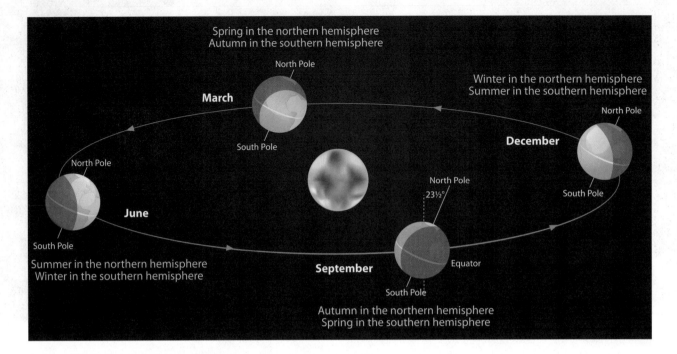

Spring in the northern hemisphere
Autumn in the southern hemisphere

North Pole

March

South Pole

Winter in the northern hemisphere
Summer in the southern hemisphere

North Pole

December

South Pole

North Pole

June

South Pole

Summer in the northern hemisphere
Winter in the southern hemisphere

North Pole

23½°

September

Equator

South Pole

Autumn in the northern hemisphere
Spring in the southern hemisphere

move in vertical lines from the equator to the poles and back. However, what is observed is a diagonal airflow with respect to the earth's axis. This is caused because the air near the equator moves faster than the air near the poles due to the rotation of the earth. The Coriolis effect due to the rotation of the earth also causes cyclones to spin counter-clockwise in the northern hemisphere and clockwise in the southern hemisphere.

Revolution

The second way the earth moves is by revolving around the sun. The path the earth takes in its revolution around the sun is called its orbit. When scientists accepted the geocentric model, they accounted for changing seasons by saying that the sun moved differently around the earth at different times of the year. But seasons are better explained by the earth orbiting the sun and the tilt of the earth's axis. The earth is not completely vertical with respect to the sun. The earth is tilted 23½ degrees from vertical. When the northern hemisphere is tilted toward the sun, the sun's rays are more direct, causing warmer temperatures in that hemisphere during the summer. When the northern hemisphere is tilted away from the sun, the sun's rays hit at a lower angle, causing less heating and therefore lower temperatures in the winter. The seasons are reversed in the southern hemisphere.

The four parts of earth's orbit

The earth's orbit is divided into four parts. The summer solstice, the first day of summer in the northern hemisphere, occurs on June 21st, when the sun's rays directly hit the Tropic of Cancer, which is an imaginary line around the earth at 23½ degrees north of the equator. The earth reaches the halfway point in its orbit on December 21st, the first day of winter in the northern hemisphere, or the winter solstice. This is when the sun's rays directly hit the Tropic of Capricorn at 23½ degrees south of the equator. Halfway between these points is the spring equinox, the first day of spring, which occurs on March 21st, and the autumnal equinox, the first day of autumn, which occurs on September 22nd.

Other observations also point to a moving earth. First, with powerful telescopes, scientists have observed something called parallax of the stars. This is where stars that are closer seem to shift their positions with respect to stars that are farther away as the earth moves through space. To understand parallax, think of standing behind a chair and looking at a picture across the room. From where you stand, the chair would be directly in front of the picture. But if you move sideways a few feet and look at the same picture, the chair would now appear to be to the side of the picture. When astronomers look at stars that are far away, they can see closer stars at the same time. If they look at the same stars several days later, the stars appear to be in different positions with respect to each other because the earth has moved. In fact, a lack of observed parallax was one argument against Copernicus when he first suggested the heliocentric model. He argued that there was a parallax but that they could not observe it because the distances to the stars were too great. He has been proven correct with the invention of powerful telescopes that can now measure these apparent movements.

Finally, it has been observed that more meteors and brighter meteors are observed after midnight than before midnight. This occurs because as the earth rotates on its axis, the area on the earth where it is between midnight and sunrise is on the forward part of the orbit. It is moving toward oncoming debris in space and more collisions will be observed during this time. These observations, as well as many others, support the heliocentric model and demonstrate the rotation and revolution of the earth.

What did we learn?

- What are the two different types of motion that the earth experiences?

- What observations can we make that are the result of the rotation of the earth on its axis?

- What observations can we make that are the result of the revolution of the earth around the sun?

- What is a solstice?

- What is an equinox?

Taking it further

- What are the advantages of the earth being tilted on its axis as it revolves around the sun?

- One argument against Copernicus's theory was that if the earth were moving, flying birds would be left behind. Why don't the birds get left behind as the earth moves through space?

Demonstrating movement

Activity 1—Purpose: To demonstrate how a rotating Earth gives hours of daylight and darkness

Materials: masking tape, volleyball or basketball, flashlight

Procedure:

1. Place a small piece of masking tape on a basketball or volleyball then hold the ball out in front of you.

2. Have another person hold a flashlight representing the sun and shine it on the ball. Slowly rotate the ball.

3. Observe when the light is shining on the piece of tape and when the tape is in the shadow or darkness. This shows how we experience day and night.

Activity 2—Purpose: To demonstrate the observed parallax of stars

Materials: None

Procedure:

1. Hold your arm straight out in front of you with one finger pointing up.

2. Using only your right eye, look at a distant object, noting where your finger is with respect to the object.

3. Close your right eye and look at the object with your left eye. Note how your finger appears to shift with respect to the distant object.

4. Repeat several times, alternating which eye is open.

Conclusion:

The different locations of your eyes represent the different locations of the earth with respect to the stars. It is easy to see the finger appear to move because the finger and the object are both relatively close to you. However, this effect is harder to see with the stars because they are so far away from the earth. Powerful telescopes are needed to see the stars clearly. With modern telescopes astronomers have observed parallax among stars, which confirms that the earth is moving through space.

🏅 Foucault pendulum

Even after scientists concluded that the earth must rotate on its axis, it was very difficult to demonstrate this movement. One idea was to drop a rock down a very deep shaft and see if it moved sideways compared to the shaft. This did not work because the depth of the shaft was very small compared to the radius of the earth, so the sideways movement was too small to measure. A similar experiment was to fire a cannon ball north to south and measure its movement east to west. Again however, the movement was too small to measure.

Eventually however, a French scientist named Leon Foucault devised a way to demonstrate the rotation of the earth. Foucault used a very long pendulum which would swing slowly. He placed marks in a circle on the floor below the pendulum. This allowed an observer to watch the path of the swinging pendulum. Over time, the pendulum appeared to change its path, but what was actually happening was the earth was rotating under the pendulum, thus moving the marks in the circle. This device is called a **Foucault pendulum**.

Purpose: To demonstrate the movement of the earth with your own Foucault pendulum

Materials: copy of "Clock" pattern; needle; thread; tape; modeling clay; tripod; swivel chair, stool, or turntable

Procedure:

1. Tape a copy of the clock pattern to the top of a swiveling chair, stool, or other turntable.

2. Place a tripod on top of the chair and center the tripod over the circle.

3. Cut a length of sewing thread long enough to reach from the center of the tripod to the clock circle.

4. Thread one end of the string through a needle and tie a knot in the thread to prevent the needle from slipping off.

5. Push the needle through a ½-inch ball of modeling clay so that a small amount of the needle sticks through the end of the clay.

6. Tape the other end of the thread to the center of the tripod so that the needle swings freely just above the circle.

7. Start the thread gently swinging across the circle from 12 to 24.

8. Smoothly turn the chair ¼ of a turn to the right. Observe the numbers that the needle is now swinging across.

9. Turn the chair ¼ of a turn more and observe the numbers over which the needle is swinging.

10. Repeat until a complete turn has been made.

Questions:

- What forces are affecting the pendulum?

- Why does the pendulum eventually stop moving?

- How does a Foucault pendulum keep moving for hours or days at a time without stopping?

Conclusion:

Although the tripod and circle are moving with the chair, the swinging of the thread is mostly unaffected by its turning. Full-size Foucault pendulums can be seen in many museums and they demonstrate the rotation of the earth in much the same way as your smaller model.

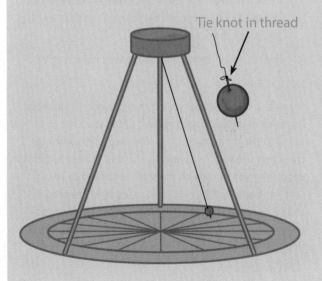
Tie knot in thread

Fun Fact

In 1852, Leon Foucault also invented the gyroscope, a special kind of top that is used in many aerospace applications.

Space Models

4

Tools for Studying Space

Do I need more than
my eyes?

What tools are used to study the universe?

Words to know:

refracting telescope   radio telescope

reflecting telescope

Challenge words:

interferometry

From the very beginning, man has enjoyed gazing at and studying the stars. Yet there is a limit to what man can understand about the universe using only his eyes. Many instruments have been developed to help track the movement of the sun, stars, and planets, as well as to view and measure the distant parts of the universe.

One of the oldest existing structures speaks of man's attempt to understand the universe. Stonehenge is an area in England where large stone slabs have been raised. The builders of Stonehenge are unknown and the exact nature of the use of Stonehenge is also unknown. However, the stones line up in such a way as to mark the summer solstice. These stones track the movement of the earth around the sun. Many other ancient civilizations also built buildings or monuments that mark the seasons.

Ancient devices

Another ancient attempt to track the movement of the sun is the sundial. This device used the shadow cast by the sun as it moved through the sky to indicate the time of day. The changing angle of

Stonehenge

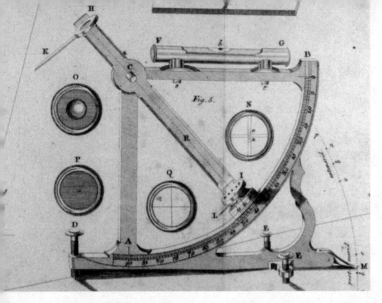

A diagram of a quadrant

Refracting telescopes

But man wanted to know more about the universe. In 1608 Hans Lippershey, a Dutchman, invented the first practical telescope. And in 1609 an Italian scientist named Galileo Galilei built his own telescope and became the first man to use a telescope for viewing the heavens. His was a very simple telescope with a lens at either end of a tube. These lenses magnified the image, allowing more accurate viewing of the stars and planets. The invention of the telescope started a new age of space exploration.

Galileo's telescope was called a **refracting telescope**. Refracting telescopes use two lenses. The first lens refracts or bends the light from the distant star to make a concentrated image. The second lens, the eyepiece, bends the light once more to make the beams parallel again. One problem encountered with this type of telescope was that false colors, called chromatic aberrations, appeared around the image due to the bending of the light. To avoid this problem, the lenses were made thinner so they did not bend the light as much, but this required the telescopes to be much longer. Some telescopes were as long as 200 feet. Today, refracting telescopes use a series of lenses that focus the different colors of light at the same point, thus reducing the false colors.

the shadow from day to day helped to indicate the seasons. Sundials were used for centuries, until the invention of more accurate clocks.

Sailors used a device called a quadrant to mark their location with respect to the stars. A quadrant is a device shaped like one fourth of a circle, with an angular scale and a moveable sight. The quadrant was used to measure the angle that a particular star made with the horizon. Coupled with accurate charts of the stars, a sailor could measure his latitude (distance north or south) with a quadrant. This navigation device was extremely useful and necessary on sea voyages that left sight of land.

Fun Fact

The mirror on the Large Binocular Telescope located on Mt. Graham in Arizona weighs over 16 tons.

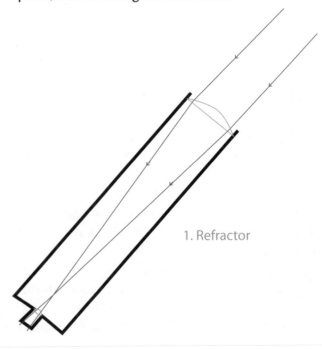

1. Refractor

Reflecting telescopes

Sir Isaac Newton discovered the reason for this chromatic aberration, or false color. It was caused because white light is composed of all colors of light combined, and as the lens bends the light, the different colors bend at different angles. So Newton decided to build a telescope that avoided this problem. He invented the **reflecting telescope**, which uses a combination of mirrors and lenses. Instead of a lens to collect the light, a Newtonian reflecting telescope uses a concave mirror to collect the light and a flat mirror to project the image on the side of the telescope where the eyepiece is.

Newton's design requires that the image be viewed from the side of the tube. A different arrangement of mirrors, called the Cassegrainian reflector, uses a concave mirror at the end of the tube to collect the light, then a convex mirror in the middle to reflect the light back to the end where the eyepiece magnifies the image. This arrangement allows the image to be viewed from the end of the telescope.

Modern telescopes

The basic design of the early refracting and reflecting telescopes is still used today. However, many improvements have been made to the mirrors and lenses, and some newer telescopes called catadioptric telescopes combine both mirrors and lenses in one unit. Also, computer technology has allowed scientists to accurately control telescopes and to observe and record the far reaches of space.

A much more recent invention is the non-optical telescope. One type of non-optical telescope is the **radio telescope**. These devices detect radio waves that are emitted from distant stars. They collect and concentrate these waves so scientists can view other characteristics of stars that cannot be viewed with the eye. These telescopes can also send radio waves and detect what is returned, much like sonar or radar, and collect more information about neighboring planets.

2. Newtonian Reflector

3. Cassegrainian Reflector

Radio telescopes

Space telescopes

One of the most important advancements in telescope technology has been the launching of the Hubble Space Telescope in 1990. This telescope was placed in orbit around the earth to allow astronomers to view the stars without the interference of the earth's atmosphere.

The Hubble Space Telescope has an 8-foot wide mirror and was built at a cost of $1.6 billion. The images from the Hubble are sent to the Space Telescope Science Institute in Baltimore, Maryland, where they are analyzed by astronomers from around the world. In addition to the mirror, Hubble is fitted with instruments that determine the temperature and chemical make-up of distant objects, as well as instruments that measure ultraviolet light, brightness, and infrared light.

When the Hubble Telescope was first launched from the space shuttle *Discovery*, it did not work

The Hubble Space Telescope in 1990, shown here as it was being released from the space shuttle cargo bay.

Refraction & reflection

Purpose: To demonstrate refraction and reflection

Materials: flashlight, magnifying glass, mirror

Procedure:

1. Go into a dark room.

2. Shine the beam of a flashlight through a magnifying glass onto a wall.

3. Observe how the beam is concentrated. Look for rainbows around the edges of the beam's outer circle.

4. Next, shine the beam of the flashlight on a mirror at an angle so that it shines onto a wall.

5. Observe the angle at which the beam reflects from the mirror. What happens to the color of the beam?

Conclusion:

The magnifying glass is a convex lens just like the refracting lens of a refracting telescope. The white light from the flashlight is separated around the edges, and shows up as rainbows on the wall. This is similar to the chromatic aberration that was observed with refracting telescopes.

When reflected with the mirror, the light should remain white. You should not see any rainbows in the reflected light. Most household mirrors are flat mirrors, which just reflect the light at the same angle at which it entered the mirror. This is the kind of mirror that reflects the image to the eyepiece in a Newtonian telescope. Concave mirrors, ones that are curved in toward the center, actually concentrate the light and reflect it in a stronger beam. A concave mirror is the type located at the end of a reflecting telescope.

Optional Activity:

If you have access to a telescope, you can use it to view objects around you during the day, and to view the stars and the moon at night (**but never look directly at the sun**). Some of the most interesting things to see with a telescope are the craters on the moon. Find out what you can about the design of the telescope. Is it a refracting or reflecting telescope? Do you view the objects from the side or the end of the telescope? How powerful are the lenses—how much do they magnify the image?

properly. It was discovered that even after a year of polishing, the telescope's mirror had a flaw that prevented it from focusing the light properly. So, in 1993, another shuttle mission was conducted to repair the telescope. This mission was a success and the Hubble immediately began sending back astounding images. Additional shuttle missions were conducted in 1997, 2002, and 2009 to upgrade the systems on Hubble. These upgrades have allowed the telescope to keep up with current technology and remain useful long past its initial anticipated lifespan. This telescope has provided, and continues to provide, startling new pictures of objects in space and huge amounts of data for astronomers to analyze.

Several other space telescopes have been placed in earth's orbit since the Hubble was launched, and others are planned for future launches. Some are optical, but many of them detect wavelengths that the earth's atmosphere prevents from reaching the ground. These telescopes allow scientists to learn more about the universe every day. Many new discoveries have been made thanks to the use of space telescopes.

Fun Fact

Many land-based observatories (like the Keck Observatory shown here) are built on high hills in remote areas to help avoid light, atmospheric interference, and pollution. The highest observatory in the world is the University of Tokyo Atacama Observatory located on the summit of Cerro Chajnantor, at an altitude of 18,500 ft (5,640 m).

What did we learn?

- What are the three main types of telescopes?
- What was one disadvantage of the early refracting telescope?
- How did Newton avoid this problem?

Taking it further

- Why do you think scientists wanted to put a telescope in space?
- What kinds of things can we learn from using optical telescopes?
- What kinds of things can we learn from radio telescopes?

Telescope advances

Since the invention of the telescope, scientists have understood that the larger you make the opening to the telescope, the more light it will gather, and thus the more you can magnify the image with less distortion. However, there are limits to how big you can make a mirror or lens for a telescope. The bigger the mirror is, the more it becomes distorted by gravity pulling on its own mass. Thus scientists have developed ways to make mirrors larger without increasing this distortion.

The two giant telescopes used at the Keck Observatory on top of Mauna Kea, a mountain on the big island of Hawaii, are 30 feet (10 m) across (pictured at right). A single mirror of this size would have significant distortion; however, these mirrors are actually a series of hexagon-shaped mirrors (shown here) that are precisely fitted together to form one large mirror. Each segment is supported by a structure that can adjust its position with respect to the segments around it. These adjustments are made twice each second. This results in a very large mirror that can gather light from very distant stars and allow the scientists to see more clearly into space.

The large mirror design is only part of the wonder of the Keck telescopes, however. The two telescopes sit 275 feet (85 m) apart. The light from

these two telescopes can be used together to give the equivalent images that a 275-foot telescope could give. The process of combining the light from the two telescopes is called interferometry. The resulting image is brighter and sharper than the image from either of the telescopes individually.

Fun Fact

Mauna Kea is home to more than 13 scientific telescopes. Most are optical telescopes, but there are infrared and radio telescopes there as well.

Purpose: To demonstrate how light pollution can interfere with telescopes

Materials: sheet of paper, black marker, car

Procedure:

1. On a sheet of white paper, use a black marker to write letters like an eye doctor's chart with large letters at the top and smaller letters at the bottom.

2. At night, have someone stand in front of a parked car that has its lights off and hold the sign just above one of the dark headlights.

3. Stand several feet in front of the car. Facing the car, shine a flashlight on the sign. Read as many of the letters as you can.

4. Next, have someone turn on the car's headlights and have the person holding the sign, hold it just above one of the headlights.

5. Again, shine your flashlight at the sign and see how many of the letters you can read.

Question:

When was it easier to read the letters, with the headlights on or off? Why?

Conclusion:

The light from the car interferes with your ability to see the sign. This is called light pollution and is why telescopes are located away from the bright lights of the city and are often on the tops of mountains in areas with few people. Light in the area around the telescope can interfere with viewing the stars.

Space Models

Galileo Galilei

1564–1642

Have you ever gone camping and looked at the sky on a clear night? It can take your breath away. The number of stars you see are past counting. The beauty and splendor of what God has put there for us to enjoy has been the topic of stories and wonder ever since God made the world.

Many men and women have looked at the stars and wanted to know more. Maybe it's because this makes them feel closer to God. Whatever the reason, Galileo Galilei was no exception. He looked at the stars and wanted to know more. What made Galileo exceptional is what he did to learn more about the stars.

Galileo was the son of a professional musician who liked to experiment on strings. Galileo was born in 1564, when his father was 44 years old. His parents felt that Galileo's mathematical and mechanical pursuits did not promise a substantial return. They wanted him to follow a more suitable profession— one in the medical field. But their hope was in vain.

Galileo did not follow the prevailing system of learning, which was always to learn by reading what the authority said on a subject and accept it as truth. To learn about nature, he was told to read Aristotle and accept what he had written as the final authority. However, Galileo wanted to learn through experiments and calculations. This way of doing things brought much controversy to his life.

In 1609 Galileo heard about a spyglass that was invented by a Dutchman and was being demonstrated in Venice. From the reports about this spyglass, and his own understanding of mathematics, he was able to build a telescope with which to observe the heavens. He is believed to be the first to use this technology to observe the stars. The first telescope he built only magnified objects 3 times, making them appear three times bigger than they appear to the naked eye. After more work, he was able to magnify objects 32 times. He later modified the telescope to view very small things, using it as a microscope, or "occhialini" as he called it. He made several of these and gave them to various people to use.

With his telescope, Galileo was able to see many new things in space that had not been seen before. He discovered the moons, or satellites, of Jupiter and saw their orbit around the large planet. Using the telescope to study Venus led to his understanding of how our solar system works, and led him to accept the model of the solar system developed by Nicolaus Copernicus. As Galileo studied the heavens, he noticed that Venus had phases like our moon. This led him to believe that the planets went around the sun and not around the earth. This was called the Copernican model and it was not well received by the leading scientists of the day. They had been influenced by Greek philosophy and viewed Galileo as endangering their positions of authority.

Many in the Church believed that the Bible taught that earth is the center of the universe, and so felt that Galileo's theories would undermine the authority of the Bible. They had interpreted the Bible to agree with the secular Ptolemaic view of the solar system. Others in the Church were at first very open to Galileo's theories, but later, due to political and personal reasons, Pope Urban VIII issued a decree that Galileo be tried for heresy (false teaching).

In 1616 he was tried by the Catholic Church and found guilty of heresy. The Church put him in prison until he died in 1642. But this was not the type of prison you might think of today. He spent most of this time under house arrest, living in the homes of his friends. Throughout this ordeal, Galileo held a strong belief in God and had a deep respect for the Church. He wrote, "I have two sources of perpetual comfort—first, that in my writings there cannot be found the faintest shadow of irreverence towards the Holy Church; and second, the testimony of my own conscience, which only I and God in heaven thoroughly know. And He knows that in this cause in which I suffer, though many might have spoken with more learning, none, not even the ancient Fathers, have spoken with more piety or with greater zeal for the Church than I."

His arrest may have slowed him down but it didn't stop him from his work. He continued to perform experiments and by the end of his life he had given science many ideas that would prove very beneficial. One of the most important ideas discovered by Galileo was the idea of inertia. This theory states that a body in motion will remain in motion unless something acts on it to stop it. This was in direct conflict with Aristotle's view that some force must continuously act on a body to keep it in motion. Galileo was later proven right.

As smart as Galileo was, he still made mistakes. He thought that the tides were caused by the earth's rotation on its axis. He did not consider the gravitational pull of the sun and moon. He also thought that comets and meteors were atmospheric phenomena instead of heavenly bodies outside the earth's atmosphere. But in spite of his mistakes, Galileo contributed greatly to our understanding in many areas of science and is considered by many as the "father of modern physics."

UNIT 2

Outer Space

◊ **Describe** the structure of the universe and galaxies.

◊ **Define** the relationship between stars and constellations.

◊ **Identify** the differences that exist among stars.

◊ **Compare** and **contrast** asteroids, comets, and meteors.

5

Overview of the Universe

How big is it?

Where do we live in space, and how big is the universe?

Words to know:

light-year

Milky Way

constellation

asterism

Challenge words:

celestial equator

prime hour circle

vernal equinox

degrees of declination

hours of right ascension

Exactly how big is the universe? Only God can answer that question. Some scientists believe that radio telescopes reach out to a distance of up to nearly 14 billion light-years, but these distances cannot really be measured. A **light-year** is a measure of distance, not time. It is the distance that light travels in a year and is equal to about 6 trillion miles (9.4 trillion kilometers), so the known universe could have a radius of at least 90 thousand billion billion miles (144 thousand billion billion kilometers). Scientists are not even sure if the universe has an end. With the invention of the telescope, man has learned

a great deal about the universe. But there are still many unanswered questions, and much of what is believed to be true about the universe cannot really be tested or directly observed because of our fixed location on earth and the great distances to objects in space.

Objects in space

We know the most about our own solar system. Our solar system consists of a sun orbited by eight planets and various asteroids, moons, and other objects. Our solar system is part of the **Milky Way** galaxy. Our sun is one of millions of stars that are revolving about the galaxy center. The Milky Way is believed to be shaped like a flat disk with arms extending out like a giant pinwheel, similar to the spiral galaxy shown here. Other galaxies are elliptical, shaped like an elongated oval. Scientists believe that there are billions of galaxies in the universe, all with billions of stars, some with planets, moons, etc.

There are also other objects in the universe including nebulae, asteroids, comets, quasars, and black holes. Scientists are just beginning to understand many of these unusual objects. But one thing that people have understood from ancient times is the movement of the stars through the night sky relative to the earth.

Constellations and asterisms

Stars have been mapped since ancient times. Ptolemy mapped 48 different star patterns around AD 150. The Greeks, Romans, and Babylonians also gave names to many of the star groupings in the night sky. Many of these names were based on the pictures that were formed by connecting certain stars together. Most of these groupings were named after mythological characters.

In 1930, the International Astronomical Union changed the way we talk about star groupings. They defined 88 constellations in the sky. A **constellation** is a region in the sky that contains stars. The entire celestial sphere has been divided into 88 regions, or constellations. All stars, whether bright, dim, or invisible, belong to (are within) a constellation, even if they contribute nothing to forming a recognizable picture. What we often call a constellation is actually an **asterism**, which is a group of stars with a recognizable pattern.

The constellation, Ursa Major ("Great Bear"), is a region in the sky that contains dozens of visible stars. Ursa Major contains the Big Dipper, an asterism made up of seven bright stars that form the pattern of a bowl and handle. Another famous asterism is the Little Dipper in the constellation Ursa Minor ("Little Bear").

Other easily identifiable constellations include Cassiopeia and Orion. By studying star charts, you can learn to locate and identify these and many other constellations.

Because of the rotation of earth and its movement around the sun, the location of various constellations with respect to a particular spot on earth moves throughout the night and from one day to another. A good star guide will help you by showing

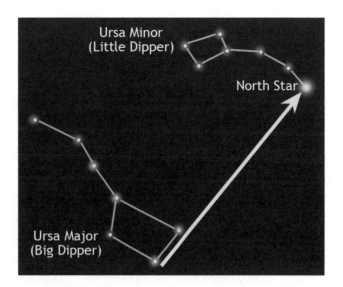

the location of constellations at various times of night and at various times of the year.

Many constellations that are visible in the northern hemisphere are not visible in the southern hemisphere. Sailors used to navigate by the stars and had to learn the different constellations in each part of the world they were likely to visit. By studying the universe, we begin to appreciate the amazing wonder of God's creation.

What did we learn?

- What is our solar system?
- Our solar system is part of which galaxy?
- How big is the universe?

Taking it further

- Why do you think our galaxy is called the Milky Way?
- Why do you need star charts that are different for different times of the year?
- Why do you need star charts that are different for different times of the night?

Observing the night sky

Review many of the most easily identifiable constellations using a good star chart. Then, on a clear night, practice using the chart to help locate and identify these constellations in the sky.

Fun Fact

Several constellations are mentioned in the Bible. Pleiades, the Bear and her Cubs, and Orion are mentioned in Job 9:9, Job 38:31–32, and Amos 5:8.

Locating stars

The whole earth has been divided into areas defined by the lines of latitude and longitude. If you want to locate any spot on earth, you just need the latitude and longitude coordinates. Similarly, the night sky has been defined by lines that are projected from the earth onto the sky. This is called the celestial coordinate system. The plane of the equator is projected out from the earth onto the sky to define the celestial equator. The prime meridian, the longitude line passing through the poles and Greenwich, England, is projected onto the sky and called the prime hour circle. The point in the sky where the celestial equator and the prime hour circle meet is called the vernal equinox.

Using these lines, the night sky map is divided into sections. The lines parallel to the celestial equator are called degrees of declination. Stars that are found north of the equator are given a positive number and those south of the equator are given a negative number. The lines parallel to the prime hour circle are called hours of right ascension. The night sky is divided into 24 sections, or hours, and the star is designated by its location left, or east, of the prime hour circle.

To locate a particular star on the star map, you just need to know its declination and right ascension. For example, the star Sirius is located at -16.7°, 6 hours 44 minutes. This means that the star is located 16.7 degrees below the celestial equator and 6 hours and 44 minutes right ascension from the prime hour circle. With coordinates, it is fairly easy to locate a star on a star map. But actually locating the star in the sky at any given time is not so easy because the earth is always moving with respect to the stars, and a chart that takes into account the date and time must be used.

Although this celestial coordinate system is useful, it is not the only way that scientists locate objects in the universe. In addition, the whole night sky has been divided into 88 areas defined by constellations. To an astronomer, a constellation is an area in the sky, not the picture defined by the stars in that area. The constellations are well defined but are not square or rectangular like the areas on a globe. Instead, they are irregular to match the patterns of the stars.

The stars within a constellation are named according to the constellation. The star is given a Greek letter

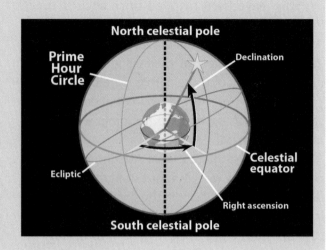

designation followed by a modification of the name of the constellation. The brightest or most important star in the constellation is usually called alpha, the second brightest beta, and so on. For example, the first star in the Big Dipper (also called Ursa Major) is thus called Alpha Ursae Majoris. The second star in the dipper would then be called Beta Ursae Majoris and so on.

There are also naming systems used to identify other heavenly objects. One system is called the Messier catalog. The objects in this catalog (nebulae, galaxies, and clusters) are each numbered and referred to by their number. So the 20th entry in the catalog would be Messier 20 or M20 for short.

Questions:

- Explain how a star map is similar to a map of the globe.

- What units are used to measure declination and ascension?

- How does an astronomer define a constellation differently than most people?

Fun Fact

Polaris, or the North Star, which is the end of the handle of the Little Dipper, does not move with respect to the earth. This phenomenon has helped sailors in the northern hemisphere navigate on the ocean for generations.

Outer Space

6

Stars

Twinkle, twinkle little star

What different kinds of stars are there?

The early study of the stars mostly involved studying the motion of the stars through the sky and charting the constellations. But since the invention of the telescope, and with the aid of modern technology, we have been able to learn a great deal about the stars. Much of what we know about stars comes from our study of the sun. It is the closest star and therefore the easiest to study. We know that stars are hot balls of burning gas. But not all stars are the same. Looking at stars with our eyes alone reveals that some stars are brighter than others and some stars have different shades of color, while others appear to be white.

Brightness and distance

Scientists describe stars by various characteristics, including brightness, distance from the earth, color, size, and motion relative to the earth. The brightness of a star as seen from the earth depends on two things: the amount of light it emits and how far away it is. One of the first astronomers to describe the differing brightness of the stars was a Greek named Hipparchus. Hipparchus assigned a number to each star to describe its brightness. He assigned magnitudes from 1 to 6, with 1 being the brightest stars he could see and 6 being the faintest. We still use the same scale to describe brightness today. However, with the aid of telescopes we can now see stars that are much fainter than Hipparchus could see and some that are brighter, so the scale for stars (apart from our sun) now goes from −1.5 (brightest star—Sirius) to 36 (faintest object in the sky). On this scale of brightness, the full moon would be −13, and the sun would be −27.

The second characteristic of a star is its distance from the earth. The closest star to the earth, not including our sun, is called Proxima Centauri, a star that is part of the Alpha Centauri system. It is approximately 25 trillion miles away from the earth. Because stars are so far away, astronomers use a unit called a light-year for measuring very large distances. One light-year is equal to the distance that light travels in one year (about 6 trillion miles). Therefore, Proxima Centauri is about 4.2 light-years away from earth. Rigel is a star that is about 810 light-years away. And stars in the Andromeda galaxy are over 2 million light-years away. Some stars are billions of light-years away.

Color, size, and relative motion

Color is the third characteristic of stars. Some stars are blue, or bluish-white, while others are yellow, orange, or even red. The color of the star is determined by the surface temperature of the star. Blue stars are the hottest, with a surface temperature believed to be approximately 54,000°F (30,000°C). White stars have a surface temperature of about 20,000°F (11,000°C), while the cooler red stars have a surface temperature that is only about 5,400°F (3,000°C). Our sun is a yellow star and is about 11,000°F (6,000°C) on the surface. Orange stars are about 7,600°F (4,200°C).

Stars vary in size as much as they vary in color. In general, the hotter and brighter stars are bigger and more dense. This is not a hard and fast rule, however, and some smaller stars are hotter than some larger stars.

Finally, stars are described by their motion through space. This measurement does not refer to the movement of the stars through the sky each night or each season, but the movement of stars relative to other stars. Because of the immense distances to the stars, they do not appear to move much, even over hundreds of years. However, some stars that were recorded 1,500 years ago by a Greek named Ptolemy, who made very accurate measurements, have changed location by as much as one degree, or two times the width of the moon.

Whether the stars are near or far, bright or dim, we can enjoy them and recognize the signature of the Great Designer as we look to the skies and see the beauty there. For more information on the stars and how they point to a Creator, do a search on the Answers in Genesis website. 🌐

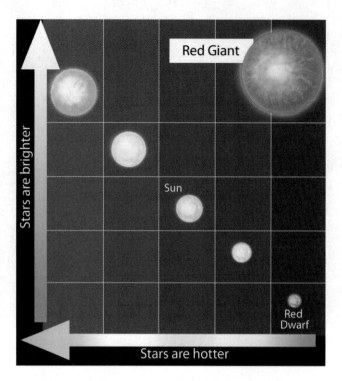

What did we learn?

- What is the unit of distance used to measure how far away something is in space?
- How far is a light-year?
- What does the color of a star tell us about that star?

Taking it further

- What causes stars to appear to move in the sky?
- How can we determine if a star's absolute distance from the earth is actually changing over time?
- Why is brightness not a good indicator of the distance of a star from the earth?

Fun Fact

Sirius emits about 25 times as much light as our sun. Rigel emits about 50,000 times as much light as our sun. But Sirius appears brighter to us than Rigel because Sirius is only 8.6 light-years away, and Rigel is 810 light-years away.

Simulating starlight

Complete the "Starlight" worksheet.

Origin of stars

Where do stars come from? You may get different answers to this question depending on whom you ask. Many evolutionists believe that stars are formed in gas clouds such as nebulae, where the particles of gas and dust clump together and eventually become so dense that they form stars. Pictures of bright areas within nebulae have been used to support this hypothesis. However, the truth is that no scientist has ever witnessed the birth of a star. Particles do not just clump together and become more dense without some outside force pushing them together. What is actually observed inside nebulae is gas that is expanding not contracting. Many scientists will admit that they do not really understand the process by which stars are formed.

So where did the stars come from? According to the Bible, God created the stars on Day 4 of the Creation Week. Psalm 8:3–4 says, "When I consider Your heavens, the work of Your fingers, the moon and the stars, which You have ordained, what is man that You are mindful of him, and the son of man that You visit him?"

Which makes sense to you? To believe the Bible or to believe men who don't really understand the process of star formation and have never witnessed a single star being formed? Take a few minutes and make a couple of calculations that may help you appreciate the situation. Scientists estimate that there are about 100 billion galaxies and that each galaxy contains an average of 200 billion stars per galaxy. How many stars do scientists estimate are in the universe? If you did your calculations right you should have come up with a number that is 2 followed by 22 zeros. Evolutionists believe that the universe is about 14 billion years old. How many stars would have to be formed each year in order for all the stars we have today to exist? This

Many evolutionists believe that stars form in nebulae, like the Orion Nebula pictured here.

would be 1.4 trillion stars per year. Divide that number by 365 days per year and what do you get? That would be about 4 billion stars formed per day, every day for the past 14 billion years. Yet today, scientists do not observe even one new star forming.

This brings up another question. How long does a star live? A star is continually using up energy and slowly burning out. The more massive a star is, the shorter its lifespan. This may seem backwards to you. But the more mass a star has, the more gravity pulls on that mass and the hotter it burns, so it will use its fuel up faster than a less massive star, which burns slower. The brightest stars we see today will burn out in about 10 million years. If the universe is 14 billion years old, how can we still see so many bright stars today? Evolutionists claim that new stars are being born to replace the dying stars, yet we do not actually see this taking place. We can believe the Bible when it says that God formed the stars at the creation of the world only a few thousand years ago.

7

Heavenly Bodies

More than just stars

What kinds of objects do we find in the universe?

Words to know:

nova

supernova

nebula

Objects in the universe can be very far apart. Astronomers have measured star systems that are 100,000 or even 1 million light-years away from earth, and they believe that other systems are billions of light-years away. Some people argue that the earth must be millions or even billions of years old in order for light from so far away to reach here. Some have speculated that the earth looked mature when it was first created, and so the starlight was created in place to reach the earth. Recently, however, a new theory has been suggested that says that due to the intense gravity at the center of the universe when it was created, time moved more slowly in earth's reference frame (predicted by General Relativity), allowing "billions of years" to pass in the outer reaches of the expanding universe while only six days passed on earth. Research into this "problem" continues, but in any case, light from the far reaches of the universe does not prove the earth to be millions or billions of years old. (See Answers in Genesis web page at answersingenesis.org

Stars

The most obvious objects in the universe are the stars. Groups of stars that appear to move together are called star clusters. Some clusters of stars are grouped closely and are called globular clusters. Other stars move together but are spread out and are called open clusters. Star clusters usually consist of thousands of stars.

Larger groups of stars are called galaxies. A typical galaxy consists of millions or billions of stars orbiting around a center. The most common shape for a galaxy is elliptical. Other galaxies are spiral shaped like the one shown bottom left, and others have irregular shapes. Our sun is part of the Milky Way galaxy. The Milky Way is believed to be about 100,000 light-years across.

Astronomers have discovered many unusual stars within these clusters and galaxies. Some stars appear to increase and then later decrease in brightness. One kind of star that varies in brightness is a Cepheid variable star. This is a star that expands and becomes brighter, and then contracts and becomes dimmer on a regular schedule of days

Elliptical galaxy

Spiral galaxy

or weeks. Varying brightness can also be caused by eclipsing binary stars, where two stars revolve around each other. When both stars are side by side they appear as one very bright star, but when one star is in front of the other, they appear to be a single dimmer star.

A **nova** is a temporary flare-up in brightness of a star. At one time, astronomers thought that a nova was an explosion in a single star. However, we now know that a nova is an eruption on the surface of one star in a close binary system. There are many types of novae (plural of nova). The brightest novae can increase their brightness by thousands of times and take months to return to normal. A much brighter eruption on a star is a **supernova**. A supernova may temporarily increase a star's brightness by millions. There are different types of supernovae. Some occur in close binary stars as novae do, but others are explosions of single stars. In 1604, records show that a star became so bright that it was visible during the day—this is believed to have been a supernova.

When a massive star explodes, its core often collapses into a neutron star. This is an extremely dense, small object. Neutron stars spin very rapidly, and emit pulses of radio waves. (If earth is lined up with these pulses, the neutron star is called a *pulsar*.) Some stars are so massive when they explode their core is crushed into a tiny point. The area around this point is called a black hole. Scientists cannot see a black hole, but they see the effects of it. They see a very dense area pulling gas into itself and emitting x-rays. The gravity in a black hole is so strong that nothing can escape it, not even light.

Nebulae

Stars are not the only interesting objects in space. There are also planets, asteroids, comets, and meteors. We will examine each of these in more detail in following lessons. Another interesting object is a nebula. A **nebula** is a cloud of gas and dust that is in space. If there are stars near the nebula, it is called a bright nebula because it glows from the light from nearby stars. The picture at the beginning of this lesson is a bright nebula. If there are no stars nearby it is called a dark nebula. Dark nebulae can only be seen because they block out a part of the sky like a shadow. Some nebulae are believed to be the remains of supernovas. The Crab Nebula was formed when a star exploded in AD 1054. Most nebulae have an irregular shape, but sometimes they can form something that resembles a known object. One dark nebula is called the Horsehead Nebula because it resembles a horse's head. One type of nebula, a planetary nebula, has a ring or disk shape. Planetary nebulae are rings of gases expanding outward from a central hot star.

Quasars

One final unusual object in space is a quasar. Quasars are relatively small objects that are as bright as an entire galaxy. They appear faint because they are very far away. Most astronomers

🧪 Making a nebula

Astronomers can see bright nebulae with telescopes because they glow from the light of neighboring stars. However, detecting dark nebulae is a little more difficult. Astronomers know where a nebula is, even if there are no nearby stars, because it blocks out the light from the stars that are behind it. To demonstrate this, perform the following activity.

Purpose: To see how dark nebulae are identified

Materials: flashlight, pencil

Procedure:

1. Shine a flashlight on the wall.

2. Have someone hold a pencil or some other object in the beam of light and observe the shadow on the wall.

Conclusion:

The shadow indicates that something is blocking the light, even if you can't distinctly see it. The shadow of the pencil shows us its shape, just as the area blocked by a nebula shows us its shape.

think they might be the centers of some distant galaxies with a super-massive black hole at the center causing some sort of energetic action. They appear to be moving away from the earth at very high speeds. There is much controversy regarding these mysterious objects.

God designed the universe to be an astounding place. It is bigger than we can imagine. It has more stars than we can possibly count. And it supplies us with unlimited hours of fascination and research possibilities. So, enjoy studying our universe. 🌐

Fun Fact

A neutron star is so dense that a tablespoon of it would weigh more than all the buildings in New York City.

🧠 What did we learn?

- What is a cluster of stars?
- What is a galaxy?
- Explain the difference between a nova, a supernova, and a neutron star.

🚀 Taking it further

- How can a star appear to become brighter and dimmer on a regular basis?
- Why does starlight from millions of light-years away not prove that the earth is old?

Distant starlight

The most popular evolutionist idea for the origin of the universe is called the big bang theory. According to this theory, about 14 billion years ago the universe came into existence when space began to rapidly expand from a tiny point, called a singularity. Within this expanding mass, planets, moons, stars, and other celestial bodies were formed.

There are several problems with this idea that scientists have not been able to adequately address. First, where did all of the matter and energy in the universe come from to begin with? Second, what caused the singularity to begin to expand? Third, if stars have been forming and dying for billions of years, why don't we see stars forming today? Fourth, how did planets, stars, and other celestial bodies form from nothing but hydrogen gas—the first element in the big bang? The laws of science tell us that particles would be spread out in all directions, and not come together to form planets and stars.

The Bible clearly states that God created the universe and everything in it. However, there is one important question that creationists are trying to answer. If the universe was created only a few thousand years ago, how can we see light from a star that is millions of light-years away? It seems that the light from that star would have originated millions of years ago, yet the Bible says that everything was created only a few thousand years ago. Although creationists disagree on what is the best answer to this "problem," there are several possibilities.

One theory proposes that the speed of light was faster in the past than it is today, so light would cover more distance in less time. This would mean that a star would not have to be millions of years old for its light to reach the earth. Not everyone agrees that this is a good explanation, but some people say it is possible. Another theory uses Einstein's theory of relativity that explains that time is not constant but is affected by gravitational pull. Thus, if the earth is near the center of the universe, a few thousand years may have passed here, while millions of years passed at the edge of the expanding universe. During the Creation Week, while six days passed from the perspective of earth, billions of years could have passed in the far reaches of space. This theory is supported by many of the observations that we see, but is still being investigated.

If scientists cannot explain how we see distant starlight, does this mean the Bible is wrong? No. There have been, and there still are, many areas of science that cannot be adequately explained. Yet, the Bible is God's Word and can be trusted.

Astronomy is the study of the objects in the universe. It is the study of planets, moons, stars, comets, and other heavenly bodies. Astronomers seek to observe and understand what these objects are made of, how far away they are from earth, how they function, and how they affect each other. Astrology, on the other hand, is not science, but is based on superstition and on occult practices. Understanding the movement of the stars and using the constellations as a navigation tool is science—astronomy. But using the stars to predict the future is superstition—astrology.

Astrology has its roots in ancient religions including the beliefs of the Babylonians, Egyptians, and Indians. Ancient people believed that heavenly bodies such as the moon, planets, and stars gave off vibrations that could affect the future of particular people. They used the alignment of the stars and planets to predict what would happen in the future. When scientists discovered how far away these heavenly bodies are, it became obvious that their vibrations could not have any effect on people on earth. However, these superstitious ideas still persist. Many people today still believe in horoscopes, which are predictions based on the movement of the stars.

Astrologers make predictions about the futures of other people. Many times these predictions are made after seeking information from a spirit guide. This is witchcraft and should be avoided by all Christians. The Bible says, "There shall not be found among you anyone ... who practices witchcraft, or a soothsayer, or one who interprets omens, or a sorcerer, or one who conjures spells, or a medium, or a spiritist, or one who calls up the dead. For all who do these things are an abomination to the LORD" (Deut. 18:10–12). Using the stars to try and predict the future is obviously against God's will.

God intended the heavens to be a source of joy and wonder. Psalm 19:1 says, "The heavens declare the glory of God; and the firmament shows His handiwork." And Job 38:33 says, "Do you know the ordinances of the heavens? Can you set their dominion over the earth?" We should study to understand the way the universe works, but we should not be superstitious in our study of the heavens. We should instead look for ways to glorify God in our study of the universe He created.

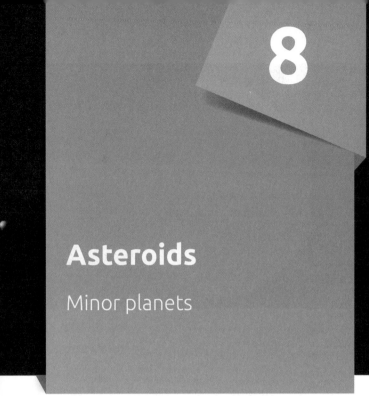

8

Asteroids

Minor planets

What is an asteroid, and where are most of them located?

Words to know:

asteroid   asteroid belt

Relative to the distance between other orbits, there is a large gap between the orbit of Mars and the orbit of Jupiter. However, this gap is not empty. It is filled with what many call the minor planets. These are large pieces of rock that orbit the sun, just as the planets do. Because when they were first discovered they looked star-like to the observers, they were called asteroids, meaning star-like. This area between Mars and Jupiter is called the asteroid belt.

We know today that the asteroid belt contains millions of chunks of rock in a regular orbit around the sun. Most of the asteroids are small, but a few are fairly large. The first and largest asteroid was discovered in 1801, and is called Ceres. Ceres is about 600 miles (965 km) in diameter. Ceres is now considered a dwarf planet. We will learn more about dwarf planets in lesson 27. Other large asteroids were discovered between 1804 and 1807. Pella and Vesta are two asteroids that are over 300 miles (483 km) across and were discovered during this time. These may also be classified as dwarf planets in the future. By 1890, with the improvement of telescopes, over 350 minor planets had been identified. Today, there are more than 600,000 known asteroids, and discovery of new ones continues at a huge rate. A little more than 19,000 asteroids have proper names. The preferred scientific word for asteroid is minor planet.

In an effort to learn more about the asteroids in the asteroid belt, a space probe named Dawn was

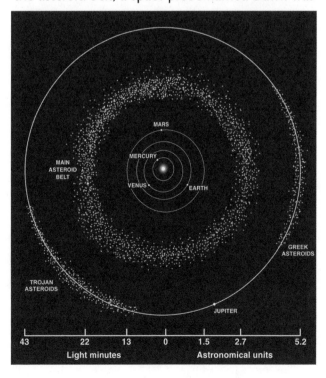

These two views of Ceres were acquired by NASA's Dawn spacecraft on Feb. 12, 2015, from a distance of about 52,000 miles (83,000 km) as the dwarf planet rotated.

launched in September 2007. It orbited Vesta from 2011–2012 and took numerous pictures and other readings of this large asteroid. Then in March 2015, Dawn entered orbit around Ceres. One of the most unexpected things Dawn discovered is that there are several very bright areas on the surface of Ceres. These bright areas appear to be reflected sunlight, but the exact reason for this reflection is unclear. The probe will continue to take photos and readings from the surface of Ceres and will remain in orbit around Ceres even after it finishes its mission.

Asteroid families

Asteroids are objects that are smaller than planets yet circle the sun in a regular orbit. Most of the asteroids in our solar system are found in the asteroid belt. However, some groups of asteroids (called families) have different orbits. The Amor Asteroids have orbits that cross the orbit of Mars. The Trojan Asteroids are in the same orbit as Jupiter.

The Apollo Asteroids cross the orbit of the earth. Hence Apollo Asteroids present the danger of a collision with earth.

All asteroids are relatively small. Because of their small mass, they do not have enough gravity to hold an atmosphere, so they are all lifeless rocks. Still, they are interesting objects to study. At one time it was suggested that the rocks in the asteroid belt may have been a planet that broke apart. But there is no evidence for this and no method that explains how a planet could have broken up and leave its pieces in its original orbit. Besides, if all the asteroids in the asteroid belt were put together, they would still be smaller than the earth's moon—not a very impressive planet.

What did we learn?

- What is an asteroid?
- Where are most asteroids in our solar system located?
- What is another name for asteroids?

Taking it further

- What is the chance that an asteroid will hit the earth?

Naming asteroids

The first person to discover an asteroid in the asteroid belt was an Italian astronomer named Giuseppe Piazzi. He named his discovery Ceres after the Roman goddess of grain and agriculture. Later discoveries were also given the names of Greek or Roman goddesses. But there were many more asteroids than there were goddesses to name them after, so scientists began to name them after famous people. The asteroid Piazzi was named after the astronomer who discovered the first asteroid. Some asteroids were named after cities, flowers, and even pets. Pretend that you are an astronomer that has just discovered five new asteroids. What would you name them? Write down your names on a piece of paper. Remember that most asteroid names have been changed to make them sound feminine. For example, Pittsburghia was named after Pittsburgh with an "ia" added to the end.

Trojan asteroids

When a group of asteroids travels in the same path, especially if it is outside the asteroid belt, the group is called a family. As mentioned earlier, the Trojan family of asteroids travels in the same orbit as the planet Jupiter. All of the asteroids in this family are named after the heroes of the Trojan War. In general, the asteroids shown to the right of Jupiter in the diagram are named after Greek heroes and those to the left of Jupiter are named after the heroes from Troy. Do some research and find out who these heroes were and what they did during the Trojan War. This war is chronicled in the book *The Iliad* by Homer. Then list some of the names of the Trojan Asteroids.

9

Comets

Look at that tail!

What is a comet made of, and how does it travel?

Words to know:

comet

What has a tail when it is near the sun, but loses it when it is far away? A comet does. **Comets** are another interesting phenomenon seen in space. Just like asteroids, comets have a regular orbit around the sun. But unlike asteroids, comets are made mostly of bits of rock and dust surrounded by ice. Comets orbit the sun once every ten to several thousand years. The time it takes to orbit the sun is called the comet's period. Because comets are seen so seldom, they were not always recognized as being the same object from one sighting to the next.

Edmond Halley (1656–1742) was the first

scientist to apply the laws of astronomy to comets. Using Newton's law of gravity, he predicted the orbits for several comets. He found that comets that had appeared in 1531, 1607, and 1682 all had

Edmond Halley

Fun Fact

In 1999 astronomers discovered 91 new comets. Six of these were discovered by amateur astronomers. So keep looking to the sky—you may discover something new.

The dust tail is blue and the ion tail is yellow in this photo.

nearly identical orbits. So he concluded that they were actually the same comet. He predicted that the comet would appear again in 1758. He died before that time. However, when the comet did show up as he predicted, the scientists named the comet Halley's Comet. It appears every 75–76 years. It was last seen in 1986. Halley's Comet has a very elliptical, or stretched, orbit that reaches nearly to Pluto.

Comets have two main parts: the head and the tail. The head of the comet has a nucleus and a coma. The nucleus contains most of the mass of the comet. It is made up of bits of rock and dust that are frozen in a ball of ice. The nuclei of most comets are less than 50 miles (80 km) in diameter. Halley's Comet has a nucleus that is less than 10 miles (16 km) across.

Surrounding the nucleus is the coma. The coma is a cloud of material that has been ejected from the nucleus. It contains gases and dust particles. It can be very large. It reflects light very well and is what allows astronomers with telescopes, and sometimes even observers without telescopes, to be able to see the comet when it passes close to the earth.

The tail of a comet consists of gases and dust particles that are forced back from the coma by the solar wind and the pressure of sunlight. Comets may have one or two types of tails. The ion or gas tail forms quickly and is made mostly of gases that are forced back by the solar wind. The ion tail goes straight out from the nucleus. The dust tail is comprised mostly of dust that is pushed by the radiation pressure from the sun. It forms slowly and curves away from the main tail. The tails of a comet always point away from the sun regardless of whether the comet is moving toward or away from the sun. As the comet gets farther from the sun, its tail shrinks, and when it is far from the sun it does not have a tail at all.

Some comets have only one type of tail. Some have both types. Some comets even have several of each type of tail. The Great Comet of 1744 had six tails!

Comets are fragile and can break apart when they are approaching the sun. Break-up can be rapid. Most comets last for only a few hundred to a few thousand years. Evolutionists cannot explain the existence of comets. If the solar system is actually billions of years old, all of these comets should have completely vaporized by now. Some scientists try to explain comets by saying there are two storehouses of comets beyond the orbit of Neptune, the Kuiper Belt and the Oort cloud, but there is no evidence to support this idea. Discovery of previously unknown comets is due to better telescopes and more astronomers searching the skies. God designed comets and put them in place at creation, and we can enjoy them today. 🌐

Fun Fact

Project Deep Impact launched a space vehicle on December 30, 2004 that impacted the Comet Tempel 1 on July 4, 2005. This impact created a large crater that allowed scientists to study the surface and interior of the comet.

Fun Fact

Comet ISON was discovered in 2012. Its path was expected to take it very near the sun in November and December 2013. Some scientists expected it to be brighter than a full moon and visible with the naked eye. However, the comet broke apart in November 2013 and was not easily visible without a telescope.

Comet model

Purpose: To make a model of a comet

Materials: small Styrofoam™ ball, tagboard/poster board, glue, glitter

Procedure:

1. Cut a small Styrofoam™ ball in half.

2. Glue it to a piece of tagboard as the nucleus of the comet.

3. Using glue and glitter, add a coma around the nucleus and one or more tails to the comet. Be sure to remember that the tail points away from the sun.

 # What did we learn?

- What is a comet?
- Who was the first person to accurately predict the orbit of comets?
- What are the two main parts of a comet?

 # Taking it further

- Why does a comet's tail always point away from the sun?
- Why doesn't a comet have a tail when it is far from the sun?
- When will Halley's Comet next appear?

 # God created comets

Comets can be powerful tools to support the Bible. Explain how what you have learned about comets can support each of the following Scriptures:

1. "Lift up your eyes to the heavens, And look on the earth beneath. For the heavens will vanish away like smoke, The earth will grow old like a garment, And those who dwell in it will die in like manner; But My salvation will be forever, And My righteousness will not be abolished." Isaiah 51:6

2. Then God said, "Let there be lights in the firmament of the heavens to divide the day from the night; and let them be for signs and seasons, and for days and years." Genesis 1:14

3. Thus says the LORD: "Do not learn the way of the Gentiles; Do not be dismayed at the signs of heaven, For the Gentiles are dismayed at them." Jeremiah 10:2

4. "In the beginning was the Word, and the Word was with God, and the Word was God. He was in the beginning with God. All things were made through Him, and without Him nothing was made that was made." John 1:1–3

Fun Fact

The NASA *Stardust* spacecraft returned from a successful mission on January 15, 2006 after retrieving actual particles of gases and dust near the head of comet Wild 2. These are being studied by scientists to help us understand the composition of comets.

Outer Space

10

Meteors

Shooting stars

What is the difference between a meteor, a meteorite, and a meteoroid?

Words to know:

meteor   meteorite

meteoroid

Have you ever watched the night sky and saw what appeared to be a star streaking across the sky? You may have said you saw a shooting star or a falling star. What you probably saw was a meteor. Meteors are objects from space that have been pulled into the earth's atmosphere by gravity. Friction from the atmosphere heats the object up, usually burning it up before it reaches the surface of the earth. Most meteors are visible at 60–80 miles (95–130 km) above the surface of the earth. Some meteors have been clocked at speeds up to 45 miles per second (72,000 m/s)!

Particles in space that are too small to be an asteroid or a comet are called meteoroids. Occasionally, an object comes close enough to the earth to get caught in the earth's gravitational pull. If the object enters the earth's atmosphere, but does not reach the ground, it is called a meteor. If the object is large enough that at least some of it survives the hot trip through the atmosphere and hits the surface of the earth it is called a meteorite. Only about 1 out of 1,000,000 meteors becomes a meteorite. Our atmosphere is part of God's provision to protect us from the debris in space.

Perseid Meteor Shower, August 12, 2013

Fun Fact

There are many craters in various locations around the earth that are believed to be the result of the impact of meteorites. The most famous crater is the Barringer Meteorite Crater near Winslow, Arizona, shown in this picture. It is 4,150 feet (1265 m) across and 570 feet (174 m) deep. The rim of the crater rises 160 feet (50 m) above the surrounding terrain. Scientists believe that the meteorite that struck the area was about 100 feet (30 m) in diameter. They believe that it exploded on impact, causing the giant crater. About 30 tons of fragments have been unearthed, but no large pieces of rock have been found.

Every September for the past several years scientists from NASA have conducted experiments near this crater because the harsh conditions there are similar in many ways to the conditions on the moon and Mars.

Your chances of seeing a meteor depend on many things. You have to be in the right place at the right time and look at the right part of the sky. However, you can increase your chances of seeing a meteor by watching the sky on particular days and at certain times of the night. Beginning in late July and peaking around August 12th of each year, the earth passes through the remains of the tail of a comet called Comet Swift-Tuttle. These meteors appear to move away from the constellation Perseus, and are thus called the Perseids. A similar meteor shower is experienced around mid-November each year, as the earth passes through the remains of the tail of Comet Tempel-Tuttle, which passes through the earth's orbit every 33 years. These meteors are called the Leonids because they always appear to streak away from the constellation Leo.

You also have a better chance of seeing meteors if you look at the sky after midnight. After midnight, your part of the earth is on the leading edge as the earth moves around the sun. Thus, your part of the earth is approaching meteoroids rather than moving away from them. This phenomenon of observing more meteors after midnight is one of the proofs that Copernicus and others used to prove that the earth is moving through space rather than being stationary.

Most meteorites are very small by the time they reach the surface of the earth. But occasionally a large meteorite manages to strike the earth's surface. The largest meteorite ever discovered is the Hoba meteorite, found in Namibia, Africa, in 1920. It weighs almost

The sky is falling

Purpose: To demonstrate how impact craters form

Materials: pie pan, flour, toys, salt, marble, golf ball

Procedure:

1. Fill a pie pan half full of flour.
2. Arrange toys to represent a town.
3. Sprinkle salt over the town and observe any damage.
4. Drop a marble on the town from a height of two feet and observe any damage.
5. Finally, drop a golf ball on the town from a height of two feet.

Questions:

- Did the salt do any damage? This represents the vast majority of the meteorites that hit the earth. Most are so small they fall as dust and are not even noticed.

- How much damage did the marble cause? This represents a few larger meteorites that occasionally strike the earth, causing some damage.

- How much damage did the golf ball do to the town compared to the marble? Did it make a crater in the flour? This represents the very rare large meteorite that can do substantial damage to the earth.

A huge meteor flew over the Urals early on February 15, 2013. The fireball exploded above Chelyabinsk, Russia. It damaged buildings and injured hundreds of people.

70 tons and is so large that no one has attempted to move it from where it landed. Studies have shown that most meteorites are made from silicates and other stone. Most of the remaining meteorites are made from iron. Rarely, meteorites are found to contain stone and iron in equal proportions.

On February 15, 2013, a meteor, which NASA described as a small asteroid, exploded over the Ural region of Russia. The large meteor entered earth's atmosphere at a shallow angle which caused most of it to burn up and resulted in an explosion over Chelyabinsk at an altitude of about 18.4 miles (29.7 km). Over 1,500 people were injured, mostly due to broken glass from windows that shattered in the explosion. Over 7,000 buildings were damaged by the shock wave. Hundreds of small fragments reached the earth's surface but most of the damage was due to the force of the explosion. This was described as a 100-year event, meaning an event like this happens on average only about once every hundred years.

Even though meteorites are relatively rare, if the earth were billions of years old, we would expect to discover hundreds of meteorites in the fossil layers of the earth. However, there have only been a few confirmed discoveries of meteorites in the fossil layers. If, as the Bible says, the earth is only a few thousand years old and most fossils are a result of the Great Flood, we would not expect to find many meteorites in the fossil layers.

A fragment of the Chelyabinsk meteorite. This specimen was found on a field between the villages of Deputatsky and Emanzhelinsk on February 18, 2013.

What did we learn?

- What is the difference between a meteoroid, meteor, and meteorite?
- When is the best time to watch for meteors?

Taking it further

- Space dust (extremely small meteorites) is constantly falling on the earth. If this has been going on for billions of years, what would you expect to find on the earth and in the oceans?
- Have we discovered these things?

What happened to the dinosaurs?

Did a meteor really cause the extinction of the dinosaurs? Many science books today suggest that a very large meteor or comet could have collided with the earth millions of years ago. They suggest that this collision put tons of debris into the air causing the climate to change significantly and the dinosaurs were unable to adapt to these changes and thus died out. But is there any evidence for this kind of an event? A collision of this magnitude would have left a gigantic crater; however, even though a few large craters have been found around the world, none has been found that is nearly large enough to change the climate on a global scale. And if the dinosaurs went extinct because of this global catastrophe, why did many other kinds of animals survive this event with no problems?

Other astronomical events have also been suggested for the demise of the dinosaurs. Some people suggest that a passing comet could have poisoned the air, or a meteorite may have landed in the ocean, causing a giant wave that washed all life out to sea. Another suggestion is that a nearby supernova exploded, poisoning the earth with deadly radiation. None of these ideas has any significant evidence to support it.

What does the Bible say about dinosaurs? You probably won't find the word dinosaur in a concordance, but you can read the following verses and get an idea of what God's Word says about the fate of dinosaurs. Read Genesis 6:19–7:5, Genesis 8:18–19, and Job 40:15–41:10. These verses indicate that representatives of the dinosaurs would have been on the Ark with Noah and were saved from the Flood, but that the rest were killed by the floodwaters. The verses in Job indicate that at least some of the dinosaurs were still alive during Job's life, so some of the dinosaurs continued to live after the Flood. However, it seems that most dinosaurs did not cope well with the changed earth after the Flood and became extinct like many other animals have in the past. For more on dinosaurs and how to explain them using the Bible, do a search on the Answers in Genesis website.

UNIT 3

Sun & Moon

◊ **Describe** the general structure of our solar system.

◊ **Distinguish** between rotation and revolution.

◊ **Describe** the basic structure and function of the sun.

◊ **Use** a model to explain a solar eclipse.

◊ **Describe** the origin and motion of the moon.

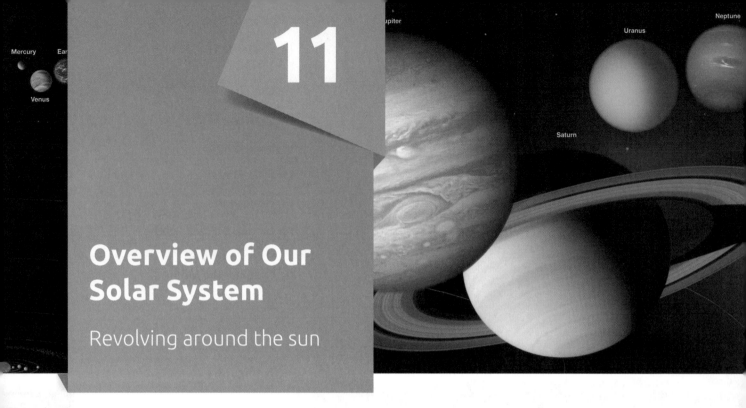

Mercury   Venus   Ear[th]   [Ju]piter   Saturn   Uranus   Neptune

11

Overview of Our Solar System

Revolving around the sun

Sun & Moon

How many planets are there in our solar system?

Challenge words:

elliptical   aphelion

perihelion

The universe is so vast and most objects in it are so far away that it is difficult for us to study them in much detail. Because of this, we are most familiar with the objects in our own solar system. Our solar system is the collection of objects that revolve around our sun. Our sun is one of millions of stars in the Milky Way Galaxy. It is located about ⅗ of the way from the center of the galaxy, in between two of the pinwheel arms.

Our solar system consists of one star (the sun), eight planets, several dwarf planets, many moons, asteroids, comets, and meteoroids. The sun is the largest and most massive object in our solar system. It is a yellow star. Its gravitational pull is what keeps all the other objects in their orbits around it.

Mercury is the closest planet to the sun. It is a dead planet. It is sun-baked and extremely hot. The surface resembles the surface of the earth's moon.

The second planet from the sun is Venus. Venus is covered with a thick layer of yellow clouds made of sulfuric acid. The third planet out from the sun is Earth. Earth is the only planet in our solar system that is able to support life. God designed this planet just for us! The fourth planet is Mars. Mars has a reddish color due to the iron oxide (rust) in its soil. It also has two tiny moons that orbit it.

These first four planets are called the terrestrial, or Earth-like, planets because they are all composed of rocky material. The first four planets are also called the inner planets. Their orbits are all relatively close to the sun. Between Mars and the rest of the planets is a large gap. As you learned in lesson 8, this gap is called the asteroid belt and is filled with asteroids. There are millions of small chunks of rock in this belt and thousands of larger rocks. The largest asteroid in the asteroid belt, Ceres, is about one-third the size of the earth's moon and is now classified as a dwarf planet.

Outside the asteroid belt are the four outer planets: Jupiter, Saturn, Uranus, and Neptune. These are also called the Jovian, or Jupiter-like, planets. This means that, like Jupiter, these four planets are all made of gas. They are not solid like the inner planets. Pluto was considered a planet until 2006 when it was demoted to the status of a dwarf planet. In 2008, Pluto was further classified as a

Relative sizes of the sun and planets

plutoid, which is a dwarf planet that orbits farther away than Neptune.

Of the outer planets, Jupiter is closest to the sun and is the largest planet in the solar system. Saturn is the sixth planet from the sun and the second largest planet. Saturn is most well known and recognized for the thousands of beautiful rings that surround it. The seventh planet is Uranus. Uranus also has a few rings. The eighth planet from the sun is Neptune, a bluish/green gas planet.

Fun Fact

With improvements in technology and increased interest in astronomy, new discoveries about our solar system are constantly being made. For example, in January 2003, scientists announced the discovery of three new moons around the planet Neptune. This was the first discovery of new moons made by a land-based telescope since 1949. Many other new discoveries have been made since the launching of the Hubble Space Telescope. In November 2012, astronomers discovered the most distant galaxy to date. It is 13.3 billion light-years from the earth. In August 1992, astronomers discovered what is believed to be the first observed planet outside our solar system. And in July of 2005, astronomers announced the discovery of what was originally thought to be a tenth planet in our solar system, but is now classified as a dwarf planet called Eris. Eris is 30% more massive than Pluto and orbits nearly three times as far from the sun.

Beyond the orbit of Neptune are Pluto and Eris, classified as dwarf planets. Because these worlds are so far away and so small, and because the first space probe to reach Pluto has not sent back much data yet, we do not know very much about them. They are believed to be terrestrial and composed of a combination of frozen methane, water, and rock.

In addition to the sun and planets, our solar system contains many moons. Several of the planets have moons revolving around them. Some of the planets have multiple moons. There are also many comets and groups of asteroids that orbit the sun. Comets have very elongated orbits and are only rarely visible from the earth.

The outer planets are much larger than the inner planets. One beneficial effect of this for Earth is that the larger planets have larger gravitational pulls and thus capture many of the meteoroids that might otherwise make it to Earth's orbit. This is another example of God's wonderful design for the universe.

What did we learn?

- Name the eight planets in our solar system.
- Name two dwarf planets.
- Which planets can support life?

Taking it further

- What are the major differences between the inner and outer planets?
- Why are the gas planets called Jovian planets?

Learning the names of the planets

You can learn the names and orders of the planets (including Pluto, the dwarf planet) by learning the following song—sung to the tune of "Twinkle, Twinkle Little Star."

Mercury, Venus, Earth, and Mars

These are the planets that dwell with the stars.

Jupiter, Saturn, Uranus, too

Neptune, Pluto, I know them, do you?

Mercury Venus, Earth, and Mars

These are the planets that dwell with the stars.

 # Laws of planetary motion

In lesson 2, we mentioned that Johannes Kepler discovered that the planets move in an **elliptical**, or squashed circle, path around the sun. This was an important discovery because it explained the observations made by many astronomers and showed that God's design was a good and orderly design. Before Kepler's discovery, many people, including Copernicus and Tycho Brahe, struggled to explain the apparent course for Mars. It appeared that Mars moved backward at times with respect to the earth. This was explained by the fact that Earth is moving more quickly through its orbit than Mars is and therefore catches up with Mars and passes it, making Mars appear to move backward (see below). Although Copernicus believed this was the case, he and others could not find a correct path for Mars.

Tycho Brahe made thousands of very accurate measurements of the location of Mars but could

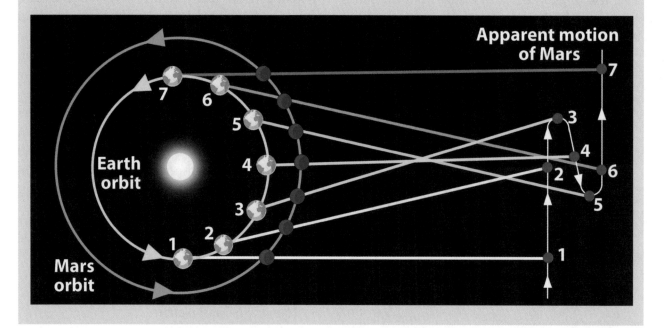

Sun & Moon

not plot its exact course. Then, near the end of Brahe's life, God arranged for Kepler to join him in his work. Kepler had been living in Austria, but when a persecution of Protestants broke out, Kepler left Austria and moved to Prague. There he went to work for Brahe. After many years of work, Kepler finally discovered that the planets move in ellipses.

Through all his work, Kepler discovered three laws that affect the movements of not only the planets, but also the moons and man-made satellites as well. Below are Kepler's three laws of planetary motion:

1. Planets move in ellipses with the sun at one focus.
2. An imaginary line from the center of the sun to the center of a planet always sweeps over an equal area in equal time.
3. The squares of the periods of the planets are proportional to the cubes of their distances from the sun.

These may sound confusing so let's look at what each of these laws means. The first law is pretty straightforward; planets travel in ellipses around the sun. The second law means that when the planet is closer to the sun it moves along its orbit faster, or covers more distance, than it does when it is further away from the sun. The third law means that the time it takes for a planet to make one orbit around the sun increases the farther away the planet is from the sun.

Because the planets do not travel in a circle around the sun, they are not always the same distance from the sun. When a planet is at its closest to the sun it is said to be at its **perihelion** (per-uh-HEE-lee-un), and when it is at its farthest point from the sun it is said to be at its **aphelion** (au-FEE-lee-un). Charts that show distance from the sun usually show the average distance the planet is from the sun. Venus and Neptune have orbits that are nearly circular, so their distance from the sun does not vary as much as planets with more stretched orbits. Pluto has a very eccentric or stretched orbit, and its actual distance from the sun may be very different from its average. Also, Pluto's orbit crosses Neptune's orbit, so sometimes Pluto is the farther from the sun and other times Neptune is the farthest from the sun. The orbits of all eight planets are in nearly the same plane around the sun. The dwarf planet Pluto orbits at about a 17° tilt compared to the rest of the planets, and the orbit of Eris is tilted by 44°. So even though their orbits may cross, the objects will never crash into each other.

Purpose: To demonstrate how Neptune's and Pluto's paths can cross.

Materials: piece of paper, tape, cardboard, two thumb tacks, string, pencil

Procedure:

1. Tape a piece of paper to a piece of cardboard.
2. In the center of the paper place two thumb tacks 3 inches apart horizontally.
3. Cut a piece of string 12 inches long and tie it in a circle and place the string around the tacks.
4. Place your pencil against the inside of the string and pull it tight against the tacks.
5. Draw an ellipse around the tacks by keeping the string tight against the tacks. This represents Neptune's orbit. Label this ellipse with the word *Neptune*.
6. Move one tack in about one inch and up about one inch.
7. Repeat the process to draw a second ellipse. This ellipse will be larger and will slightly overlap the first. This represents Pluto's orbit. Label this ellipse *Pluto*.

12

Our Sun

The center of our solar system

How large is the sun, and how hot is it?

The sun is the center of our solar system; but why is it so important to us? The sun provides light and heat to keep us alive. It provides the gravitational pull needed to keep everything in our solar system in its proper place. And the sun was designed by God to rule the day (Genesis 1:14–19).

The sun has a diameter of 868,000 miles (1.4 million km). It is approximately 100 times bigger around than the earth. The sun is so large that one million earths could fit inside it! The sun weighs about 2×10^{27} tons (that's the number two followed by 27 zeroes), which is 333,000 times as much as the earth. 99% of all of the mass of our solar system is in the sun.

Compared to other stars, the sun is a medium-sized star and is yellow in color. The surface temperature is approximately 11,000°F (6,000°C). The sun is composed mostly of helium and hydrogen. Scientists estimate that the sun contains enough hydrogen to continue burning at the present rate for 5 billion more years. As stars continue to burn, the conversion of hydrogen into helium changes the composition of the core, causing it to grow brighter with age. This is another indication that evolution is false. Evolutionists believe that life arose on earth about 3.8 billion years ago. However, the sun would have been 25% dimmer then, and the earth would have been much too cold to support life. This is called the young faint sun paradox, and shows once again that God's Word can be trusted.

Ninety-seven percent of the sun's energy is electromagnetic energy in the form of light, heat, x-rays, and radio waves. It is theorized that the other 3%

The size of the earth in comparison to the sun.

Earth to Scale

is in the form of neutrinos, which are believed to be tiny particles that can pass through matter and travel at nearly the speed of light. The energy from the sun moves in waves. These energy waves are visible to our eye if they are between 0.0004 and 0.00075 mm long, which are the wavelengths of the various colors of light. Waves that are longer or shorter than this cannot be seen with the human eye. For example, heat waves are longer and x-rays are shorter than visible light.

All of this information is very interesting, but the most important thing to realize about the sun is that God designed it and placed it in just the perfect location for us to live. The sun is just the right distance from the earth to provide heat without burning us up. It provides just the right amount of light for plants to grow and provide the earth with food. The sun may be an ordinary star, but it has an extraordinary purpose for our lives.

For more information on the sun and how it shows God's handiwork, do a search on the Answers in Genesis website.

What did we learn?

- What are the main elements found in the sun?
- What colors are found in sunlight?

Taking it further

- Why is the sun so important to us?
- How does energy get from the sun to the earth?

Viewing sunlight

The light coming from the sun has a yellow tint to it. However, Sir Isaac Newton discovered that sunlight actually contains all colors. If the sun emitted all colors equally, it would give off a pure white light. But it emits colors in the middle of the spectrum more strongly so its light appears yellow. A rainbow reveals all of the colors of sunlight. As the light passes through raindrops in the sky, the different colors of light are bent at different angles and are displayed in the rainbow.

Purpose: To create a rainbow and view all the colors of sunlight

Materials: pie pan, small mirror

Procedure:

1. Fill a pie pan with water and place it on a level surface near a window.

2. Hold a small mirror partially in the water at an angle so that sunlight that passes through the water to the mirror is reflected onto a wall.

Conclusion:

The light reflected by the part of the mirror that is out of the water will be white, but the light reflected after it has passed through the water will make a rainbow. Water acts like a prism. Different colors of light travel at different speeds through water so the colors spread out and can be seen separately. If you have a prism available, try passing the sunlight through it and see how it separates the colors, too.

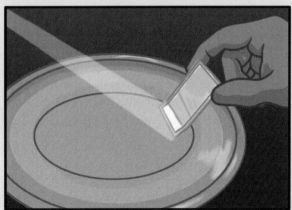

🎖 Diameter of the sun

Measuring the exact diameter of the sun is a difficult thing. The surface of the sun is constantly changing so exact measurements cannot be made. But scientists have determined that the diameter of the sun is approximately 868,000 miles (1,400,000 km). Using a little math, you can make some simple measurements and calculate the approximate diameter of the sun without needing any fancy scientific equipment. All you need is a pinhole projector.

Purpose: To calculate the diameter of the sun using a pinhole projector

Materials: needle, two index cards, tape, meter stick, ruler, calculator, "Sun Measurement" worksheet

Procedure:

1. Use a needle to punch a small hole in the center of an index card.

2. Tape the index card to the end of a meter (or yard) stick so that the card is perpendicular to the stick.

3. Tape a second card to the other end of the stick so that it is also perpendicular to it.

4. Go outside on a sunny day and place the end of the stick with the card that does not have the hole against the ground.

5. Move the top of the stick until the shadow of the top card falls on the bottom card. You should see a projection of the sun (it looks like a white circle) on the bottom card. **Do not look directly at the sun; it can damage your eyes!**

6. Use a ruler to measure the diameter of the image that is projected onto the bottom card. If the cards are taped to a meter stick, measure the diameter of the image to the nearest 1/10 of a millimeter. If the cards are taped to a yardstick, measure the diameter of the image to the nearest 1/16 of an inch.

Pin hole

Sun projection

7. Record the measurements on the "Sun Measurement" worksheet. Make at least three measurements to try to eliminate error, then find the average of the measurements.

8. Next, follow the instructions on the worksheet to determine the diameter of the sun.

13

Structure of the Sun

What is it like on the inside?

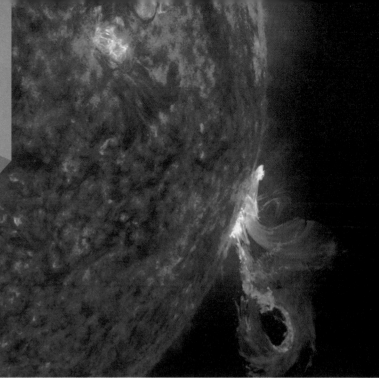

What are the different layers of the sun?

Words to know:

chromosphere	aurora australis
corona	core
sunspot	radiative zone
aurora borealis	convective zone

Challenge words:

umbra	penumbra

The sun is not just a simple ball of hot hydrogen and helium. It has a definite structure that we are just beginning to understand. The sun has an atmosphere that consists of two parts: the chromosphere and the corona. The **chromosphere** is heated plasma that extends from the surface of the sun to about 1,600 miles (2,000 km) high. The chromosphere is about 11,000°F (6,000°C) at the bottom and up to 19,000 degrees Fahrenheit (35,000 degrees Celsius) at the top. The **corona** is above the chromosphere. It spreads outward for millions of miles. The corona can reach temperatures of up to 3.6 million degrees Fahrenheit (2

million degrees Celsius). It is continually moving and changing shape.

The visible surface of the sun is called the photosphere. It consists of plasma—super heated material that is neither solid, liquid, nor gas. The surface is covered with granules, which are bubbles of hot plasma rising from the interior of the sun. The photosphere is about 10,800°F (6,000°C), but some areas of the surface are cooler than others. Areas that are

Structure of the sun

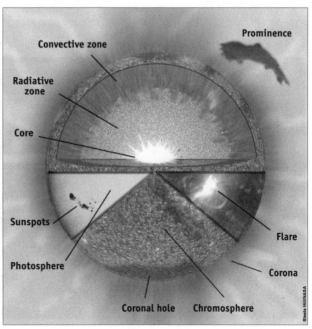

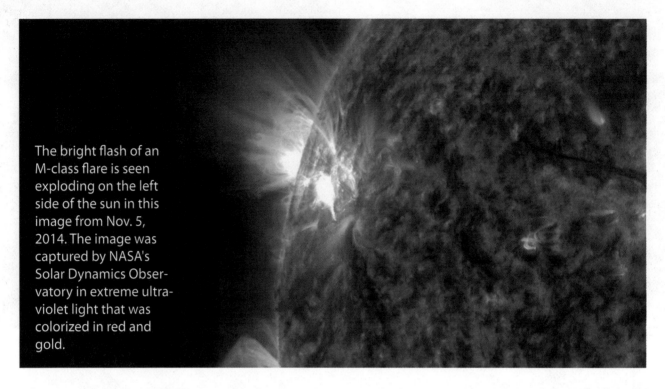

The bright flash of an M-class flare is seen exploding on the left side of the sun in this image from Nov. 5, 2014. The image was captured by NASA's Solar Dynamics Observatory in extreme ultraviolet light that was colorized in red and gold.

only about 8,100°F (4,500°C) are called **sunspots**. These cooler areas appear to be darker than the hotter areas around them. Sunspots appear to move across the face of the sun due to the sun's rotation. The sun takes about a month to rotate.

The sun's surface also experiences periods of violent eruptions called solar flares. A solar flare sends out matter, x-rays, and other energy waves that can interfere with radio transmissions on the earth. Solar flares usually last less than one hour. The emissions from these eruptions hit the earth's ionosphere and light it up. This is usually more visible near the poles. In the northern hemisphere this phenomenon is call the **aurora borealis**, or the northern lights, and in the southern hemisphere it is called the **aurora australis**, or southern lights.

A gigantic sunspot—almost 80,000 miles across—can be seen on the lower center of the sun in this image from NASA's Solar Dynamic Observatory captured on Oct. 23, 2014.

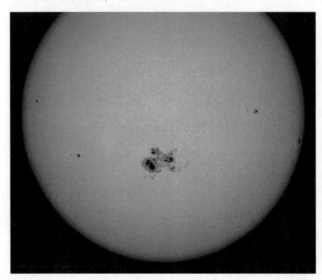

Aurora borealis over Iceland

Aurora australis over New Zealand

Fun Fact

If the scientists' model of the sun is correct, the sun loses about 6 million tons of material per second. Five million tons are converted into energy and 1 million tons are blown away in the solar wind. Because the sun uses up so much material, it is slowly wearing out. No evolutionary theory adequately explains what gave the stars their energy to begin with. Only God could have started the billions of power plants (stars) we see throughout the universe.

Scientists cannot directly observe the interior of the sun; however, they have developed a model that they think describes it. They believe that the sun's interior has three parts: the core, the radiative zone, and the convective zone. Scientists believe that the core works like a thermonuclear reactor, generating the sun's energy. They think that hydrogen atoms in the core combine to form helium atoms, which releases huge amounts of energy. This is similar to the reaction that takes place in a hydrogen bomb. It is believed that the temperature in the core of the sun is about 25 million degrees Fahrenheit (14 million degrees Celsius) and that the pressure is 340 billion times earth's air pressure.

Outside the core is the radiative zone. Energy moves outward from the core through the radiative zone as electromagnetic waves. As the energy approaches the surface it passes through the convective zone where the hot gas cools slightly, falls back to the radiative zone, gets heated again, rises to the surface, and so on. This is why the surface of the sun resembles a pot of boiling water.

As scientists continue to study the sun, they will better understand its makeup.

What did we learn?

- What are the two parts of the sun's atmosphere?
- What is a sunspot?
- Are sunspots stationary?
- What do scientists believe are the three parts of the sun's interior?

Taking it further

- What is the hottest part of the sun?
- What causes the aurora borealis or northern lights?
- When do you think scientists study the sun's corona?

Tracking the earth's movement

The earth rotates with respect to the sun. It makes one complete rotation every 24 hours. We can see this relative movement as we watch the sun move across the sky throughout the day. Another fun way to track the movement of the earth is to watch your shadow move.

Purpose: To track the movement of the sun

Materials: sidewalk chalk

Procedure:

1. On a sunny day, go outside early in the morning and make an X on the sidewalk or driveway, then stand on the X.

2. Have someone trace your shadow on the ground using sidewalk chalk.

3. Write the time next to the shadow.

4. Repeat this activity every 2–3 hours throughout the day.

Conclusion:

You will see your shadow get shorter and shorter until the sun reaches its highest point in the sky. Then the shadow will begin to grow longer in the other direction as the sun begins to set.

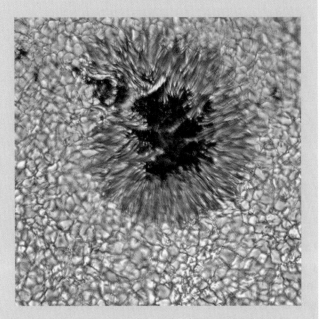 Sunspots

Sunspots are areas that are cooler than the surrounding surface of the sun. However, scientists do not fully understand what causes sunspots. They know that sunspots are associated with areas of higher magnetic fields. The magnetic field in a sunspot is about 1,000 times greater than in the rest of the sun. It is believed that this greater magnetic field expands the gas near sunspots, cooling the gas, causing the sunspots to be cooler than the surrounding areas.

The center of a sunspot is called the umbra and is the darkest area. The outer edge of a sunspot is called the penumbra and is warmer and brighter than the umbra, but not as hot as the rest of the surface of the sun (see close-up at right).

Sunspots rotate with the rotation of the sun. Because the sun is not a solid like the earth, but plasma, all of the mass of the sun does not rotate at the same speed. The mass at the equator rotates about once every 25 days but the mass near the poles rotates about once every 35 days. Thus the sunspots near the equator move across the surface faster than the sunspots that occur at higher or lower latitudes.

Some sunspots last for a few days, and other sunspots last for several weeks. Records of sunspots over the past 150 years have shown that sunspots occur in cycles. Some years there are relatively few sunspots and other years many sunspots occur. This pattern repeats approximately every 11 years. Years when there are few sunspots are called solar minimum, and when the number of sunspots peaks it is called solar maximum.

Solar flares appear to be related to sunspots because they almost always occur near sunspots and there are more solar flares when there are more sunspots; however, the exact cause of solar flares is not completely understood and therefore solar flares cannot be predicted.

You may be able to detect sunspots using your pinhole projector. Look at the projected image of the sun and see if you can detect any dark spots in the image. Your image will be very small so you may not be able to see them.

14

Solar Eclipse

Where did it go?

What causes an eclipse?

Words to know:

solar eclipse

An eclipse occurs when one heavenly body blocks the light from another heavenly body. From the earth's point of view, there are two types of eclipses. A **solar eclipse** is when the moon blocks the sun's light and casts a shadow on the earth. A lunar eclipse is when the earth blocks the sun's light and casts a shadow on the moon. We will study more about lunar eclipses in lesson 17.

A solar eclipse occurs when the moon comes directly between the sun and the earth. This can only happen when the moon is at its new moon phase. A solar eclipse happens somewhere on the earth 2–5 times each year. The moon's orbit around the earth is at a 5-degree tilt to the earth's orbit around the sun, so it usually goes above or below the plane of the earth's orbit.

When an eclipse does occur, it can be either a partial or a total eclipse. During a partial eclipse, the moon covers part of the sun's disk but not all of it. It is much more likely that a person will observe a partial eclipse than a total eclipse. Partial eclipses

happen more frequently and can be observed in a much larger area.

A total eclipse occurs when the moon covers the entire disk of the sun. Only the corona and chromosphere of the sun can be observed during the total eclipse. A total eclipse can be observed in only a small area of the earth, along a path usually about 150 miles (240 km) wide. During a total

On January 30, 2014, beginning at 8:31 am EST, the moon moved between NASA's Solar Dynamics Observatory, or SDO, and the sun, giving the observatory a view of a partial solar eclipse from space. This eclipse was not visible from earth.

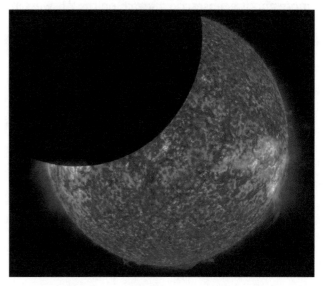

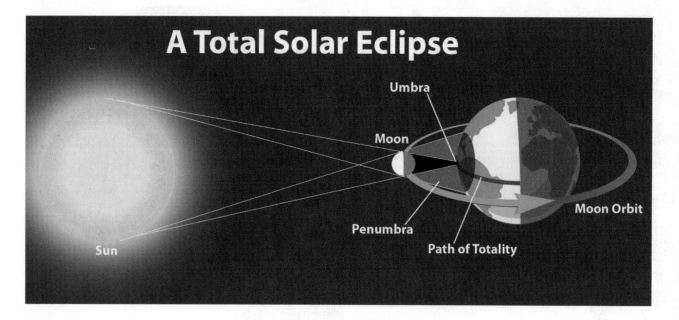

A Total Solar Eclipse

Umbra

Moon

Sun

Penumbra

Path of Totality

Moon Orbit

eclipse, there does not appear to be much change in the amount of sunlight until the sun is almost completely covered. Then the sky darkens and plants and animals begin to act as though night was falling. At totality, the sky is as dark as a moonlit night. Totality can last for as little as an instant to as long as 7½ minutes. The total time for the moon to move across the face of the sun is usually about two hours.

It is vitally important to remember that even if the moon covers the sun, there is still a significant amount of dangerous radiation coming from the sun. So, never look at the sun, even during an eclipse! An eclipse should be viewed by projecting an image of the sun on a box through a hole in one end of the box and watching the shadow. To learn more about eclipses, do a search on the Answers in Genesis website. 🌐

What did we learn?

- What is an eclipse?
- What is the difference between a partial and a total eclipse?
- How often do solar eclipses occur?

Fun Fact

There is no place in the universe quite like earth. Only on earth do the moon and sun appear to be about the same size in the sky. Although the moon is about 400 times smaller than the sun, it is also about 400 times closer to the earth. This allows the earth to experience solar eclipses. These eclipses can be accurately predicted and have been used to date events in the past. God has truly provided the sun and the moon to mark the seasons, days, and years just as He said in Genesis 1:14–15.

🚀 Taking it further

- Why do you think plants and animals start preparing for nightfall during an eclipse?
- Why can a total eclipse only be seen in a small area on the earth?
- How can the moon block out the entire sun when the sun is 400 times bigger than the moon?

Making an eclipse

Purpose: To simulate a solar eclipse

Materials: large ball, flashlight, small ball

Procedure:

1. Have one person hold a large ball such as a basketball or volleyball. This represents the earth.

2. Have another person stand 3 to 4 feet away and shine a flashlight on the ball. This represents the sun.

3. One of you hold a small ball such as a tennis ball in the middle of the light beam. This represents the moon.

4. Have the person with the "moon" move it until it blocks out the light from the flashlight, casting a shadow on the "earth."

Conclusion:

Notice how much of the earth is covered by the shadow. It will be a small percentage. Experiment with the moon in different locations. Watch what effect this has on the light reaching the earth. You will find that the moon must be in a very specific place in order to cause an eclipse.

 # Total solar eclipse

The most recent solar eclipse visible in the United States occurred on August 21, 2017. It was spectacularly visible to millions of people across the United States. This was an impressive total eclipse, lasting over 2½ minutes at maximum and visible over a path up to 71 miles (115 km) wide.

The path started in the Pacific, well north of Hawaii, and then crossed to make landfall in the U.S. in the northern half of Oregon. It then crossed Idaho, Wyoming, and Nebraska, and clipped the northeast corner of Kansas before passing right over Missouri. It also cut over the southern tip of Illinois and the western end of Kentucky, before crossing Tennessee and the western tip of North Carolina. The extreme northeast corner of Georgia was also in the path of totality.

Research past and future solar and lunar eclipses. Make a chart showing when and where the eclipses have and/or will occur. You can find information on eclipse schedules in several places. To learn more about eclipses, do a search on the Answers in Genesis website. You are likely to live in an area where you can see a lunar eclipse, but you are less likely to live in an area where you can view a total solar eclipse.

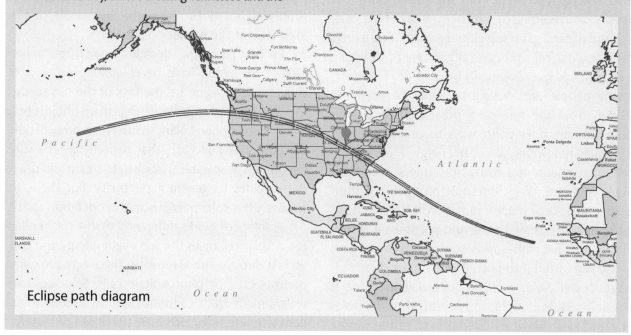

Eclipse path diagram

15

Solar Energy

Can it meet our energy needs?

How can we use the sun for energy?

Words to know:

solar energy

The sun is a giant power plant. The energy that reaches the earth from the sun heats the globe and helps plants to grow. The amount of energy that reaches the earth from the sun in only two weeks' time is equal to the energy in all of the coal, oil, and natural gas reserves in the world. Fossil fuels such as coal, oil, and natural gas cannot be easily replaced and may eventually be used up. Therefore, many people are looking to solar energy—the energy from the sun—as a possible replacement. Scientists are developing ways to collect and use this huge renewable source of energy.

Solar energy has many advantages over fossil fuels. It is cleaner—it does not produce pollution such as smoke or nuclear radiation. It is also renewable. In fact, for all intents and purposes it is infinite. And it is a high-quality source of energy that is easily converted into heat. But there are disadvantages as well. Solar energy is not always available. It is not available at night, and in areas near the poles it is not available at all during much of the winter.

Also, solar energy is very dispersed or spread out. It must be concentrated in order to be used.

For years, gardeners have used solar energy to heat their greenhouses. This is the idea behind solar collectors. Solar collectors are essentially flat boxes that have been painted black on the inside. Tubes carrying water are placed inside the boxes and then the boxes are covered with glass. As the sun passes through the glass, some of the energy is trapped. This energy heats the water as it flows through the pipes. Homes with solar panels have a nearly free supply of hot water. Also, this hot water can be used to heat the homes on cold days.

In the past few decades, many researchers around the world have been working on ways to collect and concentrate the rays of the sun so that they can be used to generate electricity, not just heat water. A solar power plant may have an array of hundreds of solar collectors that concentrate the sun's energy and heat water that turns to steam and drives the turbines to generate electricity. But there are relatively few solar power plants in operation today.

A solar cell works differently than a solar collector. A solar cell takes the sun's light energy and converts it directly into electricity. These cells are called photoelectric or photovoltaic cells. Solar cells are wafers made from cadmium sulfide, silicon, or gallium arsenide. Solar cells have two layers of material.

Many houses have solar panels on the roof to generate electricity.

Each layer has a different electrical charge. When the sunlight hits the top layer, the charges begin to flow from one layer to the other, thus creating a current of electricity. Solar cells can convert about 20–25% of the light that hits them into electricity. Researchers are trying to find ways to increase this percentage.

Solar cells work on cloudy days nearly as well as they do on sunny days; however, they do not work at night. Solar cells are used in many places. They are used to power street signs and lights, especially in remote areas where there is not a readily-available source of electricity. They are also used as back-up energy sources in many areas. Chances are you have seen a solar operated calculator that works off of the sun's light or even the light in your room. But the biggest use of solar cells is in space technology. Solar energy is abundant in space where there is no atmosphere to block the light. Solar cells are used to generate electricity for satellites, space probes, and even the space station.

More research is needed before solar energy can be used to completely replace our current sources of energy. But God has supplied us with a wonderful source of energy, and we will continue to find ways to use it.

What did we learn?

- What is solar energy?
- What are the two ways that solar energy is used today?

🚀 Taking it further

- Why is solar energy a good alternative to fossil fuels?
- Why are the insides of solar collectors painted black?
- What are some of the advantages of using solar cells in outer space?

Fun Fact

Researchers have built a solar furnace in France. This facility has thousands of flat mirrors that reflect the sun's light toward a ten story curved mirror. The curved mirror concentrates all of the sunlight at a tower. This concentrated sunlight can raise temperatures inside the tower to over 5,400°F (3,000°C). This facility is operated by the Solar Research Institute.

Solar energy

Activity 1—Purpose: To test which color absorbs the most heat

Materials: black, white, and green construction paper; baking sheet; ice cubes; "Solar Energy" worksheet

Procedure:

1. Place a piece of black paper, a piece of green paper, and a piece of white paper side by side on a baking sheet.

2. Place an ice cube on each sheet of paper.

3. Set the baking sheet in a sunny location.

4. On the "Solar Energy" worksheet, record the time you set the sheet in the sun as the starting time and the time the ice was completely melted as the ending time.

5. Answer the questions on the worksheet.

Activity 2—Purpose: To demonstrate how the sun heats water in a solar collector

Materials: two clear glasses, black construction paper, tape, two thermometers, "Solar Energy" worksheet

Procedure:

1. Fill two clear glasses with water.

2. Wrap black paper around one glass and tape it in place.

3. Place both glasses side by side in a sunny location.

4. On the "Solar Energy" worksheet, write down the starting time of your experiment.

5. Use a thermometer to measure the temperature of the water in each glass and record it on the worksheet.

6. Repeat the temperature measurement every 5 minutes for 20 minutes and record the results on the worksheet.

7. Answer the questions on the worksheet.

Solar energy

One of the problems with using solar energy efficiently is that the light from the sun is dispersed, or not very concentrated. Because the sun is far away, the light spreads out before it reaches the earth. This is good for plants and animals on the earth, but it presents some challenges for engineers trying to harness this energy. The light is not evenly distributed on the earth either. Because the earth is tilted at a 23-degree angle with respect to the sun, the rays from the sun hit the hemisphere that is tilted toward it more directly than the hemisphere that is tilted away from it. This is why summers are warmer than winters.

Purpose: To demonstrate the distribution of light on earth

Materials: hardback book, flashlight, clipboard, piece of paper, pencil

Procedure:

1. Place a hardback book upright on a table with the cover spread slightly so it will stand up.

2. Place a flashlight on top of the book and point the flashlight at a clipboard with a piece of white paper on it. Be sure that the clipboard is vertical.

3. Trace the circle of light made by the flashlight on the paper.

4. Now, tip the clipboard away from the flashlight so the light is not hitting it as directly and trace the pattern of light made by the flashlight on the paper.

Questions:

- Is the new pattern bigger or smaller than the first pattern?

- Based on what you just learned, where would be the best location for a solar energy power plant?

16

Our Moon

Is it made of green cheese?

What is the moon made of, and what is its surface like?

Words to know:

maria

Challenge words:

rays   rilles

The Bible tells us that God created the sun to rule the day and the moon to rule the night (Genesis 1:16). Although the moon lights up the night, it does not generate any light itself. Instead, it reflects light from the sun. Without the moon, nighttime would be very dark indeed.

The moon is a sphere of rock that orbits the earth once every 27.3 days, or about once per month. The word *month* comes from the old word for moon. The average distance from the center of the earth to the center of the moon is about 239,000 miles (384,500 km). The moon's diameter is 2,159 miles (3,475 km) across, less than the width of the United States. The moon is $\frac{1}{81}$ as massive as the earth and has $\frac{1}{6}$ the gravity. Because of the low gravitational pull, the moon does not have an atmosphere. Without an atmosphere, there is no

protection from the dangers of space, including extreme temperature swings and meteorites. This is why the surface of the moon is covered with craters. There are hundreds of thousands of craters ranging in size from a few inches to hundreds of miles across. A few of the craters do not appear to have been formed by impact. Some scientists think these may have been formed by past volcanic activity on the moon.

In addition to craters, the surface of the moon also has many dark areas called **maria**

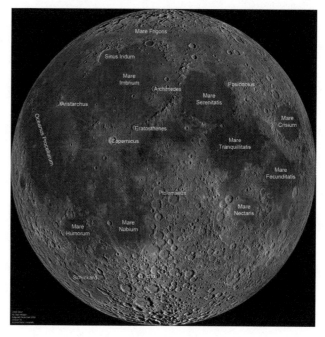

(MAH-ree-uh). This is the Latin word for seas. Early astronomers thought that these areas were bodies of water. These areas are actually broad plains that are covered with hardened lava that is darker than the surrounding area. The maria on the near side of the moon cover nearly half of the surface. Most maria are believed to be large impact craters that later filled with lava. The far side of the moon also has many craters, but most of them are not filled with lava. In addition to craters, the moon's surface also has many mountain ranges and valleys.

Fun Fact

Some people say the maria on the moon resemble a face, and thus they call the picture made by the maria "the man in the moon." Also, the pock-marked appearance of the moon has given it the reputation of being made of cheese, which, of course, is not true.

The moon that orbits earth is unique among all the moons in our solar system. It is 100 times larger than the average moon. This allows it to reflect a substantial amount of sunlight to the earth, making the night more pleasant. God truly provides for all of our needs.

What did we learn?

- Why does the moon shine?
- What causes the dark spots on the surface of the moon?

Taking it further

- Why does the size of our moon show God's provision for man?
- Why is gravity much less on the moon than on the earth?
- Why doesn't the surface of the earth have as many craters as the surface of the moon?

Reflected light

Purpose: To demonstrate how the moon reflects the sun's light

Materials: hand mirror, flashlight

Procedure:

1. Stand in a dark room holding a mirror. Observe how much light it gives off. (It should be none.)

2. Next, have someone stand across the room and shine a flashlight at the mirror. Notice how much light the mirror now gives off.

3. Experiment with different angles and positions of the mirror to the flashlight. See when the light from the mirror is the brightest and when it is the dimmest. Is there an angle at which the mirror gives off no light?

Conclusion: Remember that the mirror does not produce any light, but rather redirects the light of the flashlight. Just as the mirror reflects the light of the flashlight to our eyes, so the moon reflects the light of the sun to the earth.

Surface of the moon

The surface of the moon is marked primarily by craters, maria, mountain ranges, and rilles. The craters are indentations in the surface, usually with high sides. It is believed that most of the craters were formed when meteorites struck the surface of the moon. Many times meteorites strike with such force that they explode and sometimes even melt the surface of the moon where they land. Radiating out from many of the craters are bright streaks called rays. These rays are believed to be lunar material that was blown outward by the explosion of the meteorite. During a full moon, rays can be seen stretching out from many of the craters. Some rays stretch out as far as 1,000 miles (1,600 km).

In addition to the many craters on the moon, there are many areas called maria, which as you read earlier in the lesson are plains covered in lava. Because the maria resembled seas, they were given names that reflected weather conditions including the Sea of Rains, the Sea of Tranquility, the Sea of Storms, and the Sea of Serenity. When people look at the moon, they often claim to see pictures formed from these dark areas. The most famous of these "pictures" is the man in the moon.

The moon has a few of what appear to be mountain ranges. However, these are not true mountain ranges, but rather are raised walls of large craters and other upraised features on the lunar surface. Still, astronomers call these mountains. The highest peaks are about 3 miles (5 km) high. Many of the mountain ranges on the moon were named after the mountain ranges on earth including the Alps, Caucasus, and Carpathian Mountains.

Finally, the surface of the moon also has many valleys that are called rilles. Some rilles look like winding rivers, but do not carry water. It is believed that these rilles were probably paths for the lava that flowed in the maria. Other rilles are fairly straight and resemble fault lines on earth.

Using a pair of binoculars or a telescope, observe the moon and see how many of the features mentioned in this lesson you can observe. Also, look at the maria and see what pictures you can see on the face of the moon.

Newton & the Apple

1642–1727

Isaac Newton led an interesting life, and according to the calendar used in England at the time, he was born on Christmas Day, 1642. However, some people would disagree on his birth date because the calendar in use in England at that time was off by 10 days from the calendar in use today. By our calendar, he was born on January 4, 1643. But this did not matter to the people of that day for it was Christmas to them.

Isaac never knew his father, because he died three months before Isaac was born. His mother remarried when Isaac was two and sent him to live with his grandparents. When Isaac was about ten, his stepfather died and Isaac moved in with his mother, stepbrother, and two stepsisters for a time. He was later sent away to school and lived with a family named Clark. At this time he showed little promise in school and the school reports said he was "inattentive and idle," so he returned home.

His mother, now a woman of reasonable wealth and land, thought Isaac was now old enough to manage her affairs. He soon showed this was not the right job for him. After this failed endeavor, Isaac's uncle persuaded his mother to let him try school again. This time he stayed with Stokes, the headmaster of the school, and he did much better. He did well enough that his uncle persuaded his mother to let him go to the university.

Although Isaac's mother was fairly well off, when Isaac entered Trinity College at Cambridge in 1661, he entered as a sizar, one who works as a servant to other students. By doing this, he received an allowance toward his college expenses. It's interesting to note that at 18 he was older than most boys entering the college.

When he started at Cambridge, he was planning to receive a law degree, but sometime in college he found a whole new respect for mathematics. He was

elected a scholar and received his bachelor's degree in 1665. It was in that summer that the college was closed for two years because of an outbreak of the plague.

When the school closed, Isaac returned home and it was there he started revolutionizing astronomy, optics, physics, and mathematics. He performed many experiments and developed many mathematical formulas while waiting for the plague to pass. When the school reopened after two years, Isaac returned and earned his master's degree. It was after he returned to school that Isaac Newton began some of his most famous work.

One of Isaac's most important discoveries was that sunlight was not just simple white light but was made up of all the colors of the rainbow. He proved this by passing sunlight through a glass prism and producing a rainbow. This discovery led him to develop a telescope using mirrors instead of just lenses in order to eliminate the distorted colors caused by the lenses.

Even though Isaac Newton was a very bright man, he was not able to handle criticism very well. Because of the criticism he received from one of the other scientists in the field of optics, Newton quit the Royal Society and did not publish his findings on optics until after his critic died, some 30 years later.

This did not stop Newton from continuing his research in other areas, however. Isaac Newton is most well known for his work in physics. He was the first to come up with the idea that the earth's gravity influences the moon. He is reported to have been sitting in a garden when he observed an apple fall to the ground. This gave him the idea that the force working on the apple might also be the force that keeps the moon revolving around earth. After much research and testing, Newton devised the law of gravitation and was able to explain the gravitational pull mathematically. The law of gravitation states: "Any two bodies attract each other with a force proportional to the product of their masses and inversely proportional to the square of the distance between them." This means that heavier objects exert more gravitational pull than lighter objects and that the gravitational pull decreases the farther the two objects are from each other. This discovery helped him explain the tides and the orbit of comets, as well as the orbit of the moon.

Newton made many other advancements in the areas of science and mathematics. From 1669–1687, while he was a professor at Cambridge, he did most of his productive research. Newton is credited with laying the foundations for calculus and detailed his work on physics in his book *Philosophiae Naturalis Principia Mathematica*, or *Principia* as is it better known. *Principia* is considered by many to be the greatest scientific book ever written. In fact, Newton made so many discoveries that in 1705 he was knighted by Queen Anne. He was the first scientist so honored for his work.

Sir Isaac Newton had a deep faith in God and believed in the Bible's account of creation. In his works he expressed a strong sense of God in all of nature. In *Principia* he wrote, "This most beautiful system of the sun, planets, and comets, could only proceed from the counsel and dominion of an intelligent Being. ... This Being governs all things, not as the soul of the world, but as Lord over all; and on account of his dominion he is wont to be called "Lord God" ... or "Universal Ruler". ... The Supreme God is a Being eternal, infinite, absolutely perfect."

Although we think of Newton as a great scientist, he did not spend his entire life on research. In 1689 Newton was elected as a member of parliament representing the University and was reelected in 1701. In 1696, Isaac Newton was given a position in the government as Warden of the Royal Mint. Then three years later, he was named Master of the Mint. He was able to lead the mint through a difficult time of recoinage, and he worked to eliminate counterfeiting. In 1703 he was elected President of the Royal Society and kept that position until his death in 1727. Newton spent only 20 years of his career on science and math research, yet the discoveries made by Sir Isaac Newton helped shape science as we know it today.

17

Motion & Phases of the Moon

There's a full moon tonight

How does the moon move, and why does its appearance change in our sky?

Words to know:

new moon	waning gibbous
waxing crescent	waning crescent
waxing gibbous	lunar eclipse
full moon	

Challenge words:

near side of the moon	light side of the moon
far side of the moon	dark side of the moon

Just as the earth moves in two different ways with respect to the sun, so also the moon moves in two ways with respect to the earth. The moon revolves around the earth, and it rotates on its axis. From the perspective of the earth, the moon revolves around, or circles, the earth about once per month. The moon rotates on its axis once per month as well. This results in the same side of the moon always facing the earth. This side is called the near side of the moon. The back side is called the far side of the moon.

Because the moon orbits the earth, it is in a different position with respect to the sun each day for about a month, and then it repeats the cycle. The moon's position with respect to the sun determines how much light reflects off of its surface to the earth. Therefore, the moon appears to change shape throughout the month. These varying shapes are called the phases of the moon.

At **new moon**, the moon is between the earth and the sun. We can't see the moon at all because the sun is too bright and shining only on the far

First Quarter

Waxing Gibbous

Waxing Crescent

Full

New

Waning Gibbous

Waning Crescent

Third Quarter

side of the moon. A couple nights later, we can see a small sliver lit up on the right side of the moon. This is called a **waxing crescent**. After seven days, the right half will be lit up. This is called the first

Fun Fact

The first full moon after the autumn equinox, September 21–23, is called the Harvest Moon. The next full moon is called the Hunter's Moon.

quarter. As the moon continues to "grow" throughout the next week it is called a **waxing gibbous**. At 14 days through the cycle, the moon is at the opposite side of the earth from the sun and is considered a **full moon**. The full moon rises at sunset, and sets at sunrise. A full moon is nine times brighter than the moon when it is half lit (during the first or last quarter). The line between the light and dark sides of the moon is called the moon's terminator.

The next day, after the full moon, the moon appears to get smaller. This is called a **waning** gibbous. Then ¾ of the way through the cycle, only the left half of the moon is lit and is called the last quarter. Finally, as the moon "shrinks" further it is called a waning crescent.

Even though it takes 27.3 days to complete one orbit, the moon's cycle from one new moon to the next takes 29.5 days, or one synodic month, to complete. If you viewed the earth and moon from a location in space, you would see the moon line up with a particular point on the earth every 27.3 days. But the moon lines up between the earth and the sun the same way every 29.5 days because they are both moving around the sun as the moon moves around the earth.

Just as the moon passing directly between the earth and the sun causes a solar eclipse, so too, if the earth passes directly between the sun and the moon we see a lunar eclipse. This can only occur at full moon and only when the sun, the earth, and the moon are all directly lined up. This happens infrequently because the moon's orbit is tilted with respect to the earth's orbit. During a lunar eclipse, the moon is still visible with a slight red color. The longest lunar eclipse was recorded at 1 hour 40 minutes of complete eclipse with the moon being at least partially blocked for 3 hours and 40 minutes.

What did we learn?

- What causes the phases of the moon?
- Why does the same side of the moon always face the earth?
- What causes a lunar eclipse?
- From the perspective of space, how long does it take for the moon to complete its cycle around the earth?

Taking it further

- Why doesn't a lunar eclipse occur every month?
- What is the difference between a waxing crescent and a waning crescent?

Moon phases

Label the moon on the "Identifying Phases of the Moon" worksheet.

⛉ Observing the moon

There are some terms associated with the moon that can be confusing. Since the moon rotates and

The far side of the moon.

revolves at the same rate, the same side of the moon is always facing the earth. As we mentioned before, this is called the near side of the moon, and the back side is called the far side of the moon. You may also hear the terms light and dark sides of the moon. You may think that since the moon reflects the sun's light toward the earth that the side facing the earth would be the light side of the moon, but this is not necessarily true. The light side of the moon is the side facing the sun, regardless of the moon's position with respect to the earth. And the dark side of the moon is the side facing away from the sun. When is the light side of the moon the same as the near side of the moon? When is the dark side of the moon the same as the near side of the moon?

Because there is no atmosphere on the moon, the temperatures on the moon vary greatly. On the light side, when the sun is shining directly on the moon, the temperature can be as much as 265°F (130°C) and on the dark side of the moon the temperature can be as low as −280°F (−173°C).

Purpose: To observe and record the phases of the moon

Materials: "Observing the Phases of the Moon" worksheet

Procedure:

1. On a copy of "Observing the Phases of the Moon" worksheet, fill in today's date under the first circle, tomorrow's date under the second circle, and so on for a total of 29 days.

2. Next, fill in the time of the moon rise and moon set for each date. You can often find the moon rise and set times in your local paper or on the Internet.

3. Now that you have your chart ready, observe the moon each day for the next month. Use a pencil to fill in the part of the moon that appears dark. This will give you your own chart of the phases of the moon.

Conclusion:

After observing the moon every day for one month, you will have a better understanding of how the moon moves through the sky and how its position changes each day with respect to the sun.

18

Origin of the Moon

Where did it come from?

How did the moon get there?

Genesis says that God created the sun, moon, and stars on Day Four of creation. Yet many scientists do not accept the biblical account of creation. Evolutionists have proposed many theories to explain where the moon came from, and how it ended up orbiting the earth. However, all of these theories have significant problems.

One theory, called the Capture Theory, says the moon originally orbited the sun. Then, somehow it was dislodged from its orbit and was captured by the earth's gravity. There are no observed or credible ideas for what could have caused the moon's original orbit to be disrupted. Also, the chances that the moon would have approached the earth at just the right speed and angle to be captured are extremely slim. It is much more likely that the moon would have flown off or been pulled into the earth than to begin orbiting it.

A second theory, called the Fission Theory, says that as the earth was spinning, it spun a ball off of itself that became the moon. However, in order for the ball to escape the gravity of the earth and begin orbiting it, the earth would have had to be spinning at about one revolution every 2–3 hours. Again, this would create tremendous heat.

There is no evidence of such heat in the geologic records. Also, the composition of moon rocks is different from that of most earth rocks. If the moon came from the earth, the moon's rocks should have the same composition as the earth's rocks. Most scientists have disregarded the Fission Theory because of its problems.

A third idea, called Accretion, says that the earth, moon, and other planets were all formed when particles in a giant dust cloud started sticking together. Scientists cannot explain what would

This image from Apollo 11 shows the earth rising over the stark, scarred surface of the moon.

cause these particles to stick together. Gravity of small particles is very small, so they would not be attracted to each other by gravity. Also, the average density of the earth is much greater than the average density of the moon. If these two bodies were formed from the same gas cloud, why do they have such different densities? No one can adequately answer this question.

A fourth theory, the Impact Theory, states that something the size of Mars hit the edge of the earth, knocking off a chunk, which became the moon. This is extremely unlikely. There is no evidence that this has happened. Collisions with objects as large as planets have never been observed, and calculations have shown that the chances of a collision that would have this effect are practically zero.

All theories for the moon's existence have come up short. There are no processes observed today that can explain the existence of the moon without a Creator. The only idea that has not been shown inadequate is the one in the Bible. God created the moon and placed it in orbit around the earth. 🌐

What did we learn?

- What are four secular theories for the origin of the moon?

- Which of these theories is most likely to be true?

- What does the Bible say about the origin of the moon?

Fun Fact

The moon is slowly moving away from the earth (called recession). As the moon orbits the earth, its gravity pulls on the earth's oceans, causing tides. The tides actually "pull forward" on the moon, which causes the moon to gradually spiral outward. Today, the moon moves about an inch and a half away from the earth each year, which means that the moon would have been closer to the earth in the past. This rate of recession would have been greater in the past when the moon was closer to the earth.

Six thousand years ago, the moon would have been about 800 feet (245 m) closer to the earth (which is not much of a change, considering the moon is a quarter of a million miles away). So this recession of the moon is not a problem over the biblical timescale of 6,000 years. But, if the earth and moon were over four billion years old (as evolutionists teach), then we'd have big problems. In this case, the moon would have been touching the earth only 1.4 billion years ago, suggesting that the moon can't possibly be as old as secular astronomers claim.

Taking it further

- What are the main difficulties with the Capture Theory?

- Why do you think scientists come up with unworkable ideas for the moon's origin?

⚗ Spinning bodies

Purpose: To demonstrate why the capture theory is wrong

Materials: two tops (spinning toys), masking tape

Procedure:

1. Place a piece of masking tape on the floor. Write the letter *E* on it to represent the orbit of the earth.

2. Place a second piece of tape about three inches away and write an *M* on it to represent the moon's orbit.

3. Spin the "earth" top on the floor on the *E* piece of tape.

4. Then, start the "moon" top spinning, but not on the *M*. Try to make the "moon" top hit the "earth" top in such a way that the moon top ends up spinning on the *M* after the collision without significantly moving the "earth" top from the *E*.

5. Repeat this several times.

6. Now, start each top spinning on its designated spot.

Conclusion:

You will find that it is impossible, or nearly so, to get the tops to end up on the right pieces of tape. The actual science involved is much more complicated than this simple demonstration, yet this is how the Capture Theory tries to explain the origin of the moon. Step 6 demonstrates how God created the earth and the moon—He put them in their places.

🏅 Origin of the moon

Read the following verses and discuss what each says about the origin of the moon.

- Genesis 1:14–19
- Psalm 8:3–4
- Psalm 33:6
- Psalm 74:16
- Psalm 136:3–9
- Jeremiah 31:35

It is clear from the Bible that no naturalistic explanation will adequately explain the moon's origin because its creation was supernatural.

UNIT 4

Planets

◊ **Distinguish** between the terrestrial planets and the Jovian planets.

◊ **Describe** the basic characteristics of each of the planets.

◊ **Explain** why Earth is unique among the planets.

19

Mercury

Closest planet to the sun

What is the planet closest to the sun like?

Words to know:

terrestrial

inferior planets

Jovian

Our solar system has eight known planets that orbit the sun. All of the planets have elliptical orbits—orbits that are stretched circles. Those with solid surfaces are called **terrestrial** planets and those with gas surfaces are called **Jovian** planets, or gas giants. The planet with the closest orbit to the sun is Mercury. Mercury's average distance from the sun is 36 million miles (58 million km). Compared to the earth, Mercury revolves very quickly around the sun, making one complete revolution every 88 Earth days. But compared to the earth, it rotates slowly on its axis, making one complete rotation every 58.6 Earth days.

Mercury is a terrestrial planet. Its surface is covered with craters. This is most likely due to meteorites. Mercury is a small planet and its mass is much smaller than that of the earth; therefore, it has much less gravity and thus has almost no atmosphere to protect it from meteors like the earth does. What

little atmosphere it does have is composed of helium and hydrogen. Its lack of atmosphere also allows for extreme temperature changes on the surface of the planet. The side of the planet facing the sun can be as hot as 800°F (470°C) and the side facing away from the sun can be as cold as −360°F (−180°C). Without a substantial atmosphere, Mercury does not have any weather. It was believed that Mercury was too hot to have any water, but in 1991, a small amount of ice was discovered in very deep craters near the poles where sunlight does not reach.

Mercury was named using Roman mythology. In Roman mythology, Mercury was the messenger of the gods. The planet Mercury is the smallest with a diameter of 3,031 miles (4,877 km). Its gravity is only 0.38 times as much as the gravity on Earth. This means if you weigh 100 pounds on Earth, you would weigh only 38 pounds on Mercury. Mercury

does not have any moons.

Mercury and Venus are *inferior planets*. This does not mean there is something wrong with them, just that they have smaller orbits than the earth. From the earth, the interior planets appear to have phases just as the moon does.

For more information on Mercury and how it shows God's handiwork, do a search on the Answers in Genesis website.

 What did we learn?

- How do Mercury's revolution around the sun and rotation on its axis compare to that of Earth?
- What is the surface of Mercury like?

Taking it further

- How does a lack of atmosphere affect the conditions on Mercury?

 Atmosphere test

God provided a special atmosphere for the earth that allows life to flourish. Our atmosphere protects us from most meteors. It provides oxygen for us to breathe, circulates the air on the planet, and provides weather so we can grow food. The atmosphere also protects us from the extreme temperatures of space. Mercury's atmosphere, on the other hand, is too thin to protect it from extreme temperatures.

Purpose: To understand how the atmosphere protects the earth and how a lack of atmosphere affects Mercury

Materials: towel, hair dryer, ice

Procedure:

1. Wrap a towel around one arm.

2. Using a hair dryer on low heat, blow warm air on both of your arms. Compare the temperatures felt by each arm.

3. Next, place a piece of ice on each of your arms for a few seconds. Again, compare the temperatures felt by each arm.

Conclusion:

The towel insulates your arm from the hot air and the cold ice just as the earth's atmosphere insulates our planet from the heat of the sun and the cold of space. Without an atmosphere, Mercury's surface bakes in the sun and freezes in the shade.

 Mercury probe

For many years very little was known about Mercury. Scientists could see the planet with their telescopes, which gave them some idea of what the planet was like, but this did not answer all of their questions. Then in 1974,

NASA was able to send a space probe called *Mariner 10* near Mercury where it was able to take photos and many scientific measurements of the planet. In one year, the *Mariner 10* was able to pass by the planet three times at

Planets

three different levels, which allowed scientists to obtain valuable information about Mercury.

Scientists obtained some surprising results. First, they expected that any atmosphere Mercury may have had would have boiled away long ago, but instead, the probe detected a very thin atmosphere around the planet. Also, scientists were surprised to find that Mercury has a magnetic field. Because Mercury rotates slowly on its axis, scientists did not think that it could generate a magnetic field, yet it has a definite magnetic signature. Scientists are not sure how this field is generated.

The probe revealed that in many ways, Mercury is similar to our moon. Both objects are covered with craters. Also, both Mercury and the moon are believed to have small amounts of frozen liquid at the poles where the sun's rays do not reach. One distinct difference between the moon and Mercury, however, is their densities. Mercury is much denser than the moon. Its density is similar to the density of Earth.

Purpose: To help appreciate how little we can tell about a planet just by looking at it through a telescope

Materials: two index cards, crayons or markers, box or stack of books, tape, flashlight, magnifying glass, two clear plastic cups, water, milk

Procedure:

1. On an index card, draw a 1 inch circle and color it with many dark spots representing the craters on Mercury.

2. Set a box or a stack of books on a table and tape the index card to the box so that it is perpendicular to the table and its bottom edge is against the table.

3. Set a flashlight on the table at about a 30-degree angle to the left of the center of the card. Its light should be shining on the drawing of Mercury.

4. Hold a magnifying glass a few inches away from the drawing of Mercury at about a 30-degree angle to the right of the center of the card.

5. Hold a second index card so that the magnifying glass is between the two cards.

6. Move the card and the magnifying glass until you project a clear image of the planet onto the card.

   This set up is similar to what a scientist does to view something in space. The flashlight represents the sun and the lens in the magnifying glass represents the lens in a telescope. The card on which the image is projected represents film from a camera or electronic sensor that detects the image and displays it. This set up is not complete however. Mercury has a very thin atmosphere. So let's make it a little more realistic.

7. Place a clear plastic cup between the flashlight and the index card with Mercury on it.

   How did this affect the image on the second card? It probably blurred it  slightly. The plastic causes some of the light rays to go in different directions so the image is not as bright or clear.

8. Now add a second plastic cup between the first index card and the magnifying glass to represent the atmosphere of the earth. How did this second cup affect the image? Again, it is probably slightly blurred and dimmer than the original image. Closely observe the image on the card. What can you tell about the planet just from looking at the image? Not as much as you would like. This is why space probes are so important for understanding the objects in our solar system.

   As you will learn in our next lesson, Venus has a very thick opaque atmosphere.

9. Add water and two tablespoons of milk to the cup between the flashlight and the index card. How did this affect the image that is projected? It should block out the image.

Conclusion: Scientists cannot see the surface of Venus at all with their telescopes and have relied on space probes for pictures of its surface.

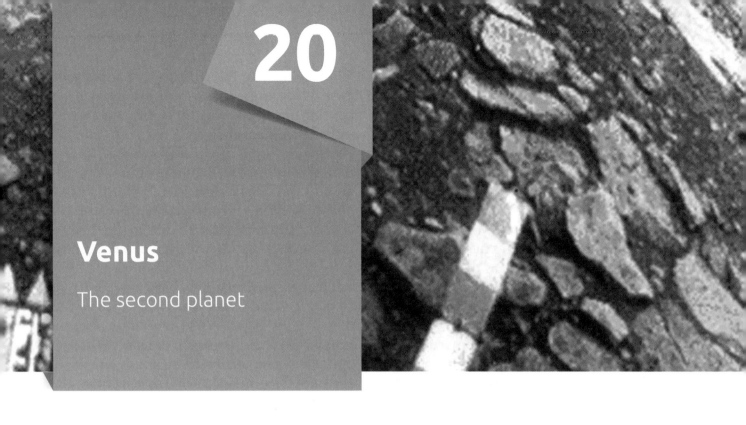

20

Venus

The second planet

What is the second planet from the sun like?

Words to know:

retrograde rotation

The second planet from the sun is Venus. This planet was named for the Roman goddess of love and beauty. Venus is sometimes called the Evening Star or the Morning Star because, besides the moon, it is often one of the brightest objects in the nighttime sky; thus it may be the first "star" to appear at sunset or the last "star" to disappear at sunrise.

Venus appears so bright in the sky because it has an atmosphere that reflects over 75% of the light that hits it. This atmosphere is 100 times thicker than Earth's atmosphere and is made up of 98% carbon dioxide and about 2% nitrogen. In addition, the sky is full of clouds made of sulfuric acid. Although this atmosphere protects the planet

Mariner 10 took this image of Venus as it flew past the inner planet. Made using an ultraviolet filter, this photo has been color-enhanced to bring out Venus's cloudy atmosphere so the human eye would see it.

from the extreme temperatures of space, because it is so thick it traps the sun's rays causing the surface to heat up. In fact, Venus is the hottest planet in the solar system, with a surface temperature of up to 900˚F (470˚C). This shows us that God provided just the right atmosphere for Earth. Mercury has basically no atmosphere at all and Venus has an atmosphere that is poisonous to humans and keeps the planet too hot. In fact, none of the planets except Earth has an atmosphere that would

Planets

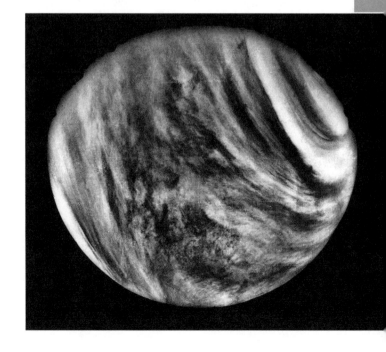

Fun Fact

Venus is 15 times brighter than Sirius, which is the brightest star in the night sky.

support life.

Venus's thick atmosphere exerts great pressure on the surface of the planet. Several space probes that were sent to investigate Venus were crushed by the atmospheric pressure as they approached the surface. However, several other probes survived the trip to the surface and sent many photos to Earth.

The first probe to safely land on Venus was a Soviet probe called *Venera 7*, but it did not send back any photos. The Soviet Union continued to send probes to Venus and the first probe to send back images was *Venera 9* which sent its photos in 1975. In 1981 *Venera 13* sent back the first color photos of the surface of Venus. These probes did not survive long under the crushing atmospheric pressure but they survived long enough to send back important information.

Other probes have used radar while orbiting the planet to map out the surface of Venus. From all of this data we know that Venus has a rocky surface with several large craters. Its atmosphere protects it from small meteors but large ones still occasionally make it to the surface. Also, we see evidence of

The greenhouse effect

The thick atmosphere on Venus acts like a greenhouse, trapping the sun's energy and heating the surface of the planet. To demonstrate this effect, follow the directions and complete the "Greenhouse Effect" worksheet.

former lava flows. This indicates that at one time there was extensive volcanic activity on Venus. It is believed that at one time the surface was covered with hundreds of volcanoes.

Because Venus is an inferior planet, it goes through phases as seen from the earth. Depending on its relative position, we can see all, part, or none of the planet reflecting the sun's light. So, just like the moon and Mercury, Venus appears to have phases. In fact, this was one piece of evidence that helped convince people that the sun, not the earth, was the center of the solar system.

Venus is the planet that is closest in size to the earth. Its gravity is 0.91 times that of Earth. Venus makes one revolution around the sun in 224.7 Earth days and rotates on its axis once every 243 Earth days, making Venus the planet with the slowest rotation in the solar system. Most planets rotate from west to east, but Venus rotates backwards, from east to west. This backwards rotation is called retrograde rotation. Venus does not have any moons orbiting it. Its average distance from the sun is 67 million miles (108 million km).

What did we learn?

- Where is Venus's orbit with respect to the sun and the other planets?
- What makes Venus so bright in the sky?
- What is a nickname for Venus?
- How many moons does Venus have?

Taking it further

- Even though Venus has an atmosphere, why can't life exist there?
- Why doesn't the earth's atmosphere keep our planet too hot?

Surface mapping

As you learned in the last lesson, it was impossible for scientists to view the surface of Venus with telescopes. However, this did not mean that scientists had no knowledge of Venus's surface. In addition to the pictures sent by the Venera probes, several other probes have determined what the surface looks like by using radar.

Radio waves can penetrate the atmosphere around Venus and return information about the surface. The probe sends out a radio wave which bounces off of the planet's surface and sends some of the radio wave back to the probe. The probe detects this reflected energy and uses the time between when the original wave was sent and when the reflected wave was received to determine how far away the surface is. The probe then sends another radio wave to a slightly different location and repeats the process. In this way the probe can determine what the surface looks like.

In 1978, a probe called Pioneer Venus used radar to map some of the planet's surface. Then from 1990 to 1994, the Magellan probe orbited

The hemispheric view of Venus, as revealed by more than a decade of radar investigations.

Venus. During this time it used radio waves to make high resolution pictures of the entire surface of Venus. Another probe called The European Venus Express also did radar mapping of the planet from 2005 to 2014. You can simulate this process by doing the following experiment.

Purpose: To understand how scientists can map the surface of Venus

Materials: shoebox, modeling clay, tape, graph paper, string, metal washer, ruler

Procedure:

1. In a shoebox, make a landscape with modeling clay. Include mountains, plains, and valleys. Be sure that the landscape does not go above the edge of the box.

2. Tape a piece of graph paper to the side of the box so that the top of the paper is even with the top of the box.

3. Make a probe by tying a metal washer on the end of a piece of string.

4. Use a marker and ruler to make marks every ½ inch on the string. Begin at the left hand edge of the graph paper.

5. Without looking into the box, lower the weight into the box until it hits something. Note which mark on the string is closest to the top of the box.

6. Remove the probe and measure how far the probe went into the box. Make a dot on the graph paper that distance from the top of the paper. For example, if the probe hit the surface of the planet 1½ inches down from the top of the box, the dot should be placed 1½ inches from the top of the paper.

7. Move to the next mark to the right on your graph paper and repeat this process. You should end up with a series of dots on the paper that when connected together resemble the landscape inside the box.

Conclusion:

From the information sent back by the radio probes, scientists discovered that Venus has mountains, valleys, plains, and craters similar to those on Earth. They saw that Venus also has what are believed to be volcanoes. They even found that Venus has two large land masses similar in size to Australia and Africa. However, Venus does not have any water. Instead of vast oceans, Venus has dry, barren plains. As much as Venus may resemble Earth in its size and form, it is very different in its ability to support life. God created a very special place for us.

21

Earth

Designed for life

What makes our home, the third planet, special?

Words to know:

satellite

Only one planet in the solar system can sustain life—Earth. Our planet Earth was designed by God to be the perfect place for us to live. However, as a result of Adam's sin in the Garden of Eden, God cursed the earth (Genesis 3); and later, because of the wickedness of all of the people of Noah's time, God judged the world with a global Flood (Genesis 6–9). This resulted in a planet that is much different from the paradise God initially created for man. However, the earth today is still a marvelous planet and a wonderful place to live!

Earth is the third planet from the sun. It revolves around the sun every 365.26 days, or one year, and rotates on its axis every 23 hours, 56 minutes and 4 seconds, or one day. It is tilted on its axis at 23 degrees from vertical with respect to the sun. The earth is an average of 93 million miles (150 million km) from the sun. All of this places Earth in the perfect position for life.

Earth is the only planet in our solar system with a significant amount of water. About 72% of the surface of the earth is covered with water. This water is necessary for life to exist. Many scientists are searching for signs of water on other planets to see if life could have existed on other planets in the past. So far, there is no indication that life exists anywhere in our universe except on Earth.

The earth has an atmosphere consisting of 78% nitrogen, 20% oxygen, 0.9% argon, and 0.1% carbon dioxide and other gases. As we learned in other lessons, this atmosphere protects the earth from the harsh temperatures of space and from many meteors that would otherwise hit the surface of the earth. But the atmosphere is special for other reasons, too. The closest layer to the surface of the earth, the first 0–10 miles (0–16 km), is called the troposphere. The troposphere is where the weather occurs. The weather patterns are vital to sustaining life on Earth. The winds and air currents move water from the oceans where it evaporates, to the land where it can water plants. The weather also

Fun Fact

There is enough water in the oceans that if all the surface features of the earth were evened out, water would cover the earth to a depth of 1.7 miles (2.7 km).

Planets

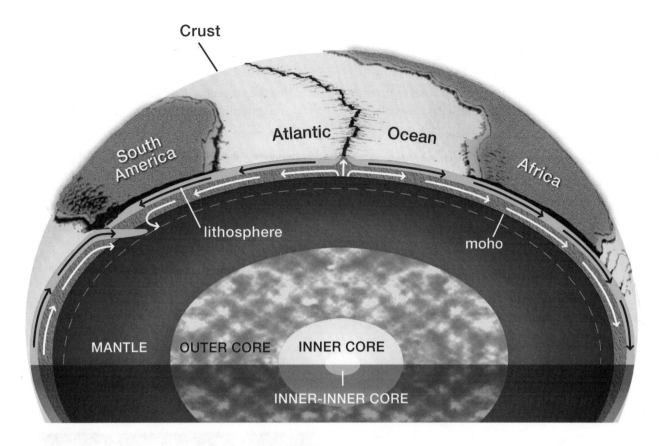

Crust

South America

Atlantic   Ocean

Africa

lithosphere

moho

MANTLE   OUTER CORE   INNER CORE

INNER-INNER CORE

helps move cooler and warmer air around so the temperatures remain more constant around the earth. There is still a difference in temperature from one part of the earth to another. The temperatures can range from −60 to 140°F (−51 to 60°C), but this is a much smaller difference than the −360 to 800°F (−218 to 425°C) experienced on Mercury.

Earth is a terrestrial planet. It has a 5–35 mile (8–56 km) thick crust of rock. This crust floats on a mantle of rock that is about 1,800 miles (2,900 km) thick. The crust is broken into pieces called plates. These plates move slightly as they float on the mantle, and this movement sometimes causes earthquakes.

The earth has one natural **satellite**—the moon. The moon orbits the earth and reflects the light of the sun to give us light at night. The earth's moon is one of the larger moons in the solar system. God designed it just right to light up the night. Earth is God's special gift to humanity.

What did we learn?

- What are some features of our planet that make it uniquely able to support life?
- What name is given to the period of time it takes for Earth's revolution around the sun?
- What name is given to the length of Earth's rotation on its axis?
- On average, how far is Earth from the sun?

Taking it further

- What are some possible reasons why large amounts of water are found on Earth but not on other planets?
- Why is it important that Earth is a terrestrial planet?

Fun Fact

At the equator, the earth is spinning at 1,000 mph (447 m/s) about its axis and moving at 67,000 mph (30,000 m/s) around the Sun.

Earth model

Purpose: To demonstrate why landmasses on flat maps often look different from the actual landmasses

Materials: globe, world map, orange, marker

Procedure:

1. Look at a globe of the earth. Notice the landmasses and the oceans. Consider how much water is on the earth and how it is needed to support life.

2. Now compare the globe to a world map. See how the landmasses and oceans near the poles have been stretched to change a round object into a flat map.

3. To make your own world map, draw the landmasses onto an orange with a marker.

4. After the marker has dried, carefully peel the orange, in one piece if possible, and flatten it to make a map.

Conclusion:

Notice how the ends of the orange peel had to be broken apart to make the peel lie flat. This is why Greenland and other land masses near the poles look larger on many maps than they really are. If possible, locate a Mercator or cylindrical projection map of the earth and compare those with the map you have.

Now enjoy a delicious snack that could only be grown on planet Earth.

Why is the sky blue?

Every child knows that on Earth the sky is blue. This is true even from space. Pictures taken from space show that our planet is a beautiful blue color. So why is Earth a blue planet?

Purpose: To demonstrate why the earth appears blue

Materials: two clear cups, milk, flashlight, water

Procedure:

1. Fill two clear cups with water.

2. Add a few drops of milk to one cup and stir the water just to mix the milk into it.

3. Take both cups to a dark room and shine a flashlight through each cup.

Questions:

- What color does the water appear to be in each cup? Why do you think this is?

Conclusion:

In the cup without milk, the water appears to be clear. In the cup with milk, the water has a pale blue color. This is because the milk droplets in the water disperse the blue light just as the air molecules disperse the blue light in our atmosphere. Our planet appears blue because the molecules in the atmosphere scatter the blue light waves more than they scatter other colors of light. This allows us to see blue more than other colors. Mars is called the red planet. Do you think this is because of the scattering of red light in its atmosphere? You will find out in the next lesson.

22

Mars

The red planet

How is the fourth planet different from Earth?

Words to know:

superior planets

More than any other planet, Mars has evoked images of aliens and ideas for science fiction novels. Mars is the fourth planet from the sun and the first of the superior planets—those with larger orbits than Earth. Mars was named for the Roman god of war, perhaps because of its red color. It has two small moons called Phobos and Deimos, named for the attendants of Mars.

Mars is about half the size of Earth. It has a diameter of 4,222 miles (6,793 km) compared to Earth's diameter of 7,927 miles (12,757 km). The gravity on Mars is nearly the same as the gravity on Mercury and is 0.38 times the gravity on Earth.

Fun Fact

Mars One is a non-profit organization based in the Netherlands that plans to send astronauts to Mars by 2025. They hope to fund this project by making it part of a reality TV show.

Although Mars is small and has little gravity, it has a very thin atmosphere. Its atmosphere is about 0.7% as thick as the atmosphere around Earth and consists mostly of carbon dioxide. Mars has polar ice caps that grow in the winter and shrink in the summer. The permanent part of these ice caps is made primarily of frozen water, but in the winter, carbon dioxide from the atmosphere freezes on top of the ice forming a layer of what is called dry ice. It is called dry ice because when frozen carbon dioxide warms up, instead of melting and becoming a liquid, it immediately becomes a gas. Carbon dioxide freezes at a much lower temperature than water

Mars has little gravity and a very thin atmosphere.

Curiosity takes a self-portrait doing its mission on Mars.

Fun Fact

The Mars Society is a privately funded organization whose ultimate goal is to establish a colony on Mars. Their purpose statement includes the following goals.

1. Broad public outreach to instill the vision of pioneering Mars.

2. Support of ever more aggressive government funded Mars exploration programs around the world.

3. Conducting Mars exploration on a private basis.

The Mars Society believes that mankind is ready and should aggressively seek ways to colonize the red planet. Apparently the U.S. government agrees, and NASA is working on projects which may lead to putting people on Mars.

does and melts at temperatures above −110°F (−79°C). The thin atmosphere does not protect the planet from harsh temperatures, which range from −220 to 80°F (−140 to 27°C).

The surface of Mars is covered with many craters, mountains, and valleys. Some valleys on Mars are much bigger than Grand Canyon on Earth. The soil contains a high amount of iron oxide (rust), which gives Mars its characteristic red color. Periodically, the warming of the sun causes winds to blow, creating giant dust storms. Eventually the storms block out enough of the sun that the temperatures even out and the wind stops, allowing the dust to settle.

We know a great deal about Mars, due mainly to the Viking landers and other space probes, such as NASA's rovers, *Spirit*, *Opportunity*, and *Curiosity*, that visited there and sent back information. The Mars rovers have found some evidence that liquid water may once have existed on Mars, but no probe has ever found any signs that life ever existed on the planet. Scientists continue to search for signs of life, and NASA plans to continue sending probes to learn as much as possible about the red planet.

What did we learn?

- Why is Mars called a superior planet?
- Why is Mars called the red planet?
- How many moons does Mars have?

Taking it further

- What causes the dust storms on Mars?
- Why doesn't the wind on Earth cause giant dust storms like the wind on Mars?
- How would your weight on Mars compare to your weight on Mercury?

Experimenting with polar ice caps

NOTE: Dry ice must be handled by an adult wearing gloves! Never touch dry ice with your bare skin.

The polar ice caps on Mars are covered with frozen carbon dioxide, better known as dry ice, in the winter. Much of this carbon dioxide evaporates back into the atmosphere in the summer. You can have some fun with dry ice and learn about Mars at the same time.

Purpose: To understand the properties of dry ice

Materials: dry ice, gloves, empty aquarium or other glass case, candle, matches or lighter, cup of water

Procedure:

1. Using gloves, place a piece of dry ice in an empty aquarium or other similar tank. Observe the "smoke" coming off of the surface of the ice.

2. Light a candle and scoop some of the carbon dioxide gas from the tank and pour it over the candle. Observe what happens.

3. Carefully drop a small piece of the dry ice into a cup of water. Observe the water "boil" as the ice turns to gas.

Questions:

- What was the "smoke" coming off of the dry ice?
- Why did the candle flame go out?
- Why did the water in the cup "boil"?

Conclusion:

Dry ice changes from solid to gas without going through a liquid phase. This process is called sublimation and is what caused the "smoke." In August 2003, Mars was closer to Earth than it has ever been. Observers using telescopes were able to see evidence of the polar ice cap sublimating. The gas brightly reflects sunlight causing the ice cap to appear brighter than the rest of the planet. Since dry ice goes directly from a solid to a gas without leaving a liquid behind, it is used for transporting many frozen foods. It is also more efficient because it keeps foods colder than water ice does.

What happened to the flame? Fire requires oxygen. The gas from the dry ice is carbon dioxide. Carbon dioxide is heavier than air so when it is poured over the candle it pushes the oxygen molecules away, causing the fire to go out.

Carbon dioxide gas is what gives soda pop its fizz. The gas is added to the liquid under pressure. When a can of soda is opened, the gas begins to come out of the liquid, making it fizzy, just like your cup of water.

Although the polar ice caps on Mars contain regular water ice, they also contain carbon dioxide. Carbon dioxide has very different properties from water.

Mars probes

More space probes have visited Mars than any other object in space. Research some of the probes that have gone to Mars and what they have discovered. Four different space agencies have successfully sent probes to Mars. These include the Soviet Union, NASA, the European Space Agency, and the Indian Space Research Organization.

You may want to start by researching the Viking landers, but be sure to find out about more recent probes to the red planet, such as *Spirit*, *Opportunity*, and *Curiosity*, as well. The NASA website is a good place to start your research. Prepare a short presentation on what you learned about Mars space probes.

Spirit looks back at its lander in Gusev Crater on Mars

23

Jupiter

The gas giant

What is the largest planet in our solar system like?

Challenge words:

vortex

Mercury, Venus, Earth, and Mars are considered the terrestrial or "Earth-like" planets. These planets are relatively small compared to the other planets in our solar system, and their surfaces are solid rock. Beginning with Jupiter, the outer planets are called Jovian or "Jupiter-like" because Jupiter, Saturn, Uranus, and Neptune are large gas planets.

Jupiter is the giant of our solar system. Its diameter is 89,372 miles (143,800 km) across compared with Earth's diameter of only 7,927 miles (12,757 km). It is 1½ times as big as all of the other planets put together. Because of its large size, it was named Jupiter after the ruler of the Roman gods. Its large mass gives it a surface gravity that is 2.64 times that of Earth.

Jupiter is the fastest spinning planet in the solar system. It rotates on its axis every 9 hours and 55 minutes. This fast rotation causes the planet to bulge noticeably at its equator. However, it is not as speedy around the sun. Its revolution around the sun takes 11.86 Earth years to complete. It is an average of 483 million miles (778 million km) from the sun.

Jupiter is composed mainly of hydrogen and helium. It has an atmosphere of hydrogen gas that is hundreds of miles thick. The temperature at the top of the clouds is believed to be –250°F (–157°C). One of the most striking features of Jupiter's atmosphere is the Great Red Spot. This spot is an area in the atmosphere the size of three Earths. Most scientists believe the Great Red Spot is a giant windstorm. It shrinks and grows and its color changes from pink to bright red. But it is in

Three Earths would fit inside Jupiter's Great Red Spot.

Planets

the same position and has the same oval shape that is has had since it was first discovered almost 300 years ago.

Jupiter's surface is made of hydrogen liquid and gas, and is believed to be 10,000 miles (16,000 km) deep. The center of the planet is very hot. This heat stirs up the liquid and gas hydrogen in a similar way to the convection experienced on the sun.

For years it was thought that Jupiter had 16 moons orbiting it, but recent discoveries have pushed that number to more than sixty. Most of these moons are very small, but four are quite large. The four largest moons are often referred to as the Galilean moons because Galileo was the first person to see them. Galileo named these moons Io, Europa, Ganymede, and Callisto. Io (shown here) has many active volcanoes. Europa is covered with ice. Ganymede is the largest moon in the solar system and is larger than the planet Mercury. Callisto is also larger than Mercury and is made of ice and rock. Astronomers discovered the smaller moons with better telescopes and with space probes. The *Voyager* space probe also discovered a ring around Jupiter that had not been seen

Jupiter's moon Io

by telescopes. It is now believed that Jupiter has four rings. These rings are made of bits of rock and dust and were most likely a result of particles that were broken off of Jupiter's moons when they were struck by meteorites. Instead of flying off into space, Jupiter's gravity pulled the particles into orbit.

 ## The giant planet

Purpose: To appreciate just how big Jupiter is

Materials: two cereal bowls, marbles (enough to fill both bowls)

Procedure:

1. Place two empty cereal bowls together to represent Jupiter.

2. Fill the two cereal bowls with marbles. The marbles represent the size of the earth.

3. Count how many marbles are in the bowls.

Questions:

- How many marbles fit in the two bowls?

- How many actual Earths do you think could fit inside Jupiter? (The answer is more than 1,300!)

Conclusion:

What other items could be used to represent different objects in the solar system? Jupiter's diameter is about 11 times bigger than Earth's diameter, and the sun's diameter is about 10 times bigger than Jupiter's. What can you find that is about 10 times bigger around than the cereal bowl? Perhaps you have a giant beach ball or other very large ball that could represent the sun. What could you use to represent the dwarf planet Pluto? Pluto's diameter is about 5 times smaller than Earth's. Perhaps a BB could be used to represent Pluto. Take a guess at how many BBs would be needed to fill both cereal bowls. Now you have an idea of how large Jupiter really is.

Taking it further

- Why does Jupiter bulge more in the middle than Earth does?
- Why can't life exist on Jupiter?
- Why are space probes necessary for exploring other planets?

 # What did we learn?

- What are some major differences between Jupiter and the inner planets?
- What is the Great Red Spot?

Great red spot

Jupiter is well known for its Great Red Spot. Recently scientists have discovered a new spot on Jupiter that some scientists have dubbed "Red Spot Jr." Beginning in 2000, three smaller spots collided and formed one bigger spot. The original spots were white and for some time the new spot remained white. Then in 2003, the new spot began to change colors and is now almost identical in color to the Great Red Spot.

Scientists do not know why these storms are red. There are many ideas but no one knows for sure. Some scientists think that the power of the storm pulls material from deep below the clouds and lifts it up to the surface of the storm, where solar radiation somehow causes a chemical reaction that turns the storm red.

Purpose: To simulate the movement of particles inside the Great Red Spot

Materials: clear cup, tea bag, pencil, water

Procedure:

1. Fill a clear cup with water.
2. Open a tea bag and pour the tea leaves into the glass.
3. Insert a pencil into the center of the glass and swirl it around quickly.

Conclusion: If you swirled the pencil properly, you created a vortex. Watch as the tea leaves are sucked into the center of the vortex. This is similar to how storms such as tornadoes and hurricanes work on Earth as well.

Planets

24

Saturn

Surrounded by
beautiful rings

What makes the sixth planet unique?

Challenge words:

shepherding moons

Saturn is the second largest planet in the solar system. Like Jupiter, it is a gas planet with an atmosphere composed mostly of hydrogen and helium. It is the sixth planet from the sun and was named for the Roman god of farming. However, Saturn is most famous for the beautiful rings that surround it.

Galileo was the first person to see the rings around Saturn when he viewed them with his telescope in 1610. However, he could not see them clearly enough to know what they were. Galileo thought that Saturn had two smaller globes circling around it because he saw what looked like "ears" on the sides of the planet. This phenomenon remained a mystery until 1659 when an astronomer named Christian Huygens was able to use a better telescope and discovered that the "ears" were actually rings around the planet.

From Earth we can see only a few rings around Saturn. However, when the *Voyager* space probe explored Saturn in 1980, it was discovered that there are actually thousands of smaller rings around the planet. The rings are composed of pieces of ice, dust, and rocks. The band of rings is 170,000 miles (274,000 km) across and less than 3 miles (4.8 km) thick. Secular scientists have not been able to come up with a good explanation as to how Saturn's rings could form. Plus, we know that the rings are eroding

Fun Fact

Saturn has a stormy atmosphere with winds clocked at about 1,118 miles per hour (500 m/s) near the equator.

quickly, so they could not have been there for millions of years. We know from the Bible that God created Saturn on Day 4 of Creation Week, about 6,000 years ago, so the rings couldn't be older than that.

In addition to the thousands of rings, Saturn also has over 60 moons, most of which have been discovered in the 21st century. One moon is large, six are medium-sized, and the rest are very small. Most of the moons are covered in ice and full of craters. The largest moon is called Titan. Titan is the second largest moon in the solar system and is bigger than Mercury. Titan has an atmosphere consisting mostly of nitrogen with a small amount of methane. It is the only moon in the solar system known to have a substantial atmosphere.

Like Jupiter, Saturn spins very quickly on its axis. It makes one complete rotation every 10 hours and 33 minutes. This fast rotation causes Saturn to bulge in the middle just as Jupiter does. Saturn averages 887 million miles (1.4 billion km) from the sun and revolves around the sun once every 29.46 Earth years. Saturn is tilted on its axis with respect to Earth in such a way that about every 14–15 years the rings are edge-on toward the earth, making them seem to disappear for a time. Saturn will line up in this way again in the year 2024.

Fun Fact

The Cassini-Huygens mission was launched on October 15, 1997. This is the first spacecraft to explore Saturn's rings and moons from orbit. The *Cassini* spacecraft entered orbit on June 30, 2004 and immediately began sending back intriguing images and data. The *Huygens* Probe dove into Titan's thick atmosphere in January 2005 and sent data for about 90 minutes after reaching the surface. The touchdown on the surface of Titan marked the farthest a man-made spacecraft has successfully landed away from Earth.

What do you see?

When Galileo first saw the rings around Saturn, he did not know what they were. He described them as ears on the planet. He knew they were not ears but could not tell what they were. He guessed that they could have been smaller satellites orbiting Saturn. Our minds interpret what we see based on what we know. If we see something we are not familiar with, our brains connect the image with something we are familiar with. For a fun example of this, look at the pictures shown here.

What do you see? In the left picture, do you see a duck or a rabbit? In the right picture, do you see a vase or two people facing each other? Most people can see either

image if they know to look for them, but different people see different things at first glance.

Taking it further

 # What did we learn?

- Who first saw Saturn's rings?
- What are Saturn's rings made of?
- What makes Titan unique among moons?

- Why did astronomers believe that Saturn had only a few rings before the *Voyager* space probe explored Saturn?
- Both Titan and Earth have a mostly nitrogen atmosphere. What important differences exist between these two worlds that make Earth able to support life but Titan unable to?

Saturn's amazing features

Since the time of their discovery, Saturn and its rings have captured people's imaginations. There are seven major bands of rings around Saturn, labeled A through G. There is also a dark area between the A-ring and the B-ring that is called the Cassini Division. Each band of rings is from hundreds to hundreds of thousands of miles wide and can contain thousands of ringlets.

With the use of space probes, scientists have been able to learn more about these rings. In 1980, the *Voyager* space probe revealed that at least two of Saturn's moons, Prometheus and Pandora, may play a part in keeping the rings in place. These moons are very small. Pandora orbits on the outside of Saturn's F-ring while Prometheus orbits between the F-ring and Saturn. It is believed that the gravity from these moons plays some role in keeping the particles in the ring in orbit around Saturn. Thus, they have been called **shepherding moons**. However, there is some indication that these moons could also disrupt the orbit of some of the particles, so more study is needed to really understand what effect these moons actually have.

In 2004 the *Cassini-Huygens* space probe began sending back images from orbit around Saturn. These data have revealed many new and interesting things about Saturn. One moon, called Enceladus, which orbits in the E-ring, was observed shooting out jets of vapor and dust from its south pole. This is now believed to be the source of the material in the E-ring. Also, many new moons and moonlets have been discovered

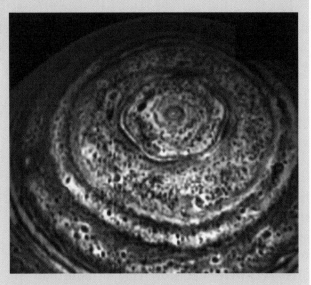

orbiting within the ring structures. There appears to be a somewhat complicated interplay between the moons and the rings. Data are still being collected and will continue to be analyzed in hopes of discovering how all these things work together.

One amazing and unique feature discovered on Saturn is a double hexagon formed in the clouds of the planet's North pole (pictured above). Scientists are unable to explain its origin or how it has maintained this shape since it was first discovered in 1981. What do you think it might be?

While we may not understand all the features of Saturn, or the workings of its moons and rings, we can rejoice in the beauty that God has created.

Planets

Uranus

Seventh planet from the sun

What is the seventh planet from the sun like?

Even before the invention of the telescope, astronomers knew of the existence of five planets besides Earth. The planets could be seen shining in the night sky. However, the planets farthest away were not discovered until more than 150 years after the invention of the telescope. The first of these new discoveries was made in 1781, when an English astronomer named William Herschel discovered Uranus (YOOR-uh-nus). He named the planet for the Roman god of the heavens.

Uranus is a pale blue color. It has an atmosphere of hydrogen, helium, and methane that completely obscures any view of the planet's surface. The atmosphere contains clouds and has winds that move from east to west at 90–360 mph (40–160 m/s). Its average distance from the sun is 1,783 million miles (2.8 billion km), and it revolves around the sun once every 84 Earth years. Since it takes 84 years for Uranus to orbit the sun, each season on Uranus is 21 years long. This may sound like a long hot summer; however, the average temperature on Uranus is −365°F (−220°C), even in the sun. Uranus is so far from the sun, that the sun's rays have little effect on it so it remains very cold.

Uranus rotates on its axis once every 17 hours and 14 minutes. However, Uranus's rotation on its axis is unique. Whereas most planets rotate with a slight tilt from vertical with respect to the sun, Uranus rotates at a nearly 90-degree angle as if it were on its side compared to the other planets in the solar system. Uranus appears to roll around the sun because of this unusual tilt. This situation is impossible, according to evolutionary ideas about the formation of the solar system, namely that the planets condensed from a rotating nebula. Secular scientists have no plausible explanation for Uranus's strange angle of rotation.

Voyager 2 is the only space probe to visit Uranus. It visited the planet in 1986. Uranus has more than 20 known moons that orbit it. Ten of these moons were discovered by *Voyager 2*. Five of Uranus's moons are relatively large and the others are relatively small. Several of the moons orbit very close to the planet. Just as the planet rotates at a 90-degree angle, so the moons revolve around the planet at a 90-degree

Fun Fact

Caroline Herschel, William's sister, became a noted astronomer in her own right—the first important woman astronomer. She discovered eight comets and three nebulae.

Planets

angle from how the moons revolve around the other planets. The moons revolve around the planet vertically. The above diagram illustrates how Uranus orbits the sun and how the moons orbit Uranus.

In addition to the moons, Uranus is also surrounded by at least 13 rings. Some of these rings have been discovered using telescopes, and others were discovered when *Voyager 2* passed by Uranus. Some of the rings contain chunks of black material that has yet to be identified. Much remains unknown about this planet because it is so far away from Earth.

For more information on Uranus and how it shows God's handiwork, do a search on the Answers in Genesis website.

What did we learn?

- What makes Uranus unusual compared to the other planets?
- How have rings been discovered around Uranus?

Taking it further

- How can we learn more about Uranus?
- Why is Uranus such a cold planet?

Rotations & revolutions

Purpose: To illustrate the unusual rotation of Uranus

Materials: ping-pong ball, two colors of paint, large ball

Procedure:

1. Paint one half of a ping-pong ball one color and the other half a different color.

2. Once the paint is dry, place a larger ball on the floor to represent the sun.

3. Practice rolling the ping-pong ball on the floor around the larger ball in such a way that it rolls along the line separating the two colors, so that one side of the ball is facing the "sun" at one side of the orbit and the other side is facing the "sun" when it is half way around the orbit, like the planet in the diagram above. This is how Uranus orbits the sun.

⚜️ Tilt and rotation

Each planet in the solar system orbits at a different angle compared to the plane in which it orbits the sun, and some planets rotate in opposite directions. Below is a chart showing the angle and direction of rotation for each planet. Use this information to make models of each planet.

Purpose: To make a model of each planet showing angle of tilt and direction of rotation

Materials: modeling clay, 8 pencils, protractor, index cards

Procedure:

1. Make a ball of clay to represent each planet.

2. Push a pencil through each ball to represent the axis of rotation.

3. Place a piece of modeling clay on the table and insert the sharpened end of the pencil into the clay.

4. Use a protractor to measure the angle of the tilt for that planet and press the clay against the pencil to hold it in place.

5. Write the name of the planet, its angle of tilt, and its direction of rotation on an index card and place the card in front of the model.

6. You can take a picture of your models to help you remember what they look like.

Planet	Angle of Tilt from Vertical	Direction of Rotation (viewed from North pole)
Mercury	0°	Counter clockwise (toward east)
Venus	3°	Clockwise (toward west)
Earth	23°	Counter clockwise (toward east)
Mars	24°	Counter clockwise (toward east)
Jupiter	3°	Counter clockwise (toward east)
Saturn	27°	Counter clockwise (toward east)
Uranus	98°	Clockwise (toward west, forward)
Neptune	29°	Counter clockwise (toward east)

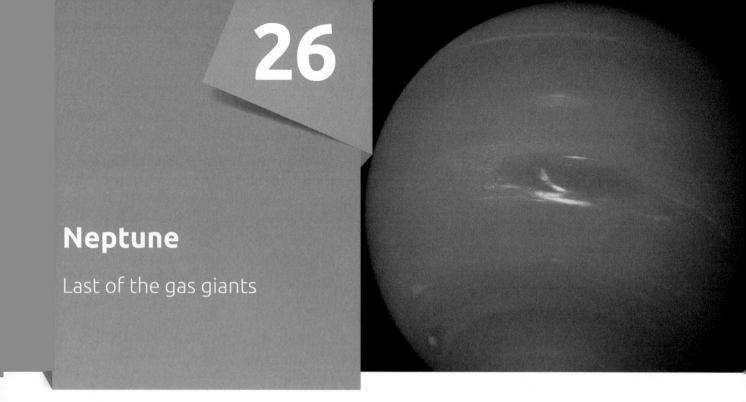

26

Neptune

Last of the gas giants

What is the farthest planet from the sun like?

Challenge words:

centripetal force

The last of the gas giants is Neptune, the eighth planet from the sun. Neptune was discovered in 1846, and named for the Roman god of the sea. It was discovered in a rather unusual way. Astronomers noticed that when they observed Uranus's location it was not always quite where they expected it to be. They theorized that the gravitational pull of another planet could be affecting its orbit. A British astronomer named John Couch Adams and a French astronomer named Jean Leverrier calculated where a planet would have to be in order to affect Uranus' orbit. When the German astronomer Johann Gottfried Galle looked in the predicted location, he discovered Neptune only one degree off from the predicted location.

Neptune is so far away that it can only be viewed with a very good telescope. It is an average of 2,794 million miles (4.5 billion km) from the sun. It is so distant from the sun that from the surface of Neptune, the sun would appear to be only a bright star. It revolves around the sun once every 164.8 Earth years and rotates on its axis once every 18 hours and 30 minutes.

Neptune has an atmosphere composed mostly of hydrogen, helium, and methane. Methane absorbs red and other colors and reflects blue so the planet appears to be blue. It has streaky methane ice clouds. And like Jupiter, Neptune had what is believed to be a giant storm in an area called the Great Dark Spot. It is believed that the winds in the Great Dark Spot blew at more than 700 mph (313 m/s). The Great Dark Spot seems to have disappeared for now. But astronomers believe they discovered a new storm in 1994, using the Hubble Telescope. Some scientists believe that the Dark Spot may actually be a hole in the clouds surrounding Neptune. Until more information can be gathered we may not know for sure what these dark spots are.

Neptune is the farthest out of the gas giants. It

Fun Fact

Neptune was discovered in 1846 (over 160 years ago). Since that time, it has made only one complete orbit around the sun, because one Neptune year lasts nearly 165 Earth years.

is nearly the same size as Uranus. It has at least four rings and 13 moons. Two of the moons are large and the rest are small. The largest moon is called Triton. Triton is about 1,700 miles (2,736 km) across, nearly the same size as our moon. Triton has a retrograde, or backwards, orbit around the planet compared to the orbits of other moons around their planets. Triton has many geysers that shoot out cold nitrogen gas and dust particles.

For more information on Neptune and how it shows God's handiwork, do a search on the Answers in Genesis website. 🌐

What did we learn?

- What similarities are there between Uranus and Neptune?
- What are two possible explanations for the Great Dark Spot?

Taking it further

- Explain how Neptune was discovered.
- What affects the color of a planet?

🧪 Reflection of colored light

Purpose: To demonstrate how different colors of light can be absorbed

Materials: three clear plastic or glass cups, red and blue food coloring, flashlight

Procedure:

1. Fill three clear plastic or glass cups with water.

2. Add blue food coloring to one cup and red food coloring to another.

3. Shine a flashlight through the clear cup of water, projecting the beam onto a wall. What color is the light? (It should be white, or perhaps a bit yellow or blue depending on the type of bulb in the flashlight.)

4. Next, shine the flashlight through the cup with blue water. What color was the light on the wall? (The light was blue because the blue water absorbed all colors except blue and allowed the blue light to pass through.)

5. Now shine the flashlight through the cup of red water. What color was the light on the wall? (The red water absorbed all colors of light except the red light.)

Conclusion: Like Uranus, Neptune's atmosphere is primarily made up of hydrogen, helium, and methane. Methane absorbs all colors of light except blue so only blue light is reflected, giving the planet a blue appearance.

Similar to our experiment, scientists can determine the elements in a planet's atmosphere by the wavelength of light that is reflected.

Centripetal force

Take a close look at the Planet Statistics on page 255. What do you notice about the length of time it takes for each planet to orbit the sun? You will notice that Mercury, the closest planet, obits the sun in only 88 days. Pluto, farthest from the sun, orbits the sun in 248 years, which is about 90,520 days. If you convert all of the orbits into days, you will see that the farther a planet is from the sun, the slower it orbits the sun. Let's see why this is.

Purpose: To see how gravity affects rate of orbit

Materials: metal washer, string

Procedure:

1. Tie a washer to the end of a string that is three feet (1 m) long.

2. Go outside away from any buildings and other people to try this experiment. Holding the string near the end, twirl the string above your head. Exert just enough force to keep the washer moving at its slowest speed. The string is applying centripetal force to the washer much like the sun's gravity pulls on the planets and keeps them in orbit.

3. Next, hold the string in the middle and repeat the experiment. Note the pressure between your hand and the string and the speed you must spin the washer to keep it moving.

4. Now, shorten the string to only a few inches and spin the washer again. It should spin very quickly. Again, note the pressure between your hand and the string and the speed of the washer.

Questions:

- Were you able to spin the washer as slowly after you shortened the string?

- How does the pressure between your hand and the string compare when the string is short and when the string is long?

Conclusion: As the string shortened, you had to exert more pressure to keep the washer spinning and its speed increased. In much the same way, the gravitational pull is greater on a planet that is closer to the sun. The gravity of the sun exerts a force on each planet called centripetal force, which is the force that causes something to move in a circle. In our experiment, the pull of the string was the centripetal force. The greater the force the faster something moves. So as the gravity decreases it causes the planet to orbit at a slower rate.

Planets

27

Pluto & Eris

Plutoids

What is Pluto, the former planet, like?

Words to know:

synchronous orbit

Pluto is very small and very far away from the sun. Because of its distance from Earth and its small size, it was not discovered until 1930. A young American astronomer named Clyde Tombaugh is credited with the discovery. Although Percival Lowell, owner of the Lowell Observatory, believed that there was a ninth planet, he was unable to find it before he died. Tombaugh, an astronomer working at the Lowell Observatory in Arizona, used Lowell's calculations and eventually found the elusive planet. It was much dimmer than Lowell expected and was thus harder to find. The name *Pluto* was first suggested by Venetia Burney, an 11-year-old school girl from England. The name

Fun Fact

Since Adam and Eve were created about 6,000 years ago, Pluto has orbited the sun about 24 times.

won out over numerous other suggestions partly because it was named after the Roman god of the underworld (who was able to make himself invisible) and because the first two letters were the same as Percival Lowell's initials.

Because Pluto is so far away, very little is known about it. It is believed to be a ball of frozen methane, water, and rock. It may possibly have a very thin methane atmosphere, but only part of the time. The gases become frozen when Pluto is far from the sun and only comprise an atmosphere when the planet is close enough to the sun to melt the gases. It is believed that the average temperature on Pluto is a cold −370°F (−223°C).

In 1978 a moon was discovered orbiting Pluto. It was named Charon after the ferryman of the dead in Greek mythology. Charon is about 50% the size of Pluto, making it very large in comparison to the object it orbits. Some people have said that Pluto and Charon should be considered a double planet system.

Charon orbits Pluto in a **synchronous orbit**. This means that Pluto and its satellite are always presenting the same side to each other. If you were to stand on Pluto, Charon would appear to hover in the sky and not move. In May 2005 the Hubble telescope was being used to observe Pluto, and scientists discovered two new satellites

Planets

NASA's *New Horizons* probe captured this high-resolution enhanced color view of Pluto on July 14, 2015.

orbiting Pluto. Additional images from the Hubble in 2006 confirmed that Pluto has two additional moons. These new moons have been named Nix and Hydra, also names from Greek mythology. More recently two additional moons, Kerberos and Styx, have been discovered, bringing the total known moons around Pluto to five.

Pluto's orbit around the sun is an elongated ellipse that actually crosses Neptune's orbit. So, for 20 out of every 250 years, Pluto is closer to the sun than Neptune. The last time this occurred was from 1979–1999. From Pluto, the sun appears to be a small bright dot in the sky.

Pluto is very small. Its diameter is only 1,425 miles (2,294 km), compared to Earth's diameter of 7,927 miles (12,757 km). It has a very small mass and is believed to have a gravitational pull of only 0.08 times that of Earth.

For many years Pluto was considered the ninth planet in our solar system. However, in 2006 the International Astronomical Union (IAU), a large group of astronomers who are largely responsible for naming new discoveries in space, changed the definition of a planet. When this happened, Pluto no longer fit the definition and was changed from a planet to a dwarf planet. If you recall from lesson 8, Ceres, the largest asteroid in the asteroid belt is also classified as a dwarf planet. Then in 2008, the IAU specified that dwarf planets that orbit the sun farther away than Neptune would be called plutoids. Many people originally objected to removing Pluto from the list of planets, but as more orbiting bodies have been discovered beyond Neptune, it appears that Pluto's designation as a plutoid will remain.

This change in designation was prompted by the discovery in 2005 of another dwarf planet

How much do I weigh?

Complete the "How Much Do I Weigh?" worksheet.

that orbits farther from the sun than Pluto and is more massive than Pluto. This body was named Eris. Rather than call Eris a tenth planet, the IAU changed the definitions, and Eris became the second known plutoid. Since then two other plutiods have been named, Haumea and Makemake. It is believed, however, that there are dozens and perhaps hundreds of heavenly bodies that fit the definition of plutoids, and many of these may be named in the future.

In addition to plutoids, astronomers have discovered thousands of planets orbiting stars outside our solar system. These planets are called exoplanets. Very few of these planet have actually been seen by astronomers. Most have been detected by how they affect the movement or the light of the stars they orbit. Beyond our solar system there could be millions of planets orbiting other stars. We do not yet possess the technology to see in detail beyond our solar system; however, we will continue to study the vastness of space and learn more about the wonderful universe God has created.

What did we learn?

- What discovery was originally considered to be the ninth planet?
- How does the gravity on Pluto compare to the gravity on Earth?
- Is Pluto always farther from the sun than Neptune?
- What is unique about how Charon orbits Pluto?

Taking it further

- Why did it take so long to discover Pluto?
- Why is Pluto no longer considered to be a planet?
- What alternate classification was given to Pluto in 2006?

New Horizons

Because the only way to get detailed information about a planet is to send a space probe there, NASA launched a probe called *New Horizons* on January 19, 2006. In 2007 *New Horizons* passed close to Jupiter and took many photographs of Jupiter, its rings, and its moons. The gravity of Jupiter was then used to increase the speed of the probe, sending it on its way to Pluto. It arrived at Pluto in 2015.

New Horizons carries seven different scientific instruments that are designed to give us information about the composition, geography, and atmosphere of both Pluto and Charon. *New Horizons* will give us the best opportunity to observe the newly discovered moons as well.

Once the probe sends back information on Pluto and Charon, it is scheduled to continue on into the Kuiper Belt beyond Pluto's orbit and send back information on what it encounters there.

Planet Statistics

One way to learn more about the planets in our solar system is to compare certain statistics. By seeing how the various planets compare to Earth, we can get a better feel for how big the other planets are, where they are located compared to Earth, and how they move.

Planet	Avg. distance from sun (in millions)	Revolution around sun	Rotation on axis	Diameter	Volume compared to Earth	Mass compared to Earth
Mercury	36 miles (58 km)	88 days	58.6 days	3,031 miles (4877 km)	0.06	0.056
Venus	67 miles (108 km)	224.7 days	243 days	7,521 miles (12,101 km)	0.97	0.82
Earth	93 miles (150 km)	365.26 days (1 year)	23 hr 56 min (1 day)	7,927 miles (12,757 km)	1.0	1.0
Mars	143 miles (230 km)	628 days	24 hr 38 min	4,222 miles (6793 km)	0.15	0.11
Jupiter	483 miles (778 km)	11.86 years	9 hr 55 min	89,372 miles (143,800 km)	1324	318
Saturn	887 miles (1,427 km)	29.46 years	10 hr 40 min	74,990 miles (120,660 km)	736	95.1
Uranus	1,783 miles (2,870 km)	84 years	17 hr 14 min	31,700 miles (51,118 km)	64	14.5
Neptune	2,794 miles (4,497 km)	164.8 years	16 hr 6 min	30,764 miles (49,500 km)	58	17.2
Pluto (dwarf planet)	3,666 miles (5,900 km)	248 years	6 days 9 hr	1,425 miles (2,294 km)	0.01	0.002
Eris (dwarf planet)	9,000 miles (15,000 km)	557 years	8 hr	1,500 miles (2,400 km)	0.01	0.003

UNIT 5

Space Program

◊ **Describe** how rockets and satellites are used by mankind.

◊ **Identify** the goals of the Apollo missions.

◊ **Identify** the major differences between the space shuttle and previous spacecraft.

◊ **Identify** the purpose of the International Space Station.

28

NASA

The National Aeronautics and Space Administration

What is NASA, and what does it do?

Words to know:

NASA

escape velocity

Challenge words:

NACA

supersonic

The study of space is a very exciting field, and although many countries and many scientific groups have contributed to our exploration of space, none has done as much to promote our understanding of the universe as NASA has. NASA, the National Aeronautics and Space Administration, is a government-funded scientific organization dedicated to exploring the universe.

NASA was founded in 1958 by President Dwight Eisenhower. It was an outgrowth of the National Advisory Committee on Aeronautics, an organization that was already working to improve aircraft. NASA's focus was not only on flying vehicles, but also on space exploration.

Throughout the 1960s, NASA's main goal was to develop the technology necessary to place a man on the moon. This was accomplished through three separate programs: Mercury, Gemini, and Apollo. We will study these programs in more detail in a later lesson. In addition to these programs, NASA also worked on weather and communications satellites.

Today, NASA is involved in many different areas of space research. There are people in NASA that design and develop better tools and technologies to use in space. These technologies are not only used by

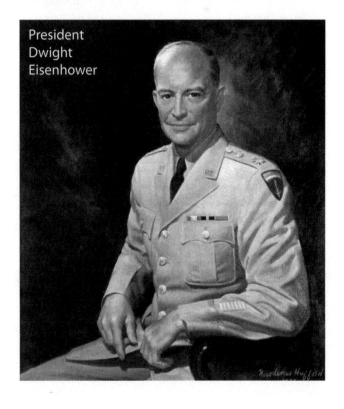

President Dwight Eisenhower

NASA but are often used to improve commercial and military space applications as well. Other groups in NASA work on projects to put humans and robots into space. A third area that NASA is involved in is collecting and analyzing data from different space related projects including data from probes, the space station, Hubble, and other missions in space. Other groups plan missions and oversee the actual launch of rockets, probes, and other items into space.

As you can see, NASA is involved in a broad scope of activities, from research and development, to space flights and data analysis. Many of these activities have had a profound impact on everyone on earth. Not only are we more aware of what is in the universe, but many of the technologies developed for the space programs have contributed to non-space developments as well.

In the 1960s NASA developed digital imaging systems to receive images from the moon. This technology led to medical imaging systems that are used to help diagnose and treat patients. More recently, NASA developed a cable system that responds to human touch. This system has been developed into a special kind of walker that aids patients with spinal cord injuries in their rehabilitation process. Another NASA invention is likely to benefit people at the gas pump. NASA developed a new flow meter process for the space shuttle. This meter is being made available to oil and gas refineries and other industries that must regulate the flow of liquids. The NASA flow meter is much more efficient than older systems and can greatly reduce the energy needed to push the liquids through the pipes. Other examples include the joystick control system used to

 # Escape velocity

In order to launch a vehicle into space, scientists had to find a way for it to escape the pull of earth's gravity. Since the earth is always pulling things toward the center of the earth, a spacecraft must be moving fast enough to overcome this force. The speed required to overcome gravity is called **escape velocity.** On earth, escape velocity is approximately 25,000 mph (40,000 km/h). So far, all spacecraft that have been launched have used rockets to generate escape velocity. However, NASA is working with the aviation industry to develop jet technology that can also propel aircraft into space.

Purpose: To demonstrate how escape velocity works

Materials: tagboard/poster board, tape, magnet, plastic lid or dish, several books, steel BBs

Procedure:

1. Cut a 4-inch wide by 12-inch long strip of tagboard or stiff paper. Fold the paper in half the long way. Now, fold each long edge of the paper back toward the fold so that the paper looks like an M. This is your ramp.

2. Tape a magnet to one end of the ramp.

3. Place the magnet end of the ramp inside the edge of a plastic lid or dish with sides.

4. Place a book under the other end of the ramp to give it a slight tilt.

5. Now, place a steel BB at the top of the ramp and let it go. Note what happens to it. If the BB sticks to the magnet, remove it.

6. Next, add another book under the end of the ramp to make it steeper. Release another BB from the top of the ramp. Note the speed of this BB. If the second BB sticks to the magnet, remove it from the magnet.

7. Add a third book to the ramp, and try it again. What happened to this BB?

Questions:

- What happened to the first BB? Why?

- What happened to the second BB? The third? Why?

Conclusion:

When the BB is moving faster it has more momentum; thus it takes more force to stop it. The first BB was probably attracted to the magnet because it was not moving fast enough to escape the magnetic pull. This is similar to the pull of gravity on a space craft. If the second or third BB was moving fast enough, the force of the magnet would not have stopped it. Similarly, if a spacecraft is moving fast enough, the earth's gravity does not have enough force to stop it and pull it back to the surface of the earth. This required speed is called the escape velocity.

maneuver the lunar vehicle, which has been adapted to automobiles, allowing disabled people to operate their cars using only their hands, and the development of scratch-resistant eyeglasses. The space industry developed a strong yet light coating to protect equipment in space. This coating was later adapted as a coating for plastic lenses that provides greatly-improved scratch resistance. As NASA develops new technologies for space research, many of these technologies will be adapted to uses closer to home.

Although NASA has accomplished many great feats, it should be noted that NASA as a whole is dedicated to evolutionary ideas. Many of its programs are being designed specifically to prove that the origins of the universe and life are naturalistic. Because of their blatant evolutionary bias, NASA scientists will interpret data to fit their old universe, naturalistic worldview and will likely miss many of the wonders that God has waiting for us to discover.

 What did we learn?

- What is NASA?
- When was NASA formed?
- What was one of NASA's first tasks?
- List at least three different types of projects that a person at NASA could work on.

 Taking it further

- How does NASA help people who are not interested in space exploration?
- How might an evolutionary worldview affect NASA's work?

 NACA

NASA grew out of an organization called the National Advisory Committee on Aeronautics (NACA). NACA was created by President Woodrow Wilson on March 3, 1915. According to President Wilson, its purpose was "to supervise and direct the scientific study of the problems of flight, with a view to their practical solution." NACA provided oversight and direction for the development of new aircraft from 1915 until it became part of NASA in 1958.

NACA was instrumental in developing many of the technologies that were used in civilian and military aircraft. NACA engineers designed better engines, better airfoils, and better wing designs. They also developed the first supersonic (faster than the speed of sound) wind tunnel to allow testing of designs for supersonic aircraft.

NACA also pioneered many of the inventions and ideas that have made flying safer. The NACA engineers designed a system to prevent ice formation on wings and propellers, and were the first to use a refrigerated wind tunnel to test their inventions under cold conditions. NACA also instituted licensing of pilots, supported

weather research to improve navigation safety, and recommended inspection and expansion of airmail.

In 1952 NACA began doing research on problems that might be encountered in space. In 1954 it worked together with the U.S. Air Force to develop a high altitude research vehicle called the X-15 (shown here). This aircraft was a rocket-propelled craft that could fly into the upper atmosphere and give researchers the chance to see what space flight might be like.

In 1958 NACA became part of the new space agency, NASA, but they continued to do aeronautic research. Today, the scientists at NASA are working on technology that will allow aircraft to go into space using propulsion methods other than rockets. In 2004, NASA engineers set air speed records for air-powered engines by flying their plane at Mach 9.6 (6,800 mph).

NACA has always believed that sharing its technology with the civilian and military aircraft designers benefits everyone. Thus, the vision of President Wilson to find practical solutions to the problems of flight continues to live on in the work that is being done by the scientists and engineers at NASA today.

Questions:

- What was NACA?

- What was its original purpose?

- What were some of the major contributions to aeronautics that were made by NACA?

Pilot Neil Armstrong next to the X-15 after a research flight

29

Space Exploration

Seeing what's out there

How do we study deep space?

Words to know:

space probe

The idea of space travel originated in science fiction. The earliest ideas were in the writings of Jules Verne, H. G. Wells, and other 19th-century authors. At that time no one took the idea of space travel seriously. However, Robert H. Goddard was influenced by these writers and began experimenting with rockets. He wrote his own book on rocket flight, called *A Method of Reaching Extreme Altitudes*, in 1919. Goddard performed the first flight of a liquid-fueled rocket on March 16, 1926. He continued his work on rockets and flew the first rocket to go faster than the speed of sound in 1935. Today, Robert Goddard is considered the father of modern rocketry. NASA's Goddard Space Flight Center near Washington, D.C., is named for him. However, during his lifetime people did not take Goddard's work seriously. It wasn't until after rockets were used during World War II that the idea of sending rockets into space took hold. After World War II, Wernher von Braun and other German scientists came to America to help develop rockets, and Soviet scientists began working on rockets in earnest as well. The earliest rockets were unreliable, but

as rockets became more reliable, a race began to see who would be the first nation to get to space.

The Soviet Union (a former northern Eurasian empire from 1922–1991, consisting of 15 Socialist Republics of which Russia was the largest) won the first lap of the race by putting the first man-made

Robert Goddard with an early rocket

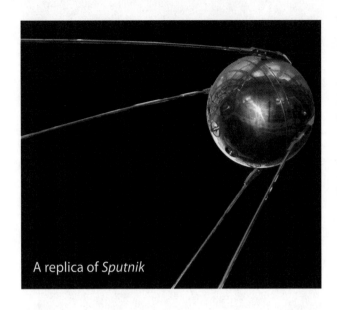
A replica of *Sputnik*

The ECHO satellite. Note the car and people at bottom center for scale.

satellite into orbit. *Sputnik*, shown here, was launched October 4, 1957. The first U.S. satellite, *Explorer 1*, was launched just a few months later on January 31, 1958. This sparked a huge interest in space and rockets around the world.

The next step was to put a man into space. Again, the Soviets were the first to do this. Yuri Gagarin was the first man in space on April 12, 1961. The first American in space was Alan Shepherd in May 1961, and the first American to orbit earth was John Glenn on February 20, 1962. The Soviets continued to lead in the space race by putting the first woman in space when Valentina Tereshkova went up in 1963, and by performing the first space walk in 1965.

These early successes by the Soviet Union led U.S. President John F. Kennedy, in May 1961, to challenge America to place a man on the moon by the end of the decade. This was a monumental task to complete in less than nine years. This was accomplished through three projects. The Mercury project had the goal of manned space flight. Each Mercury capsule held one person. There were four orbital flights in all. The second project was called Gemini and was designed for two-man space flight. Gemini taught scientists many things about space flight as well as how

people interact and work together. The third project was the Apollo project whose goal was to put a man on the moon. NASA achieved President Kennedy's goal when Neil Armstrong stepped on the moon on July 20, 1969. America became the new leader in the space race. Today, the United States continues to lead in the development of space technology and space exploration, but Russia and many other countries continue to be involved in space exploration as well.

In addition to manned space flight, the United States, the Soviet Union, and other countries worked to send scientific satellites into space to gather data about earth including data on the land, atmosphere, and weather. Other satellites were developed for communications. The ECHO satellite, shown here, was NASA's first communications satellite, launched in 1960. This work continues today with many satellites being used for scientific purposes. One of the most famous scientific satellites is the Hubble Space Telescope.

Satellites are also used for commercial purposes such as television and telephone transmission. One of the most useful types of satellite is the Global Positioning Satellite (GPS). Many cars, phones, tablets, and other electronic devices connect electronically with GPS satellites. The information from these satellites helps us to navigate nearly anywhere in the world. Governments also send up spy or observation satellites to collect information on troops, arms, and other military data. Today, space satellites have become an integral part of our daily lives.

Fun Fact

There are over 2,500 man-made satellites currently orbiting the earth.

Space Program

A third aspect of the space program is the development of unmanned **space probes**. These probes often travel to other planets that are too far away for manned visits. Most of the knowledge we have about the objects in our solar system has come from these probes. Initially, probes explored the closest object to earth—the moon. The *Luna*, *Range*, and *Surveyor* probes were sent to the moon to gather data before man was sent there. Later, probes were sent to explore the planets. The *Mariner 10* probe passed by Mercury in 1974 and 1975, and the *Messenger* probe made several flybys in 2008 and 2009 before entering orbit around Mercury in 2011. The *Venera*, *Mariner*, and *Pioneer* probes visited Venus. And in the 1990s, the *Magellan* probe sent us the most accurate information we have from Venus.

Mars has been explored by more space probes than any other planet. Over 30 probes, including the *Mariner*, *Viking 1*, and *Viking 2*, have sent back important information on the red planet. Several missions to Mars have failed, but recently the *Opportunity* and *Curiosity* rovers have sent back data from the planet's surface while the *Mars Reconnaissance Orbiter*, launched in 2005, was still sending information in

Artist's representation of *New Horizons* approaching Pluto

2015 as it orbited the planet from space. Exploring and understanding Mars is a high priority for NASA as well as for other countries. The European Space Agency (ESA) and the Indian Space Research Organization (ISRO) have also sent probes to Mars in recent years. The ESA and NASA have both proposed sending humans to Mars, possibly by 2035.

The asteroid belt and outer planets have also been explored by one or more space probes. *Pioneer 10* explored the asteroid belt and Jupiter. *Pioneer 11* and the *Cassini-Huygens* probes explored Saturn, and *Voyager 2* explored Jupiter, Saturn, Uranus, and Neptune before leaving our solar system. *New Horizons*, a probe launched in 2006, has sent back the clearest pictures of Jupiter as it passed on its way to Pluto. *New Horizons* is the first probe to explore this distant world.

Fun Fact

SpaceX is developing reusable rockets, including the Grasshopper rocket, which can take off and then land vertically in a designated area where it can be refueled and reused.

Space satellite models

Examine the pictures of the space probes and space satellites in this lesson. Then, design your own space satellite model using items around your house. For example, you could cover a Styrofoam™ ball with aluminum foil then attach toothpicks to make a Sputnik type of model, or you could form modeling clay into the desired shapes and add tagboard pieces to make the model. Space satellites come in all shapes and sizes depending on their purpose, so use your imagination. After completing the model,

explain the function and purpose of your satellite to someone.

Optional—Model Rocket

For an exciting project, you can obtain a model rocket kit from a hobby store and build and launch your own model rockets. You can learn more about rocketry from the National Association of Rocketry.

Space exploration continues to fascinate humanity. We will probably never really understand the broad expanse of the universe, but God has allowed us to glimpse its wonders through space travel. 🌐

 # What did we learn?

- Who were the first people to talk about going into space?
- Who is considered the father of modern rocketry?
- What major event sparked interest in the development of the rocket for space travel?
- Who was one of the primary developers of rockets in the United States after World War II?
- What was the first man-made object to orbit the earth?
- Who was the first man in space?
- Who was the first American in space?
- Who was the first American to orbit the earth?
- Who was the first man to walk on the moon?

🚀 Taking it further

- Why are satellites an important part of space exploration?
- Why are space probes an important part of space exploration?

 # Commercial space flights

Although government funded space programs have been the leaders in space exploration, privately funded space exploration got a giant boost on October 4, 2004. That is the day the *SpaceShipOne* completed its second flight into space in a two week period. But before we discuss this amazing machine, we must first talk about the X Prize.

Since the invention of aviation, privately funded prizes have spurred on new designs. Charles Lindbergh's famous flight across the Atlantic Ocean was in response to the Orteig Prize. In the 1920s Raymond Orteig offered a prize of $25,000 to the first person to fly non-stop across the Atlantic Ocean. In 1927, Charles Lindbergh was the first to successfully complete the trip and received the $25,000. In that same spirit, the Ansari X Prize was developed to spur research and development of privately funded space travel. The X Prize was started in May 1996, and consisted of $10,000,000 to be awarded to the first privately funded craft that could carry 3 people, fly to an altitude of at least 62.5 miles (100 km) and return to earth safely and then repeat the trip again within a 14 day period. At least 7 teams signed up to compete for the prize.

The first ship to successfully fulfill the requirements was *SpaceShipOne*. Paul G. Allen, cofounder of Microsoft, provided most of the funding and Burt Rutan's company, Scaled Composites, designed and built the ship. Burt Rutan is the same man who designed the *Voyager* aircraft that successfully flew around the world without refueling in 1986. Mike Melvill was the pilot that flew the ship on both *SpaceShipOne* trips. The costs of putting *SpaceShipOne* into space is estimated at $25,000,000.

After this successful venture, Scaled Composites joined forces with the Virgin Group to form Virgin Galactic. Virgin Galactic has continued to work on a new space ship called *SpaceShipTwo*, which is designed to carry passengers and satellites into space. Although this program has run into several problems, Virgin's owner, Richard Branson, is confident that they will overcome the problems. Many other people agree, and at least 300 people have already paid $200,000 each to become space tourists.

Another company that has been very successful in the private space market is Space Exploration Technologies Corporation, better known as SpaceX, owned by Elon Musk. In 2008 SpaceX became the first privately funded corporation to successfully launch a liquid fueled rocket into space and has made several successful launches. In 2010 SpaceX was one of two companies chosen by the U.S. government to develop an unmanned vehicle that could supply the International Space Station. On May 25, 2012 SpaceX became the first private company to send a spacecraft to the International Space Station. This craft is called *Dragon* and will continue to be used to resupply the space station. SpaceX has also developed the *Dragon 2* spacecraft, which will be used to shuttle astronauts to the ISS.

Orbital Sciences is the second private company to send a space vehicle to the ISS. Their *Cygnus* craft successfully docked at the ISS in September 2013. Both *Dragon* and *Cygnus* are expected to

SpaceShipOne

resupply ISS for many years to come. Other private companies working on vehicles for space include Bigelow Aerospace, which is working to build private expandable space stations, and Boeing, which, like SpaceX, has been awarded a contract to build a manned space vehicle to take astronauts to the ISS.

Suppose you were to build a reusable spacecraft. What would it look like? What would it be used for? Would it be manned or unmanned? Would it be used close to earth or would it go to other planets? Use your imagination, and draw a picture of your spacecraft and explain how you think it would work.

Dragon leaving SpaceX HQ in Hawthorne, California, February 23, 2015.

30

Apollo Program

First flight to the moon

What was the Apollo program, and what did it accomplish?

Words to know:

Command Module   Lunar Module

Service Module

Service Module

Command Module

To put a man on the moon and return him safely to earth was the challenge presented by President John F. Kennedy in 1961. He challenged the nation to reach this goal before the end of the decade. Against unbelievable odds, on July 20, 1969, Neil Armstrong became the first human being to walk on the surface of the moon.

In order to reach this goal, NASA, the National Aeronautics and Space Administration, first had to put a man in space, which they did with the Mercury project. Then they had to learn how to work in space, including working outside the capsule and docking with other space vehicles. All of these skills were needed for the trip to the moon. These goals were reached during ten Gemini missions. Finally, NASA was ready to reach for the moon, and the Apollo missions began.

Apollo required a completely different command and rocket system than what had previously been used. Going into orbit around earth was a very different task than flying all the way to the moon and back. First, a new **Command Module** was designed. This cone-shaped module was the control center and living space for three astronauts. Attached to the Command Module was a **Service Module** containing an engine, fuel cells, and the power system for the

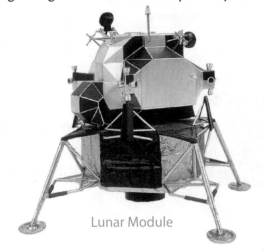

Lunar Module

Command Module. Together these two parts were called the CSM or Command and Service Module. The picture here is a model of the CSM.

A third module designed specifically for the Apollo missions was the Lunar Module. This was the vehicle used for landing on the moon's surface. It had two stages: a descent stage for landing on the moon and an ascent stage for taking off from the moon and returning to the Command Module. This picture shows a model of the LM or Lunar Module.

The CSM and LM were launched together into space by the giant Saturn V rocket. The Saturn V was a three-stage rocket that provided 7.5 million pounds of thrust. Each stage was a separate rocket engine

🧪 Two-stage rocket

The Saturn V was a three-stage rocket. Each stage was a separate engine. The first engine lifted the whole Apollo vehicle off the ground and into the air. The second stage propelled the astronauts into earth's orbit. The third stage pushed the vehicle out of earth's orbit and toward the moon.

Purpose: To make a model of a single-stage and a two-stage rocket

Materials: long string, two straws, tape, two balloons

Procedure:

1. First, we will make a single stage rocket. Put one end of a long string through a soda straw then tape the string to a wall.

2. Tape the other end of the string to the wall on the opposite side of the room.

3. Next, blow up a balloon but do not tie the end. While holding the inflated balloon, tape it to the straw with the mouthpiece of the balloon pointing at one wall.

4. Pull the straw and balloon to the wall facing the mouthpiece of the balloon.

5. Release the balloon and watch it fly across the room.

6. Now we will make a two-stage rocket. Add a second straw to the string. Tape the second straw to the first straw.

7. Tape an inflated balloon to each straw as shown. Be sure that the balloon in the back is close enough to the front balloon to hold the mouthpiece of the front balloon shut. Rolling the mouthpiece of the front balloon up will help to hold it in place.

8. Pull both balloons together toward the wall. Release the balloons. What happened?

Conclusion:

The single balloon moves the same way that a single-stage rocket does. The air pushes on the front of the balloon as it escapes out the back, propelling the balloon forward. With two balloons, the back balloon should push both balloons forward. Once the back balloon becomes smaller, the mouthpiece of the front balloon will be released and the front balloon should begin to deflate, thus increasing the speed of both balloons. This is similar to how a multi-stage rocket works on a spacecraft.

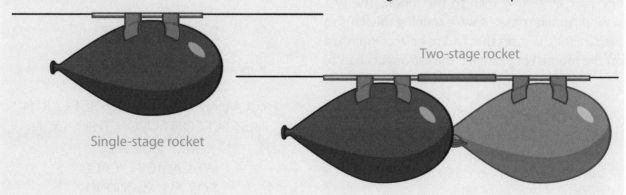

Two-stage rocket

Single-stage rocket

This bootprint made by astronaut Buzz Aldrin during the Apollo 11 mission marks one of the first steps human beings took on the moon in July 1969.

that fired after the previous engine was extinguished. Stages one and two were used to get the modules into earth's orbit. Each of these stages detached from the spacecraft after expending its fuel and fell back to earth. The third stage engine was used to propel the astronauts out of earth's orbit and to a lunar orbit around the moon. Once the fuel in the third stage was used up, it detached and remained floating in space.

Designing the Apollo space vehicle was only one part of getting men to the moon. The first several Apollo missions were training missions to prepare for the tasks that had to be accomplished on the moon. For example, the astronauts had to practice docking the lunar module with the command module in space so the astronauts could return from the moon.

At first, it looked like Apollo would be a failure. The *Apollo 1* mission was a disaster with a fire breaking out before launch, killing all three astronauts inside the Command Module. This devastating accident forced NASA to redesign the Command Module, and the next several Apollo missions were unmanned ones designed to test every piece of equipment that would be used on the trip to the moon.

Finally, *Apollo 11* was ready to put a man on the moon. Three men, Neil Armstrong, Edwin (Buzz) Aldrin, and Michael Collins were selected to man this historic mission. After reaching lunar orbit, Collins remained in the Command Module and Armstrong and Aldrin were able to land on the moon. Neil Armstrong's famous line, "That's one small step for man, one giant leap for mankind," will forever remind us of that moment when man stepped beyond the limits of earth. You can hear a recording of this statement on NASA's website. See Answers in Genesis web page at answersingenesis.org for more information.

The two men remained on the surface of the moon for 2 hours and 13 minutes. They did several experiments, collected soil and rock samples, took pictures, and left an American flag and a memorial on the moon. Then they returned to the Command Module and the three astronauts safely returned to earth. NASA had accomplished what many people believed to be impossible.

Apollo 12 and Apollo missions 14–17 were also missions that put men on the moon. Astronauts on

Fun Fact

The longest time anyone has stayed on the moon was 74 hours 59 minutes during the Apollo 17 mission.

Fun Fact

The memorial plaque that was left on the moon by the crew of *Apollo 11* reads:

HERE MEN FROM THE PLANET EARTH
FIRST SET FOOT UPON THE MOON
JULY 1969, A.D.
WE CAME IN PEACE
FOR ALL MANKIND

these missions performed additional experiments and explored different areas of the moon. Prior to the Apollo missions, no man had ever seen the far side of the moon. *Apollo 13* was an aborted mission when an explosion in the CSM damaged the module, requiring the astronauts to return home without stopping at the moon. The last Apollo mission was in 1975. It was a joint Apollo-Soyuz, American-Soviet project. There have been no manned missions to the moon since then, but in 2004 President George W. Bush announced plans for NASA to return to the moon by 2020. Currently NASA is investigating the possibility of building an outpost on the moon, but there are no definite plans to return to the moon in the near future.

 # What did we learn?

- What was the name of the NASA program whose goal was to put a man on the moon?

- What are the three modules in the Apollo spacecraft?

- What were the two parts of the lunar module designed to do?

- What was the name of the three-stage rocket used with the Apollo spacecraft?

Taking it further

- What is the advantage of a multi-stage rocket engine?

Space Program

 ## Apollo 13

Overall, NASA has had an incredible track record of safety and success. Considering how little was known about space and how dangerous it is to attempt to work in the harsh environment of space, it is amazing that the Apollo program was so successful. However, one mission clearly brought home the delicate nature of working in space. *Apollo 11* and *Apollo 12* were successful missions with men visiting the moon and returning home safely. So *Apollo 13*

was considered almost routine by many Americans who never expected there to be a problem.

The *Apollo 13* mission began fairly normally. There were some slight problems with the burn times of the second and third stage engines, but these were corrected and the astronauts began their journey toward the moon. They traveled for two days away from earth. Then suddenly things changed.

There was a loud noise inside the Command Module as an oxygen tank in the Service Module exploded. Suddenly, warning lights came on. Within three minutes only one of the three fuel cells had any power. As the astronauts checked the other systems they discovered that oxygen tank 2 had no oxygen and that oxygen tank 1 was slowly losing oxygen. This only left one oxygen tank unharmed. The astronauts knew immediately that they were in serious trouble. They knew they might not make it home.

The NASA engineers began examining the situation and working on solutions for getting the three astronauts back to earth before they ran out of oxygen and fuel. Because *Apollo 13* was most of the way to the moon, and because of the shortage of fuel, it was decided that the best solution was to continue around the moon and to use the moon's gravity to give the space module a boost back toward earth.

Apollo 13 astronauts Fred Haise, John Swigert, and James Lovell are pictured during the press conference after their ill-fated mission.

The Command Module was connected to the Lunar Module and the Lunar Module was unharmed by the accident. So to conserve energy, most systems were shut down in the Command Module and the men spent most of their time in the Lunar Module. This was not a perfect solution, because the Lunar Module was designed for only two people for two days. But three people would have to live there for four days before they could get back to earth.

The men took turns sleeping in the Command Module, but without energy the Command Module became very cold. By the time they got close to earth, the temperature in the Command Module had dropped to 38°F (3.3°C) and there was condensation over all the instruments, causing fear that something might short circuit when it was turned back on.

The astronauts had other problems to face as well. First, there was very little water available because the explosion had damaged the water tank and all three were suffering from dehydration. Also, the carbon dioxide level inside the Lunar and Command Modules was rising. Eventually, the astronauts were able to fashion an air filter out of miscellaneous parts inside the modules that helped get rid of the excess carbon dioxide.

The most frightening part of the mission may have been when *Apollo 13* had to go around the moon. At that time the astronauts were out of contact with earth for about 25 minutes. After they passed the back side of the moon and regained contact with earth, they did a short engine burn and began their trip home. As they began approaching earth, the people in Houston realized that *Apollo 13* was off course because of the continued oxygen leak from tank 1. They had to plan another controlled firing of the engines to get the ship back on course so it would not miss the earth. As the ship got closer to

The damaged *Apollo 13* service module just after it was jettisoned prior to the command module's re-entry into earth's atmosphere. As can be seen here, an entire panel was blown away by the explosion of an oxygen tank.

earth, the astronauts used the Lunar Module engines, and made the necessary course correction.

When the ship was about nine hours from splashdown, the people in Houston decided there was enough power left to fully power up the Command Module, which helped to warm things up a little. Then the astronauts brought the necessary systems on line to make the landing. Finally, as they approached the earth, the astronauts disconnected the Lunar Module, which had been their life boat for the past four days. Then they jettisoned the Service Module. As it floated away their camera was able to take some pictures of the damage done by the explosion and the astronauts saw that a whole side of the module was missing.

The astronauts were able to complete the reentry procedure and splash down safely in the ocean. Their harrowing journey was over and they were safely back home. Although the ordeal of Apollo 13 shows the courage and ingenuity of man, it also shows the beauty and care that God took in designing our world, the only place we know of where life can exist.

31

The Space Shuttle

Reusable parts

How was the space shuttle designed, and what was it used for?

After the last Apollo mission there was a six year period with no space flight by the United States. This was because a new type of space vehicle was being designed. Apollo had a huge rocket, the CSM, and the lunar module that together stood 363 feet high on the launch pad. Of this huge tower, only the CSM returned to earth. This was a very costly and inefficient design, so NASA set out to design a new space vehicle that could be reused. The result was the space shuttle.

The first space shuttle flight took place on April 12, 1981. This shuttle was called *Columbia*. Eventually four shuttles were built and quickly became the workhorses of the space program. The first four shuttles were named *Columbia*, *Challenger*, *Discovery*, and *Atlantis*.

There were three parts to the space shuttle system. First, there was the big orange fuel tank. This was the only part of the shuttle system that was not reusable. It held the liquid fuel that was used for take-off. It was 153.8 feet (46.9 m) long, 27.6 feet (8.4 m) in diameter, and was the tallest part of the shuttle system. The second part of the

shuttle system consisted of the two solid rocket boosters. These attached on either side of the main fuel tank and were retrieved and reused after each launch. The final part of the shuttle system was the shuttle orbiter. As the name implies, the shuttle was designed to orbit earth. It could not be used to

fly to the moon. It orbited at about 150 miles (240 km) above the surface of earth.

The shuttle orbiter was a delta, or triangular shaped, vehicle. It had a 78-foot (23.8 m) wingspan and was 122 feet (37.2 m) from nose to tail. The orbiter was much more spacious than the command module of the Apollo program. It had a crew cabin in the front with upper and lower decks. The upper deck was the flight deck. The lower deck had room for the astronauts to conduct experiments, eat, sleep, shower, and exercise. Behind the crew cabin was the payload bay. This large bay was often used to place satellites into orbit. It also contained a 50-foot (15 m) long robotic manipulator arm that could be used to move things around and to retrieve malfunctioning satellites. The space shuttle was used to place the Hubble Space Telescope into orbit. It was also used to repair the telescope when it did not work properly. Finally, the underside of the orbiter was covered with heat resistant tiles that protected the shuttle vehicle from the extreme temperatures experienced during reentry into the atmosphere.

Shuttle missions usually included seven crew members and lasted from 5 to 14 days. Missions

Robert L. Curbeam installs the Destiny module on the International Space Station during an EVA from space shuttle *Atlantis*.

were generally scientific in nature and included many experiments as well as launching satellites. Shuttle astronauts often performed EVAs, or extra-vehicular activities—better known as space walks. They often worked in the payload bay to perform experiments or worked on equipment. The shuttle was also used to ferry astronauts and materials back and forth to the International Space Station.

When a shuttle mission was complete, the orbiter normally landed in Florida, near Kennedy Space Center. Depending on the weather conditions in Florida, sometimes the shuttle landed

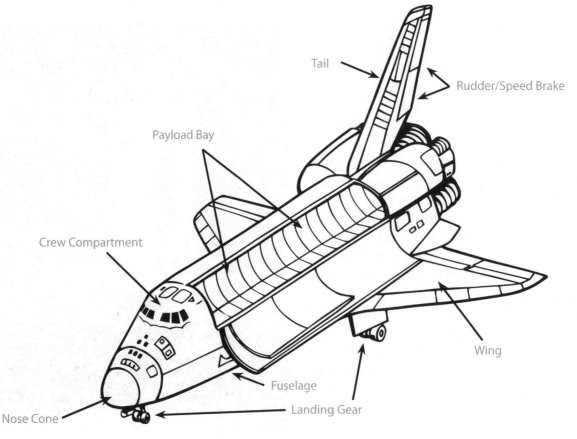

in California. If this happened, it was flown back to Florida on the back of a specially modified 747 jet.

Just as with the Apollo project, there were some heartbreaking disasters. On January 28, 1986, the space shuttle *Challenger* exploded shortly after take-off, killing all seven members aboard. The explosion was attributed to a leaking seal. After much redesign and testing, flights resumed in 1988. *Challenger* was replaced with a new shuttle named *Endeavor*. Flights continued relatively uninterrupted for over ten years. Then a second disaster occurred on February 1, 2003, when the shuttle *Columbia* burned up on reentry. NASA's three remaining space shuttles were retired in 2011 following the completion of the major portions of the International Space Station (ISS). Since that time people and supplies have been taken to the ISS by Russian spacecraft. Also, private space vehicles from companies like SpaceX and Orbital are now being used to send supplies to the ISS and will soon be able to transport people there as well.

The space shuttle

Label the parts on the "Space Shuttle" worksheet.

On January 28, 1986, the Space Shuttle *Challenger* was lost when a ruptured O-ring in the right solid rocket booster caused an explosion soon after launch. Bottom: The crew cabin was ejected into free fall by the explosion. None of the crew survived.

What did we learn?

- What was the main advantage of the space shuttle vehicle over all previous manned space vehicles?

- What were the main purposes of the shuttle program?

- What were the two main parts of the orbiter and what were their purposes?

Taking it further

- Why was the space shuttle called an orbiter?

- Why was the orbiter shaped like an airplane?

- Why did the orbiter have to be carried back to Florida if it landed in California?

Fun Fact

The original space shuttle was a prototype called *Enterprise*. This ship is now on display at the Intrepid Sea, Air & Space Museum in New York City. The *Enterprise* was used for tests beginning in 1977, but was never put into orbit around the earth.

Dedication ceremony for Space Shuttle *Enterprise*, April 27, 2015.

Orion

Now that the space shuttle program has been cancelled and with private companies now supplying the ISS, NASA has turned its attention to developing a spacecraft that can carry humans into outer space. This new spacecraft is called Orion. The Orion spacecraft looks similar to the Apollo craft but with 21st century design features.

The Orion Multi-purpose Crew Vehicle (MPCV) is designed to carry up to four astronauts to the moon, to asteroids, and perhaps even to Mars. Like Apollo, it contains a crew module (CM) for the astronauts and a service module (SM) which provides power, propulsion, water, and oxygen for the crew. It also has a launch abort system (LAS) in case an emergency occurs on the launch pad or during takeoff. If an emergency does occur, the CM can be separated from the launch rockets, and the rocket system in the LAS will get it away from the launch site so that the astronauts can land safely.

To put astronauts farther into space than they have gone before, NASA is developing a new rocket system call the Space Launch System (SLS). This new system is more powerful than any rocket ever built and will provide the force necessary to launch the MPCV into outer space.

The first test flight of the Orion system took place on December 5, 2014. It was an unmanned test and successfully launched the Orion MPCV into space where it orbited earth twice before splashing down in the Pacific Ocean where is was recovered and returned to Kennedy Space Center in Florida. The next scheduled test will also be an unmanned flight. The Orion is scheduled to make a trip around the moon and back to earth sometime in 2018. The first manned flight of Orion is not scheduled until sometime after 2021. To find out the latest about Orion, visit the NASA website.

At NASA's Kennedy Space Center in Florida, the agency's completed Orion spacecraft begins its trip to Launch Complex 37 at Cape Canaveral Air Force Station for its first test flight.

Orion is recovered from the Pacific Ocean and offloaded at Mole Pier at the Naval Base San Diego after completing a two-orbit, four-and-a-half hour test mission on December 5, 2014.

Rick D. Husband

1958–2003

The names of many astronauts are well known: Alan Shepherd, John Glenn, Neil Armstrong, Buzz Aldrin, and James Irwin to name a few. But the name of Rick Husband may never have become known if it weren't for the tragic events of February 1, 2003. Rick was the commander of the fateful shuttle that burned up on reentry, killing all seven crew members. Although many people will remember Husband for this event, the events of his life are much more important than the event that caused his death.

Rick Husband graduated from high school in 1975, and went on to earn undergraduate and master's degrees in mechanical engineering. Rick also joined the Air Force and became a test pilot and flight instructor. Rick dreamed of being an astronaut ever since he was a boy. But he was rejected by NASA three times. After the third rejection, Rick put his career in God's hands. His guiding verse was Proverbs 3:5–6, "Trust in the Lord with all your heart, and lean not on your own understanding; in all your ways acknowledge Him, and He shall direct your paths." He put his faith and his family as his top priorities and trusted in God to lead him. He decided to apply to the space program one more time and was accepted in 1994. After extensive training, Husband was assigned to be the pilot on the first shuttle mission to dock with the International Space Station in 1999.

Rick Husband was a highly dedicated astronaut. He was very intelligent, determined, and well educated. Rick gave his best to his job. He was very skilled and was well respected by all who worked with him. However, Rick's devotion to his family and faith are what he would most want to be remembered for. Although his work was important to him,

Rick remained true to his commitment to put God and his family first. Rick was a dedicated father and strong Christian man. He videotaped daily devotions for each of his children so they could continue their Bible studies while he was in space. While he and his wife were homeschooling their children, Rick was actively involved in a support group for homeschooling dads. He prayed with his crew before each mission and praised God openly from space.

Before his second shuttle mission, Rick was interviewed and said, "If I ended up at the end of my life having been an astronaut, but having sacrificed my family along the way or living my life in a way that didn't glorify God, then I would look back on it with great regret. Having become an astronaut would not really have mattered all that much." We should strive to live our lives to glorify God just as Rick Husband did. And we should remember this astronaut for his life of dedication to his faith and his family.

32

International Space Station

Reaching for freedom

Who built the International Space Station, and how does it help us?

NASA quit conducting flights to the moon after the Apollo missions were over because flights to the moon are very costly, and people at NASA believed they had learned what they could from manned flights there. Instead, NASA concentrated on shuttle flights for scientific purposes. However, most shuttle flights were 14 days or less in duration. The United States and other countries, especially Russia, have also seen the benefits of having astronauts in space for extended periods of time to conduct long-term research in a zero or micro-gravity environment.

To provide a place to conduct these long-term experiments, both the U.S. and Russia have placed space stations in orbit around earth. The first space station, called *Salyut*, was launched in 1971 by the Soviet Union. The United States launched its first space station, *Sky Lab*, in 1973. These stations were used to conduct many experiments, both for civilian and military purposes. The orbits of both of these stations deteriorated and they burned up on reentry.

In 1986 the Soviets launched a new space station called *Mir. Mir* was the first permanently manned space station. It operated for 15 years, and astronauts from dozens of nations visited and worked there. Various modules were added and sometimes removed depending on the required functions of

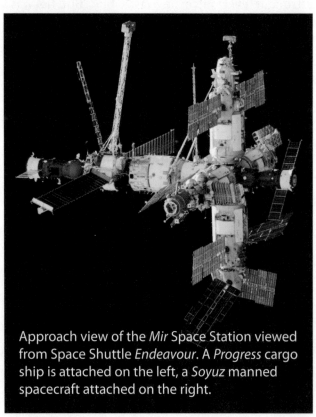

Approach view of the *Mir* Space Station viewed from Space Shuttle *Endeavour*. A *Progress* cargo ship is attached on the left, a *Soyuz* manned spacecraft attached on the right.

the station. What was learned on *Mir* provided stepping stones for the next stage in space stations.

In January 1984 U.S. President Ronald Reagan announced that NASA was beginning a new space station program that would be international in scope. This new space station was to be called *Freedom*, and was to be a joint effort between the United States, Canada, Japan, the European Space Agency, and other friendly countries. Work began on the design of space station *Freedom*. Then, after the fall of the Soviet Union in 1991, relations improved between the United States and Russia. And in 1991, President George Bush worked to include Russia in the planning of the space station.

With the addition of Russia, the name was changed to the International Space Station.

Construction on *Freedom* was originally scheduled to begin in 1995, but due to many factors, the International Space Station was actually begun in 1998. It was estimated that it would be completed in 8 years. However, shuttle flights were canceled after the *Columbia* explosion in 2003. Several parts of the shuttle were redesigned and flights resumed in July 2005.

The International Space Station has been built in stages, with U.S. space shuttles and Russian Soyuz rockets launching pieces into space where they were joined together by astronauts during space walks. The first crew to stay at the space station arrived in October 2000, and the station has been continuously occupied since that time. There are usually three crew members in the station for several months at a time. The average stay is between 128 and 195 days. Most of the occupants have been Americans and Russians; however, there have been

The International Space Station hangs above earth as seen from Space Shuttle *Discovery* after the two spacecraft separated on March 7, 2011.

Fun Fact

As of 2015 the ISS has been supported by
- 100 Russian launches
- 37 Space Shuttle launches
- 3 flights of SpaceX's *Dragon*
- 2 flights of Orbital Science's *Cygnus*
- 4 Japanese HTVs
- 5 European ATVs
- 184 space walks
- And over 215 people have visited the space station

astronauts from many other countries working in the station as well.

The crew of the space station conducts many experiments that cannot be done on earth. Some of these involve growing crystals. Crystals form more perfectly without gravity. These crystals are being used to make new medicines. Other experiments involve growing plants in micro-gravity and testing the long-term effects of micro-gravity on plants as well as people. One experiment tested the long-term effects of space walks on the lungs. Liver tissues are grown in this environment in hopes of finding better screening for patients prior to transplants. Also, various energy experiments are conducted to find new sources of energy. One of the most important results of ISS experiments is that a new method of treating cancer has been developed. These, and many other experiments, hold the promise of great advancements in science in the future. Also, more than 50,000 pictures have been taken of the planet and sent back to earth. The research done at the International Space Station is expected to yield many other useful results for society in the future.

What did we learn?

- What is the International Space Station?
- Why do countries feel there is a need for a space station?

Taking it further

- What shape would you expect a flame to be on the space station?

Water balls

One interesting observation in space is that water, which on earth conforms to whatever container it is in, actually forms balls of water in zero gravity. We of course can't observe this phenomenon on earth, but we can get an idea of how it occurs by doing the following.

Purpose: To see why water forms balls in space

Materials: water, waxed paper, toothpick or knife

Procedure:

1. Place a few drops of water about 2 inches apart on a piece of waxed paper. Note how these drops form into bubble shapes instead of flowing across the paper.

2. Using a toothpick or the edge of a butter knife, slowly push one drop of water toward another. What happens when the drops get close together?

3. Try to separate a larger drop of water into two separate drops. How difficult is this?

4. Slowly move a wet toothpick near the drop of water. What happens when it gets near?

Conclusion:

Water molecules have an attraction for each other, and one drop is pulled toward the other. In space, this attraction causes water to gather into balls, since gravity is not pulling them flat onto a surface like on earth. In our experiment, when the drops were moved closer together, they were attracted to one another. When you tried to separate them, the attraction of the water molecules prevented the larger drop from separating easily. The water drop on the paper is attracted to the water on the toothpick so the drop moves toward the toothpick even before the toothpick touches it.

🏅 Assembling the space station

Assembling the space station is a monumental task. Most items that go into space such as satellites and space shuttles are assembled on earth and then transported into space; however, the space station is too big to be done that way. It has been assembled and is continuing to be built piece by piece in space. Assembling a ship or space station in space has many challenges that are not real considerations on earth. What problems or challenges can you see with assembling a large space ship in space?

The first problem faced by astronauts is the lack of gravity. Because there is no gravity, everything must be connected to something else or it may drift away forever. Moving in space is very different from moving on earth so astronauts must train for this special environment. There is one advantage to a low-gravity environment, however. Heavy pieces of the space station, weighing as much as 35,000 pounds, would be very awkward to move on earth, but can be moved relatively easily in space because of their near weightlessness.

The second problem is no atmosphere. All assembly work must be done either by robotic arms or by space walks in space suits. The space station has a robotic arm that can be moved along a truss system to place it where it is needed. Other times space walks are necessary. Astronauts must leave the space station in bulky space suits to complete the connections and installation of the new parts for the space station, as pictured. These are problems that do not have to be dealt with on earth. This makes assembly difficult and time consuming.

A third problem is related to the first two. Because there is no other source for power and oxygen, all assembly work must be done without disrupting the power and life support inside the space station. When new power systems are added, they must be wired into the existing station without disrupting the power that is already in place. Mike Suffredini, the NASA station program manager said, "It's like building a ship in the middle of the ocean from the keel up. You've got to float and you've got to sail. All this has to occur while you're actually building the ship, and that's what the station is like."

Astronauts are up to the challenge, however. They train for months before a mission so that they can assemble the new pieces and add to the functionality of the station. The space station has been a success, and many important experiments are being conducted there. In addition, what scientists have learned from building the space station will help them if they build a permanent base on the moon and perhaps someday on Mars.

33

Astronauts

Modern-day explorers

Who are astronauts, and how do you become one?

Many children dream of being astronauts when they grow up. The excitement and adventure of traveling into space is very appealing to some. But how does a person become an astronaut?

A few traits are common to all astronauts. First, all astronauts have an education in math and science, usually in engineering, physics, chemistry, or some other technical field. So if you want to be an astronaut, you need to work hard in math and science. Also, physical fitness is very important. Your body must be in good shape if you want to be an astronaut.

Many thousands of hopeful people apply to the space program each year, but only a handful are selected to become astronauts. After being selected, an astronaut-to-be must go through several years of training before he or she is ready to go into space.

Astronauts must learn to work and live in a micro-gravity environment. This may not seem hard, but imagine trying to do a task when your tools try to float away, what you are working on tries to float away, and you try to float away, all in different directions. Even taking a shower becomes difficult without gravity to pull the water down. One way astronauts prepare for working in a weightless environment is to work in a giant swimming pool. Working in a spacesuit under water simulates working in space.

A second way that astronauts train for zero gravity is to fly in a special jet. This jet climbs to about 36,000 feet (11,000 m) and then quickly dives to about 24,000 feet (7,300 m), allowing the passengers to experience weightlessness for 20–30 seconds (shown here). They repeat this up to 40 times in one day. This often makes astronauts feel

A KC-135 aircraft, also known as the Vomit Comet, flies a special parabolic pattern repeatedly to afford a series of 30-seconds-of-weightlessness sessions.

NASA Astronaut Scott Kelly is seen inside a Soyuz simulator at the Gagarin Cosmonaut Training Center, March 4, 2015 in Star City, Russia.

sick, so this jet is nicknamed the Vomit Comet.

In addition to physical training, astronauts must learn all about the controls of the space ship and how to perform whatever experiments are required. They must understand physics and astronomy very well in order to do their jobs.

In order to survive in space, astronauts must wear space suits when not inside a space ship or space station. These suits are designed to protect the astronauts from the extreme heat and cold of space; to provide pressure, oxygen to breathe, and water to drink; and to protect them from the strong radiation found in space. These are all functions that are performed by our atmosphere on earth. Also, the space suit has communication equipment so astronauts can talk to each other. Finally, a space suit can be fitted with an EMU, Extravehicular Mobility Unit, which is a rocket pack that propels the astronaut through space. The EMU is especially helpful when working outside a space ship.

You don't have to be an astronaut to be part of the space program. The vast majority of the people involved in the space program never go into space. They include launch support staff, technical support staff, manufacturers, and teachers. Thousands of people are involved in every space launch. They are designing and building each piece of equipment, programming computers, training astronauts, planning missions, and controlling every detail required to make the mission a success. So even if you are not an astronaut, you can be involved in the space program.

Fun Fact

Space Camp in Huntsville, Alabama, is a program for children that allows them to see what it is like to be an astronaut. Participants get to try astronaut water survival, launch model rockets, and complete a simulated space mission. Some participants design experiments that might actually go onto the space station.

What did we learn?

- What are some ways that astronauts train for their missions?
- What conditions in space require astronauts to need space suits?

Taking it further

- What are some things you can do if you want to become an astronaut?
- What would you like to do if you were involved in the space program?

🧪 Space suits

Purpose: To simulate an astronaut in his space suit

Materials: winter clothing (hat, gloves, coat, snow pants, boots), hand mirror, building blocks, nut and bolt, bicycle helmet or motorcycle helmet with face mask (if available)

Procedure:

1. Pretend to be an astronaut by dressing in a full set of winter clothes, including snow pants, a coat, gloves, bulky boots, and a helmet or winter hat.

2. Now that you are fully dressed, try to perform various tasks such as building with blocks, exercising, and screwing a nut onto a bolt.

3. If you are wearing a motorcycle helmet, breathe hard inside the helmet for a few seconds. If no helmet is available, breathe onto a hand mirror. What happened?

Questions:

- How difficult was each task?
- What problems did you encounter?

Conclusion:

The snow pants are similar to the pants that astronauts wear. A coat is similar to the top half of the space suit. Astronauts wear bulky boots and gloves as well. A

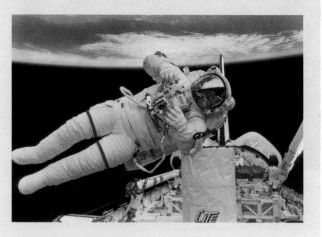

motorcycle helmet with a face mask is similar to an astronaut's helmet.

As you can tell, working would be difficult in a space suit. Astronauts must train to do their jobs in their full space suits. They often use tools that are specially designed for easy gripping by gloved hands.

Condensation appeared inside the mask or on the mirror. This is a problem that space suits have been designed to handle. Also, did you get hot while wearing all the extra clothing? Space suits are equipped to cool the astronauts when in sunlight and to warm them when in darkness.

🎖️ Research an astronaut

There have been hundreds of astronauts since the space program began. At first the astronauts were all from the military, primarily Air Force pilots. Today astronauts can be civilians, although most are still from the military. Early astronauts were chosen for their flying ability, but today, many astronauts are chosen for their scientific backgrounds in many areas.

Choose an astronaut to research. Find out about that person's background, early career, and achievements as an astronaut. You can choose any astronaut you are interested in, but in the list below are the names of a few of the most famous ones.

Present your research to your family, class, or other group.

John Glenn	Scott Carpenter
James Lovell	Judith Resnik
Alan Shepherd	Sally Ride
Michael Collins	James Irwin
Neil Armstrong	Eileen Collins
Virgil 'Gus' Grissom	Mae Jemison

Jeffery Nels Williams

1958–present

The early astronauts were considered to be heroes of space because they did things that no one had done before. They were the first to orbit the earth, orbit the moon, and walk on the moon's surface. These activities were very dangerous, and people admired these astronauts for what they did. In many ways they truly were heroes. But there are many modern-day heroes of space as well. One of these is astronaut Jeffery Williams. Williams has spent more time in space than nearly any other American, but that is not what makes him a hero. Williams is a hero because he openly stands up for his Christian faith and declares that the earth is God's amazing creation. Let's meet this modern-day hero.

Jeff Williams was raised on a farm in Winter, Wisconsin. After completing high school in 1976, he entered the U.S. Military Academy and earned a degree in engineering. He then became an aviator in the Army and served three years in Germany. After returning to the U.S., Williams earned a master's degree in aeronautical engineering. The army then sent him to Houston where he worked at the Johnson Space Center helping support the Space Shuttle program. Along the way, Jeff married Anna-Marie Moore. They have two grown sons and several grandchildren.

In 1993 Williams decided he wanted to become a test pilot for the army, so he went to test pilot school and graduated first in his class. During his career in the army Williams logged over 3,000 hours flying in over 50 different aircraft. Jeff accomplished a lot before he even became an astronaut. But becoming an astronaut was Williams' dream, and he was selected to join the NASA crew in 1996.

Williams' first trip into space took place in May 2000, when he was a member of a crew that went into space to assemble parts of the International

Space Station (ISS). During this mission Jeff conducted his first of three spacewalks, or EVAs (extravehicular activities). He spent seven hours outside the Space Shuttle moving parts into place and assembling them.

William's next job for NASA was as commander of the NEEMO3 mission. This was a training mission for astronauts, but the training did not take place in space. Instead the astronauts became aquanauts and trained in an underwater laboratory called *Aquarius*, which is located off the Florida coast in over 60 feet of water. It may seem like a strange place for astronauts to train, but there are actually many similarities between conditions underwater and conditions in space. There is no air to breathe and people must wear protective suits. Moving in water has a similar feel to moving in space. Doing things in both conditions requires great planning and special equipment. So, NASA has been using *Aquarius* for training astronauts since 2001.

After helping build the ISS, Williams finally got a chance to stay on the space station in 2006. He spent six months living in space and conducting experiments. During that time he orbited the earth more than 2,800 times. During his stay on the ISS, Williams took hundreds of photos of the earth, more photos than any other astronaut has ever taken.

Jeff was able to return to the space station in September 2009, and spent another six months in space. During his time on the space station, Williams became the first astronaut to make a live tweet from space. He also spent many hours video recording answers to questions that were submitted to the astronauts. Many of these videos can be seen on YouTube.

While Jeff Williams has had an outstanding career as an astronaut, he has done something even more important. Jeff has written a book called *The Work of His Hands: A View of God's Creation from Space*. The book uses many of the photos that Jeff took from the Space Station to tell the story of Expedition 13 from Williams' perspective as a flight engineer on the ISS. In the book he gives glory to God for the amazing world that we live in. Williams says he has learned, "vivid lessons about the meticulous goodness of divine providence, God's care for His creation, and His wisdom in ordering the universe."

Williams also has co-authored a devotional book called *Blessed is the Man: Psalms of Praise*. This book is an in-depth look at several Psalms and is intended to help train men to become men of God. This is indeed an important goal. Jeff Williams is not only a leader in space, he is a spiritual leader on earth. That makes him a true hero.

If you want to learn more about Jeff Williams, you can read his books, his blogs, or his tweets.

34

Solar System Model: Final Project

Showing what's out there

Build your own model of the solar system.

Recall from lesson 2 that models are helpful for allowing us to visualize something that is either too big or too small to easily see. You can demonstrate your understanding of the solar system by building your own model. Copernicus, Galileo, and others showed that the sun is the center of our solar system and the planets revolve around it. At one time it was believed that there were five planets besides earth revolving around the sun. With the invention of the telescope and better lenses, astronomers have detected a total of eight planets revolving around the sun, as well as other smaller objects such as asteroids and comets.

Review the order of the planets by singing the song you learned in lesson 11. You can also remember their order by learning the sentence, "My Very Excellent Mother Just Served Us Nachos" (Mercury, Venus, Earth, Mars, Jupiter, Saturn, Uranus, Neptune). Now you are ready for the fun of building your own model. 🌐

Fun Fact

The suggested lengths for the wires in the activity are convenient for making a model but are not very accurate for the actual size of each planet's orbit. If the sun's diameter were 5 inches (12.7 cm), like in our model, then the planets would actually be the following distances away from the sun:
Mercury—17 feet (5.2 m)
Venus—32 feet (9.8 m)
Earth—44.5 feet (13.6 m)
Mars—69 feet (21 m)
Jupiter—232 feet (70.7 m)
Saturn—425 feet (129.5 m)
Uranus—856 feet (261 m)
Neptune—1,341 feet (408.7 m)
And remember, the sun is a close star. Other stars are much, much farther away. Hopefully, this gives you a glimpse of just how big space really is.

🧠 What did we learn?

- What holds all of the planets in orbit around the sun?

- What other items are in our solar system that are not included in your model?

🚀 Taking it further

- Why do the planets orbit the sun and not the earth?

Final project: Solar system model

Purpose: To assemble a model of the solar system

Materials: nine Styrofoam™ balls, two Styrofoam™ rings, paint, stiff craft wire (see chart below for details)

Procedure:

1. Paint each Styrofoam™ ball and ring as follows and allow them to dry. If you have a book available with photos of the planets, you can use the pictures as guides for how to paint each planet, or use the pictures in this book.

2. After all of the pieces are dry, place the sun on the base.

3. Put Saturn's rings around Saturn.

4. Attach each planet to the sun using stiff craft wire cut to the following lengths:

    Mercury—2½ inches
    Venus—4 inches
    Earth—5 inches
    Mars—6 inches
    Jupiter—7 inches
    Saturn—8 inches
    Uranus—10 inches
    Neptune—11½ inches

5. If you want to, make small moons out of modeling clay and attach them to their planets with small pieces of wire.

6. You can also add an asteroid belt by gluing several small pieces of clay or pebbles together and then gluing them to a piece of wire 6½ inches long and placing them so that they are between Mars and Jupiter.

When your model is complete, share what you learned with your class or family.

Ball/Ring Size	Represents	Suggested Color
4½-inch ring	Base of the model	Any color you like
5-inch ball	Sun	Yellow
1¼-inch ball	Mercury	Red/brown
1½-inch ball	Venus	Reddish yellow
1½-inch ball	Earth	Blue with green/brown continents
1¼-inch ball	Mars	Red
4-inch ball	Jupiter	Red/orange—Don't forget the Great Red Spot
3-inch ball	Saturn	Peach
4½-inch ring	Saturn's rings	Striped—any colors you like
2½-inch ball	Uranus	Blue/green
2-inch ball	Neptune	Blue—May include a Dark Spot

 # Planet statistics

For each planet, make a card that can be displayed below or in front of the planet. An index card can be used for this. On each card include the name of the planet and the statistics from the Planet Statistics chart on page 255. Include any other interesting information you have learned about each planet.

Space Program

35

Conclusion

Reflecting on our universe

God created an amazing universe!

The universe is so vast that our minds cannot truly comprehend how big it is. The universe gives us just a glimpse into the awesome power of the God who created everything in it. Think about each thing that God created: stars, planets, moons, comets, asteroids, quasars, nebulae, our sun, and best of all, our planet earth. God loves us so much that He created a beautiful place for us to live and put it in a universe we can only begin to understand.

What did we learn?

- What is the best thing you learned about our universe?

Taking it further

- At the beginning of this book you wrote down some questions you had about astronomy. Check your list and see if you have found out the answers. If not, find a book or online resource for the answers.

- What would you like to learn more about? (Visit your library or search online for more information.)

- To study more about astronomy and to see how the universe declares the glory of God, do a search on the Answers in Genesis website.

Space Program

Reflecting on God's wonderful creation

Purpose: To reflect on God's creation and His goodness

Materials: blanket, flashlight, Bible

Procedure:

1. Take a blanket, a flashlight, and your Bible, and go outside on a clear night to observe the heavens and reflect on God's mighty power.

2. Spread the blanket on the ground in an area where there is not too much light. The darker the area, the better your view will be of the stars.

3. Use the flashlight to read the following Scripture passages. Reflect on each passage and thank God for His goodness as you look at the stars.

   Psalm 8:1–9
   Psalm 19:1–6
   Psalm 102:25–28
   Psalm 108:3–5
   Psalm 119:89–90
   Psalm 139:7–10

Note: this activity can be done indoors, looking out a window if weather prevents viewing the stars outside, but is not as much fun.

Our Universe — Glossary

Asterism   A group of stars with a recognizable pattern

Asteroid   A relatively small rock in a regular orbit around the sun

Astronomy   The study of the planets, moons, stars, and other objects in space

Aurora australis   The southern lights

Aurora borealis   The northern lights

Big bang theory   All that exists in our universe suddenly began nearly 14 billion years ago

Chromosphere   Sun's atmosphere closest to the sun lying just above the photosphere

Comet   A core of ice in a regular orbit around the sun

Command Module   Apollo capsule housing the astronauts

Constellation   A region in the sky that contains stars

Convective zone   Outermost layer of the sun's interior where convection currents occur

Core   Center of the sun where the thermonuclear reaction takes place

Corona   Sun's atmosphere that spreads out into space

Crescent moon   Less than ½ of the moon is lit

Equinox   First day of spring or autumn

Escape velocity   Speed required to overcome gravity

Full moon   Full circle of the moon is lit

Geocentric model   Everything revolves around the earth

Gibbous moon   At least ½ but not all of the near side of the moon is lit

Gravity   The force one body exerts on another due to its mass

Heliocentric model   Everything in our solar system revolves around the sun

Inferior planets   Planets with orbits inside or closer to the sun than earth's orbit

Jovian   "Jupiter-like," planet made of gas

Light-year   The distance light travels in one year

Lunar Module   Vehicle designed to be used on the moon

Lunar eclipse   When the earth is directly between the sun and the moon and earth's shadow falls on the moon

Maria   Basalt-filled plains on the moon's surface

Meteor   Rock or other debris pulled from space into earth's atmosphere by gravity

Meteorite   A meteor that reaches the surface of the earth

Meteoroid   A small particle of rock or other debris in space

Milky Way   The galaxy to which our solar system belongs

NASA   National Aeronautics and Space Administration

Nebula   A cloud of gas and dust in space

New moon   None of the near side of the moon is lit by the sun

Newton's law of gravitation   Any two objects exert a pull on each other that is proportional to the product of their mass, and inversely proportional to the square of the distance between them

Nova   A temporary flare-up in brightness of a star

Photosphere   The visible (light-emitting) surface of the sun

Radiative zone   Second layer of the sun's interior where energy moves outward from the core as electromagnetic waves

Retrograde motion   Movement that is backwards or opposite that of earth

Revolution   Movement of a heavenly body around another heavenly body

Rotation   Movement of a heavenly body around its axis

Satellite   Something that orbits another body

Service Module   Module attached to Command Module housing supplies and equipment

Solar eclipse   When the moon is directly between the sun and the earth, the moon casts its shadow upon earth, blocking the sun

Solar energy   Energy from the sun

Solstice   First day of summer or winter

Space probe   Man-made instrument designed to explore objects in space

Sunspot   Dark cooler area on the surface of the sun
Supernova   A very bright eruption on a star
Superior planets   Planets with orbits outside or farther from the sun than earth's orbit
Synchronous orbit   An orbit of a satellite around a rotating body, such that one orbit is completed in the time it takes for the body to make one revolution

Terrestrial   "Earth-like," planet of solid rock

Waning   Becoming smaller
Waxing   Growing or getting bigger

Our Universe — Challenge Glossary

Aphelion   Location in orbit furthest from the sun

Celestial equator   Projection of the equator onto the night sky
Centripetal force   Force that causes something to move in a circle

Dark side of the moon   Side facing away from the sun
Degrees of declination   Location above or below the celestial equator

Ellipse   A squashed circle shape

Far side of the moon   Side facing away from the earth
Foucault pendulum   A pendulum that swings independent of the movement of the earth

Hours of ascension   Location right of the prime hour circle

Interferometry   Combining light from two telescopes into one image

Light side of the moon   Side facing the sun

NACA   National Advisory Committee on Aeronautics
Near side of the moon   Side facing the earth

Penumbra   The outer, lighter region of a sunspot or shadow
Perihelion   Location in orbit closest to the sun
Prime hour circle   Projection of the prime meridian onto the sky

Rays   Bright streaks of lunar material radiating from craters
Rilles   Valleys on the moon

Shepherding moons   Moons around Saturn (or another planet) that affect the location of the rings
Supersonic   Faster than the speed of sound

Umbra   The inner dark region of a sunspot or shadow

Vernal equinox   Point that celestial equator and prime hour circle meet; the sun is here on the first day of spring
Vortex   A spiraling mass of water or air

Our
Planet
Earth

UNIT **1**

Origins & Glaciers

◊ **Describe** the origin of the earth.

◊ **Identify** unique features that make life on earth possible.

◊ **Compare** the biblical history of the world to the naturalistic history.

◊ **Describe** the problems with radiometric dating.

◊ **Describe** the formation and movement of glaciers.

1

Introduction to Earth Science

The study of our world

What does earth science include, and why should we study it?

Words to know:

astronomy

meteorology

geology

lithosphere

oceanography

first law of
thermodynamics

second law of
thermodynamics

Challenge words:

evolution

We all know where the earth is—it's all around us, right? We all know what it is—it's the planet we live on. Yet even though we are familiar with the planet we call earth and we see it every day, there are many questions that you may have about the earth. Where do rocks come from? How is a cave formed? What makes a volcano erupt? Why does it rain? How far away are the stars? Where did the universe come from? Earth science is the study of our world, and through this study scientists have attempted to answer many questions that people ask about the earth. Science has been able to

answer some of these questions better than others.

Scientists break the study of the earth into four general categories. First, there is astronomy, the study of the space in which the earth exists. Second, there is meteorology, the study of the atmosphere surrounding the planet. Then there is geology, the study of the lithosphere, or the actual solid earth itself. Finally, there is oceanography, the study of the oceans of earth. All of these studies help us to understand the wonderful world God has created for us to live on.

Although studying each of these areas will help you understand and appreciate the world on which you live, science can never answer all of your questions about the earth. We have to trust God's Word to answer some of our questions. For instance, science cannot prove where the earth came from. There are many ideas or theories that we will examine, but none of them scientifically proves where the earth came from. Only the Bible can answer that question. Genesis 1:1–2 says, "In the beginning God created the heavens and the earth. The earth was without form, and void; and darkness was on the face of the deep. And the Spirit of God was hovering over the face of the waters." The Bible goes on to tell us that God created the sun, moon, stars, sky, dry land, and every kind of plant and animal. Since no man was there and scientists cannot recreate the beginning of the world, we must trust God's Word to tell us what happened.

As you study earth science, you will find God's mighty hand all around you. Romans 1:19–20 says, "What may be known of God is manifest in them [men], for God has shown it to them. For since the creation of the world His invisible attributes are clearly seen, being understood by the things that are made, even His eternal power and Godhead, so that they are without excuse." So look for evidence of God in the world around you. You won't be disappointed.

What did we learn?

- What are the four main studies of earth science?

- What is one question mentioned in this lesson that science cannot answer about the earth?

- Why can we rely on God's Word to tell us where the earth came from?

Taking it further

- How does the first law of thermodynamics confirm the Genesis account of creation?

- How does the second law of thermodynamics confirm the Genesis account of creation?

- Read Psalm 139:8–10. What do these verses say about where we can find God?

🧪 The earth is reliable

God created the earth with reliable laws in place. As we study earth science, we can see these laws at work. Of the many physical laws at work on earth, there are two that are particularly important to understand God's plan for the earth.

The first, called the **first law of thermodynamics**, says that energy cannot be created or destroyed, only changed in form. This means that the original energy (and matter) of the universe must have been created. Only God can create something from nothing.

Another important physical law, the **second law of thermodynamics**, states that all objects tend to go to a state of rest or increasing disorganization, called entropy. That means that the universe is gradually slowing down and the energy is becoming less useful.

Purpose: To demonstrate the principle of increasing entropy

Materials: tennis ball, string, masking tape

Procedure:

1. Take a tennis ball and hold it in one hand. Hold your arm straight out in front of you and release the ball onto a hard surface. What does the ball do?

2. Now make a pendulum by taking a string and tying one end around the ball.

3. Use masking tape to tape the other end of the string to the top of a doorway so that the ball hangs at about the same height as your chin.

4. Take one step back from the doorway and gently pull the ball up until it just touches the tip of your nose. Then release it without pushing it. Be sure to stand very still. Did the ball hit you on the nose?

Conclusion:

After you dropped the ball, it bounced a few times and eventually came to rest on the floor as it lost its kinetic energy. The ball on the pendulum swung out and back without actually touching you. This is because the ball is losing energy as it swings through the air; eventually it will stop.

We observe these same principles at work on a large scale when we study planets and galaxies, and on a tiny scale when we study molecules and atoms. Everything is slowing down. If the universe was billions of years old as some people believe, we would not see the movement and organization that is evident all around us. The Bible says that God created the universe and upholds it by His power (Hebrews 1:3; Colossians 1:17). He designed our world in an orderly way, and we can trust Him to take care of it and us.

Is evolution scientific?

As you begin to study earth science, you will find that most of the books, magazines, and videos that you get from the public library or from a public school classroom state that the earth and the universe are billions of years old, that life evolved from nonlife, and that there is no power at work in nature except the natural things that we see and can test. These ideas are all part of a worldview called evolution. But these evolutionary ideas do not fit with the Word of God. The Bible clearly says that God created the earth, the universe, and all forms of life. It says that God created everything from nothing and that He did it in six days, and then rested on the seventh day. And the Bible indicates that this all took place only a few thousand years ago.

So what are we to believe? First, let's read some quotes from some evolutionists and look at what they have to say about the situation. After reading each quote below, write a summary of what that person is saying about his belief in evolution.

Professor Richard Lewontin is a geneticist and one of the world's leaders in evolutionary biology.

"We take the side of science *in spite of* the patent absurdity of some of its constructs, *in spite of* its failure to fulfill many of its extravagant promises of health and life, *in spite of* the tolerance of the scientific community for unsubstantiated just-so stories, because we have a prior commitment, a commitment to materialism. It is not that the methods and institutions of science somehow compel us to accept a material explanation of the phenomenal world, but, on the contrary, that we are forced by our *a priori* adherence to material causes to create an apparatus of investigation and a set of concepts that produce material explanations, no matter how counter-intuitive, no matter how mystifying to the uninitiated. Moreover, that materialism is an absolute, for we cannot allow a Divine Foot in the door."

Aldous Huxley was a British novelist who wrote *Brave New World* (1932). He came from a family of evolutionists. Below is a quote explaining his view of life.

"I had motive for not wanting the world to have a meaning; consequently assumed that it had none, and was able without any difficulty to find satisfying reasons for this assumption. The philosopher who finds no meaning in the world is not concerned exclusively with a problem in pure metaphysics, he is also concerned to prove that there is no valid reason why he personally should not do as he wants to do, or why his friends should not seize political power and govern in the way that they find most advantageous to themselves. . . . For myself, the philosophy of meaninglessness

Richard Lewontin, "Billions and Billions of Demons," *The New York Review*, January 9, 1997, p. 31.

Origins & Glaciers

was essentially an instrument of liberation, sexual and political."

Geoffrey Burbidge is a renowned astrophysicist and had the following to say about the big bang theory.

"Big bang cosmology is probably as widely believed as has been any theory of the universe in the history of Western civilization. It rests, however, on many untested, and in some cases untestable, assumptions. Indeed, big bang cosmology has become a bandwagon of thought that reflects faith as much as objective truth."

This final quote is from Michael Ruse who was a professor of philosophy and zoology at the University of Geulph in Canada. What is he saying about evolution?

"Evolution is promoted by its practitioners as more than mere science. Evolution is promulgated as an ideology, a secular religion—a full-fledged alternative to Christianity, with meaning and morality. I am an ardent evolutionist and an ex-Christian, but I must admit that in this one complaint—and Mr [sic] Gish is but one of many to make it—the literalists are absolutely right. Evolution is a religion. This was true of evolution in the beginning, and it is true of evolution still today.

". . . Evolution therefore came into being as a kind of secular ideology, an explicit substitute for Christianity."

Are you surprised by what these men had to say? Richard Lewontin is saying that scientists must believe in materialism to keep the Divine Foot, or God, from entering the picture. He says that there are many unsubstantiated stories and that the evidence does not necessarily compel scientists to believe in evolution.

Huxley is saying that he assumed the world has no meaning, so that he could develop a world where he could do whatever he wanted. This is the result of evolutionary thinking. If there is no God, then there is no reason not to do whatever you want. You will see a strict adherence to evolution in many people's writings because it provides a world with no meaning and thus no moral restrictions.

What Dr. Burbidge is saying is that the belief in the big bang is exactly that, a belief. There are many assumptions being used to "prove" the big bang that cannot be tested, and really don't prove anything.

Finally, Dr. Ruse is openly admitting that evolution is a religion that can be substituted for Christianity. Keep these ideas in mind when you read books that promote evolution as true. Often the things evolutionists claim to be facts are really only assumptions that are required to support the religion of evolution.

Aldous Huxley, *Ends and Means* (New York: Harper, 1937), pp. 270 ff.
Geoffrey Burbidge, "Why Only One Big Bang?" *Scientific American* 266 no. 2 (1992): 96.

Michael Ruse, "How Evolution Became a Religion," *National Post*, May 13, 2000.

2

Introduction to Geology

The study of the earth itself

What is geology, and how does it affect us?

Words to know:

physical geology	sedimentology
geophysics	paleontology
mineralogy	environmental geology

Geology is the study of the planet earth. It is the study of the structures that form the earth, the processes affecting those structures, as well as the physical history of the planet. For example, geologists study soil, rocks, mountains, and volcanoes. They try to locate particular minerals. They study and try to predict earthquakes. Geologists study glaciers and how they move. And geologists study the interaction between water, atmosphere, and the earth's surface.

The earth was perfectly designed by God to support life. What are some of the things that make earth unique? First, it contains just the right elements. No other place in our solar system has abundant liquid water, which is crucial for supporting life. Water is one of the few substances that is less dense after it freezes, allowing ice to form on the surface of lakes instead of from the bottom up, so fish and other aquatic life can survive the freezing cold. Water is a nearly universal dissolver, allowing most chemical reactions to occur. The earth is also the only planet with just the right amount of oxygen in the atmosphere to support life—too little and we would suffocate, too much and fires would burn out of control.

The earth has just the right mass to give us the needed gravity. Gravity holds the atmosphere around our planet so that we can breathe and have protection from the extreme temperatures of space. Gravity provides the needed air pressure for our bodies to function properly.

The earth is just the right distance from the sun and has just the right rotation to support life. If the earth were closer to the sun, all the water would boil away. If it were farther away, the water would all freeze. The tilt of the earth and its revolution around the sun allow for the seasons, which provide the

Fun Fact

Many of the sayings we hear have a geology basis. For example: "solid as a rock"; "I was petrified"; "That really rocks"; and "Sink like a rock." Can you think of other common sayings that are related to the earth? (Crystal clear, pure gold, far above rubies, etc.)

needed growing time for all the food we consume. All of these special features did not just happen by chance. They were the result of a loving God, who wanted to create a wonderful world for us.

You may not think geology is important to you, but geology affects your life in many ways every day. The nutrients and minerals in your food are a result of geology. Metals are used to make many things you use every day, such as tools, cars, and buildings. Petroleum is used to make gasoline to power your car, and it is used to make the many plastic items around your house. Sand is used to make glass, not to mention sandcastles. And glaciers carved many of the mountain passes that we see. So you can't avoid geology.

If geology really interests you, consider learning more about one of the following:

- **Physical Geology**—study of land formations, rocks
- **Geophysics**—study of the earth's magnetic field, heat flow, gravity, seismic waves, the earth's core
- **Mineralogy**—study of minerals in the earth's crust, moon rocks, crystals
- **Sedimentology/Paleontology**—study of sediment deposits, fossils

- **Environmental Geology**—study of the effects of humans on the earth's environment

 ## What did we learn?

- What is geology?
- What are some of the evidences that God designed the earth uniquely to support life?

 ## Taking it further

- List some ways that geology affects your life on a regular basis.
- What area of geology interests you the most?

 Geology scavenger hunt

Using a copy of "Geology Scavenger Hunt" worksheet, identify each item that is commonly found around most homes.

 ## Elements

Everything on earth is made from basic building blocks called elements. You can learn about the elements by studying a periodic table of the elements. Some of the elements you already learned about in the scavenger hunt. Other elements are less well known. You have certainly learned about silver and gold, but you may not be familiar with tantalum, osmium, or polonium. The first 92 elements listed on the periodic table are naturally occurring on the earth. The rest are man-made elements. Look at the periodic table of the elements on the next page and study it. See which elements you are familiar with and which ones you have never heard of. See which ones are naturally occurring and which ones have been made by man.

As we mentioned earlier, the food you eat contains minerals or elements that are found in the crust of the earth. Look at labels on the food in your kitchen and see how many elements you can find.

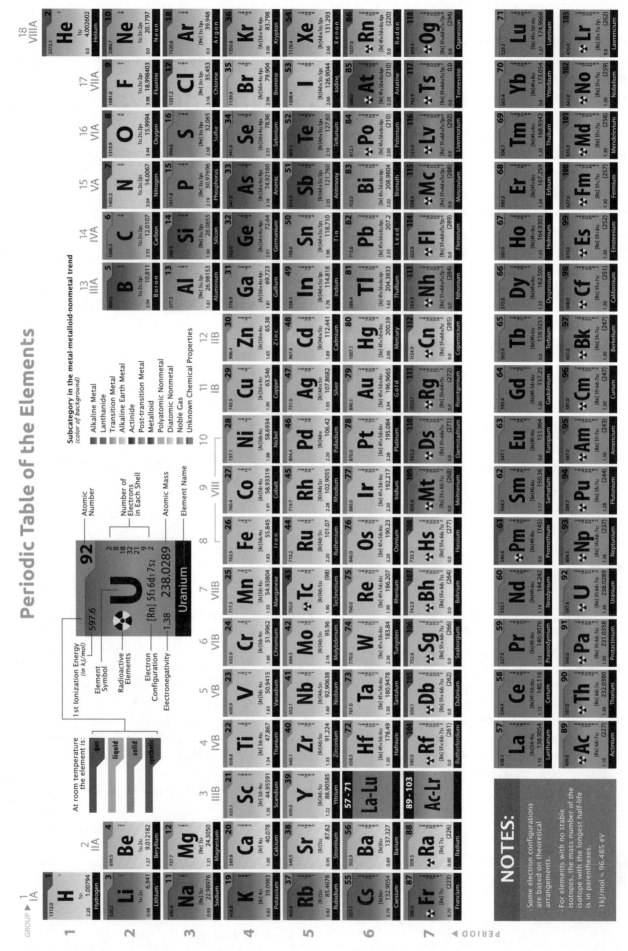

Periodic Table of the Elements

Origins & Glaciers

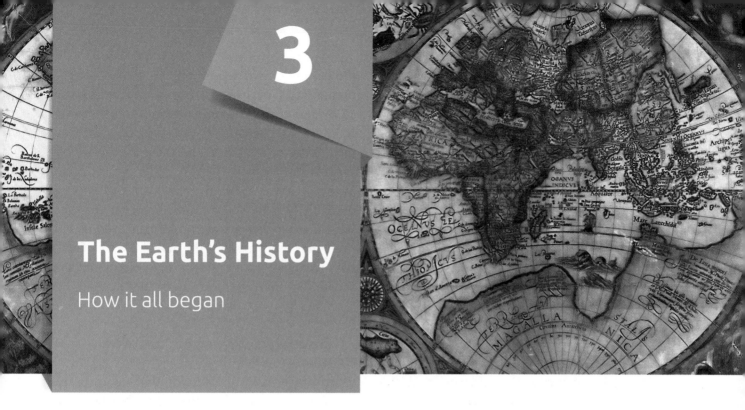

The Earth's History

How it all began

How was the earth shaped throughout its history?

Words to know:

uniformitarianism   polystrate fossil

Challenge words:

theistic evolution

No human was around to witness the beginning of the earth. And science has been unable to recreate the processes showing how the earth was formed. Therefore, people have developed many ideas about how it all began and how the earth ended up the way it is today. Among the many ideas that have been proposed, two are the most popular.

Belief systems

Creation scientists believe the biblical account of creation. The Bible says that the earth, as it is today, is the result of three important events.

1. Creation: Genesis 1 says that God created the heavens and the earth and that they were "very good."
2. The Fall: Adam and Eve sinned and God cursed the earth. The earth was changed from what it originally was (Genesis 3:17–19; Romans 8:20–22).

3. The Flood: God flooded the entire earth as judgment for man's wickedness (Genesis 6–8). Profound changes occurred to the earth, its atmosphere, and all of nature because of this Flood.

From the Bible, we learn that the earth is only about six thousand years old and that it was "very good" when it was created. The earth we see today has been deeply affected by the Fall of man and the Genesis Flood.

On the other hand, evolutionary scientists have a naturalistic view—that nature is all there is and everything happened by natural processes. They deny that there is a God that created everything. They believe that the earth is billions of years old and that life is the result of slow, natural evolution, with one kind of animal changing into another. They believe in **uniformitarianism**. This is the belief that all changes to the earth have been brought about by the processes we see today. For example, evolutionists surmise that since we observe slow erosion today, that features such as mountains and valleys must have resulted from millions or even billions of years of slow erosion. They deny a worldwide, catastrophic flood.

Evidence

Neither creation nor evolution can be scientifically proven. We must trust what God has said in His Word. He is the only eyewitness to creation! However, when we do look at the clues the earth gives us, we see that they confirm what the Bible teaches. Let's look at a few examples.

- Fossils—billions of dead things, mostly aquatic (water plants and animals), found in rock layers in every part of the earth, including on tops of mountains, in deserts, and even in Antarctica
- Large deposits of coal and oil—remains of once-living plants
- Evidence of an ice age, with many glaciers remaining
- Strata—many layers of different rock stacked on top of each other

How do we best account for these observations?

The Bible says there was a worldwide flood. This would have rapidly eroded the surface of the earth, depositing layers of sediment over every part of the earth and burying billions of organisms. This rapid covering would account for the many layers of sedimentary rock over the earth as well as the vast number of fossils in them discovered around the world. It would also account for the large oil and coal deposits that have been discovered. Finally, conditions after the Flood would have been just right to trigger an ice age.

The Flood also would have deposited sediment in the ocean. If we figure the age of the oceans by

the current rate of deposition, the sediment in the oceans would have been accumulating for less than 12 million years. This time period is much shorter than the 4.5 billion years that evolutionists claim for the age of the earth, and there is no plausible explanation for why there is not more sediment in the oceans if the earth is really billions of years old. This 12 million years is much longer than the Bible teaches that the earth has been around, but it is a maximum age, not the actual age. The Flood with its raging waters and worldwide scope would account for most of the sediment in the ocean.

Problems with evolution

Evolutionists explain that the layers of rock containing fossils formed slowly over millions of years. However, fossils only form when a creature is quickly covered with mud or sand shortly after it dies. Slow, gradual covering does not result in fossils because the dead animal is eaten by other animals or decays before it can become fossilized. Without a large-scale disaster, such as the Genesis Flood, fossils do not form very often. So evolutionists explain the abundance of fossils by saying they formed over very long periods of time. Also, the fossils of aquatic (water) creatures found on the tops of even the tallest mountains and in the deserts can be explained by the Genesis Flood. Evolutionists try to say that the level of the oceans has risen and fallen as the climate slowly changes, and that the mountains were slowly uplifted over millions of years.

Uniformitarianism also cannot explain how such vast amounts of coal and oil were formed when we do not see significant amounts being formed now. Just as with fossils, coal and oil are formed when massive amounts of plants are covered quickly and then compressed. This is more consistent with a catastrophe than with slow uniform processes.

Evolutionists say that there have been many ice ages in the past. Yet they cannot explain what triggers them or how they form. Cooler temperatures do not provide enough moisture for an ice age. So a slowly changing climate would not trigger an ice age with the formation of giant glaciers. However, the conditions necessary for the Ice Age would be just right after the Flood, due to lower temperatures on the continents and more moisture available from oceans that were warmer than today's oceans.

Finally, some strata have fossilized tree trunks that are upright through many layers of sediment that are thought to be separated by millions of years. Fossils that go through many layers of sediment are called polystrate fossils. Obviously, the trees could not have fossilized over millions of years; they would have decayed long before that, so they must have been buried rapidly and the sedimentary layers must have formed rapidly. Scientists who believe in uniformitarianism often ignore much of the data that does not support their ideas.

As a Christian, you must believe God's Word and look at the world through "biblical glasses." The Bible explains where the world came from, why it looks like it does now, and what will happen in the future. And as a good scientist, you should carefully examine all the data. When interpreted according to biblical history, all the data we have confirms what the Bible teaches. God's Word is ever true! For more evidence for a young earth, do a search on the Answers in Genesis website.

What did we learn?

- What are the two most popular views for how the earth became what it is today?

- According to the Bible, what are the three major events that affected the way the earth looks today?

- Should a good scientist disregard evidence that contradicts his/her ideas?

- Have scientists proven that evolution is true?

- Have scientists proven that biblical creation is true?

Taking it further

- How might scientists explain the discovery of fossilized seashells in the middle of a desert?

- Explain how a fossilized tree could be found upright through several layers of rock.

Flood in a jar

Purpose: To demonstrate how a flood sorts objects

Materials: large jar with lid, sand, dirt, pebbles, rocks, water

Procedure:

1. Put a handful of sand, a handful of dirt, a handful of pebbles, and a few larger rocks into a large jar. You can add some sticks, twigs, leaves, and grass as well. Do not fill the jar more than half full.

2. Fill the jar with water to within an inch of the top and tighten the lid.

3. Shake the jar for 30 seconds, and then set the jar on a level area. Observe what happens as the materials in the water settle to the bottom of the jar.

4. Wait 30 minutes and observe the jar again.

Questions:

- What did the jar look like right after you shook it?

- What do you see happening in the jar after 30 minutes?

- Did any of the leaves or twigs get buried in the mud and sand?

Conclusion:

You should observe the heavy items settling first, then the lighter items settling later. This forms layers of different materials in the bottom of the jar. This is like the layers we see in sedimentary rock formations today (shown here). The leaves and twigs that were buried illustrate how some of the plants and animals were buried during the Flood and became fossils.

Is Genesis history?

In the lesson we said that there are two basic views on how the earth came to be the way it is today, but there really is a third view that is becoming more popular. This view is called **theistic evolution**. People who hold this view claim that they believe the Bible, and they believe that the earth is billions of years old and living things evolved from simpler organisms changed over these long ages. They do not see a conflict between these two statements. They say that they believe the Bible because they believe that the account of creation given in Genesis is just figurative; that the story is poetic in nature and not to be taken literally.

Now there are many passages in the Bible that are poetic in nature. There are songs, psalms, and proverbs that are not literal history. Some of these poetic passages occur in the middle of books that are generally considered narrative or historical. So how can we tell if the account in Genesis chapters 1 and 2 is literal history or just poetic in nature?

When one examines the language used in Genesis 1–2, it has all the characteristics of historical narrative, not poetry or parable. This includes the Hebrew grammatical structure, the verbs used, the word order, etc. Plus, the New Testament writers, and Jesus Himself, refer to the events of creation, the Fall of Adam and Eve, and the Flood as real historical events.

Why is it important to believe that the world was created in six literal days? If you believe that the earth is billions of years old, even if you believe God created the earth and the things in it, you believe that death occurred before Adam sinned, since there are millions of fossils on earth that would have been formed before Adam. But the Bible says that death was the punishment for man's sin. It is difficult to reconcile the belief in an old earth with the belief in death as a punishment for sin and thus man's need for a savior. If you choose to take the creation account in Genesis as a figurative example and not literal history, how do you know when to start taking the rest of the Bible's history literally? It is important to believe the history of the Bible so that we can believe in the Savior of the Bible. Science does not confirm that the earth is old as you will learn as you study geology.

Dating Methods

How can we tell how old the earth is? Don't scientific dating methods prove that the earth is billions of years old? You might believe this if you read magazine articles, books, or the newspaper. Most dates for fossils, rocks, and other geological formations are stated as if they are proven facts. However, this is not the case. Let's examine how these dating methods work and we will see that science has not proven the earth to be more than a few thousand years old.

There are three main ways that scientists try to date different objects. Various radiometric dating methods, ones measuring radioactive elements which decay, are used for dating igneous and metamorphic rocks. Carbon-14 dating is a common method used for dating organic materials. And index fossils are used to date sedimentary rocks. All of these methods have significant problems that are often overlooked. Most of these problems lie in the assumptions that are made in order to use the dating method.

Assumptions for Radiometric Dating

Radiometric and carbon-14 dating rely on three assumptions:

1. The rate of decay of the element being measured is constant.
2. The system is isolated—none of the material being measured has entered or left the sample by any other means than radioactive decay.
3. The initial conditions are known—the scientist assumes he knows how much of the elements being measured was in the sample at the time it was formed.

Let's look as how these assumptions work with each of these methods. One common type of radiometric dating is uranium-lead dating. This method uses the fact that uranium-238 is unstable and decays to become lead-206 at a fixed rate. Half of a sample of U-238 will become Pb-206 in 4.47 billion years (this is called its half-life). Scientists have measured this rate of decay over the past ninety years or so, so we'll assume that the rate of decay is constant.

As for the second assumption, rock samples do not exist in an isolated system. Elements can leach in and out of rock areas, especially if water is flowing through them. Many samples are rejected for testing if they are suspected of contamination. And if results are unexpected, the sample is usually classified as contaminated.

And finally, it is assumed that igneous rocks have known quantities of lead in them when they are made. Therefore, any extra lead in the sample is assumed to be there because of the decay of the uranium. However, many tests on lava flows with known eruption dates have proven this to be inaccurate. For example, Indians living in Arizona about 900 years ago recorded volcanic eruptions in the area and tree rings in the area indicate that the eruptions took place about 900 years ago. When rock samples from this area were tested using radioisotope methods, they were dated at 210,000–230,000 years old. There was a much higher lead content than would be expected for rocks that are less than a thousand years old. But this is not an isolated incident. Rocks from a lava flow in Hawaii that occurred between 1800 and 1801 were dated with various methods and were given 12 different dates ranging from 1.4 million years to 2.96 billion years. None of the radiometric dating methods was even close to the actual date of only 200 years. Thus we can see that radioisotope dating is not reliable.

Carbon-14 Dating

Carbon-14 dating has similar problems. C-14 is made when cosmic rays knock neutrons out of atomic nuclei in the upper atmosphere. These displaced neutrons, now moving fast, hit ordinary nitrogen (N-14) at lower altitudes, converting it into C-14. When C-14 has been formed, it behaves just like ordinary carbon (carbon-12), combining with oxygen to give carbon dioxide, and also gets freely cycled through the cells of all plants and animals. Unlike common carbon, however, C-14 is unstable and slowly decays, changing back to nitrogen and releasing energy. This instability makes it radioactive.

Only living things contain C-14, and when an organism dies, the amount of C-14 decays slowly over time. By measuring the amount of C-14 left, a date of death is determined. Three assumptions are made in this dating technique: 1) the ratio of carbon-14 to carbon-12 in living things has been constant; 2) any change in the amount of C-14 in a substance is due entirely to radioactive decay; and 3) the decay rate of C-14 has been constant. We know that the production of C-14 can be affected by solar radiation, the earth's magnetic field, and volcanic activity. And carbon can leach out of a substance. The Flood also would have greatly upset the carbon balance by burying much plant material containing carbon.

Examples abound of items of known date that have given obviously wrong results when using carbon dating. For example, a freshly killed seal was dated as having died 1,300 years ago, and a living mollusk shell was dated as being 2,300 years old. With many examples of incorrect results, other results must be suspect as well. Finally, the carbon in a sample is almost completely gone in about 60,000 years, so samples cannot be tested with C-14 to prove extremely old dates. This creates another problem for old-earth scientists. Many items such as diamonds and coal, which are supposed to be millions of years old, have been found to contain C-14. If they were truly millions of years old, any C-14 that was originally in the sample would have decayed.

There are other radiometric methods as well, including potassium-argon, rubidium-strontium, and thorium-lead, but all such methods used for dating rocks and organic samples have significant problems, and results are often thrown out or labeled as contaminated or unreliable. Therefore, we must be careful when we read or hear that something has been determined to be millions or billions of years old.

Fossil Dating

Because sedimentary rocks are made from bits of other rocks, radiometric dating does not usually work on them. Therefore, sedimentary rocks are often dated by examining the fossils contained in them and then matching them to index fossils. An index fossil is always a particular fossil species that is found buried in rock layers over a very wide geographical area. Furthermore, the same fossil species must have a narrow vertical distribution, that is, only be buried in a few rock layers. The evolutionist interprets this as meaning that the species lived and died over a relatively short time (perhaps a few million years). Therefore, the rock layers containing these fossils supposedly only represent that relatively short period of time, and thus a "date" can be assigned according to the rock layers where these fossils are found.

The "date" relative to other index fossils and rock layers is often determined by the species' position in the evolutionary "tree of life" according to the order of fossils in rock layer sequences, but also by position relative to volcanic layers dated by radiometric methods. If the fossil in the rock sample were to be used to date the rock and then the rock layer used to date the index fossil, that is called circular reasoning and is bad logic.

All dating methods currently used to date the earth, fossils, and many other items have limitations and rely on untestable assumptions. Many have been proven to be unreliable. Old ages for the earth cannot be reliably confirmed. So, instead of accepting these dates, we should rely on God and His Word. The Bible indicates that the earth is only about 6,000 years old, and the evidence does not dispute this.

The Genesis Flood

God's punishment for sin

How did the Genesis Flood affect the earth?

According to the Bible, how the earth looks today is not the same as how the earth looked at creation. Two major catastrophes have led to changes that have greatly affected the surface of the earth. The first change happened as a result of Adam's sin against God in the Garden of Eden. Genesis 3:17–19 says that God cursed the ground, causing it to grow thorns and thistles. The original plan for the earth was for it to produce food without weeds. But all this changed as a result of man's sin.

The second catastrophe was also a result of man's sin. Genesis 6:3–8 says that man had become so wicked that God determined to flood the entire earth to destroy the human race. Noah and his family were the only humans saved from the Flood.

This worldwide Flood not only killed all air-breathing, land-dwelling animals not on board the Ark, but made major changes to the face of the earth. Layers of sediment were quickly laid down all over the world, resulting in the sedimentary rock formations and multitudes of fossils that we see today.

It is probable that the Flood was associated with the breaking up of the earth's outer crust into plates. Most scientists, both creationists and evolutionists, agree that the continents we have today used to be all one landmass. However, they disagree on what caused the landmass to break apart. Many creationists believe this was part of the Flood. This breaking apart of the land led to massive volcanic activity and earth movements that resulted in the high mountain ranges we see today.

Also, the Flood caused major changes in the climate. It is believed that before the Flood, the climate was mostly tropical worldwide. After the Flood, it was much cooler, both because of cloud formation and because of increased ash in the air due to the volcanic activity. A cooler climate, along

Fun Fact

Although the Bible gives us the true account of the Flood, many civilizations have flood stories as part of their history. For example, one of the oldest stories in existence is the Epic of Gilgamesh. This book contains a story of a man who built a boat that saved the lives of his family during a flood. The Chinese, Toltec, and Babylonian civilizations also have flood stories. In fact, there have been over 270 flood stories or records found around the world.

with more moisture from warmer oceans due to the Flood, set up conditions that led to the Ice Age.

So most of what we see on the surface of the earth, and most of what we study in geology, is a direct result of God's judgment on the earth because of man's sin. Despite these judgments, the earth is still a magnificent place to live, and an exciting place to study. But it is amazing to realize how wonderful the earth must have been at creation, before the Fall, and before the Flood.

Someday we will experience God's completed plan for the earth. Revelation 21:1–2 says, "Now I saw a new heaven and a new earth, for the first heaven and the first earth had passed away. Also there was no more sea. Then I, John, saw the holy city, New Jerusalem, coming down out of heaven from God, prepared as a bride adorned for her husband." As we look forward to this, we can study the earth we have today and still see God's mighty hand in its design.

What did we learn?

- What are some things geologists observe that point to a worldwide flood?
- What major geological events may have been associated with the Flood of Noah's day?

Taking it further

- How would a huge flood change the way the earth looks?
- Why did God send a huge flood?

Picture of the original earth

Imagine what a world with no sin might have looked like. It would probably have been very green and lush, with no weeds or unpleasant plants. Genesis tells us that everything in Eden was watered by dew and underground springs. And there was no death. We know that God declared it "very good." Now draw a picture of what you think the earth might have looked like before the Fall.

Did the Flood really happen?

The Bible says that, "Scoffers will come in the last days, walking according to their own lusts, and saying, 'Where is the promise of His coming? For since the fathers fell asleep, all things continue as they were from the beginning of creation.' For this they willfully forget: that by the word of God the heavens were of old, and the earth standing out of water and in the water, by which the world that then existed perished, being flooded with water" (2 Peter 3:3–5). According to these verses, in the last days scoffers will choose to forget that God sent a worldwide flood and claim that things are continuing today as they always have. This seems to be what is happening in the minds of many people today. But is there any evidence for a worldwide flood? Complete the "Did the Flood Really Happen?" worksheet to find out.

The Search for Noah's Ark

Have you ever wondered what happened to the Ark after the Flood? The only thing the Bible says about the Ark is that it landed on the "mountains of Ararat." It is likely that the Ark was used for building materials after the Flood or was abandoned and eventually decayed. However, there are some people who believe that the Ark was preserved in ice and still exists somewhere in the mountains of Ararat. Several expeditions have tried to locate the Ark and prove its existence but no one has successfully done so. But that does not stop people from trying.

There are many difficulties associated with a search for the Ark. The mountain that is called Mount Ararat today is about 17,000 feet (5,180 m) tall and located in a mountain range along the eastern border of Turkey. The top of the mountain is often covered with as much as 300 feet (90 m) of ice. Because of the ice and the harsh weather, there are only two months out of the year when anyone can climb the mountain, and even then it is very difficult to climb. The mountain has frequent thunderstorms and is covered with deep crevasses in the ice that may be 200–300 feet (60–90 m) deep. This makes looking for the Ark very slow, difficult, and dangerous.

Another problem with looking for the Ark is that the Turkish government must approve any search, and only a few expeditions have been approved. Once approved, the search party has to be careful of the people who live on the mountain. Some explorers have been able to get protection from the Turkish army, but this requires even more work. Few groups have attempted the search, and no expeditions have been successful in proving that the Ark still exists today.

Despite these problems, there are several accounts of people who say they have seen the Ark in the past 150 years or so. One account occurred in 1856. Three English scientists went to Turkey and hired Haji Yearman and his father to help them find the Ark. The Englishmen were atheists who had come to prove there was no Ark. According to reports, however, upon finding the Ark the scientists threatened Haji and his father with persecution if they ever told anyone what they had found. Later, Haji became a Christian and moved to California. On his deathbed, he told his good friend, Harold Williams, about the Ark. A short time later, Mr. Williams read a newspaper account of an English scientist who confessed on his deathbed that as a young man, in 1856, he and two other scientists climbed Mt. Ararat and saw Noah's Ark.

In 1883, after some Turkish explorers claimed to have stumbled on the Ark, the Turkish government sent up a group of men to locate the Ark. They claim that after entering the Ark they deiced three compartments. They reported finding large cages, big enough to house very large animals. They also found what appeared to be the ship's log carved in an ancient language on the side of the third compartment. Could this have been Noah's Ark?

Another story claims that in 1916, Lieutenant Roskovitsky of the Russian Imperial Air Force saw the Ark while flying over Mount Ararat. In 1939 *New Eden Magazine* quoted Roskovitsky as saying, "We flew down as close as safety permitted and took several circles around it. We were surprised when we got close to it, at the immense size of the thing, for it was as long as a city block, and would compare very favorably in size to the modern battleships of today. It was grounded on the shore of the lake, with one-fourth underwater. It had been partly dismantled on one side near the front, and on the other side there was a great doorway nearly twenty feet square . . . ."

Reportedly, this information was forwarded to the Russian tsar, who sent two engineering companies up the mountain. One group consisted of 50

people, and the other group consisted of 100 people. They said they found the Ark and measured and photographed it, and it compared closely to the sizes given in the Bible. The magazine article states that inside the Ark they found hundreds of small rooms and a few very large rooms with high ceilings. Other rooms had small cages along the walls with rows of small iron bars along the front of the cages. The craftsmanship showed a high level of design. The ship was made of Oleander wood. This wood belongs to the cypress family and resists rot. This type of wood, especially if it had been encased in ice most of the time since the Flood, could account for its near perfect preservation.

All the information was sent back to the tsar. But no one is sure what happened to this information. The expedition took place the same time as the Russian revolution of 1917. There are rumors that the pictures and information went to Leon Trotsky, who destroyed them and then killed the courier.

There have been other more recent sightings reported from the air. In 1960, Captain Gregor Schwinghammer and another pilot of the Turkish Air Force were on an observation flight around the mountain when Schwinghammer reported seeing "an enormous boxcar or rectangular barge visible in a gully high on the mountain." He stated that, "the Ark we saw was about 4,000 feet from the top (13,000 feet in altitude) on the southeast slope, perhaps four o'clock from due north."

In 1973 and 1976, two different high-powered intelligence-gathering satellites passed over the mountain and took some pictures. The photos supposedly show most of the anomaly trapped under the ice, with only the last section of it visible. The photos reportedly show a boat-like structure that is about 600 feet (180 m) long, but are of insufficient quality to make a certain identification.

But is it really important to find the Ark? If it does exist, it certainly would be a great archaeological find. However, we need to be careful because people tend to make such items into holy relics that are worshipped. The relic itself then almost takes the place of God in many instances. Christ actually taught that if people did not listen to "Moses and the prophets," then neither would something as spectacular as someone rising from the dead convince them (Luke 16). In other words, if people are not prepared to believe God's Word, even finding Noah's Ark would not be enough to convince them.

It certainly would be exciting to find Noah's Ark, and maybe God will allow this to happen one day. In the meantime, we need to remember that our faith is not built on the finding of the Ark, but on the inerrant Word of the infallible Creator God. For more information on Noah's Ark, do a search on the Answers in Genesis website.

5

The Great Ice Age

The age of woolly mammoths

What caused the Ice Age, and when did it occur?

Many areas of the earth show evidence of a great Ice Age, a time when much of the earth was covered with snow and glaciers. There is evidence that ice covered about 30% of the earth at one time, including northern Europe, all of Canada, much of the northern United States, all of Antarctica, and parts of New Zealand and South America. There are areas of land that have been cut out by massive ice movements. And many specimens of animals, and even people, have been found encased in ice. Even mammoths (large hairy elephants) have been found encased in ice.

Evolutionists claim that slow climate changes have resulted in many cycles of a warm climate, followed by an ice age, followed by a warm climate. They believe that the most recent ice age started over 2 million years ago, the ice advanced and retreated,

and then ended about 10,000 years ago. Creationists believe there has only been one Ice Age and that the animal remains in the ice are only a few thousand years old. There is fossil evidence to support a much warmer, more tropical climate immediately after the Flood, as well as evidence supporting a great Ice Age. However, evolutionists and creationists disagree on the age of these fossils and on the number of cycles that have occurred. Despite the disagreement about the dating methods and other evidence, scientists agree that for an ice age to form there must be two conditions: much wetter winters, resulting in large amounts of snowfall, and much cooler summers, preventing snow and ice from melting.

Scientists believe that the summers during an ice age would have been 20–40°F (11–17°C) cooler than they are today. They also believe that up to 80 feet (24 m) of snow would have fallen each year. At that rate, 40,000 feet (12,000 m) of snow could

Origins & Glaciers

Fun Fact

Even during the Ice Age, the middle latitudes had mild weather. Some people lived in the warmer parts of the earth.

Fun Fact

Job may have lived during the Ice Age. The Lord, in Job 38:29–30, said, "From whose womb comes the ice? And the frost of heaven, who gives it birth? The waters harden like stone, and the surface of the deep is frozen."

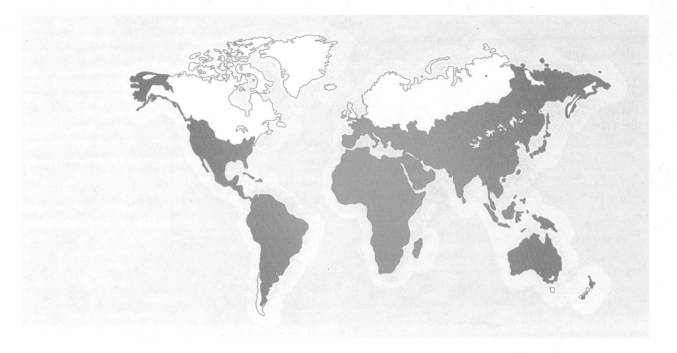

have fallen in less than 500 years. This would have compressed into 4,000 feet (1,200 m) of ice, resulting in massive glaciers. During this time people may have migrated from one area to another over land bridges that appeared because the sea level was lowered by all the ocean water now in the ice and snow on the continents. The uniformitarian idea of slow climatic changes suggested by evolutionists does not explain what would cause the temperatures to change and does not explain what would cause significantly more snowfall to occur at the same time.

On the other hand, the biblical account of the creation of the earth followed by a great Flood explains how a tropical climate was changed quickly into an ice age and eventually into the climate we see today. Prior to the Flood, the weather on the earth was much more uniform and warmer than today. During the Flood, the ocean waters were warmed by all the volcanic activity. After the Flood, conditions were just right for an ice age. The warmer oceans experienced much higher evaporation rates, resulting in large amounts of rain and snow. During the Flood there were massive volcanic eruptions, and volcanic activity continued after the Flood, spewing ash into the air, blocking some of the sunlight and causing much cooler temperatures over the entire earth, resulting in much cooler summers. These two conditions together would have resulted in an ice age. Eventually the ash settled, the waters in the oceans cooled, and the climate slowly warmed up and developed into the seasons that we have today. It is estimated that the Ice Age lasted less than 500 years. For more on the Ice Age, do a search on the Answers in Genesis website.

What did we learn?

- What two conditions are necessary for an ice age?

- How did the Genesis Flood set up conditions for the Ice Age?

- How do evolutionists explain the needed conditions for multiple ice ages?

Taking it further

- Do you think there are new glaciers still forming today?

Fun Fact

In the biblical timescale, the Ice Age would have started around the time of the Tower of Babel event (a little more than 100 years after the Flood) and lasted for several hundred years.

Ice Age crossword puzzle

Test your understanding of the climate conditions during the Ice Age by completing the "Ice Age Crossword Puzzle."

Ice Age ideas

There are several evolutionary ideas that try to explain how ice ages happen. One idea is based on the current idea that increased carbon dioxide could lead to global warming so decreased carbon dioxide in the atmosphere could lead to global cooling. However, there is no known mechanism for decreasing the carbon dioxide in the atmosphere and even if there was, this would likely only lower the temperature by a few degrees, not enough for an ice age.

Other scientists claim that the increased temperatures from global warming will affect the flow of warmer water in the North Atlantic, causing northern Europe to become colder and possibly triggering a future ice age. However, this flow has decreased by 30% in the past 50 years and has caused no noticeable change in the earth's climate.

Another idea is called the astronomical theory. The earth's orbit around the sun is an ellipse or a slightly flattened circle. The shape of the earth's orbit varies slightly over time. This changes the amount of sunlight falling on the earth. However, the amount of sunlight changes by only 0.17% at the most so this cannot account for the changes needed to bring on an ice age. Although the decrease in sunlight might make a difference of one or two degrees, it could not make the required difference of 20 to 40 degrees needed to bring about an ice age.

These ideas only account for changes in temperature and do not explain where the increased moisture and evaporation might come from. The Bible explains why there would have been greater evaporation after the Flood. Genesis 7:11 tells us that when the Flood began, "the fountains of the great deep burst forth." This means that water from under the ground burst out of the ground. The water under the surface of the earth is often much hotter than surface water. All you have to do is go to Yellowstone National Park and watch the geysers erupting to see how hot water can shoot out of the ground. This hot water, mixing with the rainwater would have greatly increased the temperature of the oceans, thus allowing for greater evaporation rates than we see today. The water would have condensed as snow and ice over the cooler continents. Since the summers were cooler, the snow didn't melt and the ice sheets continued to grow.

Purpose: To understand the extent of the Ice Age

Materials: world map, climate map, crayons or markers

Procedure:

1. Get a copy of a climate map of the world that shows areas that are currently covered with ice.

2. On a copy of the World Map color these areas dark green. This will include most of Greenland and the northernmost parts of Canada, Antarctica, as well as parts of Siberia.

3. Next, color the additional areas that were covered with ice during the Ice Age in light green. This would include Iceland, all of Canada, most of Alaska, and part of the United States including New England, Minnesota, Iowa, Illinois, Indiana, Ohio, and Pennsylvania, as well as some of the higher mountains from Colorado to California. It would also include southern parts of New Zealand and the southernmost tip of South America. You can use the map shown earlier in this lesson as a guide.

4. Make a key for your map showing what each color represents.

Conclusion: The middle and southern parts of the United States, Mexico, Central America, South America, as well as southern Europe, most of Asia, the Middle East, and most of Africa and Australia were still habitable during the Ice Age, though they would have been cooler and wetter than they are today.

6

Glaciers

Ice that never melts

What are the types of glaciers, and where are they found?

Words to know:

zone of wastage	piedmont glacier
zone of accumulation	continental glacier
valley glacier	calving

Most glaciers that formed during the Ice Age have melted, but some have just receded, and in a few areas, new glaciers continue to form and grow. Glaciers are thick sheets of ice that form in areas where summers are cool enough that the winter snows do not completely melt, and snow accumulates year after year. The weight of accumulated snow compacts the snow below it, forming it into ice.

An area where snow falls but does not completely melt is called a snowfield. Snow will melt and evaporate in the lower part of the snowfield, but snow that falls above the "snow line" does not melt and accumulates year after year. The area where snow melts is called the zone of wastage, and the area where the snow accumulates is called the zone of accumulation (see diagram on next page).

As the weight of the snow and ice increases, the effects of gravity become apparent. Gravity pulls the ice down any slope. The greater or steeper the slope, the more the ice moves down it. A glacier that spreads down a valley is called a valley glacier. If two or more glaciers move down nearby valleys and combine and spread out into a more flat area, they form a piedmont glacier.

However, more than 95% of the ice in glaciers is not in the form of valley or piedmont glaciers, but in the form of giant ice sheets called continental glaciers. These continental glaciers are mostly in Antarctica and Greenland. An ice sheet, or continental glacier, is a glacier in a relatively flat

Fun Fact

One of the largest icebergs ever measured was 208 miles (335 km) long and 62 miles (100 km) wide. That's bigger than the state of Massachusetts!

Fun Fact

Near the South Pole, the ice is about 2 miles (3.2 km) thick. And there is so much ice in Greenland that if it was spread out over the entire surface of the earth it would still be 17 feet (5 m) thick.

Fun Fact

Iceberg calving is monitored by satellites and many spectacular videos of iceberg calving can be seen on YouTube.

area that spreads out in all directions rather than flowing downhill.

Most glaciers today are found at or near the North and South poles and on very high mountain peaks. These regions remain cold even in the summer so the ice does not completely melt. Today, ice covers about 10% of the earth's surface. The world's largest glacier is on Antarctica and covers about 5.5 million square miles (14 million square km).

As glaciers move to the edge of land, they reach water. Ice is lighter than (less dense than) water so the edge of the glacier begins to float. Eventually this upward pressure causes some of the ice to break off of the glacier and fall into the water. This process is called **calving**. Pieces of ice that break off a glacier into the water become icebergs (shown above left). Icebergs often move out into the open ocean and can become very dangerous to ships. Only a small portion of the iceberg is visible above the surface of the water and the unexposed portion poses a significant danger. The most famous disaster caused by an iceberg is the sinking of the *Titanic* in 1912. 🌐

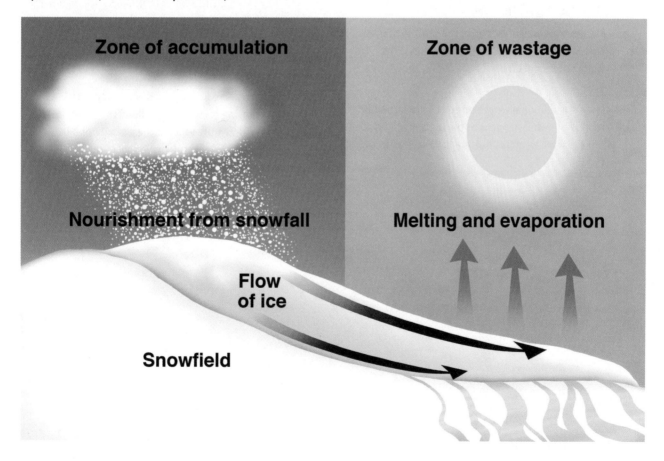

Zone of accumulation

Zone of wastage

Nourishment from snowfall

Melting and evaporation

Flow of ice

Snowfield

What did we learn?

- What is a glacier?
- How does a glacier form?
- What are the three types of glaciers?
- What is calving?

Taking it further

- Why do glaciers exist mostly at the poles and on high mountain tops?
- Why is it cold enough to prevent glaciers from melting at the North Pole, when there is 20–24 hours of sunlight during the summer?

How glaciers form

Purpose: To understand how snow can be compressed to become ice

Materials: Tall narrow jar such as an olive jar, marshmallows, cardboard, small heavy weights

Procedure:

1. Place several marshmallows on top of each other in a tall narrow jar. These marshmallows represent the snow that has fallen in the past.

2. Cut a cardboard circle that just fits inside the jar. Place it on top of the marshmallows.

3. Place a small weight on top of the cardboard disc. Note what happens to the marshmallows. The weight represents the pressure of new snowfall each year.

4. Place an additional weight on top of the cardboard. Again note what happens to the marshmallows. Continue placing weights until you have several on top of the cardboard.

5. Remove everything from the jar and examine the marshmallows.

6. What happened to the marshmallows? Have any of them stuck together? What would have happened if the jar was not there?

Conclusion:

Snow is relatively fluffy like the marshmallows. As new snow falls on top of the old snow, the weight of the new snow presses the old snow down. When the snow is pressed down enough, the water molecules stick together and change to ice. You may have experienced this when you made a snowball. If your hand presses on the snow with enough pressure you can make the snow into an ice ball.

The sides of the jar are like the sides of a valley, they keep the ice from moving outward. This allows the ice of the glaciers to flow down the valley. If the jar had not been there, the marshmallows would have spread out in all directions much more than they did. This is what happens in a continental glacier.

Changing temperatures

Glaciers experience cycles of growth and retreat depending on climate conditions. Currently most glaciers in the world are retreating; they are becoming smaller each year. However, in the past there have been extensive periods of glacier growth.

From approximately 1450 to 1850 was a period that has been dubbed the Little Ice Age. During this time period there are records that the glaciers around the world advanced nearly every year. Villages in northern Europe were destroyed by the advancing ice, and many people had to move to lower elevations. It is believed that the Vikings abandoned their homes in Greenland and Iceland and moved to other areas.

The climate change caused cooler temperatures and resulted in shorter growing seasons in many parts of Europe and North America. Rivers that normally do not freeze are recorded to have frozen many times during this time period. A famous example in America is seen in the painting of George Washington crossing the Delaware River amidst flowing ice. Today the Delaware River seldom freezes. Shorter growing seasons led to increased famine and many people died as a result.

So what caused this Little Ice Age? The exact causes are unknown, but scientists believe that there were two main factors that contributed to the colder temperatures. First, there was very little sunspot activity and the sunlight was less intense. Also, there was an increase in volcanic activity adding a significant amount of ash to the air. These two conditions combined to create a colder climate for several hundred years.

Since about 1850, temperatures have increased and growing seasons have lengthened. Glaciers have retreated in many areas. Some people see this as a natural rebound from the Little Ice Age due to reduced volcanic activity and increased solar output. However, other scientists see this as a precursor to catastrophic global warming.

The truth is that scientists don't really know how much of the warming effect is natural and how much is caused by industrialization. The actual increase in temperature over the past 100 years is about 1.2 degrees Fahrenheit (0.67 degrees Celsius). About half of this is likely to be caused by natural changes in the climate. Thus, the temperature increase due to increased carbon dioxide levels is really only about 0.6°F (0.34°C). More research is needed to really determine how much man can affect the climate and how much change is just natural cycles in temperature.

Origins & Glaciers

Sir Ernest Shackleton & the *Endurance*

Imagine what it would be like to be trapped in the ice floes around the South Pole. Imagine what it would be like to endure day after day of total darkness in temperatures down to 100 degrees below zero. Imagine what it would be like to have the ice under your feet suddenly split and break in two. This, and much more, happened to 28 men on an expedition to the South pole in 1914.

Sir Ernest Shackleton, captain of the ship *Endurance*, along with 27 other men, sailed from England on August 8, 1914, the same day that World War I began. Their goal was to be the first men to cross Antarctica on foot. They took dogs and sleds to carry their supplies, and loaded the *Endurance* with food and equipment for the dangerous journey.

They traveled south into the freezing waters of the South Atlantic. While they were still nearly 100 miles (160 km) from their landing site, the *Endurance* became trapped in the ice floes and they were unable to break free. From January–October 1915, the crew lived onboard the ship, each day hoping to see a break in the ice so they could continue their journey. But the ice just closed in tighter around them.

During this time, the crew experienced their first polar winter. Weeks passed with no sunlight. It was an endless darkness that troubled the minds of many of the men. In addition, the temperatures were very cold—often down to −100°F (−73°C).

After nearly nine months of being trapped in the ice, the pressure became too great and the ship succumbed to the ice and began to break apart. The men were forced to abandon the ship, saving what they could, and began living on the ice floes. Because of the movement of the ocean, the ice floes were not stable. Even very large pieces of ice, some a mile wide, would suddenly

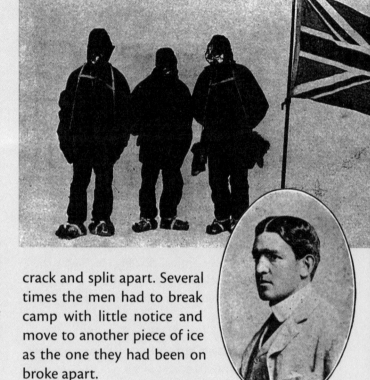

crack and split apart. Several times the men had to break camp with little notice and move to another piece of ice as the one they had been on broke apart.

The men were able to save much of their supplies along with three small boats, which they began to try to move across the ice using the dogs and sleds. This proved to be extremely difficult. And after only a few days of exhausting work, they had made very little progress toward land. They decided to let the movement of the ice take them closer to land.

After months of living on the boat and weeks of living on the ice, the food supplies became very low. They were able to survive by hunting seals and penguins and by using seal blubber for fuel. However, eventually they were forced to shoot their dogs because there was no food for the dogs. This saddened the men.

Finally, after nearly six months of living in the open, moving from ice floe to ice floe, there was enough of an opening in the ice that they were able to launch the three small boats. They were able to sail these boats between ice floes to the last island within nearly 1,000 miles (1,600 km). The island was called Elephant Island and was little more than a desolate rock. However, it was solid ground and did not split unexpectedly with the shifting of the ice. After 497 days, the crew was on solid ground again.

It was decided that the best chance they had for rescue was for six men to take one of the three open boats and try to row to the nearest inhabited land which was over 800 miles (1,285 km) away. Shackleton and five other men set sail on April 24, 1916, on a course for South Georgia Island where they hoped to get help from whalers that worked there that time of year.

On May 10, 1916, against incredible odds, Shackleton and his men reached South Georgia Island. They landed on the west side of the island and were unable to sail around the island due to bad weather. So three of the men decided to climb the giant mountains of ice to reach the whalers' camp. When they finally reached the camp, they were received as if they had risen from the dead. Despite the incredible hardship he had endured, Shackleton rested for only one day before setting out to rescue the rest of his crew.

Over the next three months, Ernest Shackleton used every resource he had to obtain ships to try to sail back to Elephant Island. Every attempt was met with defeat. Several times ships had to turn back because of the ice. A ship that was able to withstand the ice was sent from England but would take weeks to arrive. Shackleton was unwilling to wait and kept looking for another way to rescue his crew. Finally, Shackleton was able to borrow a ship from the Chilean government, and the weather cooperated long enough for them to reach Elephant Island on August 30, 1916, more than four months after he had left his crew there.

Amazingly, every man that set out on the expedition in August 1914 was rescued in August 1916. The amazing stamina and hope of these men and their trust in their captain is a story that should not be forgotten. After being rescued, every man said that he felt that there was a supernatural being that was watching over him. They all felt the presence of God throughout their amazing ordeal. Ernest Shackleton said in a speech in 1920, "I have no doubt that Providence guided us, not only across the snowfields, but across the storm-white sea that separated Elephant Island from our landing place on South Georgia. I know that during that long and racking march of thirty-six hours over the unnamed mountains and glaciers of South Georgia, it seemed to me often that we were four, not three."

To learn more about this amazing adventure and the bravery of these men, read *Endurance: Shackleton's Incredible Voyage* by Alfred Lansing.

7

Movement of Glaciers

Slowly creeping
down the valley

How does a glacier move, and what features does it create?

Words to know:

striations

lateral moraine

terminal moraine

glacial erratic

A glacier is a sheet or river of moving ice. This movement is caused by gravity. But the glacier doesn't necessarily move as one solid piece. The lower layer of ice is moldable and takes on the shape of the terrain over which it flows. This lower layer flows on a melted layer of water. However, upper layers of ice are not as compressed and are more brittle. The upper layers cannot move smoothly like the lower layers and often crack, sometimes forming huge crevasses.

Although the lower layers are moldable, the movement of the glacier does considerable damage to the terrain over which it moves. Glacier movement is nearly unstoppable due to the great mass of ice, and it levels nearly everything in its path. Glaciers dig out the sides of the valleys through which they pass, giving them a U-shaped appearance instead of the usual V-shaped appearance of most valleys.

As the edges of a glacier melt and then refreeze, the ice picks up rocks and debris that get added to the glacier. This debris acts like sandpaper on the underside of the glacier and scratches lines, called **striations**, into the ground over which it flows.

Glaciers also push rocks and debris ahead of their advance. Once the glacier quits advancing, the line of rocks that is left behind marks the farthest advance of the glacier. This line of rocks is called the **terminal moraine**. Rocks and debris are also pushed up along the sides of the glacier and are called **lateral moraines**.

Sometimes, glaciers move huge boulders as they advance. Once they begin to melt, they often leave a path of large rocks and boulders behind. Some of these rocks have been carried miles away from where they originated. An enormous boulder deposited by a glacier is called a **glacial erratic**.

Fun Fact

In general, glaciers only move a few inches per day. But sometimes they move very rapidly. One glacier on an island north of Norway averaged 60 feet (18 m) per day for three years. The fastest moving glacier ever recorded was the Kutiah Glacier, north of India, that moved 7.5 miles (12 km) in three months.

What did we learn?

- What is the shape of a valley carved by glaciers?
- How do glaciers pick up rocks and other debris?
- What is the name of the line of rocks that marks the farthest advance of the glacier?

 # Taking it further

- How might a scientist tell how far a glacier moved a rock or boulder?
- Why do glaciers often have deep cracks and crevasses?

 # Making a mini-glacier

Purpose: To observe how a glacier changes the terrain over which it flows

Materials: sand, pebbles, water, empty half-gallon milk carton, gloves

Procedure:

1. Place a handful of sand and a handful of pebbles into an empty half-gallon milk carton.

2. Fill the carton with water to within two inches of the top.

3. Place the carton in the freezer and freeze overnight.

4. When the water is frozen, remove it from the carton. Now you have a "mini-glacier."

5. Put on a pair of gloves and take the glacier to a hill. A hill with soft dirt and a gentle slope is best.

6. Place the ice at the top of the hill with the edge having the most visible sand and pebbles facing down. Then, while pressing down hard, slowly slide the ice down the hill for several feet. Notice the changes in the hill.

7. Leave the ice where it is and allow it to melt. After the ice is completely melted, look at the area where the ice had been.

Questions:

- How did the movement of the ice affect the surface of the hill?

- Can you see striations—lines made in the dirt by the sand and pebbles in the ice?

- Is there a line of dirt and rocks at the front edge of the glacier?

- What did you see after the ice melted? Is there an area of pebbles that moved with the glacier?

Conclusion: All of the features you noticed are similar to the features that glaciers make. Glaciers scrape the ground as they move and often leave behind rocks and dirt when they melt.

🏅 The force of water

As glaciers move, they greatly change the way the ground underneath the ice looks. Glacier ice melts and freezes over and over again. As the water moves into cracks in rocks and then freezes, the water expands and causes the rock to crack. Eventually, pieces of rock break off and become part of the glacier. These pieces of rock can be moved miles away from their original location. Eventually, when the glacier retreats, areas where the glacier has been look very different from how they looked before the glacier passed over them. One example of this is the Matterhorn (pictured here), one of the most famous mountains in Switzerland. It is believed that two glaciers met at this spot and both broke off large sections of the rock face, leaving behind a very pointed peak.

Purpose: To see the unyielding force of freezing water

Materials: glass jar with lid, newspaper, plastic zipper bag, freezer, work gloves

Procedure:

1. Fill a glass jar completely with water and put the lid on tightly.

2. Wrap the jar in several layers of newspaper, place it in a plastic zipper bag, and seal the bag.

3. Place the bag in the freezer and allow the water to freeze overnight.

4. After the water has frozen, remove the bag from the freezer.

5. Using work gloves, very carefully remove the jar from the bag and slowly unwrap the paper.

Questions: What happened to the jar filled with water? Why did this happen?

Conclusion: You will see that the water has broken the glass or has pushed off the top. Water expands when it freezes, and this experiment illustrates how freezing water can break rock. It may not seem that water alone could cause such devastation to a huge mountain like the Matterhorn, but over time it is possible. Glaciers are not the only place that we see freezing water causing things to break apart. Sidewalks can get cracks that expand with freezing water. Streets can also experience this problem. Water can be an unstoppable force. (Be sure to carefully dispose of any broken glass in a safe container.)

UNIT 2

Rocks & Minerals

◊ **Describe** the basic structure of the earth.

◊ **Describe** how each of the three types of rocks is formed.

◊ **Identify** the conditions required for fossilization.

◊ **Describe** the formation of fossil fuels.

◊ **Explain** why minerals are important to mankind.

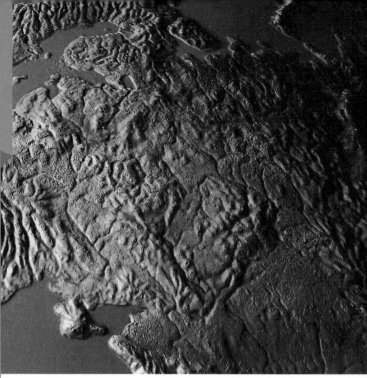

8

Design of the Earth

Blueprint for the planet

What is the earth like on the inside?

Words to know:

crust   core

mantle

How did God design this ball we call earth? How can scientists know what is inside without actually seeing it? Most of the information that we have about the interior of the earth has been obtained by studying how earthquake waves travel through the earth. Seismic waves travel at different speeds through different types of material. By studying how the waves move through the earth, scientists can make predictions about what the interior of the earth is like. There are over a million earthquakes, mostly minor, each year that scientists track to help them study the earth. Based on these observations, scientists believe that the earth is composed of three main layers: the crust, the mantle, and the core.

The **crust** is the outermost part of the earth. It is made of solid rock and is between 3 and 37 miles (5–60 km) thick. The thickest parts of the crust are under the mountain ranges, and the thinnest parts

are under the oceans. The crust is the only layer of the earth that we can directly observe. Even though several projects have attempted to drill deeply into the crust, none has ever reached the mantle. The costs and heat are too great to drill to the mantle.

In 1909 Andrija Mohorovicic (mo-ho-ro-VEECH-itch) discovered that seismic waves change speed below the crust. The area where this change occurs has been named the Mohorovicic Discontinuity or Moho for short. The Moho is the boundary between the earth's crust and the **mantle**. Scientists believe the mantle is approximately 1,800 miles (2,900 km) thick and comprises about 84% of the earth's volume. It is hotter and denser than the crust, so seismic waves travel more quickly through the mantle than through the crust. The top of the mantle is semi-rigid. The lower part of the mantle moves slowly with convection currents, which means that as the hotter mantle rises toward the surface, the cooler mantle falls toward the bottom of the mantle.

The topmost part of the mantle, together with the crust, is called the lithosphere. The lithosphere is believed to float on the more fluid central and lower mantle. Instead of being one solid piece of rock, the lithosphere is believed to be broken into 13 plates that move independently of one another.

The innermost part of the earth is the **core**. It accounts for about 15% of the total volume of

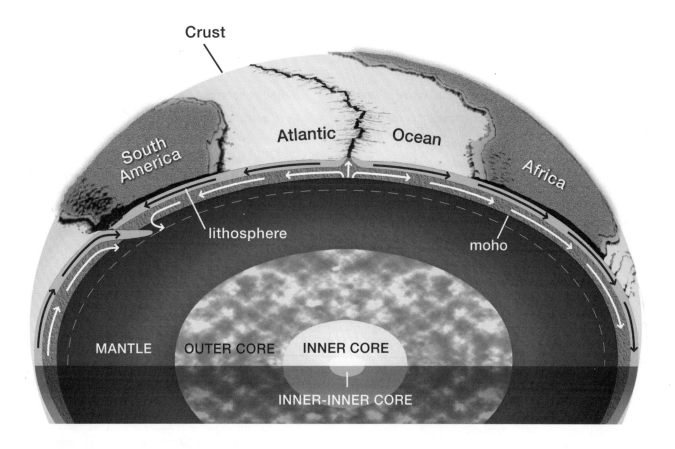

Crust

South
America

Atlantic   Ocean

Africa

lithosphere

moho

MANTLE   OUTER CORE   INNER CORE

INNER-INNER CORE

the earth. The actual composition of the core is not completely known. Creationists believe the core to be extremely hot and dense. The most widely accepted model splits the core into two parts. The outer core is believed to be liquid metal about 1,400 miles (2,250 km) thick. The inner core is believed to be a solid metal ball with a radius of about 800 miles (1,290 km). The inner core is thought to be under so much pressure that it can't melt despite the belief that its temperature may be as much as 13,000°F (7,200°C). Because the earth has a magnetic field, it is thought that the core must be mostly iron with some nickel.

Recently scientists believe they have discovered an inner-inner core. Seismic waves indicate that the inner core may actually be composed of two separate parts. The outer part lines up magnetically with the poles from north to south. But the inner part lines up magnetically from east to west. Scientists do not know why the inner-inner core has a different orientation, but they are proposing theories which they hope will explain this in the future. 🌐

What did we learn?

- What do most scientists believe to be the three main parts of the earth?

- Which is the thickest part of the earth?

- Which is the thinnest part of the earth?

- Where is the crust the thickest?

Taking it further

- Why do scientists believe the mantle is hotter and denser than the crust?

- For what other things, besides the interior of the earth, do scientists have to develop models without actually seeing what they are describing?

Making a model of earth

Purpose: To make a fun (and delicious) model of earth

Materials: large marshmallow, gumball, chocolate chips, bowl, wax paper, toothpick

Procedure:

1. Take a large marshmallow and carefully cut a small slit in one side.

2. Insert a gumball. The gumball represents the core, and the marshmallow represents the mantle.

3. Melt some chocolate chips in a microwave-safe bowl.

4. Using a toothpick, carefully dip the marshmallow into the melted chocolate. The chocolate represents the earth's crust.

5. Set your model on waxed paper to cool. After the chocolate has set, review the parts of the earth, and then eat your yummy model!

Seismic waves

Purpose: To better understand how seismic waves give scientists a picture of what is under the earth's crust

Materials: serving bowl, small bottle or jar, pencil

Procedure:

1. Fill a serving bowl half full of water.

2. Place a bottle or jar in the center of the bowl.

3. Gently tap the surface of the water near the edge of the bowl with the end of a pencil and carefully observe the direction and speed of the waves as they travel across the surface of the water. If you have difficulty seeing the waves, shine a bright light on the surface of the water.

Conclusion: The waves bounce off of the bottle and travel back toward the edge of the bowl. Similarly, some seismic waves travel through liquids and bounce off of solid objects, while others travel through solid objects and are reflected off of liquids. These various waves help scientists get a better understanding of the interior of the earth.

Earth's composition

Although scientists are not sure what the core of the earth is made of, most believe that it is probably made from iron and some nickel. This idea is based mostly on the fact that the earth has a large magnetic field surrounding it. In 1958, a scientist named James Van Allen proved that there was an area around the earth that contains a high amount of radiation. It was later shown that there are two areas reaching hundreds of miles into space that trap radiation due to a large magnetic field generated by the earth (see illustration on the next page).

The best explanation that scientists have come up with for how the magnetic field is generated is that current is flowing through the core of the earth. Thus, if the core is made of a magnetic material such as iron and nickel, this current would produce a magnetic field—essentially turning the earth into a giant electromagnet. Because of this magnetic field, many scientists believe the core must be made of mostly iron and some nickel.

In reality, scientists know very little about the core or the mantle. They know much more about the crust. Although the earth's crust contains 92 known elements, only 8 elements are found in abundance. About 47% of the earth's crust contains oxygen. This does not mean that the crust contains oxygen gas; rather, the oxygen is bonded with other elements to form the oxide minerals that make up the crust. The second most common element in the earth's crust is silicon, comprising approximately 28% of the crust by weight. Silicon is also bonded with many other elements to form the silicate rocks found in the crust. Aluminum makes up about 8%, iron makes up about 5%, and calcium, sodium, potassium, and magnesium each make up from 2–4% of the crust. The other 84 elements together comprise only 1.4% of the earth's crust.

Activity 1—Purpose: To make a pie chart showing which elements are found in the earth's crust

Materials: paper, protractor, pencil

Procedure:

1. Draw a circle on a blank piece of paper.

2. Using a protractor, from the center of the circle draw a 169 degree angle and label this piece of the pie *Oxygen*. This is 47% of the circle.

3. From one side of this angle draw a 101 degree angle and label this piece *Silicon*.

4. Continue by drawing a 29 degree angle for *Aluminum* and an 18 degree angle for *Iron*.

5. The rest of the pie, approximately 46 degrees or 12%, can be labeled as *Other*.

6. Be sure to label your chart "Elements in the Earth's Crust."

Activity 2—Purpose: To visualize how magma cools to form crust

Materials: ¼ cup chocolate chips, bowl, plastic zipper bag, cup, water

Procedure:

1. Melt ¼ cup chocolate chips in the microwave. Do not overheat them.

2. Pour this liquid chocolate into a plastic zipper bag.

3. Fill a cup with cold water.

4. Cut a small corner from the plastic bag and squeeze the liquid chocolate into the cold water.

Conclusion:

The earth's crust has been classified into two different parts: the continental crust and the oceanic crust. The continental crust is the part of the land that is not part of the ocean basins. Most continental crust is composed of granite and metamorphic rocks covered with sedimentary rocks. The ocean basin, or oceanic crust, is composed mostly of basalt, which is a darker and denser volcanic rock than granite. In your experiment you saw how the liquid quickly cooled and became a solid. This is similar to how liquid magma cools and solidifies as it enters the oceans. It is believed that the ocean basins were formed as magma squeezed up from below the crust and solidified as it was cooled by the water.

9

Rocks

Boulders, rocks, gravel, pebbles...

What are rocks made of, and how are they formed?

Words to know:

igneous   metamorphic

sedimentary

Challenge words:

vesicles

Whether you realize it or not, rock is always underneath you. Even when you are swimming in a lake or walking on a beach, even if you are mowing the grass or hiking through the forest, if you dig down deep enough, you will hit solid rock. This rock is the crust of the earth. Many of the rocks that we pick up are just small pieces that have broken off of the crust.

Rocks are very important to our lives. Rocks are the foundations on which we build our buildings, and the materials with which we build many structures. Coal is an important source of fuel. And rocks add beauty to our lives.

Rocks are a combination of one or more minerals or organic materials. A few rocks contain only one mineral, but most are a combination of two or more minerals. Scientists group rocks into three categories by how they are formed. **Igneous** rocks are formed when melted minerals, called magma, cool and harden. **Sedimentary** rocks are formed

Igneous

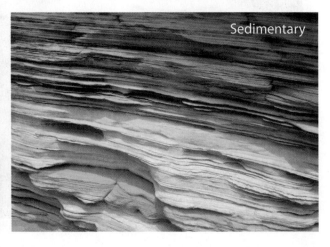

Sedimentary

Metamorphic

when layers of sediment are pressed and "cemented" together. The third type, **metamorphic** rocks, are formed when igneous or sedimentary rocks are exposed to pressure and heat. Over time, they are changed into different rocks with different minerals and structures.

Rocks are not only important for buildings and monuments, they are very important for growing plants. Soil is made from weathered and ground up bits of rocks mixed with clay, dead leaves, sticks, and small pebbles. It is important to have rocks around to make new soil.

People who like to collect and study rocks are often nicknamed *rock hounds*. For the final project in lesson 34, you will become a rock hound. So begin looking for interesting rocks to add to your collection. You will enjoy learning about rocks.

What did we learn?

- What are rocks made from?
- What are the three categories of rocks?
- How is igneous rock formed?
- How is sedimentary rock formed?
- How is metamorphic rock formed?

Taking it further

- Why are rocks important?
- Where is a good place to look for rocks?
- Why is it better to store your rock samples in a box with dividers than in a bag?

Rock cycle

All rock on earth was formed at Creation. Yet much of that rock has been recycled into other types of rock. All three types of rock can be melted to form magma. This magma can then be cooled and will solidify to form new igneous rock. Also, all three types of rock can be broken into tiny bits by weathering. Bits of sediment eventually settle and are pressed together and cemented to form new sedimentary rock. And finally, both sedimentary and igneous rock can be changed by pressure, heat, and time into various types of metamorphic rock.

Label and color "The Rock Cycle" worksheet.

Identifying rocks

There are three kinds of rocks: igneous, sedimentary, and metamorphic. If you pick up a rock from the ground, how can you tell which kind of rock it is? There are many tests that can be done to determine the exact type of rock or mineral you may have; however, there are a few common characteristics that will be helpful in making a quick determination of the type of rock.

Igneous rocks have an interlocking grain texture. You will see this clearly when looking at a sample of granite. Sometimes these grains may be of two very different sizes. Some igneous rocks have holes called vesicles. Those rocks with many holes are usually called volcanic rock (shown here). Many igneous rocks have a dark color and are heavy.

Sedimentary rocks have small pieces that are cemented together, so if you can easily rub part of the rock off with your finger it is almost certainly a sedimentary rock. Sandstone is an obvious example of a sedimentary rock. If the rock looks like small grains all glued together, then it is a sedimentary rock. Also, usually only sedimentary rocks contain recognizable fossils. Often sedimentary rocks are light colored and lightweight.

Metamorphic rocks at first glance may appear to be igneous or sedimentary rocks, but have some distinct differences. Metamorphic rocks usually have foliation or layering. Also, they often have bands of light and dark colors. They can have a large grain texture. And if you tap a metamorphic rock it will sound more like a *ching*, whereas other rocks have more of a *chunk* sound.

Now that you have an idea of what to look for, select a few rock samples that you find outside or may have around your house and see if you can determine which are igneous, which are sedimentary, and which are metamorphic. You don't need to identify exactly what kind of rocks you have, just what category each fits into.

Igneous Rocks

Fire rocks

How are igneous rocks formed?

Words to know:

magma   extrusive

lava   intrusive

Challenge words:

porphyritic

Igneous is the Latin word for *fire* **and** thus igneous rocks are fire rocks. These rocks are formed when molten or melted rock cools and hardens into new rock. This melted rock is called magma when it is below the earth's surface and is called lava once it emerges from the earth's crust. Igneous rocks can form both inside the earth's crust and on the earth's surface.

Rocks that form on the earth's surface are called **extrusive** rocks and are often nicknamed "volcanic rocks." Extrusive rocks cool quickly and therefore do not have time to form large crystals. They usually have very small crystals or no crystals at all. Pumice is a common extrusive igneous rock. It is light colored and full of holes because it cooled when the lava was full of hot gases. Because it cooled quickly, the gases were trapped inside. Eventually the gases

escaped, leaving the holes behind. These air bubbles make pumice very light, and samples can often float on water. Basalt is a heavy volcanic rock that occurs throughout the world. Obsidian, often called natural glass, is an igneous rock that cooled very quickly and has no crystals at all. However, it is often very shiny and thus looks like colored glass. Common colors for obsidian are black, brown, and red. It was often used to make arrowheads, like the one shown below.

Intrusive rocks are igneous rocks that were formed inside the earth's crust. Magma may flow upward and away from the area where it was heated to a cooler area inside the earth's crust. Because these rocks formed where the temperatures were much higher than on the surface, they cooled much more slowly, allowing crystals to grow much larger. The most common intrusive

Obsidian arrowhead

Granite

rock is granite. Granite is usually a mixture of quartz, feldspar, and mica. It is easy to see these three minerals in the granite shown above. The mica is usually black, the feldspar is pink, and the quartz is white. Granite is very strong and withstands weathering so it is often used for buildings and monuments.

Sometimes intrusive rocks form with larger crystals embedded in smaller crystals. What most likely happened to cause this was that the magma was in a warm area and the larger crystals formed, then somehow the magma was then shifted to a cooler area and cooled more quickly allowing only small crystals to form.

Igneous rocks are a part of our lives everyday. From monuments to counter tops, igneous rocks are all around us. People often use pumice stones to remove dead skin from the bottom of their feet. It is also used in abrasive (harsh) cleaning products. So keep your eyes open and look for igneous rocks in your neighborhood. 🌐

What did we learn?

- What is the difference between magma and lava?
- How are extrusive rocks formed?
- How are intrusive rocks formed?

Taking it further

- Which kind of igneous rocks have the largest crystals?
- Why is granite commonly used in buildings and monuments?
- Do all rocks sink in water?
- Why not?
- Where are you likely to find pumice?

Growing crystals

Purpose: To show what factors determine crystal size and shape

Materials: saucepan, stove, alum, two paper or plastic cups, two craft sticks, refrigerator, water

Procedure:

1. Place one cup of water in a saucepan and slowly heat it over medium heat until boiling.

2. Carefully add alum to the water until no more will dissolve or until you have dissolved about 2 ounces of alum.

3. Carefully pour half of the alum water into each of two cups.

4. Place a craft stick into each cup and put one cup in the refrigerator where it will not be disturbed for several days, and put the second cup in a location at room temperature where it will not be disturbed for several days.

5. Observe the contents of each cup every day for several days. After several days, crystals should be growing in both cups.

Questions:

- How do the crystals that formed in the refrigerator compare to those that formed at room temperature? Are the crystals the same shape? Are they the same size? Were they made of the same material?

- Why do they look so different?

Conclusion: The cup in the refrigerator will demonstrate the formation of extrusive rocks—rocks that cool quickly—and should have crystals that are smaller. The cup at room temperature will demonstrate the formation of intrusive rocks—rocks that cool slowly—and should have larger crystals. Since they both contain the same mineral, the shape of the crystals will be the same.

Identifying igneous rocks

Once you have determined that a rock sample is an igneous rock, there are several things you can look at to decide exactly which kind of rock it is.

First, examine the crystal size. If the crystals are very small or nonexistent you know that it is an extrusive rock. If the crystals are large and easily visible then you know it is an intrusive rock. Some rocks have large and small crystals in the same sample. This is called porphyritic texture. Porphyritic rocks are intrusive rocks that began cooling slowly then shifted to an area that was cooler and cooled more quickly. Pumice, basalt, and obsidian are common extrusive rocks. Common intrusive rocks include granite and diorite.

Color is also helpful in determining what kind of rock it is. Rocks containing a high percentage of silica are light colored. Rocks with a low silica content are darker. Lighter rocks high in silica include pumice and rhyolite. Darker rocks include obsidian, basalt, and scoria. Granite is a combination of quartz, feldspar, and mica. Depending on the exact combination of these minerals in a particular sample, granite can be very light or dark in color.

Some rocks have a high glass content making them very shiny. The best example of this is obsidian, which is often called glass rock or natural glass.

Finally, some igneous rocks formed from very bubbly lava. Gas bubbles were inside while they cooled; thus the rocks have a porous appearance. Porous rocks could include pumice and scoria.

Rocks & Minerals

Purpose: To test samples of igneous rocks

Materials: several samples of igneous rocks

Procedure:

1. Describe the color and the grain or crystal size for each rock.

2. Examine it for holes indicating that it had bubbles at one time.

3. Examine it with a magnifying glass and see if you can identify more than one kind of mineral in it.

4. Using a rocks and minerals guide, try to identify what each sample is.

Purpose: To better visualize the differences between intrusive and extrusive rocks

Materials: Raw sugar, brown sugar, butterscotch candy, magnifying class

Procedure:

Examine a sample of raw sugar, brown sugar, and butterscotch candy. Use a magnifying glass to closely examine each sample's structure.

What are all three of these samples made out of?

How do the crystal sizes compare for each sample?

Which sample is most likely to represent an intrusive rock?

Which sample is most likely to represent an extrusive rock?

Conclusion:

All three samples are made of sugar, yet their texture and appearances are very different. The raw sugar has large crystals; the brown sugar has very small crystals; and the butterscotch has no visible crystals at all. The raw sugar was made by slow cooling of the sugar. The butterscotch was cooled very quickly. The raw sugar represents intrusive rocks that cooled inside the crust of the earth. The butterscotch represents extrusive rocks that cooled very quickly outside the crust of the earth. The brown sugar is somewhere in between. It could represent either type of rock since small crystals can form in both kinds of rocks.

11

Sedimentary Rocks

Layers of sediment

How are sedimentary rocks formed?

Words to know:

strata   chemical rocks

fragmental rocks

Challenge words:

lithification   breccia

clast   matrix

conglomerate

Have you ever seen the side of a mountain that looked like lots of flat layers of rock piled on top of each other? Maybe you saw this along the side of the highway where the rock had been blasted away to make room for the road. If so, then you have seen sedimentary rock.

Sedimentary comes from the Latin word *sedo*—meaning to settle down. Sedimentary rocks are formed as layers of sediment are bonded together by natural cement as they settle out of a water solution. This sediment can be tiny bits of rock, sand, dirt, or seashells, along with chemicals or minerals that were dissolved in the water. Sedimentary rock usually forms in layers called strata. These layers are generally horizontal, but can become tilted as the ground shifts.

Sediment is mixed in water as the water moves over it. When the water slows down, the sediment settles to the bottom. As additional layers are deposited, the combined weight begins to press the layers more tightly together. In addition, minerals that are dissolved in the water work as a natural cement to glue the layers together. Eventually, these layers of sediment can harden and become sedimentary rock.

Most creation scientists believe that much of the sedimentary rocks on earth today were made

Sedimentary layers are called strata.

as the sediment settled from the great waters of Noah's Flood. This would account for the large number of fossils found in the sedimentary rocks around the world.

Sedimentary rocks are grouped into two categories by how they are formed. **Fragmental rocks** are formed when fragments of other rocks are cemented together with pressure. A common fragmentary rock is sandstone. Sandstone is made as bits of quartz and grains of sand are "glued" together by silica, calcite, or iron oxide. Other common fragmental rocks include siltstone and shale, which are formed from fragments of silt and clay. Bricks are a man-made rock from clay.

The second type of sedimentary rock is chemical rock. **Chemical rocks** form when a chemical that has been dissolved in the water precipitates out of the water or is left behind as the water evaporates. One type of chemical rock is dolomite, shown above. Dolomite is formed from calcium and magnesium. Limestone is one of the most common chemical sedimentary rocks. One

Dolomite

way it forms is when calcite precipitates from seawater. Many limestone deposits are filled with fossils of sea creatures. Limestone cliffs and caves can be found throughout the world.

Limestone is very important to man and has many uses. Lime is one of the key ingredients in cement. Also, real chalk is a type of limestone. However, most of today's chalk, especially sidewalk chalk, is actually made from gypsum instead of limestone. Sidewalk chalk is another man-made sedimentary rock! ◈

🧪 Making sedimentary rock

Purpose: To make your own sandstone

Materials: sand, cornstarch, water, old saucepan, stove, paint (optional)

Procedure:

1. Combine 2 cups of sand, 1 cup of cornstarch, and 1 cup of water in an old saucepan.

2. Slowly heat this mixture over medium heat, stirring constantly until it is thick.

3. Remove it from the heat and allow it to cool. When it is cool enough to handle safely, mold it into a sculpture.

4. Allow the sculpture to harden. Then, if you desire, paint the sculpture.

Conclusion:

This is similar to how sandstone is formed. The pressure of your hands is like the pressure of the water and other layers on top of the sandstone. What "chemical" was used to cement the sand together? (Cornstarch) Natural sandstone is usually cemented by calcite or silica.

Wind and water wear away exposed sandstone. Look at this picture of a sandstone arch from Arches National Park in Utah. This is a beautiful example of a landscape formation out of sandstone resulting from erosion by wind and water.

Fun Fact

In the 1400s, a special type of orange clay called *pygg* was used to form clay pottery and dishes. Often people would store their money in a pygg container. Eventually, the type of container changed but the name remained and a pygg bank became what we today call a *piggy bank*.

Making a sedimentary lunch

You can make a sedimentary lunch by layering bread, peanut butter, and jelly to form a sedimentary treat! Lunchmeat and cheese would work, too.

What did we learn?

- How are sedimentary rocks formed?
- Were all sedimentary rocks formed during the Flood?

Taking it further

- Why are fossils found in sedimentary rocks?
- Sediment is simply any small piece of something that settles out of a liquid. What sediment might you find around your house or in nature?

Lithification

The process by which sediment is turned into sedimentary rock is called lithification. Lithification involves two things. First is the compression of the sediments. This generally occurs as more sediment is deposited. The weight of the sediment above compresses the sediment in the lower layers. This compression forces out air pockets and presses the sediment grains closely together.

The second part of lithification is the cementing of the sediment grains. This can involve a number of different chemicals, but the most common chemicals that glue sediments together are silica and calcite.

As we mentioned earlier, there are two kinds of sedimentary rocks, fragmental and chemical. Another name for fragmental rocks is clastic rocks. Geologists generally refer to the fragments that are cemented together as clasts. If the clasts are fairly large, 0.08 inches (0.2 cm) or larger, the rocks that are formed are called either conglomerate or breccia (BRECH-ee-uh).

Conglomerate rocks are formed when smooth rounded clasts are glued together. Conglomerate can contain any kind of clasts, but most of the stones in conglomerate are quartz. These stones were rounded by erosion before they became part

Breccia

of the conglomerate rock. Breccia is formed when jagged or angular clasts are cemented together. Again, these clasts can be composed of any kind of igneous, sedimentary, or metamorphic rock. The material that cements the clasts together is called the matrix. The matrix may be very smooth or very grainy depending on what it is composed of.

Purpose: To make your own conglomerate and breccia samples

Materials: two paper cups, plaster of Paris, smooth and rough pebbles, spoon

Procedure:

1. In a paper cup combine ¼ cup plaster of Paris and ¼ cup smooth pebbles.

2. Add enough water to moisten the plaster. Then mix it together and press down on the mixture with a spoon to remove any air bubbles.

3. In a second paper cup combine ¼ cup plaster of Paris and ¼ cup jagged pebbles.

4. Again add enough water to moisten the plaster. Then mix it together and compress the mixture with a spoon.

5. Allow both cups to sit overnight.

6. When the mixture is dry, peel away the cups.

Conclusion: You now have a sample of conglomerate and a sample of breccia. Compare your samples with pictures of conglomerate and breccia above or in a rocks and minerals guide. How are they the same? How are they different?

12

Fossils

How do we know what dinosaurs looked like?

How are fossils formed?

Words to know:

fossil   mold fossil

cast fossil

Challenge words:

coprolite   gastrolith

One of the most interesting aspects of sedimentary rock is that fossils are often found in them. **Fossils** are evidence of plants and animals from a previous time that have been preserved in the rock.

A fossil is formed when an animal or plant is quickly covered by mud, wet sand, ice, or tar. If it is not covered quickly, the organism will decay and disappear. After it is covered, minerals may slowly replace the bones, scales, shells, and other parts of the animal that do not quickly decay. Often, all of the hard structures, and sometimes some soft structures, are replaced with minerals and become rock. A fossil is not often an actual bone from a dinosaur or other creature; it is usually a rock in the exact shape of that bone.

Because fossils only form when a creature is covered shortly after it dies, fossils do not ordinarily form.

An unusual event is required for a fossil to form. So why are fossils so common if they do not ordinarily form? The best explanation is that most fossils formed as a result of the worldwide Flood of Noah's time. Such a large flood would have suddenly covered millions of plants and animals with tons of mud and wet sand. This would result in an abundance of sedimentary rock formations filled with fossilized remains, which is exactly what we find in all parts of the world—even in Antarctica!

What can fossils tell us? They show us what kinds of plants and animals lived in the past. We see from fossils that most of the plants and animals in the past are very similar to those we see today. This is what we would expect to find since the Bible says that God created plants and animals to reproduce after their own kinds. We also see that many kinds of plants and animals no longer exist—they have become extinct.

What we do not see from the fossils is one kind of creature slowly changing into another kind. Evolution teaches that some fish eventually, over a very long period of time, developed legs to use on land. But all fossils that have been found either have fins or legs. None have been found with something in between.

The most famous fossils are fossils of dinosaur bones. Although these creatures are interesting, they account for a very small portion of all the fossils. Ninety-five percent of all fossils are marine invertebrates—mostly shellfish; 4.75% of the fossils are algae and plant fossils; 0.2375% of all fossils are insects, and 0.0124% are fish. That leaves only 0.0001% of all fossils that are mammals, reptiles, or other large creatures. And of these, 95% consist of only one bone. There are very few examples of dinosaur fossils. On a line that is 10 feet long, 9½ feet of the line would represent the marine fossils and only 1/100th of an inch would represent the dinosaur fossils. The fossil record clearly indicates conditions consistent with a marine catastrophe such as a huge flood.

Human fossils are not found in Flood rocks. There are many reasons for this. First, humans and land mammals tend to float when drowned and would not easily be covered by mud. Also, human bodies disintegrate very quickly so do not fossilize well. And finally, even if there had been 350 million people on the earth at the time of the Flood, and every one of them was preserved, there would be only one fossilized human for each 350 cubic miles (1,440 cubic km) of sedimentary rock. The chances of finding one would be very small. Besides, God said that He intended for the Flood to wipe out everybody except the eight people on the Ark.

🧠 What did we learn?

- How does an animal become a fossil?
- What are the two different types of fossils?
- What types of creatures are most fossils?

🚀 Taking it further

- How many true transitional fossils, ones showing one kind of creature evolving into another kind, have been found?
- What does this indicate about the idea that land animals evolved from sea creatures?
- What are some things we can learn from fossils?
- What kinds of things cannot be learned from fossils?

⚗️ Making your own fossils

There are two different kinds of fossils that can be found in the rocks. One kind is called a **mold fossil**. A mold is a fossil that is just the imprint of the animal or plant that has been preserved in the dried mud. For example, if an animal stepped in wet sand or mud and left an imprint, and then the imprint was filled with sediment before it was washed away, a mold fossil of the animal's footprint could be made.

The second type of fossil is what we commonly think of as a fossil, and is called a **cast fossil**. Cast fossils are made when sedimentary rock slowly replaces the bone, shell, or other hard structure of the animal.

Purpose: To make your own fossils

Materials: shell or other object to "fossilize," petroleum jelly, modeling clay, Plaster of Paris, cup, spoon

Procedure:

1. Choose a shell or other object to "fossilize."
2. Put a thin coating of petroleum jelly on the outside of the shell.
3. Press the shell into a piece of modeling clay and remove the shell. You now have a mold fossil of the shell.
4. Pour about ¼ cup of Plaster of Paris powder into a cup and stir in enough water to make a smooth, but not runny, liquid.
5. Pour this liquid into the clay cast of the shell and allow the plaster to harden for several hours.
6. After the plaster is hard, gently remove the clay. You now have a cast fossil of the shell.

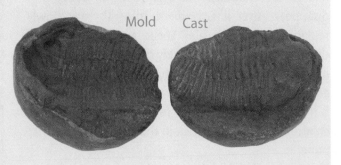
Mold   Cast

Types of fossils

Rock fossils include cast and mold fossils as you learned from the exercise you just completed. The vast majority of these fossils are bones, shells, and other hard parts of animals. But plants have left fossils behind as well. Other unusual fossils include footprints, called trace fossils. Many dinosaur and other animal footprint fossils have been uncovered in sedimentary rocks (see top photo at right). Another type of fossil is worm burrows. When animals are covered with large quantities of mud, many of them try to burrow out from under the heavy load. This sometimes results in fossilized burrows or tubes.

Petrified wood is also a type of fossil (shown at middle right). Petrified wood is formed when a tree is encased in hot silica-rich water. The chemicals seep into the wood and eventually replace all of the organic material. Other items have become petrified besides wood. Animals and even some humans have become petrified when their bodies have ended up in a location with hot silica-rich water. This form of fossilization does not take millions of years as some scientists would have you believe. Many tests have been done and petrification can happen in only a few hours to years.

Other types of rock fossils are given special names. **Coprolites** are fossilized animal dung. This may sound disgusting to you, but scientists can learn about an animal's diet by examining coprolites from that animal. Gastroliths are another special kind of fossil. **Gastroliths** are groups of smooth stones that are found inside an animal's body. We know today that some birds swallow stones to aid in digesting their food. Evidently some dinosaurs did this as well, since piles of stones have been found inside some of the fossilized dinosaur remains.

Although we said earlier in the lesson that a fossil is evidence of plants and animals in the past that have been preserved in rock, most scientists actually recognize a broader definition of fossils as just evidence of plants and animals from the past. Although most fossils are rocks, some evidence of past plant and animal life comes in other forms. A different form of fossilization occurs when an animal or plant is completely covered by something that preserves the entire creature. Many insects have been encased in amber, which is liquid tree sap. This sap eventually hardens and turns into a rock but the insect is preserved inside (see photo below). Although you may have heard that DNA can be extracted from the blood inside these trapped insects, this has not been accomplished. DNA lasts only a short time after death, and attempts to recover DNA from insects in amber have been unsuccessful.

Finally, some animals and even a few humans have been preserved in ice. It is very rare that an entire animal is frozen all at once, but a few mammoths and at least one person have been found encased in ice. Many millions of mammoth bones and parts of other animals have been found frozen. It is likely that these fossils were preserved during the Ice Age following Noah's Flood.

Fossilized footprints

Petrified wood

Insect in amber

13

Fossil Fuels

A major energy source

What are fossil fuels, and where do they come from?

Words to know:

fossil fuels

Challenge words:

geologic column

Have you ever heard the term *fossil fuels*? Did you picture a dinosaur or other creature and wonder what it had to do with fuel? **Fossil fuels** refer to coal, oil, and natural gas. All of these fuels are believed to be the result of plants that were buried in the past and, with time, heat, and pressure, changed into these forms of energy we use today.

Coal is considered by most scientists to be a sedimentary rock, although some geologists classify it as a metamorphic rock because it has been changed by heat and pressure. Either way, coal was formed from the remains of plants and thus contains a high amount of carbon that produces a large amount of energy when burned.

Evolutionists believe that coal formed when decaying plants in swampy areas, millions of years

ago, were slowly covered with sediment. The weight of the sediment layers above eventually produced enough pressure to change the plants into coal. However, there are several problems with this theory. First, carbon-14 dating of coal has shown some of it to be only a few thousand years old. Using carbon-14 dating, scientists have placed the age of some oil at only 4,200–4,900 years, which is much less than the millions of years given by evolutionists, and is about the date of Noah's Flood.

Additionally, large boulders have been found in coal deposits, indicating swift currents, not stagnant swamps, existed where the coal was formed. And finally, there are well-preserved delicate fern fossils in

One quarter of the world's coal reserves are found within the United States.

Rocks & Minerals

some coal beds, which would not be the case if these beds were formed from swamps over long periods of time. The evidence better supports the biblical view that prior to the Flood the climate was more tropical, encouraging larger plant growth than today, and that these plants were quickly buried by mud and other sediment during the Flood. These buried plants eventually changed into coal.

Contrary to what many people believe, it does not require millions of years to turn plants into coal. Coal has been formed in a laboratory in as little as eight months. All that is needed is high enough pressure and temperature. At the site of the Mount St. Helens volcanic eruption, plant debris that was buried in 1980 is already turning to peat, simply waiting for heat and pressure to turn into coal. So the large coal deposits we find today are easily explained by the Genesis Flood. (For more information on coal formation, see the Answers in Genesis web page at answersingenesis.org.)

Petroleum, or oil, is the liquid fuel formed from the remains of plants and algae. Oil is often found in sedimentary rocks containing marine fossils. Again, evolutionists say that oil formed slowly over millions of years. However, recent studies have shown that oil can form rapidly when the sedimentary layers containing the fossil plants and algae are buried deeply where the pressure and temperature extracts the liquid and gas. These often migrate into overlying layers and become trapped. Since no seal in rock is perfect, over time the liquid and gas will escape. The very existence of large oil fields, many of which have very high pressure, indicates that the fields can be only a few thousand years old, not millions of years old since the gas would have escaped and the pressure reduced long ago. In addition, oil has been formed in a laboratory in a matter of minutes or hours. All that is needed is the right amount of temperature and pressure.

Natural gas is the gas form of fossil fuels. It is

The plant debris buried in the Mount St. Helens eruption is already turning to peat.

often found along with oil and is believed to be a by-product of the oil formation process. The very existence of natural gas under pressure indicates relatively recent formation, only a few thousand years ago. The next time you hear the term fossil fuel, you can picture plants and algae, instead of dinosaurs, turning into coal, oil, and natural gas. 🌐

What did we learn?

- What is the definition of a fossil fuel?
- What three forms of fossil fuels do we commonly use?

Taking it further

- What evidence supports rapid and recent coal formation instead of slow formation millions of years ago?
- Why is finding natural gas when drilling into the ground a good indicator that oil is nearby?
- Why is the existence of natural gas an indication that oil was formed only a few thousand years ago?

Fossilized bones

Purpose: To help us understand how fossils form as minerals replace bones or shells

Materials: two sponges, shallow dish or pan, scissors, Epsom salt, food coloring (optional)

Procedure:

1. Cut two sponges into bone or shell shapes and set one piece aside to use for later comparison.

2. Place the second piece in a shallow dish or pan.

3. Pour one cup of hot water into a separate bowl and stir in as much Epsom salt as will dissolve in the hot water.

4. Add a few drops of food coloring if desired.

5. Pour the salt water over the sponge in the dish and set the dish in a location where it will not be disturbed for several days.

6. After several days compare the original sponge with the "fossilized" sponge.

Questions:

- How does the original sponge feel compared to the "fossilized" sponge?

- How does the original sponge look compared to the "fossilized" sponge?

Conclusion:

The "fossilized" sponge is larger because the holes were filled while the sponge was wet and expanded (this is a side effect of sponges and does not happen with actual fossils). Also, you should be able to see salt crystals in the holes in the sponge. This is how chemicals that harden into rock replace the bone or shell, by filling in the holes and then hardening. The "fossilized" sponge may also look white and powdery compared to the original one. Actual fossils do not necessarily have the same color as the original bone or shell.

Geologic column

Just as there is confusion about whether dinosaurs were the animals that turned into oil, there is often a lot of confusion about when and how fossils were made and when the fossilized plants and animals actually lived. In the 1600s and 1700s it was discovered that fossils of particular plants and animals were usually found together in a particular area. For example, one set of rocks may contain fossils of particular kinds of fish, shellfish, and other aquatic creatures, while another set of rocks may contain fossils of giraffes, saber-toothed tigers, and land plants. These different collections of fossils have been grouped into 12 different sets.

At that time, most scientists looked at the fossils found in different layers of rock and concluded that they were formed during Noah's Flood and that the different layers of fossils represented the different ecosystems that were destroyed during the Flood (i.e., the order of burial). This is still the view held by most creation scientists today. The layer of rocks containing primarily sea-bottom-dwelling creatures would have been buried first and formed the lowest levels of fossils. Those containing land-dwelling animals would have formed later in the Flood and would be found above the layers of aquatic fossils.

However, in the 1800s the idea that the earth is very old became popular. That is when scientists began to believe that the different layers of rock represented different time periods and that the different fossils found in each layer represent the animals that were dominant on the earth at that time. This is used to support the idea of evolution, supposedly showing that sea creatures slowly evolved into land-dwelling creatures.

Evolutionists have taken the 12 groups of fossils and stacked them one on top of another to represent a geologic timeline with the fossils in the lowest layers representing animals that supposedly lived up to 500 million years ago. It should be noted that there are few places in the world where all 12 layers are found in the order given in this geologic column. In most places, layers from only parts of this geologic column are found.

Evolutionists claim that this column demonstrates the evolution of species from simple water-dwelling creatures to complex land-dwelling creatures. However, there are no fossils that demonstrate this. First, there are no fossils that are part way between one kind of animal and another. There are no fossils of creatures that have something in between fins and legs. All fossils show animals that have either fully developed fins or fully developed legs, but nothing in between. Second, the fossils of many supposedly simple creatures show that these creatures are really quite complex. Also, many of the fossils show that even the oldest creatures are often very similar to animals that live today. This is strong evidence for fossils being formed by the Flood and not over millions of years of evolution.

Now complete the "What Would You Expect?" worksheet to see how different ecosystems could result in different animals in different fossil layers.

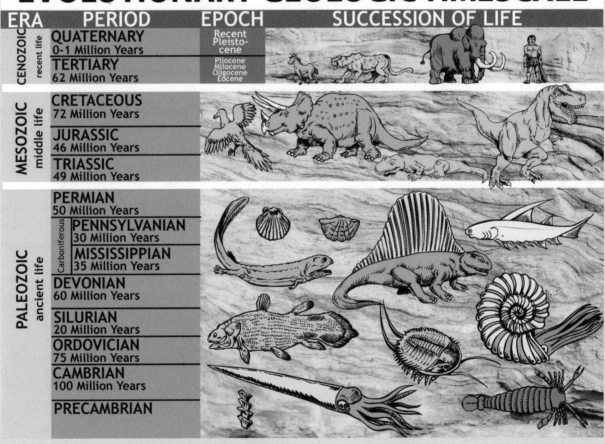

EVOLUTIONARY GEOLOGIC TIMESCALE

ERA	PERIOD	EPOCH	SUCCESSION OF LIFE
CENOZOIC recent life	QUATERNARY 0-1 Million Years	Recent Pleisto-cene	
	TERTIARY 62 Million Years	Pliocene Miocene Oligocene Eocene	
MESOZOIC middle life	CRETACEOUS 72 Million Years		
	JURASSIC 46 Million Years		
	TRIASSIC 49 Million Years		
PALEOZOIC ancient life	PERMIAN 50 Million Years		
	PENNSYLVANIAN 30 Million Years (Carboniferous)		
	MISSISSIPPIAN 35 Million Years		
	DEVONIAN 60 Million Years		
	SILURIAN 20 Million Years		
	ORDOVICIAN 75 Million Years		
	CAMBRIAN 100 Million Years		
	PRECAMBRIAN		

14

Metamorphic Rocks

Let's make a change

How are metamorphic rocks formed?

Words to know:

foliated

We have learned that igneous rock is formed when magma cools, and sedimentary rock is formed when small grains of sediment are pressed and cemented together. The third category of rock is metamorphic rock. The word *metamorphic* comes from the Greek word meaning "to change form." Metamorphic rock is igneous or sedimentary rock that has been changed into a different form. These rocks were changed due to the heat and pressure inside the earth's crust over a period of time.

Metamorphic rocks are divided into **foliated** and nonfoliated rocks. *Foliated* comes from a word meaning "with leaves." Obviously these rocks do not have leaves like trees, but they do have flattened crystals that line up in parallel layers, so they break easily into thin broad sheets that somewhat resemble leaves. A common example of a foliated rock is slate. Slate is formed when shale, a sedimentary rock, has experienced pressure and heat over time to become a very hard rock. Another foliated

rock is gneiss (pronounced like *nice*). The bands in the photo of gneiss below are clearly visible. Gneiss can be formed from several different sedimentary and igneous rocks including mudstone, siltstone, granite, and diorite.

Nonfoliated metamorphic rocks do not have lines or layers. Two common nonfoliated metamorphic rocks are quartzite and marble. Marble is limestone that has been changed. Pure marble is white, but many marble deposits contain impurities that result in the common swirled appearance often associated with marble. Marble is hard and holds a polish so it is often used for sculptures, monuments,

Gneiss, a metamorphic rock

Michelangelo's *David* was carved from marble.

floors, and buildings. Quartzite is changed sandstone. Heat and pressure rearrange the quartz crystals resulting in a very hard stone. Quartzite is the same color as the sandstone from which it came and can vary from tan to brown to red.

What did we learn?

- What are the three ingredients needed to change igneous or sedimentary rock into metamorphic rock?
- Why is marble often swirled instead of pure white?

Taking it further

- Why is metamorphic rock often used for sculptures and monuments?
- Why is metamorphic rock hard and durable?

Morphing ice

Follow the directions and answer the questions for the "Morphing Ice" worksheet.

Making marble

Purpose: To demonstrate why marble often has a swirled appearance

Materials: two or three pieces of taffy, wax paper

Procedure:

1. Unwrap two or three pieces of different colored soft candy such as taffy and place them on top of each other.

2. Wrap the candy in a piece of waxed paper and press the candy together for at least a minute.

3. Unwrap the candy and look at it.

Conclusion:

The striped appearance should resemble the swirled appearance of marble. Marble is formed when limestone is pressed and heated for a long time. The swirled appearance occurs because other types of rock may be intermixed with the limestone formation.

Types of metamorphic rocks

Complete the "Metamorphic Match" worksheet.

Artificial Islands

Natural islands develop in many ways. One of the most spectacular ways is when a volcano erupts under water and the lava builds up until it breaks the surface of the water and a new island is born. Other islands are formed when erosion wears away the land leaving the new island surrounded by water. A third way that islands are formed is when glaciers retreat and islands are revealed. Naturally occurring islands appear every few years. Some of them last, others are quickly worn away by wind and water and disappear back into the sea. But not all new islands are naturally occurring. Some islands are man-made.

One of the earliest artificial islands was built in Puget Sound near Seattle, Washington. But it wasn't made to make more land. It was the result of opening up a channel for shipping at the mouth of the Duwamish River. The builders had to do something with all the dirt they dug up, so they made an island. This project was started in 1900 and took nine years to complete. Using a process called dredging, they brought up soil from the bottom of the channel. Most of the soil, 24 million cubic yards (18 million cubic meters) of it, was used to form what is now called Harbor Island. Upon completion, the island was nearly 350 acres (140 hectares) and at that time it was the largest man-made island in the world.

Only one person lived on the soggy island for the first couple of years. He lived there with his dog, an angora goat, and about 300 chickens. He didn't own the island, but for a time no one cared. Then, in 1911, he had to leave when a shipyard was built on the island. In 1918, during World War I, two of the largest wooden steamers in the world were built at this shipyard.

The island wasn't without its problems. Because it was built on top of the river delta and the land is

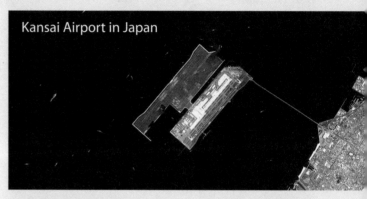

Kansai Airport in Japan

seismically unstable, it moved a fair amount during earthquakes. In 1949 parts of the island rose 16 inches (40 cm) while other parts fell 12 inches (30 cm). In the earthquake of 1965, two of the piers on the island moved one foot (30 cm) closer to Seattle. In 2001, when seismologist Bob Norris was on the island during an earthquake, he described muddy water erupting from the ground. This made him think that a water main had burst. He described what looked like geysers, shooting water into the air about 3 feet (1 m) high. He later found out that the muddy water was a result of the liquefaction of subsurface soil during the earthquake. Liquefaction is when loose soil becomes fluid-like during an earthquake.

Although Harbor Island was built because engineers needed a place to put tons of extra soil, several other man-made islands have been built for the purpose of providing more land. One of the more notable islands is off the coast of Japan, near the city of Osaka. This island was built for the purpose of making land for an airport. Japan is a rather crowded country, and airports take up a large amount of valuable land. So an island was built specifically for the new airport. The island is connected to the mainland by a 2.33 mile (3.75 km) long bridge. The bridge was built with two levels: there is a highway on the top level and a railway on the lower level. The airport only has one runway, but it can handle

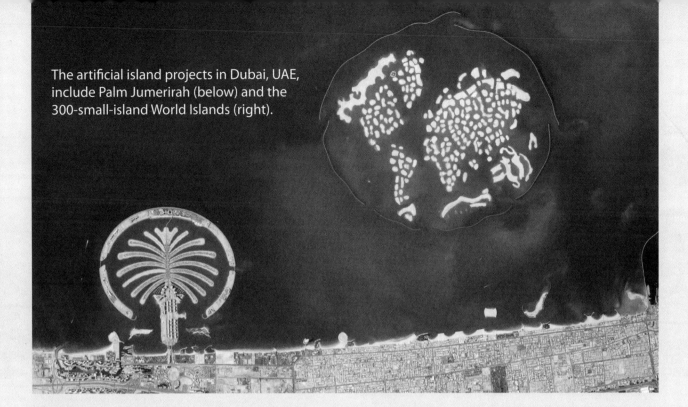

The artificial island projects in Dubai, UAE, include Palm Jumerirah (below) and the 300-small-island World Islands (right).

about 438 takeoffs and landings a day. The airport has 33 passenger gates.

The Kansai Airport opened on September 4, 1994, and has only one big problem. This 1.95 square mile (5 square km) island is sinking. The designers planned for this, however, and the airport was built with hydraulic jacks under it that can raise and lower the terminal as needed.

Although the island sank more than expected at first, the rate at which the island is sinking has greatly slowed down and the airport has been expanded. A second landing strip has been built and an updated terminal was completed in 2012. The engineers learned a lot by building the Kansai Airport, and what they learned has been used to build islands for several additional airports including the New Kitakyushu Airport, Kobe Airport, Chubu Centair International Airport, and the Hong Kong International Airport.

Although Japan has been a leader in building artificial islands there are other countries working in this area as well. Developers in the United Arab Emirates (UAE) have begun construction of several different island projects. Al Lulu Island was built off the coast of Abu Dhabi, the capital of the UAE. Although it was originally planned for tourism, it is now a private island with residential and commercial buildings.

One of the biggest artificial island projects in the UAE is the palm islands project. The builders originally planned to build three palm tree shaped islands off the coast of Dubai. The first island, called Palm Jumeirah, was completed and in 2006 the first residents moved in. This island is shaped like a palm tree with a trunk, a crown, and fronds. It is surrounded by a crescent shaped island that acts as a breakwater. The island is home to over 28 luxury hotels, private villas, restaurants, shopping malls, and more.

The second island, called Palm Jebel Ali, is about 50 percent larger than the Palm Jumeirah Island. The island itself is completed, but the development of the island was halted because of the world-wide recession in 2008. Development has slowly resumed and is expected to continue but at a much slower pace than the development of Palm Jumeirah. The third island, originally called Palm Deira, has been scaled back and is now just called Island Deira. The development of this island has been on hold since 2008.

Another interesting project in the same area as the Palm Islands is the World Islands project. The World Islands is a collection of man-made islands that when viewed from the air roughly resemble a map of the world. There are approximately 300 small islands. These islands are being sold to private developers who will develop them for tourism according to the countries that they represent.

The technology to build man-made islands is continuing to improve so we may see many more artificial islands in the future. Watch the news for new places to visit.

15

Minerals

Animal, vegetable, or mineral?

What are minerals, and how do we use them?

Words to know:

mineral

native mineral

In lesson 9 we learned that rocks are made of one or more minerals or organic materials. But what is a mineral? In order for a substance to be considered a **mineral**, it must meet all five of the following requirements.

1. Naturally occurring—not put together by man
2. Inorganic—is not and has never been alive. All plants and animals have carbon in their cells, so such carbon-based materials are considered organic.
3. Definite chemical structure—always has elements in the same proportion. For example, quartz is always two parts oxygen to one part silicon.
4. Atoms are arranged in a regular pattern—for example, a crystalline structure
5. Solid—at normal temperatures

Minerals that have only one type of atom are called **native minerals**. They are pure elements. Native minerals include most of the metals such

as gold, silver, and copper. Also, even though diamonds are made from carbon, geologists make an exception and classify them as a native mineral.

Most minerals, however, are made of more than one type of element. For example, table

Mica

Amethyst quartz

salt contains both sodium and chlorine in equal amounts. Minerals that are not composed of a pure element are called *compounds*. Most minerals are compounds.

Rocks that contain more than one mineral in varying proportions are called *mixtures*. For example, granite is a rock that contains feldspar, quartz, and mica. However, two samples of granite will likely have different ratios of the three minerals. One may have more feldspar than quartz; another sample may have more quartz than feldspar. Therefore, granite is a rock but is not a mineral. Most rocks are mixtures of minerals.

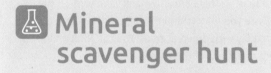

Mineral scavenger hunt

Complete the "Mineral Scavenger Hunt" worksheet.

Minerals are very important to our lives. We make many items out of minerals such as jewelry made from gold and silver. Common minerals you may find around your house include salt, alum, quartz, gold, silver, and copper. Also, our bodies need minerals to keep them healthy.

What did we learn?

- What five requirements must a substance meet in order to be classified as a mineral?

- What is a native mineral?

- What is a compound?

Taking it further

- Are there any minerals that are mixtures?

- What is the difference between a rock and a mineral?

- Is coal a mineral?

- Are all minerals considered rocks?

- Are all rocks considered minerals?

- Where are you likely to find minerals?

 # Mancala

Rocks and minerals have so many uses we could not list them all in this book, but one of my favorite ways to use rocks and minerals is to play the game Mancala. Mancala is one of the oldest games and originated in ancient Egypt or the Middle East.

Purpose: To use rocks to play Mancala

Materials: egg carton, 48 small pebbles or rocks, coin

Procedure:

1. Cut the top off of an egg carton, and then cut the top in half.

2. Tape one half to each end of the carton bottom to form a bin at each end. These are called the mancalas.

3. Place four small pebbles or stones in each of the cups in the egg carton.

The game is now set up for two players. The mancala on your right is yours and the mancala on your left is your opponent's mancala.

Game Instructions:

Flip a coin to decide which player goes first. The first player selects a cup on his side of the board and takes all of the stones out. He then drops one stone in the cup to the right of the one he took the stones out of. He continues dropping one stone into each cup in a counterclockwise direction. If he comes to the end of his side of the board, he drops a stone in his mancala and continues on around to his opponent's side of the board until he uses all of his stones. Never drop a stone in your opponent's mancala. If you drop your final stone into your mancala, you get another turn. If you have the right number of stones so that you drop your final stone into an empty cup on your side of the board, you get to move that stone and any stones that are in the cup on the opposite side of the board into your mancala. This is called a capture. You cannot make a capture from your opponent's side of the board. Continue playing until one player no longer has any stones on his side of the board. The player with remaining stones gets to place all remaining stones in his mancala. The player with the most stones in his mancala at the end of the game wins.

This is a fun game of strategy. It is simple to learn but difficult to master. There are also many variations on the rules. Once you understand the basic rules, you may want to try to play with different rules. You can look online for different variations of this game.

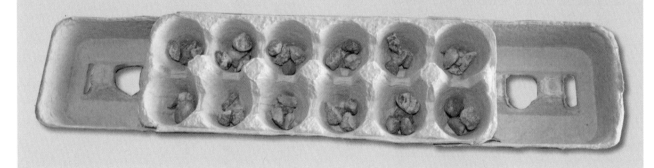

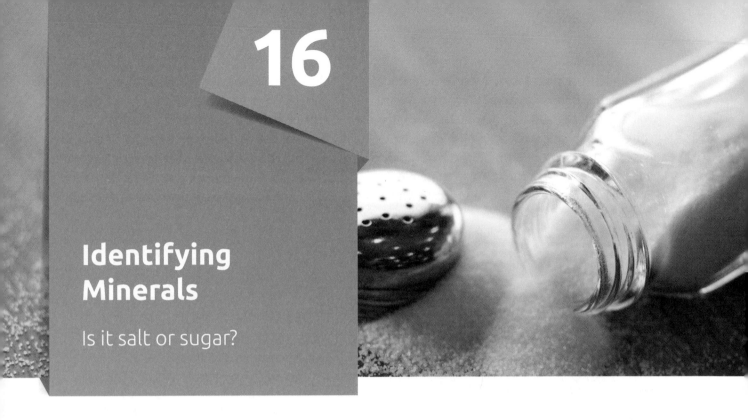

Identifying Minerals

Is it salt or sugar?

How can we identify different minerals?

Words to know:

luster   fracture

cleavage

Some minerals are easily identifiable by simple observation, while others are easily confused. With practice, you will be able to identify rock and mineral samples more easily. But even with practice, some samples can be difficult or tricky to identify. Geologists have devised a series of tests to help determine what mineral a sample contains.

- Color: This is a starting point in determining what mineral your sample contains. Some minerals have distinctive colors, especially if the samples are pure. However, color is not adequate to identify most minerals. Impurities can change the color. Quartz, for example, can be green, pink, blue, violet, or smoky. Also, oxidation, or rust, can change the outward color or appearance of a sample. Besides, many minerals have the same color as other minerals.

- Streak: A more accurate way to determine the color of a sample is to perform a streak test. Rub the sample across a piece of unglazed porcelain or ceramic tile and examine the color of the powder left behind. Even if a sample's color has been changed by impurities, its streak will remain pure. Note: minerals that are harder than the tile will not leave a streak.

- Luster: This is a description of the quality and intensity of light reflected from the surface. For example, a sample of pure copper will have a metallic/shiny luster. Other samples could have a luster classified as glassy, pearly, adamantine (sparkling like a diamond), fibrous, silky, greasy, or dull.

- Crystal shape: Minerals have a regular shape. Some minerals have hexagon, cubic, needle, or rosette-shaped crystals. Others have crystals that are too small to see with the eye. A magnifying glass is useful to help determine the crystal shape. Just as with igneous rocks, the temperature at which the mineral formed greatly affects the size of the crystals. Those formed at higher temperatures and cooled slowly have larger crystals than those that formed quickly at lower temperatures. Some minerals, which formed very quickly, may have no crystals at all.

• Hardness: A scratch test is used to determine how hard a mineral is. Something that is hard will scratch the surface of something that is softer. Using substances with known hardness will help you determine the hardness of your sample. In 1812 the German mineralogist Friedrich Mohs created the Mohs scale, which characterizes the scratch resistance of various minerals. For example, talc is one of the softest minerals and is assigned a hardness of 1 on the Mohs scale. Diamond is the hardest known mineral and is assigned a hardness of 10. Quartz has a hardness of 7, and calcite has a hardness of 3. Samples of these known minerals can help

Mineral identification

Purpose: To learn how to perform common tests used to identify minerals

Materials: Copy of "Mineral Identification" worksheet, magnifying glass, eye protection, 3 or 4 mineral samples, masking tape, penny, hammer, old drinking glass, old pillowcase or towel, unglazed ceramic tile, rocks and minerals guide

Procedure:

Use masking tape to label each mineral sample with a number. Using a copy of the "Mineral Identification" worksheet, record your observations as you perform each of the following tests.

1. Color—Record the color and any other observations for each sample.

2. Streak—Firmly press the sample against an unglazed tile and make a streak. Record the color of the powder (if any).

3. Luster—Record the luster of the sample (glassy, sparkly, shiny, oily, metallic, etc.).

4. Crystal shape—Use a magnifying glass to observe the crystal structure. Record the shape and size.

5. Hardness—Try to scratch the sample with a fingernail and a penny. Test if the sample will scratch the side of an old drinking glass. On the Mohs scale, a fingernail has a hardness of 2.5, a penny is 3.5 and glass is 5.5. Record the relative hardness of the sample. (Less than 2.5, between 3.5 and 5.5 or greater than 5.5.)

6. Cleavage—Place the sample in an old pillowcase or wrap it in a towel. **Be sure to wear eye protection such as goggles.** Use a hammer to break the sample. Observe how it cracks or breaks.

7. Using these observations and a rocks and minerals guide, try to identify each sample. Information for some common minerals is included below:

Conclusion: Performing these tests should give you a better idea of the various characteristics of different rocks and minerals.

Mineral	Color	Streak	Luster	Crystal	Hardness	Cleavage
Talc	White	White	Dull	None	1	None—thin flakes
Gypsum	White to gray	White	Pearly	Flat	2	Perfect in 1 direction
Mica	Clear to gray	Clear	Sparkly	Flat	2.5	Thin sheets
Calcite	Clear, white, pink	White	Shiny	Triangular	3	Perfect 6-sided crystals
Fluorite	White, green, pink	White	Sparkly	Cube or 8-sided	4	Perfect 8-sided
Feldspar	Pink	White	Shiny	4- or 6-sided, flat	6	Varies with type
Pyrite	Brassy to gold	Green/black	Shiny	Cubic	6–6.5	Perfect in 3 directions
Quartz	White, pink	White	Glassy	Hexagon	7	Fractures
Topaz	Colorless to green	White	Glassy	Rectangular	8	Perfect in 2 directions
Diamond	Clear	None	Sparkly	8-sided	10	Perfect in several directions

determine the hardness of your sample by using one material to try to scratch another material.

- **Cleavage**: This is a test of how well a sample breaks in straight lines. Using eye protection is a must when performing this test. Using a hammer, break the sample into two pieces. Examine the broken edges to see if the sample broke in straight lines. Samples that break in flat sheets are said to have perfect cleavage. These samples break this way because the crystals are tightly bonded in one direction but weakly bonded in another direction. An example of a mineral with perfect cleavage is mica, which breaks into flat sheets, usually with just a fingernail. Other samples may have good, fair, poor, or no cleavage. Some minerals do not have cleavage but break along smooth curves. These minerals are said to have **fracture**. An example of a mineral with good fracture is quartz, which has been used to make arrowheads and other tools.

Scientists often must perform other tests as well in order to determine the composition of a sample. However, these other tests may be difficult or dangerous to do at home. They include:

- Flame test—The color of the flame of a burning sample can help identify it.
- Acid test—Some minerals react with acids to produce a bubbling/foaming reaction.
- Magnetism—Some minerals are magnetic.
- Radioactivity—Some minerals are radioactive and can be tested with a Geiger counter.
- Glow test—Some minerals have fluorescence (they glow in ultraviolet light).
- Refraction—Some minerals bend light that shines through them.

What did we learn?

- What are some common tests used to identify minerals?
- Why is color alone not a sufficient test?

Taking it further

- Is crystal size a good test for identifying a mineral? Why or why not?
- What is the difference between cleavage and fracture?
- Why do some tests need to be done in a laboratory?
- How can you tell a sample of sugar from a sample of salt?

 ## Rocks and minerals

Recall that in lesson 15 we talked about three different categories for rocks and minerals. Specimens that contain only one kind of atom are called native elements. Specimens that contain several elements combined together to form a new substance are called compounds. Finally, if several compounds are combined together in varying proportions, the substance is called a mixture. Minerals are never mixtures; they are always native elements or compounds. Most rocks are mixtures of minerals.

Use a rocks and minerals guide to help you complete the "Is it a Rock or a Mineral?" worksheet.

17

Valuable Minerals

How much for an ounce of gold?

Which minerals are valuable and why?

As far back as we have records, and even among civilizations without written records, we see that man has recognized the beauty and usefulness of many minerals. The Bible shows that the earliest civilizations valued gold, bronze, and iron. It says in Genesis 4:22, "And as for Zillah, she also bore Tubal-Cain, an instructor of every craftsman in bronze and iron." Tubal-Cain was the great grandson of Cain and had the knowledge to work with bronze and iron. And in Genesis 2:11–12 it says that one of the rivers flowing out of the Garden of Eden also flowed through the land of Havilah, "where there is gold." Also, paintings and archaeological finds reveal many uses of gold, silver, iron, and other valuable minerals in even the oldest post-Flood civilizations. God created minerals, rocks, and gems in their various forms for man to use and enjoy.

Many of the more valuable minerals are the native minerals. Recall that native minerals are the minerals that are pure elements—they have only one kind of atom. Valuable minerals are usually expensive because they are very useful or beautiful and are limited in quantity. Generally, the more abundant an element is, the less expensive it is.

One of the most desired minerals is gold. Gold is valued for its beauty and usefulness. Because gold is one of the heaviest minerals, it has often been mined from riverbeds by panning or sluicing. In this type of mining, the miner scoops up dirt from the bottom of the river, then allows water to wash away the lighter materials, leaving the heavier gold behind. In the early gold rush days in California and Colorado, panning for gold was the easiest way to find nuggets. However, the gold in the riverbeds was soon exhausted and drilling into the mountains revealed the largest finds of gold.

Over the centuries gold has had many uses.

Men working a sluice box to find gold in the Yukon territories, circa 1900

Gold has been used for money, jewelry, and in dentistry. It doesn't tarnish or rust and it conducts electricity so it is also useful for electrical contacts in semiconductors.

Silver is more common than gold, so it is less expensive. Yet silver is still considered a precious metal. It is often used for jewelry and tableware. It is the best metal for conducting electricity, so it is used in electrical circuits. Silver is also very important in the processing of photographic film. Also, silver and gold have been used to make coins for hundreds of years. However, today most coins are made from zinc and other less expensive materials.

Another important mineral is copper. Copper is mostly mined in the form of copper sulfide ore. These ores are abundant in New Mexico and Arizona. Copper is useful for many purposes as well. Because copper conducts electricity nearly as well as silver, but does not tarnish as quickly and is less expensive, it is used for electrical wiring in most buildings. Copper pipes are used for plumbing and copper is used for making pots and pans. Copper is used for jewelry and for sculptures, as well.

Most metals, such as silver, copper, lead, and zinc are found in the earth's crust in the form of oxides or sulfides. Oxides are minerals that have combined with oxygen. Sulfides are minerals that have combined with sulfur. Ores containing these oxides and sulfides are mined and then processed to remove the native elements.

A final native mineral that is very valuable is diamond. Most minerals do not contain carbon, which is the basis of organic/living material. This is why coal is not considered a mineral. However, geologists

make an exception for diamonds and a few other minerals. Diamonds are made from pure carbon that has been crystallized. Diamond is the hardest known mineral. It is given an absolute hardness of 10 on the Mohs scale compared to glass with a hardness of 5.5 and fingernails with a hardness of 2.5.

Diamonds have perfect cleavage, allowing the light to sparkle through them. Uncut diamonds have a greasy luster, but cut diamonds have a very brilliant sparkly luster called *adamantine*. Diamonds are mostly used for jewelry. Their value is determined by their size, color, purity, and cut. Diamonds that are not useful as gems are used in other capacities. Because of their hardness they are often used on the tips of drills and saws that are used to cut other hard materials. All of these valuable minerals were created for our pleasure and use by our wonderful Creator. ✇

What did we learn?

- What are some valuable minerals?
- What is a native mineral?
- What are some important uses for gold?
- What are some important uses for silver?

Taking it further

- Why is diamond considered an exception among minerals?
- Diamonds and coal are both made from carbon. What makes them different?

Fun Fact

Valuable metals have been used for many interesting purposes. For example, the Statue of Liberty is made from sheets of copper laid over an iron framework. The dome on the Colorado state capitol building is covered in very thin sheets of 24-karat gold, called gold leaf. And although salt is very inexpensive today, during the Roman Empire salt was so valuable it was used as a form of money.

⚗ Chocolate mining

Mining is almost always required to remove valuable minerals from the earth's crust. Gold and silver nuggets are seldom found just sitting by themselves waiting to be discovered. Instead, miners must removed tons of ore—rock that contains the desired mineral—along with other elements, and then process the ore to remove the mineral.

Purpose: To appreciate the work required to mine for gold, silver, or diamonds

Materials: chocolate chip cookie, toothpick

Procedure:

1. Carefully remove each chocolate chip from the cookie by using only a toothpick.

2. After the chips are removed, describe the appearance of the cookie.

3. Enjoy the chocolate chips you "mined," and then be sure to clean up the area (by eating the crumbs.)

Questions:

- How difficult was it to "mine" the chips from the cookie?

- Does what's left over look anything like the original cookie?

Conclusion: Mining is a difficult and messy process. It can be devastating to the ecology of an area if miners are not careful. In the past, miners came and took what they wanted, leaving behind a destroyed area. Today, miners are more careful to restore an area after mining.

① Moon rocks

Some of the most precious minerals on earth did not actually originate on this planet. Moon rocks have been brought back to earth from the moon and are considered priceless because there are so few of them here. There are actually three sources for moon rocks. Most of the rocks, about 2,400 samples weighing a total of 840 pounds (380 kg) were brought back by American astronauts who visited the moon during several missions from 1969–1972. A small amount, about 11.5 ounces (326 g) were brought back by unmanned Soviet probes that visited the moon in the 1970s. And about 106 pounds (48 kg) of moon rocks have fallen from the moon to the earth as meteorites and have been recovered by private citizens and sold to collectors.

Most moon rocks are stored in a special vault at the Johnson Space Center in Houston, Texas. A smaller sample is stored at White Sands Test Facility in Las Cruces, New Mexico. These rocks are stored in a nitrogen environment to prevent them from reacting with oxygen or moisture in our air. These rocks are never handled with bare hands, but are always handled with special equipment.

In 1973, President Richard Nixon decided to make a goodwill gesture and gave a small sample of moon rock to 135 different countries as well as to all 50 U.S. states. Because moon rocks are so valuable, many of these samples are now unaccounted for and may have been stolen or sold to collectors.

Although moon rocks may look very much like earth rocks, they have a different composition. Many of the rocks are from the flat area on the moon call maria. These rocks are called mare basalts and they are igneous rocks that cooled from lava that flowed into the maria. Other rocks come from the more mountainous areas called the lunar highlands. Most of these rocks are igneous rocks containing a large amount of feldspar. A third type of moon rock is impact breccia. These rocks are believed to have been formed when meteorites struck the surface of the moon, breaking apart other rocks and melting them together from the heat of the impact.

Even though moon rocks are rare, there are several samples on display. If you visit the NASA space center in either Houston or Florida you can see samples there. Also, there are several samples on display at the Smithsonian in Washington, D.C. You can even touch one of the samples at the Smithsonian.

18

Natural & Artificial Gems

Cut stones

What are gems, and how are they made?

Words to know:

gem

Just like gold and silver, gemstones have had significant uses since the beginning of civilization. One of the most important references to gems in the Bible is in Exodus 28:15–21, when God commanded Moses to place 12 special stones on the breastplate of the high priest. There were four rows with three stones in each row. Each stone was to represent one of the twelve tribes of Israel. These gems were important for the Old Testament worship of God.

Another important reference to gems in the Bible is in Revelation 21:9–21. This passage describes what the New Jerusalem will look like. It says the foundation of the New Jerusalem will be made from jasper, sapphire, emeralds, and other precious gems.

Gems are minerals that are popular because of their beautiful colors or designs, and their ability to be polished or reflect light in a brilliant way. Most gems have perfect cleavage and can be cut in ways that reflect the light.

Popular gemstones include ruby, diamond, emerald, sapphire, topaz, and amethyst. Today, gems are used mostly as jewels and for decorations.

Naturally occurring gems are relatively scarce or limited in quantity. Therefore, they are fairly expensive. Usually, the more scarce a gem is, the more expensive it is. So, because of people's desire to possess gems, and their relative scarcity, scientists have worked to create synthetic or man-made gems.

Artificial gems

Early copies or substitutes for gems can be found as far back in history as ancient Egypt. Samples of artificial gems made from glass or ceramic have been found in many ancient Egyptian sites. Today, colored glass is less likely to be used but not completely unheard of. More recently, scientists have been successful in growing crystals from the same minerals that compose the naturally occurring gems.

In 1954, scientists produced the first man-made diamonds from carbon atoms. The temperatures required were greater than 4,800°F (2,650°C), and

the pressure was greater than 1.5 million pounds per square inch (100,000 kg/cm²). Although these copies were very close to naturally occurring diamonds, they were very small and useful only for industrial applications. More recent attempts to make man-made diamonds have resulted in larger diamonds, but ones that are not pure in color. Most substitute diamonds that are used as gemstones today are made from cubic zirconium, not carbon.

Synthetic rubies are made by melting the minerals in rubies at high temperatures and then allowing them to cool and crystallize. Many other synthetic gems are made this way as well. It is a fairly fast process, taking only months for crystals to form. However, these synthetic stones are less expensive than naturally occurring stones.

Often, synthetic gems look very similar to their natural counterparts. However, differences are easily seen under a microscope or magnifying glass. Synthetic gems are often "too perfect." Naturally occurring gems have slight imperfections. Also, synthetic gems are not as durable as the natural ones. No matter how good man's efforts are, they are a weak imitation of God's original design.

What did we learn?

- What is a gem?
- How is a gem different from a native mineral?
- How are artificial rubies made?

Taking it further

- What can you guess about the temperatures at which synthetic rubies are formed?
- Why would rubies be formed at high temperatures?
- What are some disadvantages of synthetic gems?
- Why are natural gems worth more money than artificial gems?

Breastplate worksheet

Read Exodus 28:15–21. The high priests during the time of Israel's temple worship were very important. The high priest was responsible for offering sacrifices for the sins of the nation of Israel. Today, we no longer need a high priest to offer sacrifices because Jesus was the ultimate sacrifice for our sins and Jesus has become our high priest. However, it is still important to understand the pattern of Old Testament worship.

Color the gems on the "Breastplate" worksheet. Suggested colors for each stone are listed below the picture.

Beautiful gems

Since gems are something valued for their beauty, it is helpful to actually look at gems to see how beautiful they are. Using a gems book or the Internet, look at pictures of many different gems. If you have access to a color printer or copier, make copies of the pictures and compile your own book of gems. Looking at gems on paper is good, but looking at gems in person is even better. If you have a chance, visit a jewelry store and view some of the many beautiful gems that they have available there. Also, many museums have rock and mineral collections. If you have an opportunity, visit one of these museums and view their lovely rocks and gems.

Rocks & Minerals

UNIT 3

Mountains & Movement

◊ **Identify** the period when the continents separated.

◊ **Describe** how different types of mountains form.

◊ **Describe** how earthquakes are detected and measured.

◊ **Describe** how different types of volcanoes form.

◊ **Relate** how Mount St. Helens confirms biblical geology.

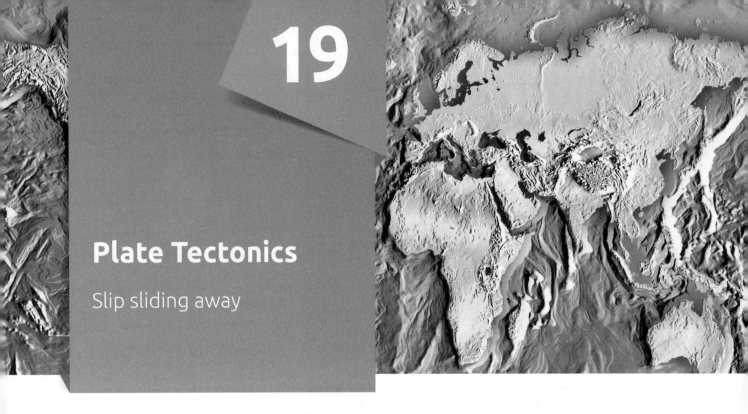

19

Plate Tectonics

Slip sliding away

What is plate tectonics and how has it affected the earth?

Words to know:

plate tectonics

Rodinia

Challenge words:

subduction zone

rifting

subduction

strike-slip faulting

Until the 1960s, most scientists believed that the earth's crust was one solid piece of rock that was completely stationary. But the idea that the earth's crust is actually several large pieces floating on the mantle has become the more accepted theory in the last 50 years or so. This idea is called **plate tectonics**.

This idea was first proposed in 1859 by scientist Antonio Snider, who suggested that the continents moved horizontally during the Flood of Noah's time. Then, in 1912 German geologist Alfred Wegener suggested that all of the continents we see today were originally one landmass. But because he could not explain what would cause the continents to move, his theory was largely ignored. Later, Arthur Holmes suggested that the earth's crust is actually

several large plates floating on liquid magma, and that slow movement of these plates, called continental drift, is what caused the single landmass to break up into the different landmasses we see today.

Creation scientists agree that there was originally one landmass and that the crust is now made up of plates that float on the magma. This original landmass has been named **Rodinia**. But most creationists reject the idea that slow continental drift is adequate to explain the movement of such

gigantic landmasses. Instead, the evidence shows that this shifting happened in a relatively short period during the Genesis Flood. This view has been called Catastrophic Plate Tectonics.

The Bible says in Genesis 1:9, "Let the waters under the heavens be gathered together into one place, and let the dry land appear." So, it appears that originally there was one landmass and one ocean. Genesis 7:11 says, "all the fountains of the great deep were broken up." The Hebrew word for "broken up" is *baqa*, which means cleaving or faulting. This could very well be describing the breaking of the earth's crust into the plates that we see today. There may have been another supercontinent called Pangaea that assembled midway through the Flood.

Creation scientists think Rodinia probably came apart early in the Flood, with its pieces slamming back into each other later in the Flood, forming a mostly submerged Pangaea. Pangaea then came apart and emerged near the end of the Flood, with its pieces forming today's continents.

It is believed that there are 13 tectonic plates: 6 major plates, each about the size of a continent, and 7 minor plates that are significantly smaller. It is also believed that many of the fold and fault mountain ranges were formed when the continental plates moved as a result of the Flood. Today, the tectonic plates move very slowly and can cause earthquakes and volcanic activity, resulting in faults and rifts in the earth.

 ## What did we learn?

- What is plate tectonics?
- How many plates do scientists think there are?

 ## Taking it further

- What are some things that are believed to have happened in the past because of the movement of the tectonic plates?
- What are some things that happen today because of the movement of the tectonic plates?

 ## Rodinia puzzle

Purpose: To see how the continents may have appeared before they broke apart into today's landmasses

Materials: tracing paper, scissors, world map, tape

Procedure:

1. Place a piece of tracing paper over a map of the world and trace the continents.

2. Cut out each of the continents and try to piece them together to form one landmass.

3. Tape the pieces together to form "Rodinia."

Plate movements

Continental drift is the name given to the movement of the tectonic plates of the earth's crust today. These plates move in three main ways. Plates can move toward each other, away from each other, or slide against each other. Each of these movements can cause earthquakes or volcanic eruptions and can have other effects on the earth's surface as well.

The collision of two plates together can create a subduction zone, and subduction occurs when one of the plates is pushed down below the other plate. The lower plate is pushed down into the earth's mantle and some of it may melt. Subduction occurs most frequently when an oceanic plate is pushed below a continental plate. Subduction is believed to be the source of much of the volcanic activity along the Pacific rim "ring of fire."

Rifting occurs when two plates move away from each other. This is occurring along the Mid-Atlantic Ridge below the Atlantic Ocean. When rifting occurs, a space opens between the plates allowing magma to push up between the plates and spread out in either direction. This forms new

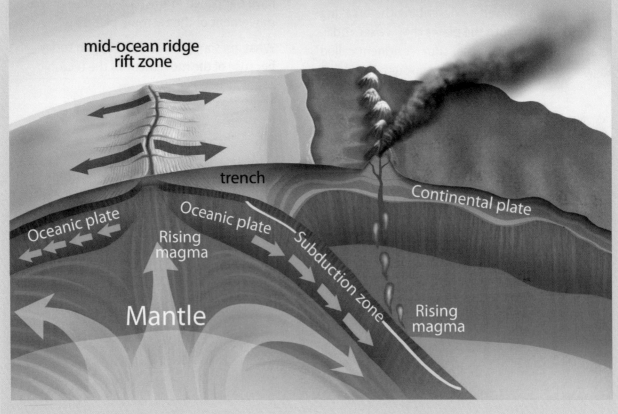

land, usually on the ocean floor. This process is often called sea-floor spreading.

The third way that plates move is horizontally against each other. This horizontal movement is called strike-slip faulting. Occasionally the plates get stuck against each other and pressure builds up. When the pressure is high enough, rocks break, and the plates lurch forward causing an earthquake.

Purpose: To demonstrate each of these plate movements

Materials: wax paper, creamy peanut butter or frosting, graham crackers

Procedure:

1. Spread a thick layer of creamy peanut butter or frosting on a piece of waxed paper. This represents the magma of the earth's mantle.

2. Place two graham crackers on top of the peanut butter to represent two tectonic plates.

3. Slide the crackers together and push one of them under the other. This represents subduction. Watch how the "magma" moves as the "plates" move.

4. Next, smooth out the peanut butter and set two crackers next to each other.

5. Move the crackers away from each other and watch as a space develops between the plates.

6. Push up from below the waxed paper and watch the peanut butter squeeze up between the plates. This movement represents rifting.

7. Finally, smooth the peanut butter out again and place two crackers next to each other.

8. With the edges pressed together, push one cracker away from you and pull the other cracker toward you. This represents strike-slip faulting. Watch for crumbs that are generated and look at how the peanut butter is moved around.

Conclusion: These exercises should give you an idea of what happens as the plates move. Remember that these plates today generally move very slowly, much more slowly than they would have moved during the Flood.

20

Mountains

Don't make a mountain out of a mole hill

What is a mountain?

Words to know:

elevation   actual height

You have probably been told, "Don't make a mountain out of a mole hill." This means don't make a problem bigger than it really is. But how can you tell if something is really a mountain or a just a hill? A mountain is an area of land that naturally rises higher than the surrounding land. It usually has steep sides rising to a summit. Mountains are taller or higher than hills in the same general area. The designation of *mountain* or *hill* is often dependent on the area in which the rise occurs. For example, a 500-foot rise in Wyoming would be called a hill because the nearby Rocky Mountains are thousands of feet tall, but a 400-foot (120-meter) ridge in New York is called the Watchung Mountains.

When describing a mountain, two different terms are often used. First, the elevation of a mountain is the height of the summit above sea level. For example, Mount Everest (shown here) has an elevation of 29,028 feet (8,848 m) and is said to be the highest mountain in the world. The second measurement for a mountain is its actual height. This is the difference between the elevation of the summit and the elevation of the base of the mountain. Because Mount Everest has such a high base, its actual height is only about 12,000 feet (3,650 m). On the other hand, Mauna Kea in Hawaii, has an elevation of 14,000 feet (4,260 m) but an actual height of 33,000 feet (10,000 m). How can its actual height be higher than its elevation? The base of Mauna Kea is 19,000 feet (5,740 m) below sea level!

A series of mountains in a given area is called a mountain range. And a group of mountain ranges is called a mountain system. The highest mountain system is the Himalaya-Karakoram system, between India and China. More than 95 of the 109 mountain peaks in this system are over 24,000 feet (7,300 m) in elevation, including Mount Everest.

The longest or most extensive mountain system is the Mid-Atlantic Ridge, which extends for 10,000 miles (16,000 km) under the Atlantic Ocean. It goes almost from pole to pole. To see it you have to be a deep sea diver because it is found on the floor of the Atlantic Ocean.

Some of the most famous mountain ranges in America include the Cascade Range in Oregon and Washington, the Sierra Nevada in California, the Rocky Mountains in Idaho, Wyoming, Colorado and New Mexico, and the Appalachian Mountains that run from Maine to Georgia.

 # What did we learn?

- What is a mountain?
- What is a mountain range?
- What is the difference between actual height and elevation of a mountain?

 # Taking it further

- Where are the mountains with the highest elevations located?
- Is a 700 foot rise a mountain or a hill?

 # Famous mountains

Complete the "Famous Mountains" worksheet.

Mountain ranges

The world today has many mountain ranges. These mountains play many important roles. Mountains have unique habitats for animals. They provide timber for us to use. Mountains also affect the weather in many areas. So it is important to know where the major mountain ranges are around the world.

Obtain a copy of a world map. Using an atlas or topographical map of the world, draw and label the following mountain ranges on your copy of the world map. Save this map for future lessons.

Major Mountain Ranges of the World

Alps	Caucasus Mountains
Ural Mountains	Himalaya Mountains
Great Dividing Range	Atlas Mountains
Andes Mountains	Sierra Nevada Mountains
Rocky Mountains	Appalachian Mountains

Mountains & Movement

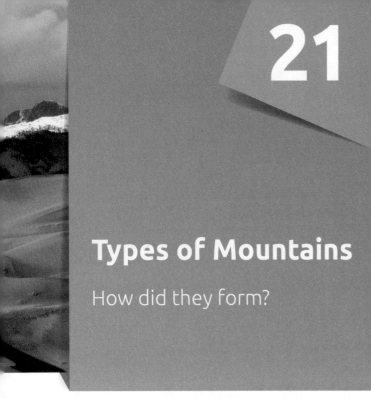

21

Types of Mountains

How did they form?

How are the different types of mountains formed?

Words to know:

depositional mountain	fold mountain
erosional mountain	fault

Challenge words:

basin	anticline
dome	syncline
monocline	

Where did mountains come from? Did God create the mountains the way they are today or have they changed over time? Not all scientists agree on how the mountains were formed. Genesis 7:19–20 says that the floodwaters covered the high mountains to a depth of 15 cubits (about 20 feet). So we know that God created the earth with some mountains. However, there is evidence that most of the mountains we see today formed as a result of the Flood and its aftermath.

Mountains are classified according to how scientists believe they were formed. Most mountains are classified as either depositional, erosional, or fold and fault mountains. **Depositional mountains** are ones that form from accumulated rocks, volcanic lava and ash, sand, or other material. Volcanic mountains are the most likely to be observed as they are being formed. Erupting volcanoes can deposit lava, ash and rocks to form new mountains in a very short period of time. One of the most well-known examples of a volcano forming a mountain occurred in a farmer's field in Mexico. In 1943, this volcano suddenly appeared and deposited over 1,400 feet (425 m) of material in only one year's time. The picture below is Diamond Head, an extinct volcano on Oahu, Hawaii.

Other depositional mountains are formed when wind and water deposit lighter materials. For example, sand dunes are hills and mountains of

Volcanic depositional mountain

Erosional mountain

Fold mountain

sand that have been deposited by wind and water. Finally, some of the mountains were formed as glaciers dragged large amounts of debris, depositing it in an area as the ice melted.

The second way that mountains form is through erosion. Erosional mountains are also called residual mountains. These are mountains that remain after the surrounding material has eroded away. Erosional mountains, like the ones in this picture, are usually flat on top and have steep sides. Most creation scientists believe that erosional mountains are a direct result of the Flood. The floodwaters laid down hundreds and even thousands of feet of sediment that formed into sedimentary rock. As the waters of the Flood receded, much of this rock

was washed away. The remaining hardened rock became the residual mountains that we see today.

Although there are many examples of depositional and erosional mountains, it is believed that most mountain ranges were formed by folding and faulting. The picture above demonstrates fold and fault mountains. Many scientists believe that when two tectonic plates, or sections of the earth's crust, push against each other, pressure is applied to the rocks. Eventually the rocks will either break or snap, resulting in an earthquake, or they will bend (called folding) or slip (called faulting). When the rocks bend and push up they form fold mountains. When they slip along a fault or crack in the earth's surface, and one section pushes up higher than another, fault mountains are formed.

Although these are the commonly accepted classifications for mountains, there is considerable disagreement and room for much more research in this area. This is one area that creation scientists, those who accept the Word of God as true, can do more investigation and gain better understanding of God's creation. 🌐

Fun Fact

The largest mountain in our solar system is on Mars. Olympus Mons rises 78,000 feet (24 km) above the surrounding plain. Its base is more than 300 miles (500 km) in diameter.

Sand dunes are a type of depositional mountain.

What did we learn?

- How are depositional mountains formed?
- How are erosional mountains formed?
- How are fold and fault mountains formed?

 Taking it further

Identify each mountain as either depositional, erosional, or fold. (Outside research is necessary for this question.)

- Mount St. Helens
- Bryce Canyon
- Sand Dunes National Monument
- Rocky Mountains
- Grand Canyon
- Mount Everest

Paper fold mountains

Purpose: To demonstrate how fold mountains form

Materials: newspaper or paper towels

Procedure:

1. Lay a few sheets of newspaper or paper towels on top of one another.

2. Slightly moisten the paper by sprinkling a small amount of water on the papers.

3. Place your hands on opposite edges of the papers, and then slowly push your hands toward each other. What happens?

4. Repeat by smoothing out the papers and pushing at different speeds and in slightly different directions.

How does the change in pressure affect the look of the mountains that are formed?

5. After you have formed the shape of mountains you like, allow the paper to dry for several hours to see how mountains retain their shape after they are dry.

Conclusion:

The papers should push up in the middle, forming fold mountains. This is similar to how many scientists believe that many mountain ranges were formed. They believe that when two tectonic plates collide by being pushed form opposite sides, the land is pushed up and crumpled in the collision zone, forming mountains.

Fold types

As you just learned, most of the mountains we see today are either fold or fault mountains. We will discuss faults more in the next lesson. For now we will take a look at the forces that produce the different fold mountains that exist around the world. The type of folding that has occurred in fold mountain formation may not be obvious from the surface of the mountain; however, erosion, mining, or roadwork can expose the inside of a mountain, and the folding of the layers of the mountain become apparent.

There are five basic types of folding that can occur. If a downward force, such as gravity,

overcomes other surrounding forces an area can sink resulting in a basin. This would appear to be a rounded depression in the earth, thus forming mountains around it. If a force is directly upward from inside the earth, a dome of rock can form. This would result in a rounded hill or smooth looking mountain.

If forces push up on one side of a rock formation and down on the other side, the rocks will rise up on one side and be compressed on the other. This forms what is called a monocline. If forces are applied from opposite sides of the rock formation and the rocks bend instead of break, they can either bend

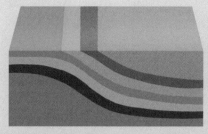

Monocline

Anticline

Syncline

upward or downward. If the rocks bend upward the formation is called an **anticline**. If the rocks bend downward the formation is called a **syncline**.

The shape of the sedimentary layers gives scientists a clue as to how the mountains were formed. To better understand how this works perform the following experiment.

Purpose: To understand how the layers in a mountain can indicate how it was formed

Materials: Four or more colors of modeling clay, knife

Procedure:

1. Roll or press each color of clay into a 6-inch circle.

2. Layer the circles by placing them one on top of another. This represents the layers of sediment as they were deposited by the Flood waters.

3. Apply pressure to the sides of the layers forcing the layers to move up or down. Experiment with differing amounts of pressure at different locations. Just like in the previous experiment this represents what happens when tectonic plates collide.

4. Once you have your mountains formed, cut off small parts of the top and sides of the mountains with a

It is believed that much of the folding of sedimentary rock occurred during or shortly after the Flood while the rock layers were still soft.

knife. This represents how some rock is removed by erosion. What do you observe?

5. Finally, make a vertical cut from the top to the bottom of one part of the mountain and remove the clay from one area. How do the layers look? Did you form an anticline or syncline? How about a monocline?

6. Draw a picture of the layers inside your mountain. Label the type of folding that occurred. Use the pictures in the lesson to help you.

Conclusion:

The shape of the layers in sedimentary rock formations can indicate what direction the forces came from and how the sediments responded while the layers were still soft and pliable like they would have been after the Flood. When rock is removed, such as when it is blasted away to make room for a road, these layers become visible to us and show us that the Bible is true and can be trusted.

22

Earthquakes

Shake, rattle, and roll

What are earthquakes and how are they caused?

Words to know:

earthquake	epicenter
aftershock	tsunami
focus	

Challenge words:

footwall	reverse fault
hanging wall	thrust fault
normal fault	strike-slip fault

Have you ever felt the ground move under your feet, seen the light fixtures swinging from the ceiling or heard dishes rattle in the cupboard without someone touching them? Probably not, unless you have experienced an earthquake. An earthquake is the rapid movement of the earth's crust. Elastic strain builds up in the rocks deep in the earth's crust as tectonic plates move against each other. This movement can be horizontal or vertical. When the strain becomes too great, the rocks break apart and rebound off of one another. This movement results in what we call an earthquake.

Earthquakes happen frequently, several times each day. However, most earthquakes are too weak for a person to detect. A few times a year, an earthquake occurs that is strong enough to feel, and occasionally strong earthquakes occur that can cause severe damage and even loss of life. Often, severe earthquakes are followed by many smaller quakes called aftershocks. Aftershocks may occur for several weeks after the original earthquake.

The center of activity for an earthquake is called the focus. The area on the surface of the earth above the focus is called the epicenter. The amount of damage or destruction caused by an earthquake depends on the location of the epicenter and the magnitude or strength of the quake. Earthquakes in uninhabited areas cause little damage. However, earthquakes in densely

Fun Fact

The longest tremor recorded in the United States was four minutes long. It occurred in Alaska in March 1964. Most earthquakes last less than one minute. About two weeks before the earthquake, Kodiak bears in Alaska awoke from hibernation and left the area even though it was earlier than they normally awaken.

populated areas can cause widespread destruction and death. Even though the ocean is uninhabited, earthquakes that originate under the ocean can be the most deadly. These quakes can trigger huge waves called **tsunamis**. Tsunamis can be only two or three feet (0.5–1 m) high in the open ocean, but they grow much higher as they approach land. They can travel at speeds up to 500 miles per hour (224 meters per second) and cause extensive damage. Land-based earthquakes near the ocean can generate tsunamis as well. On December 26, 2004, an undersea earthquake in the Indian Ocean caused a tsunami that devastated the shores of Indonesia, Sri Lanka, South India, Thailand and other countries with waves up to 100 feet (30 m) high and killed more than 283,000 people.

Earthquakes move out in waves from the epicenter. These waves move like ripples in a pond when a rock is dropped into the water. Earthquake waves travel up to 16,000 mph (7,150 m/s) through rock and more slowly through soft sand and mud. There are three types of earthquake waves. P waves, or primary waves, are the fastest waves. They move through the ground like sound waves. S waves, or

Earthquake-proof buildings

One of the major causes of death during an earthquake is the collapse of buildings. In America, in areas where earthquakes are likely to happen, buildings are often designed to withstand the movement of the earth. They are specially reinforced and some are even built on shock absorbers. However, in third world countries, many buildings are built with inferior designs and poor materials, and they easily collapse.

Purpose: To demonstrate the advantages of different building designs

Materials: 10–20 building blocks

Procedure:

1. Build a corner of a building using building blocks arranged as in the first picture.

2. Gently shake the table on which the blocks are placed.

3. Increase the intensity of the "earthquake" until some of the blocks fall over.

4. Repeat this process for each of the building designs and note what happens.

5. Now, build a building of your own design and test its strength.

Questions:

- Which design was the strongest?

- Which design was the weakest?

- How did your design compare to the others?

- What might architects do to help make buildings stronger?

- What shape of building is more likely to withstand an earthquake?

secondary waves, move more slowly. S waves distort as they pass through rock. The final type is called L waves, or long waves. L waves travel on the surface of the earth and often cause most of the damage.

Earthquakes most often occur along boundaries of tectonic plates. Faults are often found along these boundaries as well. A fault is a crack in the rock where the earth has moved. At one time, scientists thought these faults caused earthquakes. Today, we know that earthquakes cause the faults. One of the most famous faults is the San Andreas Fault, which runs from San Francisco, California south into Mexico. It is 700 miles (1,125 km) long and is located where the Pacific and American plates meet.

In God's original "very good" creation, earthquakes probably didn't exist. God cursed the creation because of Adam's sin (Genesis 3, Romans 8), and as a result we now experience natural disasters, such as earthquakes and hurricanes. Below is a list of some of the deadliest and most destructive earthquakes in recent history:

- November 1, 1775: Lisbon, Portugal—60,000 died. Damage occurred all the way down to North Africa. Most deaths were due to flooding caused by tsunamis.
- October 28, 1891: Mino-Owari, Japan—7,000 died
- April 18, 1906: San Francisco, California—5,000 died. Water pipes broke from the earthquake, preventing firefighters from putting out a fire that burned for several days.
- September 1, 1923: Yokohama, Japan—200,000 died. Most deaths were caused by fires that could not be put out.
- July 28, 1976: Tangshan, China—240,000 died

The quake registered 8.2 on the Richter scale and was felt 500 miles (800 km) away.

- September 19, 1985: Mexico City, Mexico—4,000 died

Most deaths were due to poor construction of buildings that collapsed on the people.

- December 7, 1988: Armenia—55,000 died

500,000 people were left homeless. The quake registered 6.8 on the Richter scale, followed four minutes later by a quake of 5.8 magnitude.

- May 21, 2003: Algiers, Algeria—3,000 died

A quake of 6.5 magnitude brought down many buildings on the people of Algeria.

- December 26, 2004: Indian Ocean off the coast of Sumatra—283,000 died
- May 12, 2008: Sichuan China—7.9 magnitude quake – 70,000 died
- January 12, 2010: Haiti—at least 230,000 died, estimates are as high as 316,000 deaths
- April 25, 2015: Nepal—9,000 people died. A 7.9 magnitude earthquake caused extensive damage and triggered many avalanches including an avalanche on Mount Everest that killed at least 19 people, making it the deadliest day on the mountain. There were many aftershocks including a quake with a magnitude of 7.3 on May 12 which killed an additional 200 people.

What did we learn?

- What is believed to be the cause of earthquakes?
- What is an aftershock?
- What name is given to the area on the earth's surface above where an earthquake originates?
- What is a fault?

Taking it further

- How does the type of material affect the speed of the earthquake waves?
- How does this change in speed help scientists "see" under the earth's crust?
- Why are earthquakes in the middle of the ocean so dangerous?

Faults

Faults often occur because of earthquakes. Stress among the rocks causes a break in the rocks and a sudden shift causes the rocks to move. This movement can leave a crack in the earth's surface. It is also believed that faulting has caused the formation of many of the mountain ranges around the world.

There are three basic kinds of faults that can occur. If the break is at an angle from top to bottom then the rocks generally move vertically with respect to each other. If the break is vertical, then the rocks tend to move horizontally.

If you look at the normal fault below, the right side (the side below the fault) is called the footwall and the left side (the side above the fault) is called the hanging wall. When forces are applied, the footwall and hanging wall move with respect to each other. If the hanging wall moves up with respect to the footwall, this movement is called a normal fault. If the hanging wall moves downward with respect to the footwall, it is called a reverse fault or a thrust fault. Reverse faults are nearly vertical while thrust faults are nearly horizontal. If the crack is vertical and the rocks move horizontally with respect to each other, this is called a strike-slip fault.

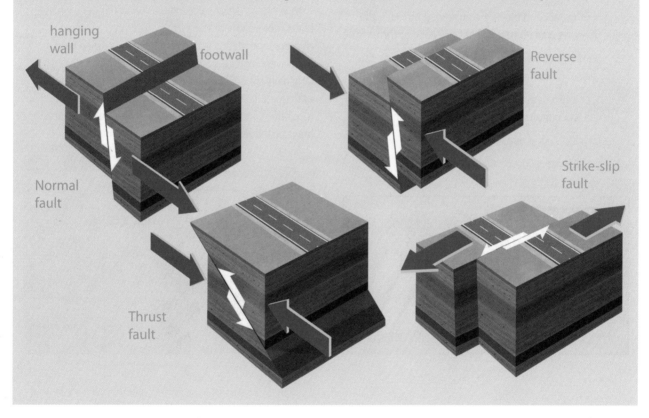

Mountains & Movement

Purpose: To demonstrate each of these kinds of faults

Materials: three colors of modeling clay, knife

Procedure:

1. Make three identical layers of clay about 1 inch thick from each of three different colors of clay.

2. Make three clay "sandwiches" with one color on top, a different color in the middle, and the third color on the bottom. These layers represent different layers of sedimentary rock.

3. Cut the first block of clay at an angle from top to bottom as shown in the diagram and slide the hanging wall down to represent a normal fault.

4. Cut the second block the same way, but slide the hanging wall up to represent a reverse or thrust fault.

5. Finally, cut the third block vertically and slide the pieces horizontally to represent a strike-slip fault.

Purpose: To demonstrate how mountains can be formed when faults move away from each other

Materials: 5 or 6 books (all of the same size would be best), ruler

Procedure:

1. Have someone set the books side by side on a table with the spines of the books on top forming a smooth surface. These books represent rock layers.

2. Measure the width of the stack of books.

3. The person holding the books should allow the books to tilt to one side at an angle of about 40 degrees.

4. Measure the width of the books now. Do they occupy more or less space? What does the surface look like now? (How do the books look from the top?)

Conclusion: This exercise shows what happens when faults move apart or the earth's crust stretches. Two changes take place. First the total area occupied by the rock layers is greater. Second, the surface has changed. Originally the surface was relatively smooth and flat. But as the rock layers moved and stretched to fill in the area, mountains and valleys were formed. This demonstrates how the movements of faults can form mountains.

23

Detecting & Predicting Earthquakes

Predicting the "Big One"

How can we measure and predict earthquakes?

Words to know:

seismograph

Predicting when and where an earthquake will strike is a very difficult task. Scientists are still not able to predict earthquakes with much accuracy. However, people have been able to detect and measure earthquakes for a long time. In AD 132, a Chinese philosopher named Zhang Heng built the first earthquake-detecting instrument, or seismoscope, on record. It was a large bronze vessel shaped somewhat like an urn. It had a pendulum hanging inside it that would swing if the earth moved. This pendulum would hit small brass balls that were on the sides of the urn. Where these balls landed indicated the direction and strength of the quake.

The first seismograph was built by Luigi Palmieri in 1856. In 1902 a British scientist named John Milne began setting up a worldwide network of seismographs. By 1913 he had seismographs in 40 locations, including Spain, Syria, Brazil, and Hawaii. Information was sent from each of these locations to Milne's laboratory in England where he was able to compile the information and begin to determine with some accuracy the origin and strength of earthquakes. Today, there are thousands of seismographs around the world. The information gathered at each of these sites is coordinated by the National Earthquake Information Center in Golden, Colorado.

A seismograph is an instrument with a large mass attached to a flexible rod. A light attached to the mass traces a line on a rotating drum that is covered with photographic material. If the earth moves, the drum will move with it, but the mass will not move. Some seismographs use pen and paper instead of light and photographic paper; however, the idea is the same.

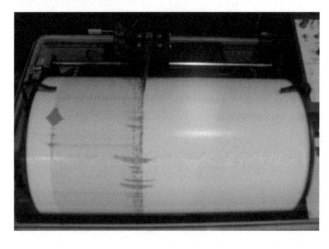

In 1935 Charles Richter defined the scale that is used to measure the magnitude or strength of an earthquake. The Richter scale is not a linear scale. An earthquake with a magnitude of 3 is 31.6 times stronger than one with a magnitude of 2. A magnitude 4 quake is 31.6 x 31.6 or nearly 1,000 times stronger than a magnitude 2. An earthquake with a magnitude of 5 or greater is considered a serious earthquake, but those with a magnitude of 7 or greater are very strong and usually cause severe damage. The undersea earthquake that caused the tsunami in the Indian Ocean in December 2004 was estimated to be a magnitude of 9.3. The Richter scale uses the distance the seismograph is from the epicenter of the earthquake and the maximum amplitude of the movement of the needle to determine the magnitude of the quake.

The Richter scale is the most important measurement of earthquakes for scientists. However, most people are more concerned about the amount of damage done by an earthquake. So, in 1902 an Italian named Giuseppe Mercalli defined a scale of intensity that describes the amount of damage done by an earthquake. The Mercalli Intensity Scale assigns a number from 1–12 to an earthquake. An earthquake with an intensity of 1 is not felt, an intensity of 4 causes dishes to rattle, an intensity of 9 damages foundations and breaks pipes, and an intensity of 12 causes total destruction.

The magnitude of an earthquake is only one element determining the destructiveness of an earthquake. The damage done is also dependent on the location of the quake with respect to population, and the length of the tremor. A short earthquake with a large magnitude may not cause as much damage as a longer quake with a smaller magnitude. Buildings can often endure vibration for a few seconds, but cannot stand up under prolonged shaking.

Because accurate prediction of earthquakes could save lives, many scientists continue to gather data and develop models to aid in prediction. Since 1985, the U.S. Geological Survey has been working on a project near Parkfield, California, which is located along the San Andreas Fault. The area is filled with equipment including seismometers, laser reflectors, magnetometers, and strain meters

Collapsed sections of the Cypress viaduct after the 7.1 Loma Prieta earthquake in 1989

designed to detect and record any changes in the earth. In 2005 a hole was drilled nearly 2.5 miles (4 km) into the earth's crust and sensors were installed to detect very small movements in the crust. Scientists hope to use all of this data to someday be able to predict earthquakes before they happen.

Despite these efforts, however, all scientists can do today is detect earthquakes as they occur. All prediction methods have proven to be imprecise and unreliable. Only God knows when and where earthquakes will occur. Man has learned to build buildings that are better able to withstand the shock of an earthquake, but he cannot predict the movements of the earth. 🌐

What did we learn?

- What is the difference between the magnitude and the intensity of an earthquake?

- What are three factors that determine how much damage is done by an earthquake?

- Explain how a seismograph works.

- What people group was first to record earthquake measurements?

Taking it further

- What are some ways people have learned to prepare for earthquakes?

- What should you do if you are in an earthquake?

Making a seismograph

Purpose: To build your own seismograph

Materials: 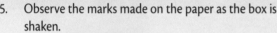 tape, paper, rolling pin, shoebox, pencil

Procedure:

1. Tape a piece of paper around a rolling pin.

2. Set the rolling pin on top of a shoebox.

3. Have one person slowly rotate the rolling pin while a second person holds a pencil so that the tip touches the paper but the pencil does not touch the shoebox.

4. Have a third person gently shake the box from side to side. Be sure to shake the box in different directions.

5. Observe the marks made on the paper as the box is shaken.

Questions: How does this affect the marks on the paper?

Conclusion: Only movement along the length of the rolling pin will show changes in the markings. Notice that the bigger the movement of the box, the longer the markings on the paper. An actual seismograph uses paper with special markings showing the Richter scale, making it easier to determine the magnitude of an earthquake.

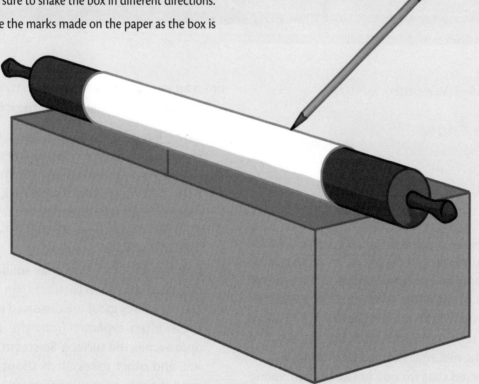

 # Earthquake locations

It is interesting to see where earthquakes happen. If you have access to the Internet, you can do a search to find locations of recent earthquakes. One web site that shows the locations of recent earthquakes is from the U.S. Geological Survey. Once you have found where the most recent earthquakes have occurred, use an X to mark the locations on the world map that you made showing mountain ranges around the world. Do you notice any sort of pattern to the location of the earthquakes?

24

Volcanoes

Fire mountains

Why does a volcano erupt?

Words to know:

caldera

dormant volcano

active volcano

extinct volcano

Another natural phenomenon closely associated with moving tectonic plates, and often occurring in the same areas of the world as earthquakes, is the eruption of volcanoes. The word *volcano* comes from the name of the Roman god of fire—Vulcan. *Volcano* can refer to the hole that lava comes out of and also to the mountain formed by that lava.

It is believed that friction between the moving crustal plates and the mantle below them allows the mantle to grow hotter. When the magma heats up, it expands and when the pressure builds up, the result is often a volcanic eruption. Magma, melted rock that is 30–120 miles (50–195 km) below the earth's surface, expands until it finds a vent or channel through the crust to the surface of the earth. Magma that reaches the surface is called lava.

Volcanoes can erupt very suddenly and violently, or they can gently pour out their contents relatively quietly. Sometimes the pressures within a volcano cause earthquakes prior to an eruption, and other times an eruption occurs without any warning at all. Volcanoes can emit any or all of the following:

- Lava—liquid melted rock, with temperatures from 1,300–2,200°F (700–1,200°C). Lava can rush downhill at speeds up to 35 mph (15.6 m/s).
- Ash—tiny fragments of solid rock, less than 0.2 inches (0.5 cm) in diameter
- Cinders—larger fragments of solid rock, 0.2–1 inch (0.5–2.5 cm) in diameter
- Bombs—blobs of lava that solidify in the air and hit the earth as rock
- Gases—many gases are dissolved in the magma. These often separate from the magma as it approaches the surface. So steam, carbon dioxide, and other gases often shoot out of a volcano. Steam quickly condenses as it hits the cool atmosphere, and sometimes this water mixing with the soil can cause severe mudslides.

Lava, ash, and mud harden as they cool and form mountains around the exit of the volcano.

Fun Fact

Mount Rainier, the highest peak in Washington State, is a volcano that still steams, but it last erupted in the 1800s.

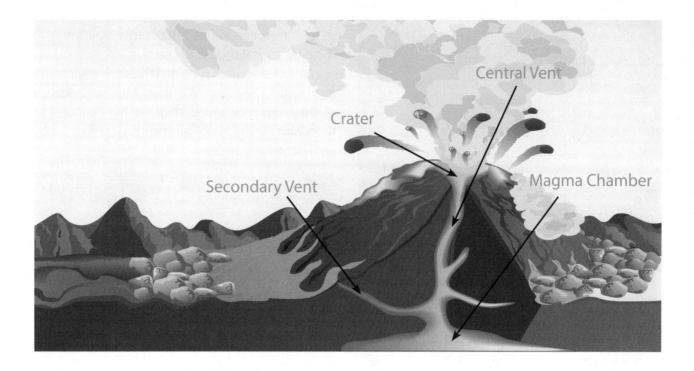

Central Vent

Crater

Secondary Vent

Magma Chamber

Although these mountains can take different shapes and forms, the basic structure of all volcanoes is the same. A volcano has a magma chamber under the earth's crust. It has a central vent, which is a tube or channel through which the magma is forced to the surface. And finally, it has a crater, when very large called a caldera, which is a bowl-shaped depression around the mouth of the volcano. This crater forms when a cone that was formed at the mouth of the volcano by the cooling lava later collapses. Some very active volcanoes sometimes develop secondary vents through which the magma may also escape.

Volcanoes are classified by their activity into one of three categories. Active volcanoes are ones that have erupted at least once in the past 50 years. Dormant volcanoes are ones that have not erupted in the past 50 years but are expected to erupt in the future. Extinct volcanoes are ones that have not erupted in the past 50 years and are not expected to erupt again in the foreseeable

Volcano model

Purpose: To make a model of a volcano

Materials: empty bottle, baking sheet, baking soda, newspaper, vinegar, red food coloring (optional), tape

Procedure:

1. Place an empty bottle in the center of a baking sheet or other tray with sides.

2. Pour one teaspoon of baking soda into the bottle.

3. Crunch up newspaper and place it around the bottle to form a mountain with the bottle in the center and tape the paper to the bottle. (The only part of the bottle that should be visible is the mouth of the bottle. Be sure all paper is on the baking sheet and not hanging over the edge.)

4. Pour ½ cup of vinegar into a measuring cup and add a few drops of red food coloring, if desired.

5. Pour the vinegar into the bottle and watch your volcano erupt! Be sure to clean up your mess when you are done.

Conclusion: The bottle represents the magma chamber under the newspaper crust. The mouth of the bottle is the vent. Although we are not heating the "lava," the reaction between the baking soda and the vinegar produces carbon dioxide gas that expands and finds its way out of the bottle "volcano," just like heated magma in a real volcano.

there have been about 1,300 active volcanoes in the past several thousand years.

Not all volcanoes form on land. Many volcanoes form under the ocean. We often don't see evidence of their existence unless they get high enough to form islands. The Hawaiian Islands were formed by underwater volcanoes.

What did we learn?

- What are the three stages or states of a volcano?
- Describe the three main parts of a volcano.
- Give the name for each of the following items that is emitted from a volcano:
  1. Liquid or melted rock
  2. Tiny bits of solid rock
  3. Pieces of rock from 0.2 to 1 inch (0.5–2.5 cm) in diameter
  4. Blobs of lava that solidify in the air
  5. Steam and carbon dioxide

Taking it further

- How might a volcano become active without anyone noticing?
- How are volcanoes and earthquakes related?
- How certain can we be that a volcano is really extinct?

future. Volcanoes may be very active, erupting over and over again, and then suddenly stop and remain dormant for hundreds or possibly even thousands of years. Classifying a volcano as extinct is tricky. Some volcanoes that were believed to be extinct have suddenly and unexpectedly come back to life.

More than 500 active volcanoes exist today. Most of these are found along an area called the "Ring of Fire," an area encircling the Pacific Ocean. More than 125 of these active volcanoes are in the island country of Indonesia. It is estimated that

Fun Fact

Tambora, in Indonesia, erupted in 1815 killing 92,000 people. It put 80 times as much debris into the air as the eruption of Mount St. Helens did in 1980.

Volcano locations

Today you are going to finish your world map by adding some of the more famous volcanoes to your map. Draw a small smoking mountain in each location and label each of the following volcanoes on your map. Use a world atlas or the Internet to help you locate each volcano, if necessary.

- Mount St. Helens—Washington State
- Mt. Vesuvius—Italy
- Mauna Loa—Hawaii
- Krakatoa—Indonesia
- Mt. Pinatubo—Philippines

- Mt. Etna—Sicily
- Mt. Fuji—Japan
- Kilauea—Hawaii
- Akutan—Aleutian Islands (near Alaska)
- Santa Maria—Guatemala
- Mount Erebus—Antarctica
- Bezymianny Volcano—Kamchatka, Russia

Do you notice a pattern to the locations of these volcanoes? Most of them are located around the edge of the Pacific Ocean. This is called the "Ring of Fire" for a good reason.

Mt. Vesuvius

Smoke, ash, choking fire, and mothers dying in an effort to protect their children. These scenes are forever recorded in the stones, mud, and ash that covered the city of Pompeii during the destructive eruption of Mt. Vesuvius in AD 79. But that wasn't the first time Mt. Vesuvius had erupted, nor would it be the last. The volcano was recorded by both Greek and Roman scholars and was known to have destroyed many small towns around it before that time. So why is this eruption so famous? First, it is famous because of the way the volcano covered the towns of Herculaneum and Pompeii, and second, because of the eyewitness account of the eruption.

A young man called Pliny the Younger, who lived from AD 61–113, recorded the account of this event. He was about 18 years old when this event took place. At the time, his uncle Pliny the Elder was commander of the Roman fleet at Misenum. Misenum was across the Bay of Naples from Pompeii, a distance of about 25 miles (40 km).

On the afternoon of August 24, AD 79, Pliny the Younger's mother drew Pliny the Elder's attention to an unusual cloud. Pliny the Elder climbed up to where he could get a better view of the cloud. The cloud was described as pine tree shaped with a long trunk. It appeared to rise out of one of the mountains, but he could not tell which one. Some of the cloud was white while other parts of it were dark like patches of dirt or ash. Having a scientific bent, he was determined to get a closer look at this unusual sight.

He ordered his boat to be made ready and asked if Pliny the Younger wanted to go along. The boy chose to stay behind and study. As he was about to leave, Pliny the Elder received a letter from Tascius's wife Rectina. She said she was terrified. Her villa lay at the foot of Mt. Vesuvius and she had no way out of Pompeii except by boat. She wanted Pliny to send a boat for her. Historians are not sure who she was, but she must have been important to Pliny. Instead of just investigating the

smoke cloud, he decided to launch all of the boats under his command. He then hurried into the face of danger, to a place others were fleeing, to save as many people as he could. He did not show his fear if he had any. As he traveled toward Pompeii, he continued his observations of the volcano, dictating what he saw.

As the boats got closer, more and more ash and rocks began falling on them. His helmsman urged him to turn back, but he said, "Fortune helps the brave." A good wind made it easy for his boats to put in near Pompeii, but it also made it impossible for his boats, or any of the other boats, to leave at that time. Upon his arrival he gave comfort and courage to those around him. To help lessen the fear around him, he asked to be taken to the baths where he relaxed. Later he dined with friends.

As night came on, it became more apparent that flames were lighting up different parts of Vesuvius. To calm people down, he said the flames were from the deserted homes of those who left in a hurry with hearth fires still going. He then rested for the night. It was said that those who passed his door that night heard him snoring. During the night, stones and ash built up against his door, and if he had slept any longer he would not have made it out of his room.

He and his companions decided to try for the open sea but when he got down to his boat he found the weather to be as rough and uncooperative as before. He sat down to drink some water, and then upon standing, he collapsed. The exact cause of his death is unknown. It is not known if any of his boats made it out of the harbor, but someone survived in order to relay his account which was recorded by his nephew, Pliny the Younger.

The city of Pompeii was covered with cinders and ash and was unseen for at least 1,500 years. Because the city was quickly covered with ash, much of the city was preserved. The ruins that have been uncovered in the last 50 years give us a very complete picture of what Roman life was like. Herculaneum was also covered at the same time, but instead of being covered with ash, it was covered with mud, which did much damage, making it more difficult to uncover.

Over the years, Mt. Vesuvius has continued to be very active. Since that day in AD 79, Mt. Vesuvius has had at least 28 other major eruptions. But because of Pliny's eyewitness account, and the many artifacts uncovered in Pompeii, the eruption of AD 79 remains the most famous.

25

Volcano Types

Is there more than one?

What are the different types of volcanoes?

Words to know:

shield volcano   composite volcano

cinder cone   geothermal

Challenge words:

continental flood basalts

What is the first thing you think of when you hear the word volcano? Is it lava? Lava is a very important component of volcanoes. There are two kinds of lava that can flow from a volcano. The first kind, aa (pronounced "ah-ah"), carries sharp chunks of rock called *scoria*. Aa cools very quickly and builds up quickly. The second type of lava is pahoehoe (pronounced "pa-hoy-hoy"). This type of lava forms a smooth skin on top, allowing the hot lava to flow beneath it. It is usually about three feet (1 m) thick and cools into ropy patterns. Some volcanoes pour out lava in a more or less continuous flow. Other eruptions are very explosive—sometimes blowing the top off of the mountain.

The types and amount of lava flowing from a volcano determine its shape. Although all volcanoes have the same basic internal structure, all volcanoes do not have the same external shape. The shape of the mountain formed by the volcano differs according to what is emitted from the volcano.

A **shield volcano** has gently sloping sides. A shield volcano is formed when mostly lava is emitted. Shield volcanoes are usually found on tectonic

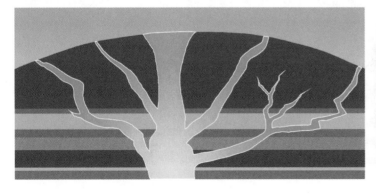

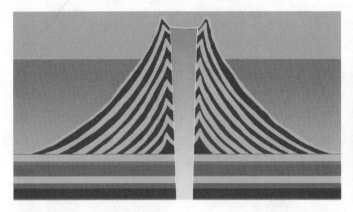

Capulin in New Mexico is an extinct cinder cone volcano rising more 1,000 feet from its base.

plates that are moving apart instead of rubbing against each other. Mauna Loa and Mauna Kea, both part of the Hawaiian Islands, are examples of shield volcanoes.

Cinder cones are formed when a volcano emits mostly ashes, cinders, and bombs. Cinder cones have steep sloping sides and are usually smaller than other types of volcanoes. Paricutin, a volcano that suddenly formed in the middle of a farm in Mexico, is an example of a cinder cone volcano.

Most volcanoes, however, are **composite volcanoes**. These are formed when a volcano alternates between emitting mostly lava and mostly solid material. Composite volcanoes usually have a symmetrical cone shape. Composite volcanoes are most often found near subduction zones, areas where one plate is sliding under another. Mount Fuji, Mount St. Helens, and Mount Vesuvius are all examples of composite volcanoes.

Although volcanoes can be extremely dangerous and destructive, they have many beneficial side effects. The ash and other chemicals enrich the soil. Volcanic soil is very fertile. Also, many volcanic areas have large deposits of sulfur, which is needed in the manufacturing of rubber and fertilizers. Volcanoes offer a source of **geothermal** (heat) energy. Hot vents near underwater volcanoes create unique ecosystems in the ocean. Some species of plants and animals can only survive near these vents. And finally, volcanoes form new land.

One of the most beautiful results of volcanic eruptions is the black sand beaches of Hawaii. Black sand is formed when hot lava hits the cool seawater and shatters into tiny crystals. It is black because of the high amount of iron oxide in the lava.

Some of the more famous volcanoes include:

- Mount Vesuvius, Italy—Erupted in AD 79, completely covering the cities of Herculaneum and Pompeii with 20 feet (6 m) of ash and mud. It has erupted several times since then.

- Kilauea, Hawaii—Has been continually erupting since 1983, causing the island of Hawaii to continue to grow.

- Mount Pinatubo, Philippines—Erupted in June 1991. The amount of ash put into the atmosphere is credited with lowering the temperature around the world that year.

The June 12, 1991, eruption column from Mount Pinatubo, taken from Clark Air Base.

- Krakatoa, Indonesia—Erupted in 1883. It is one of the largest eruptions in recorded history. The ash and rocks created huge tsunamis. The eruption of Krakatoa is believed to be the loudest sound heard on Earth, and was reported to have been heard over 3,000 miles (4,800 km) away. The explosion was so big that it destroyed about two-thirds of the island.

What did we learn?

- What are the three shapes of volcanoes, and how is each formed?
- Where are most active volcanoes located today?
- What are some of the dangers of volcanoes?
- What are some positive side effects of volcanoes?

Taking it further

- How do black sand beaches form?

Cool volcano

Purpose: To create a delicious ice cream volcano

Materials: half gallon of ice cream, pie pan, chocolate syrup, cookie crumbs, chocolate chips

Procedure:

1. Allow a half gallon of ice cream to soften slightly.
2. Place the ice cream in a pie pan and shape it into your favorite volcano shape.
3. Place it in the freezer for about four hours.
4. Remove it from the freezer and scoop out a crater.
5. Fill the crater with chocolate syrup "lava" and allow it to flow down the sides.
6. Decorate it with cookie crumb ash and chocolate chip bombs. Why not take a picture of the masterpiece before you enjoy eating your cool volcano?

Volcanoes of the past

There have been several very large volcanic eruptions in modern history, including the eruption of Krakatoa and the eruption of Mount St. Helens. However, these volcanoes are very small compared to volcanoes of the past. About 1,800 years ago Taupo erupted in New Zealand. It produced about 30 times as much ash as Mount St. Helens did. The caldera produced by this volcano is now called Lake Taupo and is approximately 238 square miles (616 sq. km.). But an even bigger caldera exists in Yellowstone National Park. This caldera is so large that it must be viewed from a satellite to really see its complete size and shape. A volcano this large likely put 60 times more ash into the air than the Taupo volcano, making it a very large volcano indeed. There are no active volcanoes even close to this size today.

In addition to these large calderas, there are extensive areas of land covered in **continental flood basalts**, which are believed to be lava flows from extremely large shield volcanoes. Areas covered with these lava fields are called traps. The Deccan Traps of India are covered with lava rock that is over a mile (1,600 m) thick and covers nearly 200,000 square miles (518,000 sq. km.) of the country. The Siberian Traps in Russia are even thicker and cover more land.

So, where did all this lava come from? Uniformitarian scientists—those who believe in slow changes over very long periods of time—cannot adequately explain what happened. They point to rifting in the oceans and shield volcanoes that are formed there and say they are a key to the past. However, the slow movement of tectonic plates that occurs today could not possibly produce the amount of lava needed to form these gigantic lava fields.

Creation scientists on the other hand can explain what likely happened. The Bible says that when the Flood began, the fountains of the deep broke forth. This is likely the source of much of

The caldera at Yellowstone National Park as seen from the Space Shuttle *Endeavor* in 1994.

the water for the Flood, but it is also likely the source for much of the lava in the continental flood basalts. Catastrophic plate tectonics, the rapid moving of the earth's plates during the Flood, would allow huge quantities of lava to gush forth from the earth, creating these amazing features.

For a fun experiment, with your parent's permission, take an unopened can of soda outside, shake it up for about 15 seconds, then hold it so that the opening is facing away from you and anyone else around you, and quickly pop the can open. Shaking the can causes pressure to build up inside the can just as moving tectonic plates cause pressure to build up inside the earth. Opening the can releases the pressure and allows the contents to come shooting out. This is what happens when lava and hot gases find a vent through the earth's crust and come shooting out.

26

Mount St. Helens

God's gift to scientists

What can we learn from the eruption of Mount St. Helens?

At 8:32 a.m., on May 18, 1980, after being quiet for 123 years, Mount St. Helens, in southwest Washington State, suddenly burst into life. The explosion that blew off the north side of the mountain was heard up to 200 miles (320 km) away. The summit was lowered by 1,300 feet (400 m), as rock was blown off. The avalanche of rock was followed by a flow of hot gas and ash rushing down the side of the mountain. The explosions lasted for nine hours. Millions of tons of ash were shot 15 miles (24 km) into the atmosphere. Ash darkened the skies across the northern USA and southern Canada for two months. The energy released by this eruption was equal to that of 33,000 atomic bombs, or 400 million tons of dynamite. There had been small earthquakes in the area for two months before the eruption, but no one expected the explosive display that occurred.

The eruption of Mount St. Helens was a frightening event, but it was exciting as well. Many consider it a gift to scientists, since it has given us much scientific knowledge that could not be gained anywhere else. Much of the data collected at Mount St. Helens reveals how catastrophes such as Noah's Flood can explain much of the geology we see today.

Formation of sedimentary rock

When an evolutionist looks at sedimentary rock with hundreds of thin layers, he believes that the layers were deposited slowly over millions of years. However, the eruption of Mount St. Helens deposited over 25 feet (7.6 m) of debris, mostly composed of thin layers of ash, in only one day! There is evidence that there was extensive volcanic activity associated with the Genesis Flood. Similar catastrophic sediment transport activity could account for much of the sedimentary rock formations we see today. Mount St. Helens showed us that these formations can form very quickly as a result of a catastrophe, instead of slowly over millions of years.

Ash from Mount St. Helens darkened the sky in nearby U.S. states and Canadian provinces. The 1815 eruption of Tambora in Indonesia spewed millions of tons of ash into the atmosphere. The following year, the New England states, Canada, England, and France all experienced snow in June and frost in July as a result of that eruption. It is therefore likely that the massive amounts of ash put into the atmosphere due to volcanic activity at the time of the Flood contributed greatly to the cooler summers needed to form the great Ice Age after the Flood.

Mountains & Movement

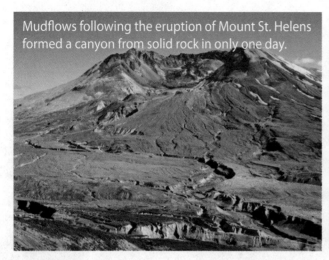
Mudflows following the eruption of Mount St. Helens formed a canyon from solid rock in only one day.

Floating logs on Spirit Lake

Formation of canyons

Another evolutionary idea that has been challenged by Mount St. Helens is the idea that canyons are formed by millions of years of erosion from the rivers flowing through them. Mudflows following the eruption of Mount St. Helens carved a canyon 100 feet (30 m) high and 100 feet (30 m) wide through solid rock in only one day! This canyon has been nicknamed "Little Grand Canyon." This event is forcing scientists to rethink how the actual Grand Canyon may have been formed. Creation scientists believe that the canyon was made by a huge amount of water in a short period of time—not by a small amount of water over a long period of time.

Spirit Lake

Spirit Lake is located at the foot of Mount St. Helens, and some very fascinating things are happening there. First, a whole forest of trees was wiped out by the blast. After the blast more than 10,000 logs were floating on Spirit Lake, and as they became waterlogged they began floating upright, with their root ends pointing down. After only ten years these logs began to settle into the layers of sediment at the bottom of the lake, many of them settling upright with their root ends on the bottom of the lake. This may explain how many fossilized tree trunks became fossilized in a vertical position through many layers of sediment. Evolutionists have not been able to adequately explain these formations, called *petrified forests*, with millions of years of slow deposition. A similar formation called Specimen Ridge, in Yellowstone National Park, had been interpreted by evolutionists to show 50 million years of activity, but Mount St. Helens showed that one catastrophe could account for this type of formation in only a few years.

As scientists continue to study the area around Mount St. Helens, they are finding more and more evidence that catastrophic processes can account for much of what evolutionists have claimed requires millions of years to form. Scientific evidence confirms the Bible's history. 🌐

🧠 What did we learn?

- Describe some of the ways the data collected at Mount St. Helens is challenging evolutionary thinking.

🚀 Taking it further

- How did the ash from the eruption of Mount St. Helens affect the weather in 1980?
- How could volcanic activity have contributed to the onset of the Ice Age?

Fun Fact

In the 1880s a volcanic eruption in New Zealand buried a village. Sixty years later a fossilized hat, a fossilized bag of flour, and a fossilized ham were dug up. Fossils do not require millions of years to form!

Mountains & Movement

Volcano word search

Using a copy of the "Volcano Word Search," review the meaning of each word as you find it in the puzzle.

 # Predicting eruptions

Mount St. Helens began erupting again in September, 2004. However, this eruption was very different from the explosive eruption of 1980. The eruption began with small earthquakes and steam coming from the vent of the volcano. Lava began pouring into the crater on October 10, 2004. For the next three years lava continued to ooze from the volcano. Various rock and ash formations built up and later collapsed along the top of the mountain. Small earthquakes accompanied this eruption from time to time. The lava stopped flowing in January, 2008, and in July, 2008, the eruption was considered finished.

Because 57 people died in the 1980 eruption, it would be nice if scientists could predict another violent eruption before it happens. However, volcanoes are unpredictable right now. In order to gain better understanding of what is going on underneath the volcano, scientists have placed 17 sensors around the mountain in hopes of detecting movement that might lead to an explosion.

Some of the instruments are placed in 6-inch (15-centimeter) wide, 800-feet (244-meter) deep holes in various locations around the crater. The instruments include strainmeters to detect tiny amounts of ground deformation, which could indicate pressure or strain in the rocks, and tiltmeters to help detect any movement of the rocks. A global positioning satellite (GPS) system consisting of nine GPS units is connected to the system to detect any movement of the ground on the surface. All of the sensors are connected to a computer system in Boulder, Colorado, where scientists can view and analyze the data in the hopes of predicting future volcanic eruptions.

UNIT 4

Water & Erosion

◊ **Identify** the source of energy for geysers.

◊ **Describe** the different types of erosion and their effects.

◊ **Describe** the formation of soil and its major components.

◊ **Explain** the formation of Grand Canyon from a biblical view.

◊ **Identify** the different types of cave formations.

27

Geysers

Heated ground water

What is a geyser, and how does it work?

Words to know:

geyser   fumarole

hot spring   mud pot

spouter

Old Faithful is probably the most famous geyser in the world. Anyone who has been to Yellowstone National Park has most likely been able to observe the majestic spray of the hot water shooting into the sky. But many people do not realize that this phenomenon is closely associated with volcanoes and earthquakes.

Geysers are a result of heated ground water. Underground water can be heated one of two ways. Scientists have observed that the interior temperature of the earth rises about 87°F (30.5°C) per mile. This is called the thermal gradient of the earth. So, as water seeps deeper into the earth, its temperature becomes hotter and hotter. The second way that water is heated is by magma rising closer to the surface. As the magma rises, it heats the rocks and water around it. Magma most frequently rises to the surface near joints in the tectonic plates.

Just like air, hot water rises and cold water sinks. This property causes geysers as well as many other interesting phenomena. The most common manifestation of heated ground water is a **hot spring**. In a spring, heated water rises or bubbles to the surface. Springs are relatively calm. **Spouters** are more active hot pools. In a spouter, water continually bubbles and gives off steam. Sometimes the water is superheated and reaches the earth's surface as steam only. This is called a **fumarole**, or steam vent. Fumaroles can sometimes be very noisy as the steam pushes its way to the surface. Heated ground water often contains hydrogen sulfide, giving the pools and springs the smell of rotten eggs.

Different temperatures of water promote growth of different algae and bacteria resulting in

hot springs

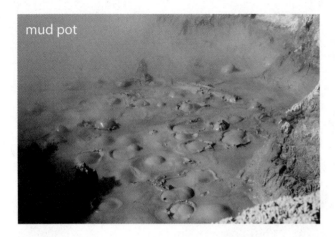
mud pot

Terraces at Mammoth Hot Springs

myriad colors in hot springs. The colors can change from the center of the pool to the edges as the cooling water spreads out. Many hot springs have a rainbow appearance.

If a hot spring contains more dirt than water, it becomes a **mud pot**. Steam bubbles to the surface and spatters out. Often the dirt in mud pots contains minerals that make the mud different colors. These mud pots are often called *paint pots* and can make a beautiful display. Occasionally, a mud pot forms a cone that can become clogged. When this happens, pressure builds until mud and steam erupt out of the top. This is called a *mud volcano*. It is a similar phenomenon to an actual volcano, but mud volcanoes are usually very small compared to lava volcanoes.

Finally, the most spectacular display of heated water is the geyser. Hot water erupts from underneath the ground and can shoot hundreds of feet into the air. Geysers form where rock containing ground water in long twisting chambers is heated by magma which lies as little as 2 to 5 miles (3.2–8 km) below the surface. The water is heated to as much as 400ºF (205ºC). This super-heated water expands and builds up pressure. When the pressure of the super-heated water becomes

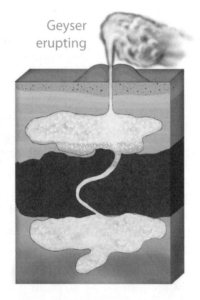
Geyser erupting

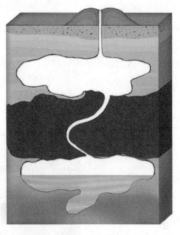
Underground chambers filling with water

greater than the weight of the water above it, the water is forced through a vent leading from the underground chambers to the surface. After an eruption, the chambers begin to refill with water and the process starts over.

Some geysers such as Old Faithful erupt regularly, more or less on a schedule. Old Faithful's next eruption can be predicted based on how long the previous eruption was. If the most recent eruption lasted 2.5 minutes or less, the next eruption will be about 65 minutes later. If the most recent eruption was more than 2.5 minutes long, the next eruption will be about 91 minutes later.

Other geysers erupt irregularly and their eruptions cannot be predicted. Irregular geysers occur because their underground plumbing is shared with other pools or geysers. For example, sometimes another geyser in Yellowstone, Daisy Geyser, erupts for about three minutes every 1½ to 3 hours while Bonita Pool quietly overflows. At other times, Bonita overflows heavily with small eruptions and Daisy erupts very seldom. These two geysers share the same underground water system, thus preventing Daisy from erupting consistently.

Water from hot springs often dissolves minerals from the rocks

The heated water in areas such as Yellowstone provides unique habitats for animals and plants that would not normally live in the area. Some fish can live in water as hot as 104ºF (40ºC), and may be able to tolerate temperatures as high as 110ºF (43ºC) for a few minutes. Even with an ability to live in such warm water, the fish still can't live too close to the hot springs, but must live downstream from the source of heat.

Also, in the dead of winter when most areas are free of insects, flies live near the hot springs. They fly up and down near the hot springs trying to keep their body temperatures just right. If they move even a few feet away from the spring they will die in minutes.

This same heat can also keep small protected pockets of grass, mosses, and flowers alive all winter. Some flowers can even bloom in the middle of winter due to the heat.

through which it flows. Then, after it reaches the surface and evaporates, the minerals are left behind. Geysers often form or leave behind mounds of geyserite—a material made from silica. You can find another beautiful example of mineral deposits left by heated water in Yellowstone at Mammoth Hot Springs (pictured on p. 394). Here beautiful terraces of travertine, or calcium carbonate, have been left behind as the water flows down the hillside. The basic color of the terraces is white but the edges display a rainbow of colors as the different temperatures of water encourage the growth of algae and bacteria in various shades of brown, green, red, yellow, and blue.

Half of all the geysers in the world are found in Yellowstone National Park. Nearly all geysers are found in only four places: Yellowstone, Kronotski National Park in Russia, North Island in New Zealand, and Iceland.

What did we learn?

- What are some ways that heated ground water shows up on the surface of the earth?

- Explain how a geyser works.

- How is a mud pot different from a hot spring?

Taking it further

- How might a scientist figure out which irregular geysers are connected underground?

- Why do some hot pools have a rainbow appearance?

- Can you tell the temperature of the water just by looking at a pool?

Make a geyser

Purpose: To make a geyser

Materials: cup with water, flexible soda straw

Procedure:

1. Fill a cup with water and take it and a soda straw outside.

2. Fill the straw with water and hold your finger over the end of the straw to prevent the water from spilling out.

3. Place the other end of the straw in your mouth and point the straw up in the air and blow out the water. You have made your own geyser!

4. Refill the straw with water and repeat.

Conclusion: The straw represents the underground plumbing that fills up with water. The air from your lungs represents the pressure produced when the heated water expands. Refilling the straw and repeating represents what happens with many geysers such as Old Faithful, as water refills the underground chambers.

🏅 Geothermal energy

Geysers, fumaroles, and hot springs are all associated with volcanic activity. Even though there may not be any active volcanoes in the area, magma is closer to the surface in areas with these features than in other parts of the earth. The magma heats the groundwater, turning it into steam. This creates a unique opportunity for generating electricity. Steam is used in power plants to turn the turbines that generate electricity, so power plants have been built in many of these areas to take advantage of the naturally occurring steam.

Geothermal power station

Geothermal energy is used in many places around the world, mostly near the edges of tectonic plates. In Iceland, over 80% of all homes are heated with geothermal energy. Geothermal power plants have also been built in the United States, New Zealand, Japan, China, Africa, and Europe.

One area north of San Francisco, California, is called The Geysers. Although there are no actual geysers in this area, there are abundant hot pools and fumaroles, indicating that magma is close to the surface. The first power plant was built at The Geysers in 1955 and today the power plant produces enough electricity for 750,000 homes.

To understand how this power plant works, you first need to understand the geology of the area. Magma is only a few miles below the surface of the earth. This magma heats the rocks around it and as water seeps into the ground above, it is heated as well. Above the area with the ground water is an area of hard rock that traps the underground heated water. This causes the water and steam to build up pressure below ground.

Holes have been drilled two miles deep through the cap rock into the rock containing the steam. These holes act like drinking straws, drawing the steam up out of the ground. The steam is then passed through a filter to remove any impurities, and then it is used to turn the turbines. After passing through the turbines, the steam is cooled and the water is returned to the ground. Approximately 25% of the water taken from the ground is recycled and the rest is lost to evaporation. This is a very efficient way to generate electricity since it does not require the burning of any other fuel to turn water into steam.

Areas with geothermal power plants must have trapped steam, but do not necessarily have geysers. A geothermal power plant was built in North Island, New Zealand where there were many geysers. There used to be 200 active geysers, but today there are only 12 active geysers. This is partially due to the building of power plants and partially due to earthquakes that have changed the underground plumbing of the area. However, because steam is still available, the power plant still works.

Questions:

- Why are geothermal power plants mostly located near edges of tectonic plates?

- Would you expect geothermal power plants to experience more or fewer earthquakes than other power plants?

- Why is geothermal energy considered a renewable resource?

28

Weathering & Erosion

It's wearing me down

What causes weathering and erosion?

Words to know:

weathering

erosion

frost heaving

Challenge words:

oxidation

The second law of thermodynamics says that all systems tend toward maximum entropy or total disorder. The Bible says in Psalm 102:25–26, "Of old You laid the foundation of the earth, And the heavens are the work of Your hands. They will perish, but You will endure; Yes, they will all grow old like a garment. . . ." Contrary to evolutionary claims that there is a continuous change toward higher life forms and increased order, what we actually observe are destruction, extinction, and loss of energy. We can easily observe that the surface of the earth is wearing out just by observing the rocks and hills. The surface wears away through three different processes: weathering, mass wasting, and stream erosion. We will discuss weathering in this lesson and the other processes in the following lessons.

Weathering is the natural process of wearing down and breaking apart rocks. **Erosion** is the transport of weathered materials. Rocks can be broken down by either chemical or mechanical means. The most common form of chemical erosion takes place when certain minerals react chemically with acids. Limestone, in particular, dissolves quickly when it comes in contact with acids. Two commonly occurring acids are carbonic acid and humic acid. Carbon

dioxide mixes with water to form carbonic acid, and decaying plants produce humic acid. These weak acids chemically dissolve many of the rocks they come in contact with.

Mechanical weathering is the second means by which rocks can be worn down. Different forces break off pieces of rock or even crack huge rocks apart. Water is the main mechanical force that breaks up rocks. Water fills small cracks in rocks. When it freezes, water expands about 8%, thus increasing the size of the crack and forcing small bits of rock to break off. After the water melts, more water can enter the larger crack. When this freezes, the crack is again enlarged. After many cycles, the water and ice eventually break the rock apart.

This freezing/thawing cycle also occurs underground. The expanding water can push rocks upward. The melting ice allows loose soil to fill in under the rock. The next freezing cycle pushes the rock up further. This process is called **frost heaving**. Rocks can be pushed to the surface from as much as 18 inches (45 cm) below ground each winter. Farmers must deal with new rocks in their fields each spring because of this process.

A third mechanical weathering force is one you might not expect. Plant and tree roots can place continuing pressure on rocks and can force cracks to expand and rocks to break apart.

Finally, wind is a strong mechanical weathering agent. Strong winds can blow debris against rock faces, breaking off bits of rock. This results in many beautiful rock formations but can also ruin the paint on the side of your car or wear away the words on a sign. Weathering forces are constantly at work on the surface of the earth, wearing down the rocks and changing the face of the planet.

What did we learn?

- What is weathering?
- Describe the two types of weathering.

Taking it further

- How does freezing and thawing of water break rocks?
- In what ways do people use water or other materials to remove the surface of something in a process similar to mechanical weathering?

Weathering at work

To observe different types of weathering, perform the experiments and answer the questions on the "Weathering" worksheet.

Chemical weathering

There are many types of chemical weathering. You have already learned about acids that can weather various materials. But water is also a chemical weathering agent. Many substances can be dissolved in water and thus eroded away as water flows over the soil and rocks. Oxygen also contributes to chemical weathering. Many metals, especially iron, react with oxygen. This is called oxidation.

When iron combines with oxygen it is called *rusting*. Rust is much weaker than iron so it is more easily eroded. Thus, when oxidation occurs it increases the rate at which erosion takes place. The rate of oxidation is affected by the amount of water available as well. Rusting happens more quickly in a humid environment than in a dry environment.

Complete the experiment described on the "Chemical Erosion" worksheet. This demonstrates the effects of rust on iron and the effects of humidity on rust rates. Soil and rocks in many areas are worn away because of oxidation.

29

Mass Wasting

The force of gravity

How does gravity cause erosion?

Words to know:

mass wasting   landslide

creep   avalanche

Challenge words:

rock glacier

Weather related forces such as acid rain, freezing water, and wind are not the only forces wearing away the surface of the earth. Gravity is a slow but powerful force constantly pulling on everything on the surface of the earth. Gravity pulls on people and animals, which keeps us from floating away. It holds our atmosphere in place, allowing us to breathe. Yet, gravity also constantly pulls soil, rocks, trees, etc., down the sides of hills or mountains. The movement of large masses of soil is called **mass wasting**.

Some mass wasting is slow. Soil is pulled down some slopes at a rate of only an inch or so each year. This slow process is called **creep**. We cannot actually see the soil creep, but we can observe telephone poles, fence posts, and other structures that have been pushed by the moving soil so they are no longer vertical. Creep is most obvious on steep slopes with loose soil.

Mass wasting can sometimes occur very rapidly. When large amounts of rock and debris are pulled down a slope rapidly it is called a **landslide**. Landslides occur when the force of gravity overcomes the adhesion or friction of the rock surfaces. Landslides often happen unexpectedly with little or no warning. Thus, they can be very dangerous.

Heavy rains that loosen the bonds between rock layers can trigger landslides. Earthquakes can also trigger landslides. The 1964 Alaskan earthquake

A landslide

triggered at least 78 landslides. And in 1959, an earthquake in Montana triggered a landslide that flowed down the mountain, across a valley, and partially up the neighboring mountainside, damming the river flowing through the valley and creating a huge lake. Mass wasting or landslides that include large amounts of ice and snow are called avalanches.

What did we learn?

- What is mass wasting?
- What is slow movement of the soil and rocks down a slope called?
- What is rapid or sudden movement of the soil and rocks called?

Taking it further

- How does water affect mass wasting?
- How might weathermen predict when the avalanche danger is high?

Observing mass wasting

Purpose: To observe the effects of gravity on soil

Materials: baking tray or large baking pan, soil, rocks, water

Procedure:

1. Cover the bottom of a baking pan with soil and rocks.
2. Lift the edge of the pan one inch and observe the movement of the soil.
3. Lift it two inches and again observe the movement of the soil.
4. Continue raising the side of the pan until the soil begins to slide across the bottom. Soil moves more quickly down a steep slope due to gravity.
5. Now place the pan on a flat surface and spread the soil evenly on the bottom of the pan.
6. Again, lift the edge of the pan, but this time shake it as it is lifted to simulate an earthquake. Observe what happens.
7. Again, replace the soil and lift the edge of the pan an inch or two.
8. This time slowly pour water on the soil along the raised edge.

Questions:

- Did the soil slide at a lower angle when you shook it?
- Did more of the soil move at one time?
- How did pouring the water affect the movement of the soil?

Conclusion: This activity simulates how landslides occur during an earthquake or heavy rains. Gravity constantly pulls on the soil on hillsides, and when the ground shakes or it rains, the soil is loosened and pulled down the hill. Earthquakes and heavy rains can often cause landslides.

Rock glaciers

Mass wasting can occur slowly or quickly. One form of slow mass wasting is creep. Another form of slow mass wasting occurs in rock glaciers. As the name would imply these are formations of rock and ice. A rock glacier is different from an ice glacier in that it consists mostly of rock instead of ice and does not necessarily exist in areas with substantial snowfall.

A rock glacier (shown below) can either be a core of ice that is covered with a massive amount of rock, or a massive amount of rock with ice cementing the pieces together. Sometimes a rock glacier can form when a rock slide covers a glacier and becomes imbedded in it. Other times a rock glacier forms when water flows through a pile of rock and debris and then freezes, thus holding the rocks together.

Rock glaciers are only found in areas with steep slopes and cool enough summertime temperatures so that the ice does not completely melt. Most rock glaciers in the United States are found in Colorado and Alaska. Rock glaciers are also found in other mountainous areas around the world.

Active rock glaciers contain a substantial amount of ice and move the rocks and soil slowly down the mountainsides and valleys. Rock glaciers can move from as little as a few inches per year to as much as 15 feet (5 m) per year. Inactive rock glaciers contain a small amount of ice but are no longer moving. Fossil rock glaciers have no ice remaining in them, so the rocks are generally not moving.

Rock glacier "Gorodetsky" in the northern Tien Shan, China

Water & Erosion

30

Stream Erosion

The power of moving water

Water & Erosion

How does moving water cause erosion?

Words to know:

stream erosion   terracing

gradient

Erosion is the gradual wearing away of rocks. This can be caused by water in the form of rain, or wind blowing debris against an exposed surface. But running water is the most powerful eroding force in nature. This form of erosion is called stream erosion. A stream is any body of water that flows regularly, from a tiny creek to a large river. Floodwaters can be extremely destructive and erode surfaces very quickly. A canyon 100 feet (30 m) wide and 100 feet (30 m) deep through rock was eroded away in only one day by the mud-flows and water triggered by the eruption of Mount St. Helens. But water does not have to be flood-strength to be a powerful force.

Water flows downhill due to the pull of gravity. The difference between the height of the source, or headwaters, and the lowest level, or mouth, is called the gradient. The higher the gradient the

steeper the incline is and the faster water will flow down it. As water flows across the surface of the earth, it breaks off and picks up pieces of rock and other debris. The faster the water moves, the larger the pieces of debris it can carry. Eventually, as the water slows down, it can no longer carry the rocks, soil, and silt, and it drops the particles, usually at the bottom of a lake or ocean.

Slow moving streams that flow along relatively level ground tend to move in long curves that resemble a snake, like the one pictured here. But even slow moving streams erode and deposit dirt, sand, and other particles. The soil is eroded from the outside of the bank's curves where the

402 • God's Design: Heaven & Earth

water is flowing more quickly and deposited on the insides of the curves where the water flows more slowly. This action constantly changes the course of the river.

Often, when rivers and streams flood and overflow their banks, they deposit rich silt along the edges of the stream as the waters recede. This flooding cycle has been very beneficial to farmers along the Nile, Ganges, and Yangtze Rivers for hundreds of years. However, flooding can carry huge amounts of eroded soil away and can also cause extensive damage.

According to the U.S. Department of Agriculture, the United States loses more than 2 billion tons of topsoil each year to erosion. Topsoil is not

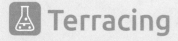 Terracing

Purpose: To demonstrate how terracing prevents erosion

Materials: three baking dishes, soil, plant material, cup of water, thick book

Procedure:

1. Fill three baking dishes with soil.

2. In the first, press the soil firmly against the bottom of the dish.

3. In the second dish, mix leaves, grass, or other plant material into the soil and press it against the bottom of the dish. Also, sprinkle some of the plant material across the surface of the soil.

4. In the third dish, build terraces in the soil, pressing each level firmly against the bottom of the dish.

5. Elevate one end of each dish several inches by setting the end on a thick book. The three dishes should be elevated the same amount.

6. Slowly pour water along the top edge of the soil in each dish. Compare the amount of soil erosion seen in each dish.

Questions:

- Which dish experienced the most erosion?
- Which experienced the least erosion?
- What effect did the leaves and grass have on the flow of the water?
- How did this affect the erosion of the soil?

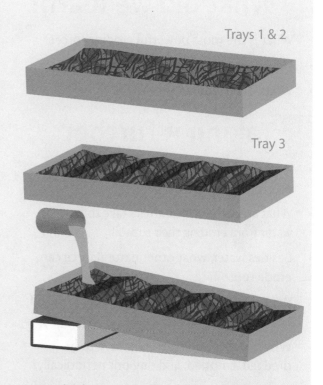

Trays 1 & 2

Tray 3

- How did the terracing affect the flow of the water?
- How did terracing affect the erosion of the soil?
- What do you think is the best way to prevent soil erosion due to running water?

Conclusion: Soil erosion should be most obvious in the pan without plants or terraces. It should be least obvious in the pan with the terraces. Terraces help to slow down the water so it cannot carry the soil away as quickly.

easily replaced, so farmers and other conservationists work to keep soil from eroding away. One way that farmers conserve soil is to plow cross-ways to the flow of the water to help slow down the flow. In very steep areas, terracing is used to control the flow of the water. **Terracing** is the cutting of level areas into the side of the hill so that the fields resemble giant stairs (shown at right). Also, farmers often alternate crops so that one section of a field is planted with tall plants such as corn and the next section is planted with short ground cover crops such as alfalfa. This also helps to stop the erosion of the topsoil by slowing the flow of the water. Finally, steep hillsides are often planted with grass or other ground cover that has spreading roots to help hold the soil in place. 🌐

What did we learn?

- What is the most powerful eroding force?
- How does gravity cause stream erosion?
- What is the gradient of a river?

Taking it further

- Why are farmers concerned about soil erosion?
- What are some steps farmers take to prevent water from eroding their topsoil?
- Besides water, what other natural force can erode topsoil?
- What can farmers do to protect their topsoil from wind erosion?
- Why do lakes and reservoirs have to be dredged, emptied, and dug out periodically?

Fun Fact

In the 1930s the Western United States experienced one of the worst droughts in recorded history. The farmers' fields dried out and the wind began to blow. This period of time is often called the Great Dust Bowl. Sometimes the wind picked up so much dirt that giant clouds of dust engulfed entire towns. Farming practices changed significantly as a result of the Dust Bowl. Today's farms are much less likely to experience a dust bowl as severe as in the 1930s.

🏅 Stream erosion

Purpose: To observe the effects of stream erosion

Materials: soil, water, oven, 3 paper cups, pencil

Procedure:

1. Get a half cup of soil from your yard and add enough water to make a thick mud.

2. Form the mud into 8 equal sized balls and bake your mud balls in an oven at 275°F for 1 hour or until they are dry.

3. Prepare 3 paper cups. Use a pencil to punch 8 holes evenly spaced around the side of cup A near the bottom so that water will drain out the sides of the cup.

4. Use the pencil to poke 10 or 12 small holes into the bottom of cup B.

5. Punch 4 larger holes in the bottom of cup C.

6. Place four of the dirt balls into cup A and place cup A in a baking dish.

7. Hold cup B about 4 inches above cup A.

8. Pour 1 cup of water through cup B and let the water rain down on the balls in cup A. After the water has drained out of cup A, examine the balls. How do they look compared to how they looked before running the water over them? Are pieces broken off? Have any of them crumbled? Examine the water in the baking dish. Are there any small pieces of rocks and soil in the dish?

9. Clean out the baking dish and cup A so you can use them for the second part of the experiment.

10. Place the last four dirt balls into cup A and place this cup in the baking dish.

11. Hold cup C, the one with the bigger holes, about 4 inches above cup A.

12. Pour 2 cups of water through cup C into cup A. After the water has drained out of cup A, examine the balls. How do these balls compare to the balls from the first experiment? Are they more eroded? How did the flow of water in the second experiment compare to the flow of water in the first experiment?

Conclusion: The water should have been flowing faster in the second experiment. Also, there was more water. So you should have seen more erosion of the second set of dirt balls. Imagine what would have happened to the dirt balls if they had been bombarded with water from the sink in a constant flow. The balls would have been completely disintegrated. Thus, you can see that flowing water greatly affects erosion.

The time when there was the greatest amount of water flowing across the surface of the earth was during and shortly after the Great Flood. We have evidence of the floodwater's eroding power all around us. Just look at pictures of Grand Canyon, Bryce Canyon, and many other rock formations that were obviously formed by water erosion.

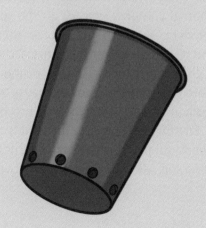

Water & Erosion

31

Soil

Isn't it just dirt?

What is soil made of?

Words to know:

humus

Challenge words:

porosity   permeability

Soil is fun for making mud pies, is home for earthworms, and makes it necessary to wash your car. But soil is also a precious resource needed for growing plants. Erosion plays two major parts with respect to soil. Erosion can devastate an area by moving topsoil away and depositing it in the ocean where it can no longer be used to support plant life. On the other hand, God designed erosion to play a crucial role in the formation of new soil as well.

Soil is formed from sand, silt, clay, and bits of decayed plants and animals. Weathering, particularly wind and water, breaks apart bits of rock to form the sand and clay that is used in the making of new soil. The ratio of sand to silt and clay depends greatly on the rocks in the area. Areas with mostly quartz rocks will have sandy soil. Areas with large deposits of mica and feldspar tend to have higher amounts of clay in the soil. Areas near rivers tend to have silt that is deposited during flood stages. Regardless of the type of soil, whether sandy or clay, it must contain **humus**—decayed plant material—in order to grow plants.

In areas that are not cultivated, plants wither, decay, and return nutrients to the soil. Farmland, however, must have nutrients added back into the soil since cultivating generally removes most of the plant material from the soil. Farmers add nutrients back into the soil by applying chemical fertilizers or by spreading animal compost (waste) on the soil. Sometimes, farmers grow crops just to plow them into the soil and thus replace lost nutrients. Other times, farmers grow crops such as beans, peanuts, or sweet potatoes that enrich the soil as they grow.

God originally created the earth with topsoil. The Garden of Eden would not have been able to support the wonderful plants described in Genesis 1–2 without good soil. Much of the soil was moved

Fun Fact

Five tons of topsoil spread over an acre is only as thick as a dime.

Fun Fact

An average soil sample contains 45% minerals, 25% water, 25% air, and 5% organic matter.

around during the Genesis Flood, and other soil has been washed into lakes, rivers, and oceans by stream erosion. However, since that time, some soil has been created by weathering. The weathering of rocks and the decomposing of plants and animals are wonderful ways God designed the earth to replace lost soil.

Weathering that produces new soil is a slow process. However, other soil has been created more quickly. Volcanic eruptions often deposit large quantities of nutrient-rich ash, which is able to support plant life within only a few years after the eruption. Also, retreating glaciers often leave large amounts of fertile soil behind.

Despite the negative effects of erosion, God has created ways for life to flourish on the earth.

What did we learn?

- What are the major components of soil?
- What is the most important element in soil for encouraging plant growth?

Taking it further

- What type of rocks would you expect to find near an area with sandy soil?
- What type of rocks would you expect to find near an area with clay soil?
- How does a river that regularly floods, such as the Nile, restore lost topsoil?
- What are some ways that farmers restore nutrients to the soil?

Examining soil

Purpose: To examine what soil is made of

Materials: potting soil, yard soil, magnifying glass

Procedure:

1. Spread out a small amount of potting soil on a flat surface and closely examine it with a magnifying glass. What do you observe?

2. Now examine a small amount of soil from your yard with the magnifying glass. What observations do you make? Was it a lighter color?

Questions:

- How did the potting soil differ from the soil in your yard?
- Which soil do you think will be better for growing plants?

Conclusion: You probably noticed a black color, moist texture, lots of plant material, white specks (vermiculite for holding in moisture), and maybe some small rocks in

the potting soil. The yard soil probably had more "dirt" or ground up rock, less plant material, more rocks, and a drier texture.

The best way to improve soil, to make it better for growing plants, is to add more humus or decayed plant material to the soil. Plant material is clearly visible in this sample of potting soil above.

Soil study

Soil plays a very important role in life on Earth. Without productive topsoil, plants would not grow and life would cease to exist. You have already learned that the composition of soil varies from one area to another depending on the rocks that are abundant in the area. The acid level of the soil also varies from one area to another. In areas that receive large amounts of rainfall, the water tends to react with chemicals in the soil to produce acid. So soil in wet areas is generally more acidic than soil in dry areas. Also, large amounts of rainfall can wash away some of the nutrients in the soil. So soil in dry areas may actually be more fertile than soil in wetter areas.

Another factor that can affect plant growth is porosity. Porosity is a measure of the pores or air spaces in the soil. If there are very large air spaces, the soil is said to have high porosity or to be very porous. Porosity affects how quickly water flows through the soil. The rate at which water flows through soil is called permeability. The water will flow through porous soil very quickly so it has high permeability. If there are only very small air spaces the soil is nonporous or has low permeability. Water will sit on top of this kind of soil and will drain very slowly. Plants generally do better in soil with medium permeability so that water drains through the soil but not too quickly.

Purpose: To determine what kind of soil you have in your yard

Materials: soil from your yard, four paper cups, newspaper, colander, fine-mesh strainer, pencils, baking sheet, stopwatch, liquid measuring cup, "Permeability of Soil" worksheet

Procedure:

1. Get 2–3 cups of soil from your yard or garden.

2. Number four paper cups from 1 to 4.

3. Place about ½ cup of soil in cup 1.

4. Place a sheet of newspaper on the counter, and then place a colander on top of the newspaper.

5. Pour the rest of your soil into the colander. Shake the colander until no more soil will fall out. Pour what is left in the colander into cup 2.

6. Pour the soil from the newspaper into a fine mesh strainer.

7. Hold the strainer over a second piece of newspaper and shake it until no more soil will fall out.

8. Pour what is in the strainer into cup 3 and pour what is on the newspaper into cup 4. You have now separated your soil according the sizes of the particles in the soil.

9. We are now going to test the permeability of each of your soil samples. Make sure you have the same amount of soil in each cup by removing soil from the cups that have more soil until all four cups have the same amount.

10. Follow the directions below and record your observations on the "Permeability of Soil" worksheet.

11. Use a sharp pencil to make four holes in the bottom of each cup. Try to make all the holes as close to the same size as possible.

12. Set two pencils parallel to each other in a baking sheet. Set cup 1 on top of the pencils.

13. You are going to pour 1 cup (8 ounces) of water through your soil sample. Use a stopwatch to time how long it takes for water to flow through your soil sample. Start the timer as soon as water starts dripping out the bottom and stop it when water quits dripping. Record this time on the worksheet under "Water Flow Time."

14. Pour the water from the baking sheet into the measuring cup to see how many ounces of water flowed through your sample. Some of the water will remain in the soil. Record this amount on your worksheet under "Water Flow Amount."

15. Repeat this procedure with each of the other samples, recording your time and volume of water for each trial on the worksheet.

16. Finally, calculate the permeability of each sample by dividing the volume of water by the flow time to give you ounces per second. Answer the questions at the bottom of the worksheet.

32

Grand Canyon

Lots of time, little water or lots of water, little time?

How was Grand Canyon formed?

One of the most fascinating areas to study on Earth is Grand Canyon in Arizona. This wonder of nature is 277 miles (446 km) long, 4 to 18 miles (6.5–29 km) wide and up to 1 mile (1.6 km) deep. This huge canyon is a wonder to behold and is also the source of great debate between evolutionists and creationists.

Evolutionists claim that the Colorado River, which flows through the bottom of the canyon, eroded the rocks around it to form the canyon over millions of years. Evolutionists also claim that the many layers of sedimentary rock observed in the canyon walls were deposited slowly over hundreds of millions of years prior to this slow erosion. They claim that the evidence in Grand Canyon is very clear that the earth is very old and that the canyon was formed by "a little water and a lot of time."

On the other hand, scientists who accept the biblical account claim just the opposite. They say that the evidence points to "lots of water and a little time." The many layers deposited in the canyon walls contain numerous fossils. These most likely were deposited by the great Flood of Noah's day. Most of the fossils are sea creatures—indicating an

ocean once covered the entire area. Genesis 7:19–20 says, "And the waters prevailed exceedingly on the earth, and all the high hills under the whole heaven were covered. The waters prevailed fifteen cubits upward, and the mountains were covered." So even the driest parts of Arizona were covered with water during the Flood.

In many places in Grand Canyon, the rock layers are bent, or as a geologist would say, "folded," This folding has taken place without cracking the rock. Folds like this indicate that the folding had to happen soon after the layers were deposited, while the material was still soft and pliable. This shows

Folded rock layers

that the deposition and the upheaval responsible for the folding were in fact one event. If the folding took place millions of years after the material was deposited, the sediment would have hardened and would have broken and cracked when it was folded.

Creation scientists believe that a very large lake formed above the current location of the canyon after the Flood. Sometime later, the land dam holding back the lake broke, resulting in a huge flow of water. This would have resulted in the erosion that carved the huge canyon. Both evolutionists and creationists agree that erosion formed the canyon, yet they disagree on the amount of water and the time needed to accomplish this.

Evolutionists have a difficult time supporting some of their ideas. For example, where did all of the eroded material from the canyon go? If a relatively small, slow moving river eroded millions of cubic yards of rock, it should have deposited the silt and debris somewhere within or just outside the canyon, yet no such deposits have been found. On the other hand, a large flood of water would have carried the debris far away.

Also, radiometric dating techniques used by evolutionists show lava layers between other rock layers deep in the canyon to be more than 1 billion years old. The same dating technique has shown the uppermost, recent lava flows, to also be more than a billion years old. These dating techniques are obviously flawed and unreliable. They do not prove the canyon to be millions or billions of years old.

Many of the fossils found in Grand Canyon indicate a fast moving water current was present when the plants and animals were covered. This does not fit with the uniformitarian theory that says all the fossil layers were formed slowly over millions of years.

Although scientists see the same evidence, they draw very different conclusions about Grand Canyon. But God's Word tells us we can trust His wisdom rather than man's. For more information on Grand Canyon and how it confirms the biblical record, do a search on the Answers in Genesis website.

What did we learn?

- What is the main controversy between evolutionists and creationists concerning the formation of Grand Canyon?
- What evidence shows radiometric dating methods to be unreliable?

Taking it further

- What event at the eruption of Mount St. Helens supports the biblical view of how Grand Canyon was formed? (Hint: Review Lesson 30.)
- How can scientists look at similar data and draw different conclusions?
- How can we know what to believe when scientists disagree?

Grand Canyon model

Look at the picture of Grand Canyon on the previous page. Notice the beauty of this area. The canyon is not just a crevice with steep walls; there are many gorges and cutouts that run perpendicular to the flow of the river. Make a model of Grand Canyon using modeling clay. Build the model on a piece of paper and color the river at the bottom of the canyon with a marker.

Moving water is one of the most destructive forces in nature, especially if it is moving quickly. Fast moving water can cut through rock very rapidly. However, slow moving water erodes rock very slowly. So, do you think Grand Canyon was formed quickly by lots of fast moving water, or slowly by a slow moving river?

Evidence of catastrophe

Creation scientists have been studying the aftermath of the Mount St. Helens eruption for more than 20 years now and have concluded that the evidence provided there confirms that a time of great catastrophe could account for much of the geologic features we see. Specifically, the evidence from Mount St. Helens supports the ideas that vast amounts of sedimentary rock could have been formed in a short time period and the floodwaters could account for many of the canyons we see today. These conclusions support many of the biblically-based ideas about Grand Canyon. However, Mount St. Helens is not the only source for these ideas. Grand Canyon itself indicates a massive flood took place there in the past and supports what the Bible says as well.

Grand Canyon stands as a monument to the biblical record if you only have the eyes to see it. Grand Canyon is special. Since so much of the rock has been stripped away, we can see the rock layers from the very bottom to the top and see a history of creation, Noah's Flood, and the time since the receding of the floodwaters.

As you learned in lesson 13, evolutionists have developed what they call the geologic column to describe the long time periods represented in the fossil layers. In Grand Canyon many of these layers of rock are easily visible, yet they do not tell of millions of years; instead they tell of a great catastrophe. There are many areas where layers of rock are found piled on top of perfectly flat lower layers. If the lower layer had been eroded for millions of years, it would not be perfectly flat. However, floodwaters could have quickly eroded the lower layers and then deposited the next layers of sediment. These layers of rock are not isolated to a small area either. These flat layers extend for up to 200 miles, showing that the water that deposited them covered a large area.

The fossils found in Grand Canyon also speak of catastrophe and flood. Fossilized footprints found in the Coconino Sandstone indicate that the animals who made the prints were still alive and walking across wet sand, and then their prints were quickly covered over with sediment. This is not something that happens slowly over millions of years. Also, in a side canyon called Nautiloid Canyon there is a large area containing fossils of hundreds of nautiloids—sea creatures with cigar-shaped shells. Many of the fossils show the shells oriented from north to south. This indicates a fast-moving current when these animals were buried. This is consistent with a flood and not with slow deposition over long periods of time.

As we study the special features on Earth such as volcanoes, canyons, and fossils, we see more and more evidence that God's Word is true.

Fossilized amphibian or reptile footprints found in sandstone layers in Grand Canyon

One of the many nautiloids found in Nautiloid Canyon

33

Caves

Underground wonderlands

How are caves formed?

Words to know:

lava tube	stalagmite
sea cave	column
sandstone cave	flowstone
solution cave	curtain
stalactite	

Caves are caverns underground. They can be small or large, but they are almost always filled with beautiful formations. There are about 17,000 caves in the United States. Over 200 of these are "show caves" that are open for public tours.

Caves are divided into four categories. Lava tubes are caverns that were formed as the outer layers of lava cooled while the hot lava continued to flow through it. After the volcano stopped erupting, the lava flowed away, leaving a hollow tube surrounded by cooled rock. Moving water has

formed two other kinds of caves. Sea caves were formed by the pounding of the waves against the rocks along the shore. And sandstone caves were formed at the base of cliffs by moving water.

The fourth and most common kind of cave is a solution cave. These are caves made primarily within limestone, dolomite, marble, and gypsum. The causes of solution cave formation are another geological event about which scientists disagree. It is obvious that many existing caves are being enlarged by erosion due to underground water flow. However, there are several ideas about how these caves originally formed.

Some creation scientists link cave formation to the Flood. Large amounts of acidic water could have seeped through limestone deposits, rapidly forming

Fun Fact

- Mammoth Cave in Kentucky is 348 miles (576 km) long and is the longest known cave.
- Kentucky has the most extensive network of caves in the United States.
- There are also many caves in the area of New Mexico near Lechuguilla Cave.
- Mammoth Cave and Carlsbad Caverns have both been designated as National Parks.

Fun Fact

People who explore caves are called spelunkers.

Water & Erosion

caverns underground. Evolutionists believe that the slow process of dissolving limestone by carbonic acid over millions of years is what formed most of these caves. We see both ground water erosion and carbonic acid dissolution occurring in caves today.

Regardless of how the caverns themselves were formed, we can easily observe how the many beautiful structures (called *speleothems*) inside caves are formed. Water, passing through limestone, dissolves some of the minerals in the rock. As the water drips into the cave, the water evaporates, leaving calcium carbonate (calcite) behind. This mineral is the main ingredient in limestone.

Calcite deposits in caves can take many forms. When the formation hangs down from the ceiling, it is called a **stalactite**. When it builds up from the floor of the cavern, it is called a **stalagmite**. When a stalactite and a stalagmite grow together into one formation, it is called a **column**.

Other times, a thin layer of water flows over the surface of the cave leaving behind wavy formations like in the picture here. These formations are called **flowstones**. Flowstones that hang from the ceiling are called **curtains**. Flowstones can also be formed on the walls and floors of caves.

Pure calcite is white and many formations in caves are white. But impurities often get mixed into the calcite, giving these formations many beautiful colors including brown, orange, yellow, and red.

Evolutionists claim that cave formations grow very slowly, about one cubic inch (16.4 cc) in 150 years. And in dry caves, the calcite formation is very slow. However, many wet caves have very active calcite formation. Crystal Spring Dome, located in Carlsbad Caverns, experiences calcite growth of about 2.5 cubic inches (41 cc) per year. Also, bats have been found encased in stalagmites and stalactites. A bat that became trapped in a stalactite or a stalagmite would have decayed before being encased if formation were very slow. However, bats that are completely covered with calcite had to have been caught where the formation of calcite was very rapid.

Fun Fact

How do you remember which formation is which? You can remember that stalacTITES hold "tightly" to the ceiling and stalagMITES are something you "might" trip over. Another way to remember these: stala**g**mite has a g, and is attached to the ground; stala**c**tite has a c, and is attached to the ceiling.

Growing stalagmites & stalactites

Purpose: To grow your own stalagmites and stalactites

Materials: hot water, Epsom salt, cotton string, two paper or plastic cups, cardboard, scissors

Procedure:

1. Fill two cups ¾ full with hot water.

2. Stir Epsom salt into each cup until no more will dissolve.

3. Cut a 16-inch piece of string and completely submerge the string in one of the cups, then remove it.

4. Place one end of the string in each cup.

5. Place the cups on a piece of cardboard so that the string hangs down a little between the cups without touching the cardboard. Place this set-up in an area where it will not be disturbed for several days.

6. Observe the string and the cardboard every day for several days. After several days, what do you observe?

Conclusion: Crystals should be forming on the string and on the cardboard below it. This is a similar process to the one in which stalactites and stalagmites are formed. In a cave, water dissolves minerals in the limestone. As the water reaches the ceiling of the cave, some of it drips to the floor. As the water evaporates from the floor or ceiling, it leaves calcite crystals behind. These crystals build up on top of each other and form stalactites and stalagmites.

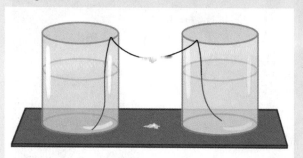

Although evolutionists point to the many formations in caves as evidence of an old Earth, we can observe that rapid formation is very possible. Conditions after the Flood would have been much wetter than today, resulting in rapid calcite formation in many caves. Caves demonstrate the truth of God's Word; they do not refute it. For more information on cave formation, do a search on the Answers in Genesis website.

What did we learn?

- How are the beautiful formations in caves formed?

- What is a stalactite?

- What is a stalagmite?

Taking it further

- What evidence do we have that formations in caves can develop rapidly?

- Why is it likely that calcite formations would have formed rapidly after the Flood?

- Besides in caves, where can calcite deposits be found?

Cave research

Do a research project on your favorite cave. Find out all you can about it and make a presentation to share what you have learned with your friends and family. If you do not have a favorite cave, you can choose one from the following list.

- Kazumura Cave—Hawaii
- Mammoth Cave—Kentucky
- Anemone Cave—Maine
- Carlsbad Caverns—New Mexico
- Lava Beds National Monument—California
- Waitomo Cave—New Zealand
- Dead Sea Caves—Israel

34

Rocks & Minerals Collection: Final Project

Putting it all together

Do you want to become a rock hound?

You have learned about the wonderful planet we call Earth. This amazing globe was designed by God to be the perfect place for all living creatures. In the beginning, God created it "very good," but Adam's sin brought a curse on the land, and the Genesis Flood reshaped the surface of the planet. Our beautiful home has mountains and ocean basins, rocks, streams, and hills. The beauty of caves, volcanoes, and geysers all help us recognize God's majesty and glory, and remind us of His judgment on sin. To help you remember the wonders of the planet around you, take what you have learned about rocks, gems, and minerals and make a display to share with others.

To become a rock hound, all you have to do is collect rocks you find on the ground and learn more about them. If you want, and you have permission, you can dig for rocks with some simple tools including a hand shovel and a mason's hammer. Be sure to wear eye protection! You will also want to have a box in which to store your samples and a rocks and minerals guidebook to help you identify the different rocks you collect. Being a rock hound can be a very enjoyable hobby. 🌐

🧠 What did we learn?

- What are the three types of rocks?
- What is a native mineral?

🚀 Taking it further

- What are some of the greatest or most interesting things you learned from your study of our planet earth?

- Read Genesis chapters 1 and 2. Discuss what was created on each day and how each part completes the whole.

- What earth science topic would you like to learn more about?

⚗️ Rocks & minerals collection

Step 1:

Collect samples of rocks and minerals. Be sure to get at least one or more samples from each of the following categories.

Minerals: Minerals are naturally occurring solids that are inorganic and have a definite atomic structure.

- Native Minerals—Pure element having only one kind of atom. Examples include gold, silver, copper, tin, and iron. If samples are too expensive to put into your display, find a picture to include.

- Compound—Two or more elements bonded together. Examples include salt, alum, and quartz.

Gems: These are minerals that are valued for their perfect cleavage and brilliance.

- Natural gems have formed inside the earth with no help from man.

- Artificial gems have been developed by man as an inexpensive substitute for the natural gems. They often contain the same materials and crystal structure.

- Gems may be too valuable to include in your display, so find pictures of gems and include the pictures in your collection.

Rocks: These contain one or more minerals and/or organic materials.

- Igneous—formed by the cooling of liquid magma or melted rock

- Sedimentary—formed from bits of broken rock, shells and other material

- Metamorphic—formed by transformation of igneous or sedimentary rock by heat and pressure over time

Places to look for samples include:

1. Your kitchen
2. Around your house
3. In your yard
4. On a hike
5. Jewelry
6. Coins

Step 2:

Once you have collected several samples, identify each sample using a rocks and minerals guidebook, if necessary. You may want to perform some of the tests you learned about in lesson 16 to help you identify your samples.

Step 3:

Prepare your display. You can display your samples in many different ways. You can glue the samples or photos to poster board or tagboard; you can use a box and make dividers from cardboard to separate sections of the box; or you can purchase a plastic container with dividers or small compartments. Maybe you have a better idea for displaying your samples. The important thing is to make it neat and easy to show to someone else.

Group your samples together by type. For example, make one part of your display for minerals, another for gems, another for igneous rocks, etc. Neatly label each sample with what it is and where you found it.

Optional:

Include some of the following:

- Possible uses for each sample
- Estimated value if the sample is valuable
- Chemical makeup of compounds
- Any other interesting facts about the sample

Step 4:

Show your collection to someone else and share the wonder of God's creation with them.

Water & Erosion

35

Conclusion

The wonder of our planet earth

Recognizing God's hand in designing our planet

The planet Earth was specially designed by God to support life. No other known planet can support life. Although we cannot prove scientifically that God created the earth because we cannot recreate that event, the Bible tells us that He created it, and we can see that the evidence points to a Designer. The complexity of the earth and of all life on it demands that an Intelligent Designer, not natural processes, made the world around us. We can be very thankful that we can know and love that Designer—Jesus, the Creator of the universe.

What have you learned in your study of the earth that has demonstrated the truth of the Bible and revealed God's design to you? Make a list of these items.

Read Psalm 139:8–10. Then pray and thank God for these revelations.

Where can you look to see more evidence of God's mighty hand on the earth? Keep your eyes open for more examples of God's design for heaven and earth.

Our Planet Earth — Glossary

Active volcano   One that has erupted at least once in the past 50 years

Actual height   Difference between the elevations of the summit and the base

Aftershock   Smaller earthquakes occurring after a major earthquake

Astronomy   Study of space

Avalanche   Sudden movement of large amounts of ice and snow

Caldera   Crater or bowl-shaped depression at the mouth of a volcano

Calving   Pieces of ice breaking off a glacier into the water

Carbon-14 dating   Dating of organic materials by measuring carbon-14 levels

Cast fossil   Fossil made when animal or plant material is replaced with rock

Chemical rock   Sedimentary rock formed by chemicals precipitating from water

Cinder cone volcano   Formed from mostly ash and cinders

Cleavage   When a rock breaks in a straight line

Column   Formation when a stalactite and stalagmite grow together

Composite volcano   Formed from alternating layers of lava and ash

Continental glacier   Giant ice sheet

Core   Center of the earth

Creep   Slow movement of dirt and rocks

Crust   Outer shell of the earth

Curtains   Flowstone that hangs from the ceiling of a cave

Depositional mountains   Mountains formed from debris

Dormant volcano   One that has not erupted in the past 50 years, but could erupt again

Earthquake   Rapid movement of the earth's crust

Elevation   Height of summit above sea level

Environmental geology   Study of the effects of humans on the earth's environment

Epicenter   Location on surface of the earth above the focus

Erosion   Transport of weathered materials

Erosional mountains   Mountains that have been formed by erosion

Extinct volcano   One that is not expected to erupt again

Extrusive   Igneous rocks that form on top of the earth's crust

Fault   Crack in the earth's crust

First law of thermodynamics   Matter cannot be created or destroyed, only changed in form

Flowstone   Thin layer of minerals covering a surface of a cave

Focus   Location of the origin of an earthquake

Fold and fault mountains   Mountains formed by movement of tectonic plates

Foliated rocks   Metamorphic rocks that break in straight lines along crystal structures

Fossil fuel   Fuel formed from dead plants or animals

Fossil   Rock or mineral structure that has the same shape as a formerly living plant or animal

Fracture   When a rock breaks in a smooth curve

Fragmental rock   Sedimentary rock formed when fragments are glued together

Frost heaving   Process of freezing and thawing that pushes rocks up to the surface

Fumarole   Steam vent where steam escapes from underground

Gem   Minerals that can be polished and reflect light

Geology   Study of the earth

Geophysics   Study of the earth's magnetic field, heat flow, gravity, seismic waves, the earth's core

Geothermal   Heat from inside the earth

Geyser   Erupting steam and water due to underground pressure of super-heated water

Glacial erratic   Very large boulders moved by a glacier

Gradient   Difference in height between the headwaters and mouth of a river or stream

Hot spring/Hot pool   Heated water that flows up from underground

Humus   Decayed plant matter

Igneous   Rocks formed from magma

Index fossils   Particular fossils used to date sedimentary rocks

Intrusive   Igneous rocks that form inside the earth's crust

Landslide   Sudden movement of large amounts of dirt and rocks

Lateral moraine   Debris pushed up along the sides of a glacier

Lava tube   Cavern formed by volcanic eruption

Lava   Liquid rock on top of the earth's surface

Lithosphere   The solid earth

Luster   Quality and intensity of reflected light

Magma   Liquid rock inside the earth's crust

Mantle   Semirigid part of the earth between the crust and the core

Mass wasting   Movement of rocks and soil due to gravity

Metamorphic   Rocks formed when atomic structures of igneous or sedimentary rocks are changed

Meteorology   Study of the atmosphere

Mineral   Naturally occurring inorganic material with crystalline structure

Mineralogy   Study of minerals in the earth's crust, moon rocks, crystals

Mold fossil   Fossilized imprint of a plant or animal

Mud pot   Hot pool containing more dirt than water

Native mineral/Native element   Minerals containing only one element

Oceanography   Study of Earth's oceans

Paleontology   Study of fossils and ancient life forms

Physical geology   Study of land formations, rocks

Piedmont glacier   Glacier formed when two valley glaciers meet

Plate tectonics   Theory that the earth's crust is composed of several moving plates

Polystrate fossil   Fossil passing vertically through many layers of sedimentary rock

Radiometric dating   Dating of igneous and metamorphic rocks by measuring radioactive elements

Rodinia   Original landmass

Sandstone cave   Cave formed at the base of cliffs by moving water

Sea cave   Cavern formed by erosion due to waves

Second law of thermodynamics   All objects tend to go to a state of rest or disorganization

Sedimentary   Rocks formed from sediment

Sedimentology   Study of sediment deposits/fossils

Seismograph   Equipment used for detecting earthquakes

Shield volcano   Formed from mostly lava

Solution cave   Cavern formed by erosion due to underground water

Spouter   Active hot pool that shoots out small amounts of water

Stalactite   Calcite formation on ceiling of a cave

Stalagmite   Calcite formation on the floor of a cave

Strata   Layers of sediment that form sedimentary rock

Stream erosion   Erosion due to running water

Striations   Scratches made in the ground by a moving glacier

Terminal moraine   Debris pushed ahead of a glacier

Terracing   Cutting of level areas into a slope

Tsunami   Giant water waves triggered by earthquake

Uniformitarianism   Belief that all changes have been brought about by the processes we see today

Valley glacier   Glacier that flows into a valley

Weathering   Natural breaking apart of rocks by chemical or mechanical means

Zone of accumulation   Part of glacier where snow does not melt

Zone of wastage   Part of glacier where the snow melts

Our Planet Earth — Challenge Glossary

Anticline   Upward folding of strata due to sideways pressure

Basin   Depression in the crust formed by downward pressure

Breccia   Sedimentary rock formed with jagged clasts

Clasts   Fragments of rock cemented together to form sedimentary rock

Conglomerate   Sedimentary rock formed with smooth clasts

Continental flood basalts   large areas of land covered in deep layers of basaltic lava

Coprolite   Fossilized animal dung

Dome   Formation due to upward pressure

Evolution   Worldview allowing only naturalistic causes for everything we see

Foot wall Rock below a fault

Gastrolith   Smooth stones found inside fossilized animals

Geologic column   Twelve groups of strata containing fossils the evolutionists claim represent the geologic time line

Hanging wall   Rock above a fault

Lithification   Process which turns sediment into sedimentary rock

Matrix   The material cementing sedimentary rock particles together

Monocline   Folding of strata due to upward pressure on one side and downward pressure on the other

Normal fault   Hanging wall moves up with respect to footwall

Oxidation   Chemical reaction involving bonding with oxygen

Permeability   The rate at which water flows through soil

Porosity   Measure of the pores or air spaces in soil

Porphyritic   Rock containing both large and small crystals

Rifting   Where two tectonic plates move away from each other

Rock glacier   Formation containing mostly rocks held together by ice

Strike-slip fault   Where two plates move horizontally against each other

Subduction/Subduction zone   Area where one tectonic plate slides under the edge of another

Syncline   Downward folding of strata due to sideways pressure

Theistic evolution   Worldview that God used the process of evolution to bring about what we see today

Thrust fault/Reverse fault   Hanging wall moves down with respect to footwall

Vesicles   Holes or air or gas spaces found in igneous rock

Index

Photo Credits

1   Shutterstock.com
3   Getty Images/iStockphoto
5   Credit NASA, ESA, and the Hubble Heritage Team (STScI/AURA)
7   Getty Images/iStockphoto
9   Getty Images/iStockphoto
11   Getty Images/iStockphoto
13   ©2008 Jupiterimages Corporation
14   ©2008 Jupiterimages Corporation
16   ©2008 Jupiterimages Corporation
17   ©2008 Answers in Genesis
19   ©2008 Jupiterimages Corporation
20   ©2008 Jupiterimages Corporation
22   Public domain
23T   ©2008 Jupiterimages Corporation
23B   ©2008 Jupiterimages Corporation
25   ©2008 Jupiterimages Corporation
26   ©2008 Jupiterimages Corporation
27T   ©Medioimages/Photodisc
27M   Getty Images/IStockphoto
27B   ©2008 Jupiterimages Corporation
28L   Getty Images/iStockphoto
28R   ©2008 Jupiterimages Corporation
31T   Getty Images/iStockphoto
31B   ©Sirer | Dreamstime.com
32   ©2008 Answers in Genesis
34   ©2008 Jupiterimages Corporation
35   ©2008 Answers in Genesis
37   ©2008 Jupiterimages Corporation
38   Getty Images/iStockphoto
40   ©2008 Jupiterimages Corporation
43   Getty Images/iStockphoto
44   ©2008 Jupiterimages Corporation
45   ©2008 Answers in Genesis
46   ©2008 Answers in Genesis
47T   ©2008 Jupiterimages Corporation
47B   ©2005 Hemera Technologies
50T   Credit NOAA Photo Library
50M   ©2008 Jupiterimages Corporation
50B   ©2008 Jupiterimages Corporation
51   ©2008 Jupiterimages Corporation
52   ©2008 Jupiterimages Corporation
53T   ©2008 Answers in Genesis
53B   Getty Images/Purestock
54TL   Getty Images/iStockphoto
54TR   Getty Images/iStockphoto
54BL   Credit NOAA Photo Library
54BR   Getty Images/iStockphoto
56   ©2008 Answers in Genesis
57   Credit NOAA Photo Library
58   Credit NOAA Photo Library
59   Getty Images/iStockphoto
60T   ©2008 Jupiterimages Corporation
60B   ©2008 Jupiterimages Corporation
61   ©2008 Answers in Genesis
63   ©2008 Jupiterimages Corporation
64   ©2008 Answers in Genesis

65   ©2008 Answers in Genesis
67T   ©2008 Jupiterimages Corporation
67B   ©2008 Jupiterimages Corporation
68   ©2008 Answers in Genesis
70   Getty Images/iStockphoto
71T   ©2008 Jupiterimages Corporation
71B   Getty Images/Dorling Kindersley RF
72   Getty Images/iStockphoto
73L   Credit NOAA Photo Library
73R   Credit NOAA Photo Library
74   Credit NOAA Photo Library
75T   Getty Images/Stocktrek
75B   ©2008 Answers in Genesis
76   Credit NOAA
78   Credit NOAA Photo Library
79   Credit NASA
80   Credit NOAA/NWS/NWSFO Lubbock, Texas
81   Getty Images/iStockphoto
82T   Public domain
82B   Creative Commons | Hannes Grobe 19:02, 3 September 2006 (UTC)
83   Public domain
86   ©2008 Jupiterimages Corporation
88T   ©istockphoto.com/Nancy Nehring
88B   Credit US Department of Commerce
89L   Getty Images/iStockphoto
89TR   Credit NOAA Photo Library
89BR   Credit NOAA Photo Library
91T   Credit NOAA Photo Library
91B   Credit NASA
92   NASA/Tony Gray and Tim Powers
93   Credit NOAA
94   Credit NOAA
96   Credit NOAA Photo Library
99   ©2008 Jupiterimages Corporation
100   ©2008 Answers in Genesis
101   ©2008 Jupiterimages Corporation
102   ©2008 Jupiterimages Corporation
103   ©2008 Jupiterimages Corporation
104   Public domain
105   ©2008 Jupiterimages Corporation
106   Getty Images/iStockphoto
107   Creative Commons | James Grellier
108   ©2008 Jupiterimages Corporation
109   ©2008 Answers in Genesis
112   Credit NOAA Photo Library
114T   ©2008 Jupiterimages Corporation
114B   ©2008 Answers in Genesis
115T   ©2008 Answers in Genesis
115BL   Credit US Navy/PH1 Bauer, Bart A.
115BR   Credit USMC/Cpl. Megan Angel
118   ©2008 Jupiterimages Corporation
119   ©2008 Answers in Genesis
120   ©istockphoto.com/Kamilla Mathisen
121T   Getty Images/iStockphoto
121B   ©2008 Jupiterimages Corporation

123   Credit USGS
124T   Creative Commons | Dani 7C3
124B   ©2008 Jupiterimages Corporation
126   Getty Images/iStockphoto
127T   Getty Images/moodboard RF
127B   ©2008 Jupiterimages Corporation
128   Public Domain
129T   Public Domain
129B   Credit NOAA Photo Library
131T   Public Domain
131B   Credit NOAA Photo Library
132   ©2015 Answers in Genesis
133   ©2008 Answers in Genesis
135T   ©2008 Jupiterimages Corporation
135B   Credit: IFE, URI-IAO, UW, Lost City Science Party; NOAA/OAR/OER;
136LA   Credit LCDR Eric Johnson, NOAA Corps
136LB   Credit NOAA/Monterey Bay Aquarium Research Institute.
136LC   Image courtesy of Expedition to the Deep Slope 2007, NOAA-OE
136LD   Credit: Andrew David, NOAA/ NMFS/SEFSC Panama City; Lance Horn, UNCW/NURC - Phantom II ROV operator.
136RA   Credit LCDR Eric Johnson, NOAA Corps
136RB   Credit NOAA Okeanos Explorer Program
136RC   Credit NOAA OKEANOS Explorer Program , 2013 Northeast U. S. Canyons Expedition
136RD   Credit: NOAA Okeanos Explorer Program, INDEX-SATAL 2010
137   Credit NOAA Okeanos Explorer Program
138   Getty Images/iStockphoto
139   Public Domain
140   Credit: Pacific Ring of Fire 2004 Expedition. NOAA Office of Ocean Exploration; Dr. Bob Embley, NOAA PMEL, Chief Scientist.
141   ©2008 Jupiterimages Corporation
142T   Getty Images/iStockphoto
142B   Credit NOAA/Richard B. Mieremet, Senior Advisor, NOAA OSDIA
143   Getty Images/iStockphoto
145   ©2008 Jupiterimages Corporation
151   Credit NASA, ESA, and the Hubble Heritage Team (STScI/AURA)
153   Credit NASA
154   Getty Images/iStockphoto
156T   ©2008 Jupiterimages Corporation
156B   Getty Images/iStockphoto
157L   Getty Images/iStockphoto
157R   ©2008 Jupiterimages Corporation

CHARLOTTE MASON INSPIRED
ELEMENTARY CURRICULUM THAT CONNECTS CHILDREN TO
AMERICA'S PAST... AND THEIR FUTURE!

Through this unique educational style, children develop comprehension through oral and written narration, and create memories through notebooking and hands-on crafts. This is not just facts and figures; this is living history for grades 3 through 6.

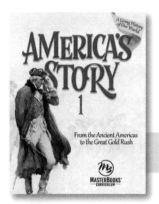

FROM THE ANCIENT AMERICAS TO THE GREAT GOLD RUSH

Part 1: Begins at the infancy of our country and travels through the founding of our great nation, catching glimpses of the men who would become known as the Founding Fathers.

America's Story Vol 1   *Teacher Guide*
978-0-89051-979-0   978-0-89051-980-6

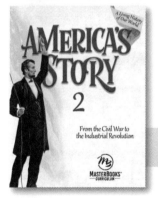

FROM THE CIVIL WAR TO THE INDUSTRIAL REVOLUTION

Part 2: Teaches students about the Civil War, the wild West, and the Industrial Revolution.

America's Story Vol 2   *Teacher Guide*
978-0-89051-981-3   978-0-89051-982-0

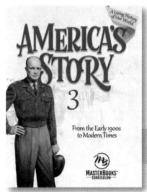

FROM THE EARLY 1900s TO OUR MODERN TIMES

Part 3: Carries the student from the turn of the 20th century through the early 2000s.

America's Story Vol 3   *Teacher Guide*
978-0-89051-983-7   978-0-89051-984-4

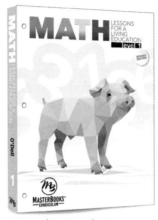
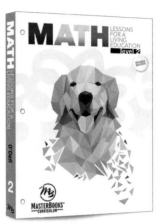
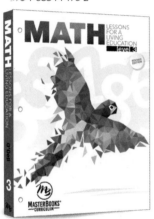

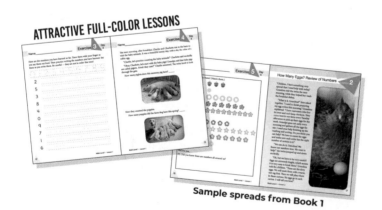
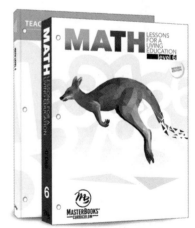

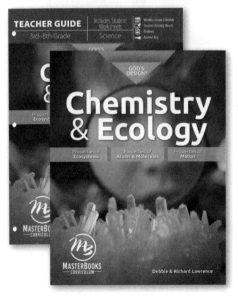

Daily Lesson Plan

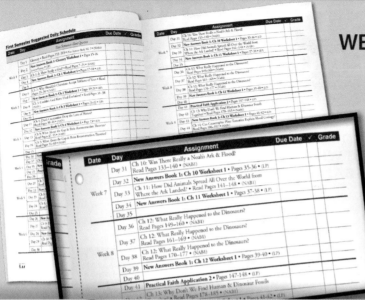

WE'VE DONE THE WORK FOR YOU!

PERFORATED & 3-HOLE PUNCHED

FLEXIBLE 180-DAY SCHEDULE

DAILY LIST OF ACTIVITIES

RECORD KEEPING

"THE TEACHER GUIDE MAKES THINGS
SO MUCH EASIER AND TAKES THE
GUESS WORK OUT OF IT FOR ME."

☆☆☆☆☆

HOMESCHOOL
Master Books® Homeschool Curriculum

Faith-Building Books & Resources
Parent-Friendly Lesson Plans
Biblically-Based Worldview
Affordably Priced

Master Books® is the leading publisher of books and resources
based upon a Biblical worldview that points to God as our Creator.

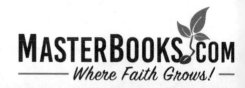